INTRODUCTION TO COMMERCIAL RECREATION AND TOURISM

An Entrepreneurial Approach

FIFTH EDITION

JOHN C. CROSSLEY,
LYNN M. JAMIESON, AND
RUSSELL E. BRAYLEY

Production Coordinator: Angie Patton
Interior Design: Janet Wahlfeldt
Cover Design: Michael Morgan
Editor: Cindy McNew

ISBN: 1-57167-567-1   978-1-57167-567-5
Library of Congress Catalog Card Number: 2006938018

Sagamore Publishing L.L.C.
804 N. Neil St. Suite 100
Champaign, IL 61824
www.sagamorepub.com

10 9 8 7 6 5 4 3 2

Contents●●●●

PART 1
INTRODUCTION TO COMMERCIAL RECREATION
AND TOURISM: AN ENTREPRENEURIAL APPROACH

PART 2
INITIATING and MANAGING COMMERCIAL RECREATION AND TOURISM

PART 3
INDUSTRY PROFILES

Acknowledgments••••

The authors wish to acknowledge the efforts of individuals who contributed to the development of the new text. Individuals who contributed "Spotlights" at the end of the chapters are Dr. Catherine DeLeo, Dr. Mary Wisnom, and Dr. Theresa Love. Their "Spotlights" are definitely highlights, particularly since many of them illustrate the success of students from commercial recreation and tourism academic programs.

We would also like to credit Dr. Joseph Bannon, Mr. M. Douglas Sanders, and the staff of Sagamore Publishing for their great patience and support. We also want to thank the individuals and organizations that contributed slides and prints. Each photo in the text lists a credit for their contribution.

Finally, we would like to thank the numerous industry professionals who contributed ideas and material, the numerous university faculty who have provided suggestions, and the many students who have said they found the past editions to be readable and actually useful in their career interests!

Introduction••••

This text is a revision and update of the fourth edition of *Introduction to Commercial Recreation and Tourism*, and it continues the themes of that edition. As in all the previous editions, the "entrepreneurism theme" is the primary focus of this text. In the fourth edition, we added "Tourism" to the title and we continue with that focus for this text. We divide this industry into three major components: the Travel Industry, the Hospitality Industry, and the Local Commercial Recreation Industry, and we will continue to use the term commercial recreation and tourism to refer to the entire industry.

The purpose of this edition remains the same as the first four editions: to provide an introduction to the scope, characteristics, and management aspects of the commercial recreation and tourism industry. We intend to offer a blend of conceptual and practical material to help achieve a basic understanding of this diverse industry. While some of the content is oriented toward large and established businesses, the text is also applicable to smaller businesses and organizations. We hope that many future commercial recreation and tourism entrepreneurs will gain some useful ideas in these pages.

As in earlier editions, this text will avoid coverage of content that is usually included in other texts such as recreation philosophy, leisure behavior theory, activity leadership, generic recreation programming, management theory, staff supervision, facility planning/design, legal liability, accounting principles, and so on. However, we will cover several topics that have received little attention in other commercial recreation and tourism texts. These topics include entrepreneurial strategies, applied economic concepts, business start-ups, steps of the feasibility study, operations management, and several specific types of programs in commercial recreation and tourism. We present this material in a logical sequence from general to specific.

The first three chapters provide an introduction to the overall commercial recreation and tourism, industry including history, definitions, economic impacts, profile of the entrepreneur, entrepreneurial strategies, economic concepts, challenges, and general strategies to overcome barriers.

Chapters 4 through 8 present content about the initiation and management of the commercial recreation and tourism enterprise. The information is intended to have general application to the overall industry, even though there are some differences between the diverse subindustries. Content includes business start-up strategies, feasibility studies, financing sources, financial management, marketing, operations management, and some specific types of programming.

Chapters 9 through 11 narrow the focus to three categories of the industry: travel, hospitality, and local commercial recreation. Each chapter examines the status, operations, trends, and opportunities in numerous specific types of industries. Another reason to hold this content until the end is to buy time to allow students to investigate these industries on their own as part of a major class project. An industry report is a good idea for a project or term paper, particularly if the student relates the text content to examples found in the student's desired area of career employment.

The final chapter examines the future of the commercial recreation and tourism industry and suggests some strategies for students who seek careers in this area.

The authors updated much of the content, particularly the content that related to specific industry data. On the other hand, conceptual content that remains relevant was changed little. Many new references were used for the new material

This text was developed for a variety of purposes. The primary use is, of course, as a textbook for an introductory course in commercial recreation and tourism. The text could also function as an introduction to the overall industry for majors in travel/tourism or hotel management. Whatever the academic use, a course instructor should try to supplement the text concepts with local examples.

Hopefully, the text may also be of value to investors and practitioners in specific industries who seek an overview of the entire commercial recreation and tourism industry. Although there are many separate subindustries, it is very common for success in one industry to be related to events in another industry. For example, hotels, restaurants, and shops in a ski destination probably won't fill up if the ski mountain itself is not updated with modern high-speed lifts or snowmaking equipment to guarantee a good base for the Christmas season. Similarly, all these businesses may be very dependent on a single airline company to fly tourists in for their ski vacations.

It should also be pointed out that the choice of gender nouns "he" or "she" throughout the text was made by random selections. As the commercial recreation and tourism industry matures, males and females seem to be less relegated to stereotypical roles either as staff, managers, or owners.

Part •••• 1

INTRODUCTION TO COMMERCIAL RECREATION AND TOURISM

An Entrepreneurial Approach

Chapter•••• 1

What Is Commercial Recreation and Tourism?

A BRIEF HISTORY OF COMMERCIAL RECREATION AND TOURISM

The commercial recreation and tourism field has a phenomenal economic, social, cultural, and personal impact. As of 2004, world travel and tourism accounted for almost 74 million jobs (2.8% of all employment), and 1.54 trillion dollars (U.S.) in direct spending, which is 3.8% of the world's combined gross national product (World Travel and Tourism Council, 2004). Of course, expenditures for local commercial recreation, including restaurants, add additional billions of dollars of direct economic impact. Let's see how this huge and complex mega-industry started thousands of years ago.

Early Travel and Commercial Recreation

While family and community recreation activities have existed in one form or another since prehistoric times, the same cannot be said for commercial recreation and tourism. The invention of money by the Sumerians in Babylonia and their development of trade are probably the beginnings of the modern era of travel. Early travel, however, was primarily for war or business purposes. Few recreation seekers would put up with the discomforts and dangers of travel in those days.

In the Egyptian, Assyrian, and Babylonian civilizations, recreation included hunting, horse racing, wrestling, boxing, archery, music, dancing, and drama. To provide these opportunities, the ruling classes employed free men or forced slaves to work. Similarly, the affluent people of the early Greek civilization sponsored paid athletes to compete in a variety of sports events. The Romans also used slaves and professionals to provide music, drama, and dance. Their Colosseum in Rome was the site of 100 daylong sport spectacles each year.

Eventually, the Greeks and Romans improved roads and naval travel in order to control their empires. With these improvements, tourism became safer and more comfortable. This theme of military technology literally paving the way for tourism has been repeated throughout history.

As early as 334 B.C., Alexander the Great attracted 700,000 tourists in a single season to Turkey, where they were entertained by acrobats, animal acts, jugglers, magicians, and circus performances. The ancient Greeks traveled to the Olympic Games, to spas, to festivals, and to the pyramids in Egypt. These and other events provided an early stimulation for travel other than for commerce or defense (About.com, 2005). Romans also traveled extensively, having 175 holidays for leisure and recreation. It was possible to cover up to 100 miles per day on the paved roads and even more by ship. Roman tourists were much like today's tourists, using guidebooks, employing guides, visiting the pyramids, shopping for souvenirs, and leaving graffiti behind (Goeldner, Ritchie, & McIntosh, 2000). Early tourists stayed in guest rooms that were part of private dwellings or in commercial inns. Housing, feeding, and entertaining the travelers became an important industry. About this time, seaside resorts and spas with medicinal waters became popular destinations.

Middle Ages and the Renaissance

With the decline of the great empires, tourism also declined. The wealthy class diminished in number, roads deteriorated, and the countryside became overrun with bandits and thieves.

In the Middle Ages, tourism-related travel came to a virtual standstill. Similarly, the emphasis on religion and abstinence resulted in a dry spell for many of the recreational pursuits of the classical period. Nevertheless, some forms of commercially oriented recreation did exist. The nobility engaged in tournaments, gambling, feasting, and watching entertainers.

During the Renaissance's revival of learning and cultural arts, more travel occurred. Fairs, exhibitions, operas, theater, and beer gardens were popular. The working class played soccer and attended prizefights, cockfights, and bear baiting. The affluent participated in ballroom dance, tennis, and games. "Travel for education" was introduced and was exemplified by the "grand tour." It became fashionable for young aristocrats, as well as members of the rising middle class, to travel and study throughout Europe, Egypt, and the Holy Land. Sometimes these grand tours took up to three years and included indulgence in recreation and revelry.

The roots of the amusement park industry were also in Europe, where pleasure gardens developed outside major cities. One such park, known as Bakken, near Copenhagen, began in 1583 and is still open today.

Travel for health also became important during the Renaissance. At first, only the infirm went to the hot springs or spas to drink or bathe in mineral waters. Later, people began to go in order to dry out from alcoholism and other urban leisure vices. Next, entertainment, recreation activities, and gambling were added. Dozens of spas grew to become high-quality resorts. Switzerland, for example, had over 100 spa-resorts.

It is important to note that there was no clear distinction between private/commercial recreation and government-sponsored recreation throughout history to this point. Many of the trips taken by nobility were actually financed by government funds. Similarly, feudal kingdoms sponsored some of the festivals, contests, and mass entertainment events provided for the working class and peasants. Church involvement in local and national governments further complicated the separation of church, state, and private enterprise.

Early Travel and Consumerism

In 1841, Englishman Thomas Cook chartered a train to carry 540 people to a temperance convention. Although Cook made no profit for himself on that trip, he saw the potential in arranging travel for others. By 1845, Thomas Cook had become the first full-time travel excursion organizer. In 1846, he took 500 people on a tour of Scotland and later arranged for over 165,000 people to attend the Great Exhibition in Hyde Park, London. A "Cook's Tour" was likely to turn up anywhere. Switzerland, the Nile, the Holy Land, Mount Everest, India, Norway, and Yellowstone Park were a few of the destinations. Cook was dedicated to making his tours as interesting and convenient as possible. One of his greatest achievements was to conduct a 212-day Round the World tour involving steamship travel across the Atlantic, a stagecoach from the east to west coasts of America, a paddle steamer to Japan, and an overland journey from China to India (Spartacus Educational Homepage, 2005). To allow access to cash while away from home, he invented "circular notes," which later became known as traveler's checks.

19th Century Commercial Recreation and Tourism

It is well known that during colonial times, Americans hunted, fished, held shooting contests and horse races, held dances and theater events, and went to taverns for cockfights, boxing, and gambling. All this occurred in spite of prohibitions by Puritan-based laws. The Southern colonies were less Puritan, but most recreation was a privilege of the wealthy. By the 1800s, the energy of America was still being spent primarily to build the new nation. Travel was not easy, but as stagecoach lines developed, taverns and inns were built along the routes. The inns provided food, drink, and sleeping accommodations. Soon, enterprising innkeepers learned to see the value of providing recreation and entertainment in the form of festivals, contests, and cultural events. They in turn served to attract more visitors and increase profit from lodging, drink, and food. In urban areas, people began to arrange competition in tennis, boxing, cockfighting, drinking, and other activities. By the late 1800s, dance halls, shooting galleries, bowling alleys, billiard parlors, beer gardens, and saloons flourished. Professional sports teams were formed. Many cities had red light districts offering prostitution, gambling, and other vices. In such an environment, commercial recreation deservedly gained an unsavory reputation. In response, city councils passed restrictive ordinances, including "blue laws," which closed recreation enterprises on Sundays. It was also in this environment that public parks and recreation became a major social movement.

The amusement park industry shifted to America, where amusements were built at the ends of trolley lines. These included picnic areas, dance halls, food service, games, and some rides. In the late 1800s, the first Ferris Wheel was introduced at the 1893 World's Fair in Chicago.

By the early 1900s, science had led to the invention of the phonograph player and silent motion pictures. There were over 10,000 motion picture theaters in the United States by 1910, and 10 million people a week attended them (Chubb & Chubb, 1981).

Travel and commercial recreation were uplifted by improvements in transportation, specifically the railroad and later the automobile. Railroads carried urban residents to amusement parks on the outskirts of town and to major resorts across the country. In many cases, the amusement parks and resorts were built by the railroads to stimulate travel volume. For example, Sun Valley, Idaho, was built by Averell Harriman and the Union Pacific Railroad. Many resorts along the southeastern coast of the United States were similarly filled by tourists traveling by rail. Also, the new development of a series of national parks became a tremendous attraction for tourists.

The automobile provided additional mobility and independence for American tourists. Vacationing by auto became the great American middle-class tradition. The auto also opened a whole range of local recreation opportunities. Urban and rural residents alike could drive to movie theaters, sporting events, and many other commercial recreation attractions.

Commercial Recreation and Tourism in the Last Half Century

A healthy economy plus technological innovations continued to fuel growth in commercial recreation after World War II. The average workweek decreased, while discretionary income increased, thus providing opportunity and means to enjoy new forms of recreation.

Perhaps the greatest technological advances again involved travel. Construction of the U.S. interstate highway system greatly expanded the area accessible to American tourists, and airlines enabled even more distant destinations to be reached easily. Some resort areas, such as Las Vegas, Central Florida, and Colorado experienced tremendous growth due to improved accessibility.

Other technological advances also had huge impacts on commercial recreation. Electronic innovations generated a huge home entertainment industry of television, stereo equipment, video recorders, and computers. Synthetic materials improved the performance and durability of ski equipment, golf clubs, skateboards, and sports balls of all types. Theme parks and water theme parks capitalized on a variety of innovations. Service innovations, such as time-sharing, have also had significant impact. Undoubtedly, the future holds a continuing variety of new facilities, products, and services.

Post 9/11 and Influence of Terrorism and War

Along with many other aspects of modern life, commercial recreation and tourism were impacted greatly when the two towers of New York's World Trade Center were demolished by Arab terrorists on September 11, 2001. Almost immediately, the world of travel changed. Air travel dropped 10% for the year, replaced by driving vacations and increases in recreational vehicle sales. Travelers became more cautious about where to travel and placed the greatest amount of importance on feeling safe. New York City rebounded one year later although an overall decline was still felt.

The impact of 9/11 and the war against terrorism caused increased security measures, changes in travel destination, and most importantly, changes in perception about travel, safety, and many other aspects of our society. In fact, international air travel to the United States did not return to pre-9/11 levels until 2005 (Neff, 2005; Adams, 2005).

Common Themes Throughout History

Several themes appeared throughout the preceding section about the history of commercial recreation and tourism. These themes include the following:

- Commercial recreation has existed when people have free time, discretionary income, and access to leisure products and services.
- Many of the technological innovations for travel and for recreation products were first developed for military purposes and then adapted for commercial use.
- The fortunes of certain industries such as restaurants, lodging, and entertainment are closely linked to travel and tourism.
- When economic conditions sour, when travel is inconvenient or unsafe, or when services are inadequate, there are declines in many types of commercial recreation and tourism.
- Some people have been willing to pay for leisure services regardless of inflation or recession.

The significance of the above themes is related to the nature of history. Scholars always tell us that history tends to repeat itself. Therefore, we should expect to see those themes repeated in the future of commercial recreation and tourism.

DEFINITIONS

The previous section mentioned how the provision of recreation throughout history has been an undefined mix of governmental (public) and private efforts. Figure 1-1 illustrates a continuum depicting the traditional difference between public agency recreation and private/commercial recreation. It must be realized that few public park and recreation agencies exist in the pure/traditional form at the left of the continuum. Most have evolved a little or a lot toward the middle and include some quasi-government agencies that have characteristics of both the public and private sectors. A similar pattern has emerged in the private sector, because a greater service orientation now exists for many businesses. Also, some large commercial recreation and tourism developments are given tax incentives and/or government-funded infrastructure improvements as enticements to locate in a given area. The characteristics analyzed here include philosophic orientation, service origin, financial base, originating authority, and service focus.

Figure 1-1
Public-Private Recreation Continuum

Public Recreation		Private Recreation
Free, necessary service for society	Philosophic orientation	Profit-making business
Social welfare movement, conservation ethics	Service origin	Consumer desire and willingness to pay
Tax revenue	Financial base	Private capital plus fees revenue
Governmental bodies; citizen boards	Originating authority	Individual initiative
Nonrestrictive, open to collective community interest	Service focus	Can focus on any special market segments

Philosophic Orientation. Public recreation is based on the value of recreation as a necessary service for society. Private sector recreation is provided to make a profit for a business.

Service Origin. Public recreation began as a social welfare movement, and public parks had roots in conservation ethics. Private recreation originated as a business response to people who desired to travel and/or purchase leisure products and services.

Financial Base. Taxes and grants have traditionally provided the bulk of public recreation finances. On the other hand, private recreation is funded by private capital and operated through fees revenue.

Originating Authority. City councils, county commissions, citizen boards, and other legislative bodies create public park and recreation departments. Individual initiative is the source of private recreation business.

Service Focus. Public recreation must be open to the collective interest of its community. On the other hand, private recreation can focus on any special market interest that it chooses.

Based upon this continuum, a definition of commercial recreation may be developed that differentiates it from public recreation. Definitions for commercialized public recreation, entrepreneurial recreation, and tourism are also included in this section.

Commercial Recreation

Obviously, commercial recreation is the provision of leisure experiences with the intent of making a profit. While this definition covers the basic revenue orientation, it does not really differentiate between public and private provision of the service. This is a distinction that must be made, since private enterprise must overcome barriers that do not similarly affect government-sponsored recreation.

While most government agencies charge fees for recreation, such fees seldom cover capital development and full overhead costs. These are major cost factors that private enterprises cannot escape. Government also has the advantage of using tax revenues to subsidize its revenue-generating activities. Similarly, nonprofit organizations such as YMCAs often have community fund-raising campaigns and other charitable donations as revenue sources. Another important difference is that public recreation agencies and nonprofit organizations do not have to pay property taxes and income taxes. Private enterprise, however, is often taxed a substantial amount to conduct business.

To account for the differences between public and private orientations, the following is offered as a definition for *commercial recreation*:

> *The provision of recreation-related products or services by private enterprise for a fee, with the long-term intent of being profitable.*

In addition to the aforementioned public/private distinction, this definition offers two other key points. First, "recreation-related" may be interpreted very broadly and may include any product or service that either directly or indirectly supports a leisure pursuit. This interpretation means that leisure-related aspects of the travel and hospitality industries (including hotels and restaurants) can be included within the broad framework of commercial recreation. Of course, a significant part of both the travel and hospitality industries serves the business traveler, and much of the restaurant industry (part of the hospitality industry) serves a fundamental nutrition purpose. However, it must be recognized that there is an extremely large leisure component of these industries.

The second key point is that the "long-term intent" is to be profitable. This recognizes the fact that commercial recreation is not always profitable; it may fail. It may also take a company many years to become profitable, because it may have to overcome very high start-up costs. Some companies may never be profitable on a day-to-day operational basis, but may yield large profits through the long-term appreciation of their land and facilities.

Commercialized Public Recreation

What can we call governmental and nonprofit recreation organizations that are operated in a commercial manner? *Commercialized public recreation* is the term suggested for this concept, defined below:

> *The provision of selected recreation-related products or services by a governmental or nonprofit organization in a commercial manner, with much or all of the costs covered by fees, charges, or other non-tax revenues.*

A key point of this definition is that the overall agency may operate under traditional funding sources, but that "selected" aspects may be operated in a commercial manner. An example of this would be a city parks and recreation department that funds its parks through tax revenues but expects its recreation programs to be self-supporting through fees. Further evidence of commercialized public recreation exists when selected recreation functional units are separately operated as enterprises such as golf courses, driving ranges, water parks, batting cages, and many other facilities.

Entrepreneurial Recreation

It is a premise of this book that private, public, and nonprofit organizations can all operate in an entrepreneurial manner. The term *entrepreneur* is commonly used in reference to a person who starts a small business. This definition, however, can exclude government and nonprofit organizations that initiate recreation services by utilizing entrepreneurial strategies. Key identifiers of entrepreneurial approaches can include environmental scanning for trends and changes that present opportunity. The entrepreneur then utilizes common managerial functions to exploit those opportunities for profit or financial self-sufficiency. Therefore, the following definition is offered for *entrepreneurial recreation*:

The actions of a recreation-related organization that searches for trends and changes in its environment, then brings together and manages resources to exploit those changes as an opportunity.

It is a premise of this book that entrepreneurial activity can exist within a governmental organization as well as within a corporate structure.

Tourism

As explained in greater detail in Chapter 9, *tourism* is:

The activities of persons traveling to and staying in places outside their usual environment, for leisure, business, or other purposes.

In most cases, a person's usual environment is their area of residence. It is important to note that this definition is not limited to leisure travel. The person traveling for business, education, religion, or other purposes is just as likely, perhaps more so, to spend money on transportation, lodging, food, and beverage as the leisure traveler does. Further, the travelers for business and other purposes often include significant leisure time and expenditure on their trips.

The tourism industry is defined as the broad industry composed of a loose network of businesses and other organizations that serve tourists. These other organizations can include government agencies that serve tourists directly or serve the overall interests of the tourism industry. Examples would be convention and visitor bureaus, national parks, regional airports, and the like. The hospitality industry is often considered to be part of the tourism industry, but sometimes it is considered a unique and separate industry.

This text will use the term *commercial recreation and tourism* to refer to the entire overlapping collection of businesses and other organizations that serve the recreation and/or tourism purposes of individuals.

TYPES OF COMMERCIAL RECREATION AND TOURISM

According to the definitions presented in the previous section, commercial recreation and tourism may include such diverse businesses as resort hotels, movie theaters, sporting goods stores, airlines, racquet sport clubs, dance studios, craft shops, restaurants, travel agencies, casinos, and campgrounds. Obviously there are commonalities and interrelationships between some of these enterprises. On the other hand, some have little or no relationship to the other types listed. This diversity makes it very difficult to grasp the breadth of the industry and understand its components. What is needed is some structure or logical classification system into which the many industries can be grouped. Such a system allows a better organized study of commercial recreation, because similar industries often have similar problems, trends, and management practices.

An Industry Classification System

The following classification system demonstrates the overlapping nature of many of the categories suggested previously. This is essential if one is to gain a realistic grasp of a complex, diverse, and interrelated industry. Consider for example: Is a ski resort in the hotel, travel, entertainment, restaurant, retail, or recreation program business? It could be all of those and serve local residents as well as tourists. The classification system has three main components: *travel/transportation*, *hospitality*, and *local commercial recreation*. Each of the components has its "purest" aspects, and each has subindustries that overlap with the other component classifications (see Figure 1-2). The key to the classification system is that each major industry has certain common characteristics, but that some components of an industry overlap with another industry. Furthermore, in some cases, certain business categories have relevance to all three industry components. These industries are located in the middle overlapping area of the three industry circles.

The Travel Industry has as its primary function the movement of people and the provision of travel-related services. The purest forms of this industry are the airlines, rental cars, bus lines, and railroads that move tourists as well as business travelers. This industry overlaps with local commercial recreation when retail products and recreation activities are provided for tourists. Examples are heli-ski services, river guide trips, souvenir shops, and RV dealers. The travel industry overlaps with hospitality when lodging, food, or other amenities are provided for tourists. Examples are cruise ships, campgrounds, and historical attractions. It is important to note that the term *tourism industry* is not used for this industry segment. That is because the tourism industry is broader in nature than just travel and hospitality. As mentioned previously, *tourism* could also include many of the industry *facilitators*. and even part of the local commercial recreation industry that serves tourists.

The Hospitality Industry has as its primary function the provision of accommodations, food and beverage, and related amenities. The purest forms of this industry are hotels and motels, restaurants, resort condominiums, taverns, RV parks, campgrounds, and recreation communities. Hospitality can overlap with the travel industry as previously mentioned. It also overlaps with local commercial recreation when recreation activities are provided at restaurants, camps, or other hospitality settings that predominantly serve local residents. Examples are leisure theme restaurants, sports day camps, and hunting day lodges.

The Local Commercial Recreation Industry has as its primary function the provision of retail products, entertainment, and recreation programs for people in their home communities. The purest forms of this industry include fitness centers, dance studios, sporting goods stores, movie theaters, and small amusement parks. As previously mentioned, local commercial recreation can overlap with the travel and hospitality industries.

Figure 1-2
The Commercial Recreation and Tourism Industry

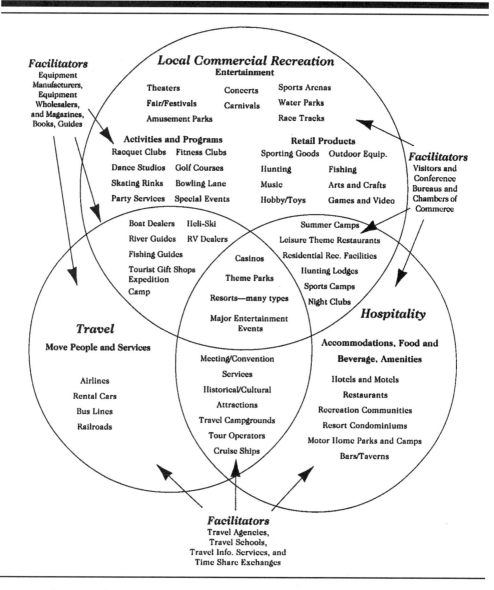

Facilitators
Equipment Manufacturers, Equipment Wholesalers, and Magazines, Books, Guides

Local Commercial Recreation
Entertainment

Theaters   Concerts   Sports Arenas

Fair/Festivals   Carnivals   Water Parks

Amusement Parks   Race Tracks

Activities and Programs

Racquet Clubs Fitness Clubs

Dance Studios Golf Courses

Skating Rinks Bowling Lane

Party Services Special Events

Retail Products

Sporting Goods Outdoor Equip.

Hunting Fishing

Music Arts and Crafts

Hobby/Toys Games and Video

Facilitators
Visitors and Conference Bureaus and Chambers of Commerce

Boat Dealers Heli-Ski

River Guides RV Dealers

Fishing Guides

Tourist Gift Shops

Expedition Camp

Casinos

Theme Parks

Resorts—many types

Major Entertainment Events

Summer Camps

Leisure Theme Restaurants

Residential Rec. Facilities

Hunting Lodges

Sports Camps

Night Clubs

Hospitality

Travel

Move People and Services

Airlines

Rental Cars

Bus Lines

Railroads

Meeting/Convention Services

Historical/Cultural Attractions

Travel Campgrounds

Tour Operators

Cruise Ships

Accommodations, Food and Beverage, Amenities

Hotels and Motels

Restaurants

Recreation Communities

Resort Condominiums

Motor Home Parks and Camps

Bars/Taverns

Facilitators
Travel Agencies, Travel Schools, Travel Info. Services, and Time Share Exchanges

Facilitators of many types support the three main industries. Some facilitators, such as travel agencies, travel schools, and time-share trade services, support the hospitality and travel/transportation industries. Other facilitators, such as equipment wholesalers, publishers of leisure-oriented magazines, and writers of "how to do it" craft books, support the local commercial recreation industry. Further, facilitators that chiefly support hospitality and local commercial recreation include convention and visitor bureaus and chambers of commerce. Facilitators are covered within the chapters of this text according to the type of industry they support most.

All of these industries overlap when accommodations, food, activities, retail shops, and entertainment are provided for both tourists and local residents. This occurs in many types of resorts, at major entertainment events such as an NFL Super Bowl, and at large theme parks.

PARTICIPATION AND EXPENDITURES IN THE RECREATION, LEISURE, AND TOURISM INDUSTRY

Depending upon which organization collects the data, the terms *recreation industry, leisure industry,* or *tourism industry* may be used. For this text, we will simply refer to it collectively as the *recreation, leisure, and tourism industry.* Data regarding participation and expenditures in this large and complex industry are important in order to assess the present and to make projections for the future. Such data is used in

- feasibility studies for new or expanded facilities or programs;
- operational decisions involving demand estimates, pricing, marketing, employment of seasonal staff, and so forth;
- projections by government for sales taxes, hotel occupancy taxes, and so on;
- policy decisions by governmental agencies; and
- lobbying efforts of industry/trade associations.

Unfortunately, the data produced through measurement of the recreation, leisure, and tourism industry are often inconsistent. There are problems in measuring both participation and expenditures. For example, different definitions are used for recreation, leisure, travel, and other categories, and those definitions can change over the years. Also, some agencies have a bias regarding the topics they survey and the methodology they use. Finally, it is difficult to separate leisure-related expenditures from business expenditures for topics such as hotels, restaurants, airlines, gardening, and so on.

Even though there are problems in measurement, it is possible to gain a general idea of the participation and expenditure levels for major categories of recreation in the United States. The next two sections will present several studies of recreation, leisure, and tourism participation and expenditures.

Recreation, Leisure, and Tourism Participation

Figure 1-3 presents the results of an annual nationwide study conducted by the Roper Starch organization (2004). The figures show the percentage of Americans age 18 or older who participate in various outdoor recreation activities. It should be noted that this participation may occur at public recreation facilities as well as commercial recreation/ tourism facilities. Note that the participation rates have not changed much in recent years. Only a few activities appear to have increased. However, if children and teen participation had been included, it is expected that activities such as snowboarding would have shown significant growth. Unfortunately, rates of participation in the arts, hobbies, team sports, and social activities were not included in the Roper Starch study, and there appears to be no comprehensive nationwide study that addresses the entire leisure industry. For comparison, a survey by the National Sporting Goods Association (2004) shows that the following sports would have been included in the top 15 most popular activities had they been included in the Roper Starch survey: exercising with equipment (18%), bowling (15%), billiards/pool (11%), workout at a club (11%), basketball (10%), and aerobic exercising (10%).

Recreation, Leisure, and Tourism Expenditures

As noted previously, data regarding expenditures for recreation, leisure, and tourism vary significantly from source to source. Perhaps the most comprehensive source is the Economic Census conducted by the U.S. Census Bureau. Figure 1-4 presents the expenditure levels, number of businesses, and number of employees (both full-time and part-time) in most of the major categories of recreation, leisure, and tourism.

Figure 1-3
Outdoor Recreation Activities
(Percentage of Adults Participating During the Year)

Activity	1995(%)	1999(%)	2003(%)
Walking for fitness/recreation	45	42	46
Driving for pleasure	36	35	43
Swimming	31	40	41
Picnicking	29	32	38
Fishing	24	28	28
Bicycling	20	22	22
Running/jogging	16	16	19
Hiking	18	15	18
Campground camping	16	21	18
Outdoor photography	15	12	17
Wildlife viewing	15	15	16
Bird watching	11	11	16
Visiting cultural sites	NA	16	15
Golf	12	12	13
Motor boating	9	11	10
Backpacking	12	10	9
RV camping	8	8	9
Hunting	7	8	8
Canoeing/kayaking	5	7	8
Wilderness camping	NA	NA	7
Off-road vehicles	5	7	6
Tennis	9	6	6
Target shooting	6	7	6
Motorcycling	5	6	6
Horseback riding	5	6	6
Riding Jet Skis	NA	5	5
Mountain biking	5	6	5
Downhill skiing	6	4	4
Water skiing	6	4	4
In-line skating	4	5	3
Rock climbing	4	3	3
Sailing	3	3	3
Snorkeling/scuba diving	3	4	3
Rowing	2	1	3
Cross-country skiing	3	1	2
Snowmobiling	3	2	2
Snowboarding	NA	3	2

Source: Roper Starch (2004); NA = Not Available

Public parks such as Yosemite National Park stimulate billions of dollars of spending for commercial recreation products and tourism services. (Photo: J. Crossley)

The $1.09 trillion total in Figure 1-4 represents a huge segment of the U.S. economy. It is, however, a figure that is not necessarily accurate and is certainly not complete. Those figures do not include the leisure-related portion of the $250 billion that Americans spent at gasoline stations or the leisure-related portion of the $445 billion spent at department stores. Added to that would be the leisure-related portion of over $160 billion of expenditures for home computers and software, online and mail-order shopping, residential swimming pools, and many other products and services (U.S. Census Bureau, 2004). If just one third of these expenses were leisure related, the grand total would be almost $1.4 trillion a year! Considering that government census data has a two- or three-year lag from initial research to publication, the above figures could easily be another 10% higher due to monetary inflation and minimal growth by 2005. Therefore, it seems safe to conclude that recreation, leisure, and tourism in the United States is a $1.5 trillion industry at the least. This is a tremendous figure that illustrates the size of this huge and diverse industry.

Figure 1-4
Recreation, Leisure, and Tourism Expenditures
from 2002 Census Data

Category	Sales ($ billions)	Establishments (thousands)	Employees (thousands)
Eating and drinking places	322.0	504.4	8,315
Traveler accommodations	126.1	50.9	1,771
Airline transportation*	111.2	NA	NA
Motion picture services	62.0	19.1	275
TV, radio, etc.	48.9	23.5	231
Lawn and garden stores	31.0	21.1	171
Liquor stores	27.8	28.9	133
Sporting goods retail	25.0	22.2	188
Book and music stores	22.6	19.7	201
Spectator sports	21.9	4.3	107
Gambling industries	20.2	2.2	162
Auto rental	19.0	4.9	123
Hobby, toy, and game	18.4	12.5	163
Golf courses/country clubs	17.4	12.2	311
RV dealers	15.0	3.1	36
Fitness and sports centers	14.8	25.0	441
Boat dealers	12.4	5.5	40
Arts and sports promoters	12.1	5.4	104
Other travel services	12.0	2.8	68
Amusement parks and arcades	9.6	3.2	123
Video/DVD rental	9.4	18.7	150
Travel agencies	9.4	21.7	147
Performing arts companies	9.4	10.7	138
Artists and performers	9.3	15.9	55
Museums/zoos/nature parks	8.6	6.7	122
Water passenger transport	8.6	0.4	17
Pet shops	7.6	7.6	74
Athletic footwear stores	7.3	6.1	64
Other amusement and recreation	5.8	13.2	85
Bowling centers	4.9	3.1	82
Photographic studios	4.9	14.6	66
Musical instrument stores	4.9	4.5	33
Art dealers	4.4	6.3	22
Photo finishing labs	3.9	4.7	47
Sewing and needlework stores	3.9	5.4	40
Arts and sports agents/managers	3.7	3.3	18
Marinas	3.5	4.3	28
Tour operators	3.1	3.1	32
Camera shops	3.1	2.8	19
Airport operations	2.7	1.4	38
Limousine service	2.6	3.9	37
Sports and recreation instruction	2.4	9.1	55
Fine arts schools	2.3	9.2	61
Skiing facilities	1.8	0.4	71
Recreational goods rental	1.8	0.6	8
Scenic transport	1.8	2.5	22

(continued)

Figure 1-4 (continued)
Recreation, Leisure, and Tourism Expenditures
from 2002 Census Data

Category	Sales ($ billions)	Establishments (thousands)	Employees (thousands)
Charter bus service	1.7	1.2	29
RV parks and campsites	1.7	4.2	19
Luggage/leather stores	1.7	1.6	10
Recreation and vacation camps	1.7	3.2	24
Consumer electronics repair	1.5	3.5	20
Pet care services (except vet.)	1.5	8.1	33
Convention and visitor bureaus	1.0	1.2	11
Totals	$1,091.3	974.1	14,640

Sources: all U.S. Census Bureau (2004), except as noted * Corridore (2004)

ECONOMIC, SOCIAL, AND ENVIRONMENTAL IMPACTS OF COMMERCIAL RECREATION AND TOURISM

On a world-wide basis, recreation and tourism, including its direct and indirect activity, accounts for over $4.2 trillion in gross domestic product and is the world's largest industry. According to the World Travel and Tourism Council, the industry employs 215 million people and accounts for almost 10% of the world's combined gross domestic product (World Travel and Tourism Council, 2004).

Within the United States, impacts are similar in importance. Commercial recreation and tourism is one of the top three industries in every state. Tax revenues generated just from tourism are about $95 billion. International tourism has a foreign trade surplus of about $3 billion, thus helping to ease the overall U.S. trade deficit (Travel Industry Association of America, 2005).

Within this huge industry, most expenditures occur in the private sector. Only about two to five percent of the industry expenditures occur through local, state, or federal government agencies. However, the importance of the role of government in the economics of the industry is much greater. Consider that government lands are often leased to commercial enterprise as the sites for many types of resorts and tourist attractions. Further, governmental agencies are in a position to provide many incentives for business development such as tax deferments, support of infrastructure, and other mechanisms. At the local level, many expenditures at retail sporting goods stores and arts and crafts shops are for equipment used in sports leagues and crafts classes sponsored by city park and recreation departments.

Positive Impacts—Commercial recreation and tourism has many positive impacts on a given community. These include the following:

- Employment opportunities increase.
- Local economy is stimulated through increased commerce.
- Outside capital (new businesses, new investors for existing businesses) is attracted.
- Property values often increase.

- Tax revenues (property, sales, and hotel room taxes) increase.
- Recreation opportunity for local residents increase.
- The economic multiplier improves when locals stay in their community for their own recreation.

Negative Impacts—Commercial recreation and tourism can also have negative impacts:

- Many types of commercial recreation and tourism have high failure rates and/or short life cycles, thus resulting in unemployment and decreased economic contribution to the local community.
- The local infrastructure (roads, sewers, utilities, etc.) can become overburdened, thus requiring capital improvements that cost huge sums of money.
- Crime can increase because tourists can be easy prey, and transient-type employees may be more crime-prone.
- Increased land values can backfire on young residents wishing to buy property for the first time.
- Natural resources can be overused to the point of ruining the attraction that is the center of the commercial recreation and tourism industry.
- Undesirable types of commercial recreation may appear, trying to capitalize on increased traffic to the prime commercial attraction.
- Local culture in rural or remote areas can be harmed.
- Residents may become disenchanted with their own community.

Ultimately, each community must assess both the pros and cons of commercial recreation and tourism development. Zoning regulations, pricing of business permits and licenses, and other local government regulations can encourage or discourage a commercial recreation and tourism enterprise.

Additional content regarding economic impact is covered in Chapter 3, and additional content regarding social and environmental impact is covered in Chapter 9.

An Indian Crafts Shop in Cherokee, North Carolina features ceramic piggy banks: What are the impacts of this type of tourism products? (Photo: J. Crossley)

THE ROLE OF GOVERNMENT IN COMMERCIAL RECREATION AND TOURISM

As mentioned in the previous section, government is concerned with the success of commercial recreation and tourism because of its economic impact on the community. In addition to assessing property taxes, sales taxes, and fees for licenses and permits, government at all levels is involved in the regulation of private enterprise. Government has a duty to protect the public interests and therefore establishes standards and regulations for many aspects of business operation. The topic of government regulation is addressed in greater depth in Chapter 4.

While taxes and regulations are necessary evils for commercial recreation and tourism, there are many positive relationships possible between government and private enterprise. These relationships could be grouped into three categories: *complementary relationships*, *cooperative arrangements*, and *planning relationships*.

Complementary Relationships

Government has occasionally expanded its scope of service into traditional areas of private enterprise. In some cases where local government has offered commercial-quality bus tours, fishing trips, and fitness facilities, lawsuits have been filed charging government with unfair competition. Government is not structured to meet all the recreation needs of all people. Also, the resources of government are stretched too thin, and conditions are not getting better. Therefore, government has acted to complement the efforts of private enterprise in order to provide the maximum recreation opportunity for its residents. Specific complementary actions by government can include the following:

- Provide, maintain, and/or regulate the infrastructure (roads, waterways, utilities, etc.) that supports commercial recreation and tourism.
- Promote tourism and commercial development.
- Provide public facilities where residents can use recreation equipment purchased from retail outlets.
- Provide low-cost introductory programs; advanced levels can be offered by commercial enterprises.
- Refer people to commercial recreation opportunities.

Cooperative Arrangements

There are many types of cooperative arrangements where government and private enterprise can interact directly to provide recreation facilities or programs. Examples include the following:

- public agency programs conducted at commercial facilities;
- commercially organized programs conducted at public agency facilities;
- cosponsorship of promotional events and special events;
- loaning or sharing of equipment, supplies, or staff expertise;
- leasing concessions for food, beverage, or other amenities;
- contracted management of entire facilities or entire programs;
- cooperative facility development;
- financial assistance, such as low-cost loans or property tax abatements; and
- leasing of public land for commercial recreation and tourism development.

Planning Relationships

Long-range planning for recreation and tourism is best served when government and private enterprise work together. Unfortunately, this does not always happen. Nevertheless, the following guidelines indicate areas where mutual planning efforts can be beneficial:

- Commercial recreation and tourism business representatives should be involved in public hearings concerning recreation and natural resources.
- Commercial recreation and tourism representatives should be active in the community, serving on advisory boards, planning commissions, and so forth.
- Comprehensive plans at the local and state levels should include the input of commercial recreation and tourism owners and managers.

KEY TRENDS IN THE RECREATION AND TOURISM INDUSTRY

Government, private enterprise, society, and environmental factors all interact constantly to create an ever-changing environment for the commercial recreation and tourism enterprise. Events of the past set the stage for the future, whether we choose to pay attention or not. Throughout this text, several trends and themes will appear constantly. Chapter 12 focuses specifically on trends and opportunities for the future. Some of these trends are introduced here to alert the reader to them:

- International, national, regional, and local economic conditions affect the ability of people to spend for recreation and tourism.
- Demographic changes underlie significant changes in the market for recreation and tourism.
- Resource availability will affect almost all forms of commercial recreation and tourism.
- Sustainability of natural resources and culture needs to gain equal importance with long-term financial sustainability as a goal of recreation and tourism development.
- Foreign policy, war, and terrorist activity and violence will alter tourists' choices of destinations.
- New technology will continuously revolutionize travel and recreation, and entirely newconcepts/products will emerge.
- New trends in recreation and leisure activities spread globally from one culture to another and will affect consumer demand for different activities.

Obviously, these are not earthshaking revelations. They are, however, trends and themes that will arise constantly and affect the commercial recreation and tourism manager's efforts to develop a profitable enterprise. If a manager does not deal with these trends, dramatic problems and business failure can result.

THE COMMERCIAL RECREATION AND TOURISM EXPERIENCE

Ultimately, the objective of a commercial recreation and tourism enterprise is to become profitable. Some managers, however, may limit their opportunities for profit by defining their business too narrowly. Others may have a terrific business concept but fail due to undercapitalization or inefficient operation policies. For example, a mountain bike tour operator is missing his full potential if he sees his business only as leading high-quality bike tours. There are additional revenue opportunities available. Managers should look at their companies in light of the total recreation and tourism experience.

There are five major steps or components of the recreation and tourism experience: (1) anticipation, preparation, and planning; (2) travel to; (3) on-site participation and/or purchase; (4) travel from; and (5) recollection. These steps may all be defined further to reflect an understanding of what motivating factors encourage one's pursuit/choice of a leisure experience.

Continuing with the mountain bike tour example, the traditional manager would concentrate only on the third step, on-site participation. On the other hand, the resourceful manager would see the potential to serve the consumer at each step of the recreation experience. Examples of this aggressive approach are given for each component.

The anticipation, preparation, and planning stage would include the manager selling products or services that help the consumer prepare for a recreation/tourism experience. This could include

- instructional classes to show people how to maintain and repair their bikes,
- "how to do it" books and tapes to instruct and prepare the participant,
- guidebooks showing trails, natural history, and so on; and
- equipment tune-up and repair services.

The travel to and travel from stages would suggest an opportunity to sell an entire vacation package that includes airfare and/or van transportation to the bike tour departure site, plus hotel accommodations prior to departure. A mountain bike tour operator could accomplish this through a cooperative arrangement with a local travel agency. If the bike tour business was large enough, it might even include a travel agent on staff.

On-site sales are the mainstay of the mountain bike tour operator's business, but revenues could be boosted by selling related products. For example, bikes and camping equipment could be rented or sold.

The Recollection stage suggests opportunities for the business to sell products or services that help the consumer relive the enjoyable experience. Ideas for the bike tour company could include

- cameras, film, photography accessories, and film developing;
- photos and videos of the trips;
- T-shirts, caps, and other souvenirs of the trip; and
- membership in a club or bike association.

All commercial recreation and tourism enterprises should analyze the potential for products and services that target each of the five steps of the recreation and tourism experience. Sometimes this extra effort can have a significant impact on the overall profitability of the business. Prime examples of this in other businesses include (1) commercial photographers at resorts and on cruise ships; (2) souvenir shops at resorts; (3) instructional classes at crafts and fabric shops; and (4) travel agencies sponsoring travel clubs and travel classes and selling passport photos, guidebooks, maps, travel games, and travel videos.

SUMMARY

Commercial recreation and tourism is the provision of recreation- and/or tourism-related products or services by private enterprise for a fee, with the long-term intent of being profitable. Public and nonprofit organizations can also provide recreation and tourism in a commercialized manner. Whether serving public, private, or nonprofit organizations, the entrepreneurial manager can exploit changes in the environment to create new recreational opportunities.

Throughout history, the provision of commercial recreation and tourism has paralleled the availability of free time, discretionary income, and transportation. Technological advancements such as railroads, autos, airplanes, plastics, and microchips have created huge industries. In the process, recreation and tourism has grown to become one of the nation's largest industries. Annual expenditures in the United States probably exceed $1.5 trillion, but differences in definition and methodology make it difficult to assess how big the industry actually is. It is certain, however, that recreation is one of the top three industries in every state.

The development of commercial recreation and tourism can have very positive impacts on a community, including attraction of outside capital, increase of the tax base, creation of new jobs, and the improvement of the local infrastructure. Negative impacts can also occur, including failure of businesses, overburdening of the infrastructure, and abuse of the environment. In order to protect public interests, the government regulates and taxes commercial recreation and tourism businesses. Government should also interact with commercial recreation and tourism by providing complementary services, by establishing cooperative ventures, and by including private sector representation in the planning process.

Most commercial recreation and tourism businesses tend to focus their efforts on only one aspect of the leisure experience. The aggressive manager will exploit revenue opportunities by providing products or services at many stages of the experience, including preparation, travel to and from, and recollection, as well as at the traditional on-site stage.

SPOTLIGHT ON:

Michelle Kelthy, Executive Spa Director
by Mary S. Wisnom, PhD

Founded in 1983, the Ritz-Carlton Hotel Company has grown from one hotel to over 50 luxury hotels and resorts worldwide. The Ritz-Carlton properties are best known for their magnificent surroundings and service of unbeatable quality. The Ritz-Carlton Resort in Naples, Florida, is consistently honored as one of the finest resorts in the world and has had the distinct honor of having received both the prestigious Exxon Mobil Five Star and AAA Five Star Awards for over 15 years.

In 2000, the Ritz-Carlton Naples resort expanded its facility to include a state-of-the-art spa. Encompassing more than 51,000 square feet and three floors, The spa offers a full spectrum of services including hot and cold plunge pools, steam and sauna rooms, tiled spa tubs with waterfalls, a sun deck and mineral pool, fitness center, mind and body studio, 33 treatment rooms (offering over 90 treatments), salon, retail space, locker facilities, and H2O, the spa café. Shortly after opening its doors, The Spa was winning its own awards, including in 2001 being named the "#1 Best Hotel Spa in the United States" by *Travel & Leisure Magazine*.

The Spa at the Ritz-Carlton, Naples, boasts highly skilled therapists and staff. There is even a Spa Concierge to assist guests in choosing the perfect treatment or combination of treatments to best suit their needs. The treatment rooms are appointed with Frette linens, down comforters, and other luxurious touches to further enhance the experience. The individual responsible for the operation of The Ritz-Carlton Spa, Naples, is the executive spa director, Michelle Kelthy. Michelle has a management staff of eight and operations staff of over 100 to help keep The Spa running smoothly. It is Michelle's goal to ensure that each Spa experience is a "vacation for your mind, body, and soul."

Michelle Kelthy has spent 20 years in the spa industry. Originally from the United Kingdom, Michelle started her career working in and managing a hair salon outside Liverpool, England. She then entered the cruise industry, managing salon and spa facilities aboard ships. Michelle completed a 10-year career in the cruise industry as regional manager of onboard spa facilities working out of cities such as Vancouver, San Juan, and Miami. In 2000, Michelle moved to Bangkok, Thailand, where she worked for Starwood Hotels and after one year moved to start the first Elemis Day Spa in Hong Kong's business district. It was at this time that Michelle immersed herself in learning Asian therapies and, along with the spa industry, began to move away from aesthetic treatments to more holistic treatments. Michelle joined the Ritz-Carlton Hotel Company in 2003, operating The Spa at the Ritz-Carlton, San Juan Hotel, The Spa & Casino in Puerto Rico, and in 2005 she took the position in Naples.

It is certainly an exciting time to work in the spa industry. According to Aesthetics Medical, Inc., in 2000, the size of the U.S. spa industry was estimated at over 12,000 locations. That number was increased to over 17,000 by 2003. According to Michelle, the best part of her role as executive spa director is the opportunity to help and heal people. "Starting out as a therapist, I've learned how much I love to help people achieve their goals." Michelle said she feels lucky to be around her staff, whom she describes as being "passionate about helping others." She states that passion is essential for anyone interested in working in the spa industry.

This spotlight on Michelle Kelthy illustrates the benefits of working in this distinct area of the commercial recreation and tourism industry. A career in the spa industry takes a desire to help people, great attention to detail, dedication to expanding your knowledge of this quickly growing industry, and as always, a passion to please the customer.

REFERENCES

About.com. (2005). Ancient history of the Olympics. http://ancienthistory.about.com/cs/olympics/a/aa021798.htm

Adams, M. (2005, April 27). International travel flies high as demand soars. *USA Today*, p. E1.

Chubb, M., & Chubb, H. (1981). *One third of our time? An introduction to recreation behavior and resources.* New York: John Wiley & Sons.

Corridore, J. (2004, May). Industry surveys: Airlines. *Standard & Poor's Industry Surveys, pp. 1-31.*

Goeldner, C., Ritchie, J. R., & McIntosh, R. (2000). *Tourism principles, practices, philosophies (8th ed.).* New York: John Wiley & Sons, Inc.

National Sporting Goods Association. (2004). Ten-year history of selected sports participation. http://www.nsga.org/

Neff, C. (2005, May/June) "Post 9/11 Travel" Via Magazine. http://www.viamagazine.com/

Roper Starch. (2004, January). Outdoor recreation in America, 2003. Washington, D.C.: The Recreation Roundtable. http://www.funoutdoors.com/

Spartacus Educational Homepage. (2005). Thomas Cook. http://www.spartacus.schoolnet.co.uk/BUcook.htm

Travel Industry Association of America. (2005). Economic impacts of travel and tourism. http://www.tia.org/Travel/econimpact.asp

U.S. Census Bureau. (2004). 2002 economic census. Washington, DC: U.S. Census Bureau. http://www.census.gov/econ/census02/

World Travel and Tourism Council. (2004). Travel and tourism's economic impact. http://www.wttc.org/

Chapter ••••  2

The Entrepreneur

The word *entrepreneur* has become a buzzword in popular literature, business-related literature, and as part of many course titles in university business schools. A study by management consulting firm Ernst & Young (Williams, 1999) found that 78% of "influential" Americans believe that entrepreneurship will be the defining trend of the 21st century. Although we use the term frequently, do we really know who the entrepreneur is? Where does she get her ideas? How does she develop those ideas into a fledgling business? What strategies does she follow to manage the new enterprise to success? These and other issues are the focus of this chapter.

WHY STUDY THE ENTREPRENEUR?

Small business has become an increasingly larger segment of the nation's economy and may now represent up to 80% of all businesses. Therefore, it is advisable to become more aware of the traits, successes, and issues surrounding the entrepreneur. Unfortunately, only a few studies have provided a direct link with entrepreneurial success and the recreation and tourism field. It is logical, however, that a study of characteristics of entrepreneurs in general should help us understand a little more about their path to success.

Misconceptions About the Entrepreneur

Several times a year we see newspapers or television shows highlight an individual who has become a successful entrepreneur. The most newsworthy stories often tell about a high school or college dropout who turned a bright idea into a million-dollar business. Variation A of this story is that the entrepreneur slaved 20 years to make a dream come true. The more glamorous variation B tells how the entrepreneur gambled everything his or her family owned on a long shot that came through.

In motion pictures, we often see the entrepreneur portrayed as the sociable huckster who, with no sense of guilt, exploits friends or swindles strangers. This popular version shows the entrepreneur with an "easy come, easy go" attitude. Another popular view is that the entrepreneur has such an instinct for the business that he or she never needs to be analytical. Finally, some people think that the entrepreneur is motivated primarily by money and will do anything to make a buck.

These views of the entrepreneur may be popular for newspapers, television, and motion pictures, but they do not square with facts. Research has shown the entrepreneur to be quite different from the popular misconceptions.

Hendricks (2005) notes the following myths and realities about what an entrepreneur needs:

1. *Myth*: You must have big money. *Reality*: Starting a business at home, contracting out for services, and other strategies may prevent the need for large capital investments.
2. *Myth*: You must have a deep management team. *Reality*: A streamlined organization is simple and agile.
3. *Myth*: You must have a technological composition advantage. *Reality*: This is not necessarily so, given the many niches one can fulfill in any given market.
4. *Myth*: You must tap into a hot market. *Reality*: Even a stagnant industry still is an industry where opportunities for innovation may abound.

PROFILE OF THE ENTREPRENEUR

Entrepreneurs are individuals with a unique combination of personal drive, skills, intelligence, and the nerve to go it alone. They are very aware of and/or study the environment, especially social change, market trends, technological advancements, and economic conditions. They find some sort of change or trend that can be exploited as an opportunity. After careful study and analysis, the entrepreneur finds resources, brings them together, and manages them in such a way as to create something new and different. In this perspective, entrepreneurism is just the opposite of a risky "easy come, easy go" venture. Rather, entrepreneurship is a well thought out shift of resources from an area of low productivity to an area of potentially higher productivity and higher financial yield. While there is still an element of risk, careful scrutiny of the market and careful planning of the business helps to reduce the risk. Modern entrepreneurs have the ability to size up a venture, ease into it, and leave it, when it is at a plateau.

Psychological Portrait of the Entrepreneur

Many profiles of entrepreneurs are oriented toward inventors and manufacturers. However, the following characteristics, from a wide variety of sources, are thought to apply to the generic portrait of an entrepreneur (Business Town, 2001; Kulzer, 2000; and Smith, 1998). Entrepreneurs typically

- are self-confident and persistent in the pursuit of their objectives;
- are motivated to create something unique on their own;
- dislike someone else having authority over them;
- are impatient and drive themselves and everyone around them;
- are comfortable in stressful situations and are challenged rather than discouraged by setbacks;
- are willing to make personal and family sacrifices in order to succeed;
- are sensitive to good ideas;
- view money as a resource and as a way of keeping score, but not as a motivating source;
- are mentally tough and recognize their own limitations;
- are more concerned with people's accomplishments than their feelings;
- prefer individual sports over team sports;
- are competitive, but compete against self-imposed standards;
- can comprehend complex situations and can work on multiple tasks;
- are realistic, accepting things as they are, and dealing with them accordingly;
- are not troubled by ambiguity because they are good problem solvers;
- are realistic, calculated risk takers, but not big gamblers;
- have the ability to delegate tasks to others;
- are better innovators than operators of a mature venture;
- have common sense and are intelligent, but not necessarily on academic tests;
- are good networkers but have little need to join group affiliations;

- are able to take a long-term perspective and see the "big picture";
- have courage to surround themselves with strong people without bruising their own egos; and
- are basically honest and ethical.

Characteristics of Leisure Service Entrepreneurs

It may be that commercial recreation and tourism entrepreneurs have the same characteristics of other entrepreneurs in general, but there may be some differences. Berrett, Burton, and Slack (1993), in a study of sport and leisure service entrepreneurs, found that no particular economic planning preceded their success. Entrepreneurs of sport and leisure businesses tended to de-emphasize growth potential in favor of remaining a small, viable operation. It is possible that this also reflects a lack of training to develop feasibility studies, but it also may point to the fierce dedication many leisure service entrepreneurs have toward their business operations.

Commitment to the quality of the product or service was the "key to success" that the sport and leisure entrepreneurs most often emphasized. Most of those entrepreneurs also suggested a commitment to the employee. A third factor was that personal financial rewards were a lower priority than the intrinsic rewards of operating a business.

The Spirit of Entrepreneurship

Very few people will perfectly fit the previously mentioned psychological portrait. In fact, some persons may match only half of the characteristics and yet become successful entrepreneurs. What then is the "bottom line" that all entrepreneurs must possess? Many authorities believe that the energy and spirit of the entrepreneur is the key factor. A lot of people have good ideas, but there are few who have the tremendous drive to actually do what it takes to make the dream become a reality.

It may be that there is a "window" in life for most people when the time is right to break away from an organization and start their own enterprise. This is a time when the spirit of entrepreneurship overlaps with competence and experience. At too young an age, a person may have enthusiasm but lack business experience and self-confidence. By the early 40s, however, this person is usually embedded in a career and facing many family and financial commitments. Even though the experience factor exists, the entrepreneurial spirit may be lost, and it is too late to break away into a new venture. On the other hand, once a person becomes a successful entrepreneur, the spirit can be rekindled with each new venture. Some entrepreneurs are still putting deals together at the age of 80.

A breakaway from the corporate or bureaucratic world also may mean that to be successful one needs to break rules, or at least be creative in "pressing the limits" or boundaries of conventional thought. While rules are there, exceptions to the rule may be capitalized on to create a unique, successful situation. The spirit may reside in this comment: "Rule breaking may, in fact, be inescapable for fast growth entrepreneurs, many of whom attribute their success specifically to being unlike anything that has been seen before" (Hendricks, 2005b).

SYSTEMATIC ENTREPRENEURSHIP AND SOURCES FOR INNOVATION

Entrepreneurs do not just pull successful ideas out of thin air. They are usually very familiar with a certain industry and find ways to improve that industry's products or services. According to a survey by the National Federation of Independent Business, 60% of entrepreneurs get their ideas from their experience on a prior job or from an area of strong personal interest. An entrepreneur may also understand a particular market segment very well and create products or services to fulfill unmet needs. Another approach occurs when the entrepreneur correctly anticipates social, demographic, or economic changes that lead to opportunities.

A special events company is contracted to provide pregame activities such as big-glove boxing at a university football game. (Photo: J. Crossley)

In all three of the above situations, innovation occurs. We can define *innovation* as any act that endows resources with new capacity to create wealth. A common thread is that the entrepreneur is closely in touch with his or her environment. In his classic text *Innovation and Entrepreneurship*, world-renowned management guru Peter Drucker (1985) suggested that the successful entrepreneur monitors the environment and engages in "systematic innovation." This means a purposeful and organized search for changes in the environment and then a systematic analysis of the opportunities that such changes may offer. Drucker further suggested eight sources for innovation. Although written 20 years ago, Drucker's ideas are totally valid today. These sources are presented here in descending order of reliability and predictability. It is important to note that the first four sources of innovation (the unexpected success or failure, incongruities, process needs, and industry and market structure) are internally oriented. That is, a person working within a given industry would be in the best position to observe these opportunities. On the other hand, the last four types (demographics, changes in perception, new knowledge, and the bright idea) are all externally oriented, and industry outsiders can capitalize on these opportunities.

Source 1: The Unexpected Success or Failure

The unexpected success or failure of a company's products or services can point to new opportunities. No other area offers richer opportunity, because it is less risky, and the pursuit is less arduous. This is because a company usually has its structure and resources in place sufficiently to capitalize on this type of innovation. Yet this method of innovation is often neglected because it may not be seen, even by insiders.

For example, the manager of a sporting goods store in Texas carried a small line of ski equipment, mainly as a convenience to some of his regular customers. Over several years, his ski equipment sales doubled, but he did not really notice the change and did not increase his product line. Meanwhile, another store manager monitored her sales more carefully. "Why would ski sales in Texas increase?" she asked. From customers she learned that cheap air fares had made it easy for Texans to reach Colorado. This manager increased her line of ski equipment each year until she became the "ski center" for miles around. The unexpected success of this product line eventually contributed to a huge increase in profitability.

The key aspect of this source of innovation is that the entrepreneur must become aware of the unexpected occurrence. Then, action must be taken to capitalize upon the circumstances.

Source 2: Incongruities

An incongruity is a discrepancy or a dissonance between an existing situation and what should logically be happening. There is an underlying fault that may not manifest itself in sales figures or reports. If the entrepreneur discovers the incongruity, it can be exploited with a new product or service or by trying a new approach with an existing product or service.

A city in Virginia conducted an extensive youth sports program. In the autumn, this program did not include soccer, but there was a tackle football program with 65 teams. This football program was very expensive, and the participant fees did not come close to covering the cost. Meanwhile, a community survey showed virtually no interest in soccer. "How could this be?" asked the city recreation supervisor. After all, he reasoned, soccer is a popular and inexpensive youth sport all over the country, including neighboring cities. A community survey showed soccer near the bottom of the list of sports interest, and no one in the city of 110,000 had ever appeared before the advisory board and asked for a soccer program. The recreation supervisor decided to challenge this incongruity by starting a youth soccer league. Within three years there were 72 teams, and the program fees covered all costs. Throughout this period, football registration did not drop. An incongruity had been met with a new program that found an entirely new market segment.

Source 3: Process Need

This is a task-focused innovation that perfects a process that already exists by replacing a weak link or by redesigning an existing process around new knowledge. When this innovation occurs, it becomes the "obvious" solution that people just did not think of. To be successful, the need must be understood, and there must be high consumer receptivity to it.

Movie theaters make about half of their profits from concession stand revenues. During sellouts of popular movies, the crowd at the concession stand gets so long that many latecomers forego a purchase in order to find seats. One theater manager observed the concession process and found a way to cut service time by 40%. First, soft drink service was redesigned to a self-serve format. Even if some people abused this approach, the product cost was minimal. Second, all items were priced so that when tax was added, the amount would be $3.00, $3.50, or $4.00. This made it much quicker to handle the customer's payment. As a result of these process innovations, more people could be served during the peak periods, and concession sales increased.

Source 4: Industry and Market Structures

This source of innovation requires that managers of a company ask themselves: "What is our business?" The idea is to search for a flaw in the basic nature of the industry. This strategy is particularly effective when an industry has been dominated by a few large companies who have become unchallenged and arrogant. An innovative newcomer then gains a foothold in the market with a simple but important change that appeals to customers. If the innovation is successful, it is difficult for the larger companies to change quickly and mobilize for a counterattack.

Joel Benard-Cutler and David Fialkow opened The Vacation Outlet as a very different kind of discount travel company. They felt that the "discount travel industry" had a basic flaw. They believed that many people shy away from discount travel agencies because of a perception of low quality or suspicion that it could be a travel scam. Therefore, they decided to build an upscale business that offered travel savings, not cheap travel. Through bulk purchase of space at a limited number of deluxe resorts, they were able to offer savings of several hundred dollars to people who care more about value than price (Hyatt, 1991).

Source 5: Demographics

Of all the externally oriented strategies, innovations based on demographic changes are the clearest and have the most predictable consequences. Demographic shifts have long lead times and are measured by numerous organizations from which data is readily available. However, a problem is that other entrepreneurs can have access to the same demographic information. Therefore, it becomes a question of which entrepreneur best interprets and exploits the demographic shifts.

One of the clear demographic trends is the great increase of women in business, including sales and management positions that require frequent travel. In response to this trend, several hotel chains have developed rooms oriented to the needs of the female business traveler. These include design for increased security; small meeting rooms that are separate from the bedroom; and bathrooms with double sinks, built-in hair dryers, and other conveniences.

Source 6: Changes in Perception

When changes in people's perceptions take place, facts do not change, but meanings do. For example, the physiological benefits of exercise have been known for years. However, in past years, staunch adherence to weight lifting or distance running was not considered normal. Now, the perception of fitness has changed. Fitness is now associated with quality of life and social interaction. As a result of this change in perception, many companies that have exploited the fitness industry have done very well.

There is a major problem with this strategy, however. Timing is critical. Nothing is more dangerous than to be premature in exploiting a change of perception. A company can go broke if it puts money into an idea before the market is ready and receptive. On the other hand, it can be equally disastrous to enter a market after it has peaked. The best approach in exploiting a change of perception is to start small and appeal to a very specific market.

Source 7: New Knowledge

Innovations based on new knowledge are the "superstars" of entrepreneurship. Although new knowledge does not have to be scientific or technology-based, these have been the glamourous areas of recent years. In many cases, it is a convergence of several different kinds of knowledge that results in a success. The airplane, for example, was a convergence of the gasoline engine and modern aerodynamics. Advances in computer chip technology have generated a vast array of product innovations such as digital cameras, DVD players, "smart dolls" that learn phrases, global positioning systems for boats and cars, virtual reality games, and many other products.

An important characteristic of knowledge-based innovation is the long lead time required to bring an idea to the marketplace. This can mean great expense, and if the idea is not right the first time, the entrepreneur may be out of business. The next entrepreneur, however, may take the failed idea, add a missing ingredient, and be successful.

Another problem is the "receptivity gamble." A knowledge-based innovation may not be what the public wants. The entrepreneur is gambling that the public will be receptive to the idea when it is developed. There is also the problem that some entrepreneurs get infatuated with their own technology, regardless of what the public wants.

For these reasons, knowledge-based innovation is very risky. The risk can be reduced, however, if this strategy can be combined with one or more other sources for innovation.

Source 8: The Bright Idea

Seven out of every 10 patents filed belong in this category. These are often simple ideas such as zippers or pull tabs on beer cans. Examples of recreation industry "bright ideas" include the hula hoop and Frisbee. Unfortunately, the bright idea is the riskiest and least successful form of innovation. Only 1 in 500 bright ideas makes significant revenue.

Bright ideas are typically unorganized and out of sync with any particular market demand. This is not a strategy upon which an entrepreneur should focus. However, society does need those rare 1-in-500 ideas that make it big.

DEVELOPING THE ENTREPRENEURIAL CONCEPT

According to Scott Molander (2005), successful former owner of Hat World, the *Investor's Business Daily* "10 Secrets to Success" are a constant guide for his enterprises. The 10 secrets are:

1. How you think is everything. Think success, not failure. Beware of a negative environment.
2. Decide upon your true dreams and goals. Write down your specific goals and develop a plan to reach them.
3. Take action. Goals are nothing without action. Don't be afraid to get started. Just do it.
4. Never stop learning. Go back to school or read books. Get training and acquire skills.
5. Be persistent and work hard. Success is a marathon, not a sprint. Never give up.
6. Learn to analyze details. Get all of the facts, all the input. Learn from your mistakes.
7. Focus your time and money. Don't let other people or things distract you.
8. Don't be afraid to innovate: Be different. Following the herd is a sure way to mediocrity.
9. Deal and communicate with people effectively. No person is an island. Learn to understand and motivate others.
10. Be honest and dependable; take responsibility. Otherwise, numbers one to nine won't matter.

Once an entrepreneur has an innovative concept, it must be developed into a workable product or service. Although Chapter 4 details the practical steps of starting a business and developing a feasibility study, we should first examine some of the general aspects of developing an innovative idea into an entrepreneurial success. The "Four Faces of the Entrepreneur" are necessary for this process to occur, and this also applies for the entrepreneur within an existing organization.

Four Faces of the Entrepreneur

There are four very different roles that must be filled for an innovative concept to become an entrepreneurial success (Von Oech, 1986). These are the roles of the explorer, the artist, the judge, and the warrior.

The Explorer enjoys the search for ideas. This can include an in-depth analysis of a person's own field of expertise, or a search of entirely different fields for "crossover" ideas. A systematic application of Drucker's "Sources of Innovation" would be a good way to start.

The Artist transforms what the explorer finds into a working concept. An imaginative artist considers many variables to create a product or service plan that will attract customers and satisfy the benefits they seek.

The Judge evaluates the artist's concept and may modify it. Questions the judge asks involve the market, the costs, the time required to implement the idea, the resources available, and the chance of success. It is important for the judge to strike down the ideas that are not well founded.

The Warrior goes to battle for the ideas that the judge approves and does whatever it takes to implement the idea. The warrior must have passion for the idea and be able to fight a long time.

Each of these four faces depends upon different entrepreneurial characteristics. For best results, the entrepreneur needs to have all four faces, because one weak face can ruin the venture. For example, if the entrepreneur isn't a good explorer, he or she will not see opportunities. On the other hand, if the judge is not analytical and realistic, then too many bad ideas will exhaust the warrior.

The key to this concept is that the entrepreneur needs all four faces to succeed, or help from other people will be needed. For example, a partner who is analytical and experienced could help mold and modify the entrepreneur's idea into a workable business concept. In another scenario, an entrepreneur might be an excellent judge and warrior who counts upon a "think tank" of business associates or consultants to come up with new ideas.

CHALLENGES WORKING AS AN ENTREPRENEUR WITHIN AN ORGANIZATION

While many entrepreneurs start their own business enterprises, many more people have entrepreneurial characteristics and work within an existing framework in the corporate or public organization. These individuals can apply many of the same entrepreneurial concepts to their workplace. Such people have been called "intrapreneurs." There are, however, certain barriers to face within organizations, particularly those organizations that have grown to become bureaucratic in nature. Some of these challenges include:

- resistance to change,
- resentment of individuality,
- red tape that makes it difficult to operate quickly and entrepreneurially,
- discouragement of creative ideas,
- little tolerance for risk,
- insufficient research and development funding,
- lack of incentives for innovations, and
- overemphasis on accountability.

In order to overcome these barriers, the intrapreneur should follow the ideas of Loeb (1995) and others.

Serve Three Types of Needs: the needs of the customers, the organization, and the intrapreneur. Obviously, it must be an idea that customers will purchase, but it must also fit within the organization's overall philosophy, resources, and strategies. It must also provide profits or savings that are acceptable. Finally, the idea must be one that the entrepreneur finds interesting and personally compatible.

Allow Time to Develop the Idea. If time cannot be found within the regular workweek, the entrepreneur must be willing to work overtime, and probably without extra pay.

Develop a Business Plan. This will demonstrate that the idea has been thoroughly researched before large resources are committed to implementation.

Find Allies and Sponsors. These people should be carefully and quietly sought. They can help "pirate" resources within the organization and buffer the intrapreneur from attacks.

Avoid Premature Publicity. Internal jealousy could wreck any good idea and bring greater penalties if the idea fails.

Get Small Decisions. Never ask for a decision larger than one needed to take the idea one step further. Don't try to sell a big untested idea.

Recognize Your Own Weaknesses. Get expert help to complement your strengths.

Rewards Are Essential. If financial rewards are not possible, the organization might provide travel expenses to conferences, public and peer recognition, and "release time" from regular work to continue to be entrepreneurial.

ENTREPRENEURIAL STRATEGIES FOR THE MARKET

Once an entrepreneurial innovation has been developed, it needs to be brought to the marketplace. Again, Peter Drucker's classic *Innovation and Entrepreneurship* (Drucker, 1985) suggested the entrepreneurial strategies below, which are still relevant.

"Fustest With the Mostest"

A Civil War Confederate cavalry general once said that the key to victory was to "git thar fustest with the mostest." Drucker borrowed this phrase to name this strategy that aims at leadership and dominance of a new market. The entrepreneur basically tries to capture an entire market by being first on the scene with an innovation.

Entrepreneurs using this strategy must continue to research and innovate if they are to fight off competition. If they set prices too high, then even more competitors will be encouraged to enter the market. And, like a moon shot, this strategy must be right on target during development, or it will be way off by the time a huge promotional program is launched. Small water theme parks popped up all over the country in the mid-1980s, and most were successful for a while, until bigger ones were built in the same area.

The "fustest with the mostest" strategy will fail more often than it will succeed and should be used only for major innovations. If it is successful, it is highly rewarding, but overall it is not the dominant strategy for marketing an innovation.

"Hit 'em Where They Ain't"

This strategy is based on the assumption that "fustest with the mostest" will fail more often than it will succeed. An entrepreneur will wait until someone else has established something new but has not achieved the ultimate design. The entrepreneur then develops the idea one step better and captures the market. Continuing with the water theme park example, small parks with a few slides did not compete well when new parks included different slides, "lazy-river" rides, shallow spray pools, and other improvements designed to appeal to a whole family.

Similarly, a large company may be first on the scene with a product and try to "cream the market" with high prices. A newcomer could simplify or modify the idea, offer it at a lower price, and steal part of the market away. Some discount hotel chains have done this in high-priced resort areas. They offer basic accommodations for the budget-minded tourist and gain excellent occupancy rates.

Ecological Niches

This strategy aims at control or practical monopoly in a small segment of a market. It may be so inconspicuous that no one tries to compete. An ecological niche may be based upon a specialty skill, product, or service. For example, a ski tuning service picks up tourists' skis at Salt Lake City hotels at night and returns them freshly waxed the next morning. The ecological niche can also be based upon a specific market.

There could even be a niche within a niche. For example, Jerron Atkin takes service one step further than even small bicycle specialty shops. Jerron provides full-service bicycle repairs and tune-ups from his home-based shop, and he provides same-day service that includes bike pickup and return to customers' homes. Because his shop overhead costs are very low, his prices undercut those at the bicycle stores (Brophy, 1996).

The problem with the ecological niche strategy is that it cannot sustain full control if the specialty market grows to become a mass market. New competitors enter the picture when volume and profit margins grow. This strategy, however, is an excellent one for an entrepreneur with a special service and/or a low overhead operation. The key is to find that unmet ecological niche and serve it well.

Changing Values and Characteristics

This strategy involves converting an established product or service into something new by changing its utility. In this way, a new customer is created. Time-share resorts capitalize on this and attract consumers who generally could not afford their own vacation homes. Time-sharing offers the security of ownership and relatively fixed prices, with the flexibility of trading for different locations. To capitalize on this entrepreneurial strategy, it is critical to know the market and know what the consumer values.

"Doggie Day Care" services have taken the traditional kennel concept to a whole new level. Instead of simply keeping a pet temporarily housed and fed, the pets are trained, exercised, socialized, and pampered. High-price/high-service operations help the pet owners reduce their sense of guilt in leaving their animal "children" behind for the workday. They are not putting their dog in a kennel; they are enrolling it in a day camp!

ENTREPRENEURIAL MANAGEMENT

Although Chapter 7 details a variety of strategies for commercial recreation and tourism ventures of all types, it seems appropriate to include here some ideas from several notable entrepreneurs about how they manage their businesses. The ideas come from Courtland Logue, who has started 28 businesses (Nulty, 1995); Herb Kelleher, the cofounder and CEO of Southwest Airlines (Lancaster, 1999); Jack Kirkham, inventor and manufacturer of the Springbar tent (Wharton, 1994); and Scott Molander, founder of Hat World (Molander, 2005).

1. Your business should be built around honesty and integrity.
2. Stick to what you know, but grow to know more.
3. Find a bank or other financial institution you can rely on, and one that can rely on you.

4. Hire employees who will appreciate your philosophy; especially hire people with positive attitudes who enjoy helping others.
5. Treat your employees well by caring for them in the totality of their lives, not just at work.
6. Give employees the license to be themselves and the opportunity to be entrepreneurs.
7. Earn the trust of your customers by treating them fairly and with appreciation. Your employees will follow this lead if your employees also feel appreciated and treated well.
8. Strive for excellence. Being the best is more satisfying than being the biggest.
9. Always put part of your earnings back into the business. This is essential in order to grow and/or become debt free.
10. Plan ahead: specifically for tomorrow, generally for a year, and conceptually for 5 to 10 years.
11. Watch your business like a hawk and know the numbers (financials).
12. As you get larger, get more systematized, but fight bureaucracy.
13. If you make a poor decision, correct it immediately.
14. You can learn as much, if not more, from a bad situation than a good one, whether personal or professional.
15. Review a decision as "What is the worst possible outcome, and can I live with that outcome?"

Sketch artists in parks and malls draw upon the creative talents and entrepreneurial spirit of the artist-business person. (Photo: J. Crossley)

ENTREPRENEURSHIP IN PUBLIC SERVICE ORGANIZATIONS

Service institutions such as public park and recreation departments need to be just as innovative and entrepreneurial as a private business. The problem is that service institutions often have cumbersome structures, procedures, and traditions that are greater barriers than are found in even the most bureaucratic of private companies. Specific obstacles that many public service institutions face include the following:

- They are dependent on a multitude of constituents and find it difficult to focus on specific market segments.
- Service institutions exist to serve the interests of their entire community and see their mission as moral rather than as economic (and subject to cost/benefit justification).
- They usually want to do more of the same and resist abandoning anything. The demand to innovate is perceived as an attack on their basic service commitments. Labor unions almost always fight innovation.
- Service institutions have budgets that have been appropriated by a higher authority (city council, county commission, etc.) rather than budgets based on their results (i.e., revenues).

In spite of the barriers mentioned, there is hope for entrepreneurism in service institutions. The key is to develop entrepreneurial philosophies and policies that will guide the operation of the service institution. Suggested policies are presented here.

- Have a clear definition of the organization's mission. Programs and projects must be considered as temporary strategies to fulfill the mission. Innovative programs might serve the mission better.
- Have realistic goals. It is impossible, for most practical purposes, to serve all the recreation needs of all the residents or constituents.
- The failure to achieve objectives must be considered an indication that the objectives could be wrong. They may need modification or elimination. It is not rational to budget more money for repeated failures.
- Build policies and procedures to search for opportunity. View change as an opportunity, not as a threat.
- Consider the privatization (contracting out) of facilities, programs, or services, if they cannot be managed efficiently and effectively by the institution.

ASSISTANCE FOR ENTREPRENEURSHIP IN RECREATION AND TOURISM ORGANIZATIONS

Because many public recreation professionals do not have entrepreneurial backgrounds, it may be advisable to seek assistance. For general business advice, any office of the Small Business Administration (SBA) can help, as can the business school of almost any university. Consultation is also available in many communities through local chapters of the Service Corps of Retired Executives or the Active Corps of Executives. Both organizations provide consultation for free or for low fees. The following URLs may be useful:

http://www.bplans.com
http://www.indianaventurecenter.org
http://www.sbinformation.about.com
http://www.nvca.org

http://www.sba.gov
http://www.businessfinance.com
http://www.accel.com
http://home.americanexpress.com

http://www.garage.com
http://www.mbda.gov
http://www.nbia.org
http://www.eonetworking.org
http://www.svn.org

http://www.tannedfeet.com
http://sbdcnet.utsa.edu
http://www.sls.lib.il.us
http://www.lowe.org
http://www.c-e-o.org

SUMMARY

People hold many misconceptions about entrepreneurs: that they are con men, hucksters, and gamblers who dropped out of school but got lucky with a business venture. Research, however, supports a much different profile. The entrepreneur is more likely to be an honest, well-educated individual who wants to create something unique on his own and is willing to work very hard to do it. While entrepreneurs are not big risk takers, they are realistic gamblers if the odds are in their favor. Primarily, they are "doers" who make things happen after they study situations very carefully. A successful entrepreneur must be an explorer of ideas, an artist for developing the idea, an unbiased judge of the idea, and a warrior who fights for the idea.

Entrepreneurs can also exist within an organization and are sometimes called "intrapreneurs." These entrepreneurs face additional barriers in the organization but have some additional assets to work with. Most importantly, the intrapreneur needs freedom, a trusting sponsor, and a system of rewards.

Systematic entrepreneurship is the organized search for changes in the environment that will present opportunities. Peter Drucker (1985) suggested eight strategies that are sources of innovation for the systematic entrepreneur: the unexpected success or failure, incongruities, process needs, industry and market structures, demographics, changes in perception, new knowledge, and the bright idea. Drucker further suggested several strategies to bring the innovations to market: "fustest with the mostest," "hit 'em where they ain't," ecological niches, and changing values and characteristics.

Recreation service institutions face certain barriers but can still be innovative and entrepreneurial. The key is to develop philosophies and policies that allow the organization to have "entrepreneurial elbow room" rather than be restricted by bureaucracy. A variety of consultation services and publications can provide assistance for the commercial recreation and tourism entrepreneur.

SPOTLIGHT ON:

Scott Molander—HAT WORLD and Beyond

Scott Molander knows firsthand what it is like to take an idea for a new business and turn it into a $100 million company. For most of his life, Molander has been fascinated by the retail world, looking for creative and profitable ways to reach the consumer with unique products.

In 1995, Molander and Glenn Campbell cofounded Hat World, Inc. Over the past nine years, Hat World has experienced phenomenal growth and is now widely recognized as the undisputed leader in specialty athletic headwear. With 500 stores located in malls, streets, outlets, tourist destinations, and airports across 46 states in the United States and with new stores being developed in overseas markets like Hong Kong, Korea, and China, Hat World continues to be the market innovator as well as the leading performer financially.

As executive vice president, Molander played an integral role in the company's growth and diversification and was very involved in key initiatives like raising capital from outside investors, acquiring key competitors, launching Hat World's e-commerce business, managing the distribution center, and identifying and negotiating prime geographic locations for expansion. The company's acquisition of their biggest competitor, Lids!, in 2001 catapulted their revenue from $45 million to $120 million. Hat World now has $200 million in revenue and employs 200 people in Indianapolis and over 2,300 people worldwide.

During these incredible years of growth, Molander and his Hat World colleagues were awarded the prestigious Indiana Entrepreneur of the Year Award in two categories—Emerging Company in 1999 and Retail-Wholesale Company in 2002. They were also given the yearly Enterprise Award by the *Indianapolis Business Journal* in 2003. In April of 2004, Genesco, Inc., a Nashville-based provider of footwear and accessories, acquired Hat World. Company headquarters and distribution center remain in Indianapolis.

Molander recently left Hat World to spend more time with his wife and daughter, take some well deserved vacations, look at some new venture opportunities, and/or launch his next big idea.

To assist aspiring entrepreneurs, Molander has provided Tips from an Entrepreneur:

1. You can learn as much, if not more, from a bad situation than a good one, whether personal or professional.
2. Treat employees the same as you would want to be treated.
3. Never think you know everything. Always seek advice both personally and professionally.
4. Teach your employees and let them do their job.
5. Whenever I review a decision I think, "What is the worst possible outcome and can I live with that outcome?"

Reprinted with permission from Sue Atmeir; Indiana Venture Center's e-newsletter, Sept. 1, 2004 http://www.kelley.indiana.edu/jcei/entrepreneur/molander.html 4/25/2005

REFERENCES

Berrett, T., Burton, T., & Slack, T. (1993). Quality products, quality service: Factors leading to the entrepreneurial success in the sport and leisure industry. *Leisure Studies, 12,* 93–106.

Brophy, S. (1996, November 18). Come and get it. *Salt Lake Tribune,* p. D1.

Business Town. (2001). Profile of an entrepreneur. Business Town.com, LLC. http://www.businesstown.com/entrepreneur/article1.asp

Drucker, P. (1985). *Innovation and entrepreneurship.* New York: Harper & Row Publishers.

Hendricks, M. (2005a, April). Honor Roll. *Entrepreneur,* pp. 68–78.

Hendricks, M. (2005b, April). The fast lane. *Entrepreneur,* p. 67.

Hyatt, J. (1991, June). Words from the wise. *Inc.,* pp. 50–65.

Kulzer, T. (2000). Profile of an entrepreneur. http://www.eglassceiling.com/wib2/ww645.htm

Lancaster, H. (1999, July 31). Managing your career. *Wall Street Journal,* p. B1.

Loeb, M. (1995, December 11). How to make your CEO buy your idea. *Fortune,* p. 210.

Molander, S. (2005). Words of wisdom from successful entrepreneur—Scott Molander. http://www.kelley.indiana.edu/jcei/entrepreneur/molander.html.

Nulty, P. (1995, July 10). Serial entrepreneur: Tips from a man who started 28 businesses. *Fortune,* p.182.

Smith, C. (1998). An entrepreneur's question: Is there a view from the top? Catalyst Financial Planning & Investment Management. http://www.catystim.co/entrepreneur/winter98_view.html

Von Oech, R. (1986). *A kick in the seat of the pants* (audio tape). Menlo Park, California: Tape Data Media, Inc.

Wharton, T. (1994, July 24). Jack Kirkham's tents shelter 50 years of devotion. *Salt Lake Tribune,* pp. F1, F3.

Williams, G. (1999, April). 2001: An entrepreneurial odyssey. *Entrepreneur,* p.106–113.

Chapter  3

The Nature of Commercial Recreation and Tourism

The entrepreneur who desires to start a new venture in commercial recreation and tourism may have previous business experience in other types of enterprises and will quickly discover that there are many similarities with other types of business. It will, however, also become clear that there are many important differences, and the key to success for the entrepreneur is to understand and appropriately respond to both the similarities and the differences. The entrepreneur must understand the basic nature of commercial recreation and tourism, including the problems and challenges of the industry itself, the constraints that consumers and potential consumers experience, and a host of other relevant economic and consumer behavior concepts particular to the industry. This chapter examines these concepts in order to develop a basic understanding of the nature of commercial recreation and tourism. It must be emphasized that this chapter deals with general concepts and should not be viewed as a substitute for more in-depth coursework or study in business-related subjects. Specific applications of these concepts to various types of commercial recreation and tourism can differ, and later chapters will investigate many of the subindustries in greater depth.

CHALLENGES IN THE COMMERCIAL RECREATION AND TOURISM INDUSTRY

It has been generally observed that approximately 60% of all new enterprises do not last 5 years. In the first 3 years after establishment, nearly 25% of new enterprises fail, and many of those do not even survive long enough to celebrate an anniversary. While this may seem like an alarmingly high failure rate, there are many good reasons for a business succeeding or failing. Given the slightly higher failure rate for businesses in commercial recreation and tourism, it would seem that there are many more reasons to anticipate a lower rate of corporate survival. The successful commercial recreation and tourism enterprise is the one that has recognized and responded to a variety of significant challenges.

There are several underlying challenges in the commercial recreation and tourism industry that contribute to the difficulty in operating a successful venture. First is the fact that this business is dependent upon discretionary income. This is compounded by the seasonal nature of many recreation industries. Furthermore, there may be cyclical periods of good and bad years. Even within a good season, there are intermittent flurries of activity and offsetting slow periods. These and other challenges will be examined in this section.

Dependence on Discretionary Income

The U.S. Census Bureau (2005a) defines *disposable income* as the current income received by persons from all sources minus their personal contributions for social insurance, personal tax, and non-tax payments such as passport fees, fines, forfeitures, and donations. In other words, it is the earned money over which a person has control. Disposable income is an important variable in predicting overall consumer spending, but when it comes to spending for commercial recreation and tourism services, a more significant predictor is discretionary income. *Discretionary income* is the residual disposable income available to households after they have paid for housing, food, and other necessities. Discretionary income is money that may be saved or spent on "nonessentials" such as jewelry, education, or recreation. It might be argued that education or recreation are essential to well-being, but expenditures in these categories are still considered to be discretionary, because they can be deferred so much more readily than expenditures for food or housing.

There are periods of time when the economy sags and people have less to spend or they choose to restrain their leisure spending. The effects of an economic downturn can be quite severe in certain locales. For example, in the late 1970s and early 1980s, the steel- and auto-producing areas in Michigan, Ohio, and western Pennsylvania were in depressed economic conditions. In the middle 1980s, the farm belt and oil-producing states suffered their own regional recessions, while the east and west coasts flourished. The Persian Gulf War and a new economic recession in 1991 combined to reduce tourism revenue through most of the United States In the mid-1990s, the west coast of the United States had its turn to experience an economic downturn. The terrorist attacks on New York City and Washington DC in 2001 had an almost crippling impact on the travel, tourism, hospitality, and commercial recreation industries. In all such difficult economic times, a commercial recreation and tourism business may find it a challenge to survive simply because the money needed to fuel the industry is not available.

Substitution. A problem associated with discretionary products and services is that they are subject to consumer substitution. This notion of substitutability refers to the extent to which recreation activities can be interchanged in order to satisfy the user's motives, wishes, and desires. Consumers may substitute goods and services in order to try something new, different, cheaper, safer, better, or more convenient. Some people, however, are hard-core enthusiasts for certain activities and are not likely to substitute unless key elements of that activity (such as price or availability) change dramatically. Expenditures for most necessities, on the other hand, are less subject to substitution.

Target Market. Although intuitive, the commonly held yet false belief is that young urban professionals constitute the target market with the most discretionary income. This young, active group of consumers does enjoy a relatively high level of personal income, but only a small part of it is disposable or discretionary because of taxation and the high level of essential demands (especially housing and child-raising expenses) on that income. The largest market segment with high discretionary income is made up of professional adults in the 45–64 year age range. More than one half (53.9%) of this group of potential consumers is classified as having relatively high income (U.S. Census Bureau 2005b). Further, the majority have low or no mortgage payments and few or no children at home. The impact of housing costs and child-raising expenses on discretionary income is further emphasized by the fact that nearly half of Americans over 65 years old are classified as having low relative income, but record the highest per capita discretionary income.

The Consumer Research Center also noted that discretionary income tends to be higher among college graduates, homeowners, suburban dwellers, and households with two or more wage earners. In these statistical categories, the young professional, as well as the professional preretirement adult, stand out as the favored markets for commercial recreation. It must be remembered, however, that these groups are not the majority of the U.S. population. The majority of the population, although financially more secure than in previous years, still struggles to have the level of discretionary income that can confidently be interpreted by the commercial recreation and tourism industry as protection from periodic recessions, regional economic problems, and substitution behavior.

Seasonal Nature of Recreation

Many commercial recreation and tourism businesses have a highly seasonal orientation. This may be because the product is weather- or natural resource-dependent (e.g., skiing, river rafting, or trophy fishing), or because the supply of consumers is regulated by seasonal conditions (e.g., public school schedules, employment demands, or traditional celebrations like Christmas or New Year's Eve). Additionally, a commercial recreation and tourism enterprise may seasonally limit its services based on the fluctuating availability of employees (especially those operations that rely on college student workers). The several white-water rafting companies operating on the New River in West Virginia, for example, experience their peak season when the weather is warm, primary and elementary schools are in summer recess, trained guides are available, water is released into the river, and adults are more likely to vacation. Seasonal fluctuations in the supply and demand of commercial recreation products also occur if a business retails items such as sporting goods, toys, or tourist gifts. Figure 3-1 illustrates some of the high and low seasons in the recreation industry.

Note that, although Figure 3-1 suggests one high season (demand approaches or exceeds capacity) and one low season (capacity far exceeds demand) for each type of recreational facility, some parts of the commercial recreation and tourism industry have several peak seasons, and most facilities have "shoulder seasons" wherein the capacity is reduced or smaller markets replace those served during the high season(s). For example, a resort that enjoys a mid-winter high season for skiing and snowboarding may also have a high season for youth in its summer camp, mountaineering, or trail riding programs. Additionally it may be completely full for a 2- or 3-week period coinciding with college spring break. The same resort may have a shoulder season in the fall or late spring during which it caters primarily to a conference or business meeting market. Furthermore, there may also be some regional exceptions, such as the Miami area, where hotels enjoy a

Figure 3-1
Examples of Seasonality in the Recreation Industry

Type of Facility	High Season	Low Season
Campgrounds/trailer parks	May to Aug.	Nov. to Dec.
Multipurpose health and athletic clubs	Oct. to March	July to Aug.
Racquet/tennis clubs	Nov. to March	May
Public golf course (non-municipal)	May to Sept.	Nov. to Feb.
Resort hotel/motel	June to Aug.	Nov. to Jan.
Theme/amusement parks	May to Aug.	Nov. to March
Private golf/country club	April to Sept.	Jan. to Feb.
Sports/recreational camps	June to Aug.	Nov. to March
Zoos	April to Sept.	Nov. to Feb.

January to March high season (in contrast to summer high seasons just about everywhere else in the United States).

Technological advances can reduce or eliminate some seasonal limitations. In Winnipeg, Canada, for example, there is a three-tier golf driving range inside a huge, air-supported dome. It does excellent business throughout the winter, while all other courses in that golf-loving city wait for the retreat of the snow and the return of warm weather (usually not until late April or early May).

There are numerous problems created by a seasonal fluctuation in business. It is very expensive to keep a facility open, and expenses such as utilities and labor may not be balanced by off-season revenue. Even if a facility closes for the off-season, there are probably fixed expenses for rent or mortgage, insurance, and administrative overhead. Management's main concern then is managing cash flow. If the revenues drop below expenses, is there enough residual revenue to carry the business through? The alternative may be to take out a short-term loan.

Although severe storms destroyed much of the resort, the Manta Ray Bay Hotel built a new swimming pool as part of their recovery plan. (Photo: J. Crossley)

Operation of a seasonal business has its problems even during the busy season. Employees may have to be imported from other areas and provided with housing. Transportation into the area during periods of bad weather must be reliable enough so that customers can get in and out. Amenities related to a visitor's comfort, such as air-conditioning, heating, and entertainment, must function flawlessly.

Increasingly, commercial recreation and tourism businesses are attempting to create a year-round market for their product or service. This may be achieved by carrying different product lines (e.g., a sportswear store may carry tennis apparel in summer and ski apparel in winter), reducing prices, conducting major special events, or expanding facilities for different purposes. Many commercial recreation and tourism facilities continue to invest millions of dollars into making their facilities attractive for year-round use, especially for shoulder season markets. Such investments should respond to the carefully measured demand for different combinations of amenities, benefits, and services expressed by different target markets.

Cyclical Nature and Unpredictable Variations

Commercial recreation and tourism enterprises, whether seasonal or not, have normal cycles of business activity in which participation increases or decreases. In some cases, movement through these cycles is very gradual, and it is relatively easy to manage the business over a long period of sustained growth or to diversify a business during a long and gradual decline. A greater challenge comes when the cycles move rapidly and/or unexpectedly or when unpredicted variations occur. In this field, the movement of business cycles is most often related to either weather or market interest.

Weather in some locales runs in cycles, which can play havoc with commercial recreation and tourism. Ski resorts have been hurt numerous times by lack of snowfall, although artificial snowmaking has helped to reduce this problem. Droughts, hurricanes, rains, jellyfish, mosquitoes, and other natural phenomena periodically hurt various types of commercial recreation and tourism business.

The market's interest can be difficult to measure and predict. Some recreational products, such as Super Balls and Rubik's cubes, have been relatively short-lived fads, while Frisbees and skateboards have had multiyear success. Some fads, like the yo-yo, come and go without any apparent rhyme or reason. Sports apparel styles can also have short- or long-term cycles. Businesses can be hurt if they are too heavily dependent on the sales of a particular product or service that goes into a period of rapid decline.

It is important to understand what makes business cycles occur and to learn the art of predicting their consequences. It is just as important to avoid being caught off guard through disregard of cycles of activity that can add to the simplicity or difficulty of achieving success.

Intermittent Nature

Even during peak season, a commercial recreation and tourism business is likely to have intermittent periods of heavy and light participation. These periods coincide with certain days of the month, days of the week, and hours of the day.

Paydays in blue-collar communities and cities with military bases are often followed by a flurry of discretionary spending. Similarly, money is more available in urban core cities and in retirement communities following the receipt of monthly welfare and social security checks.

Weekends account for more than half of the volume of some commercial recreation and tourism businesses. This is mostly due to the standard Monday through Friday work-and school week. Holidays can be peak periods of activity for resorts, but can also be days when some retail stores, restaurants, and local attractions are closed.

Many commercial recreation and tourism businesses have busy periods and slow periods during each day. Racquetball and sports clubs for example, typically have good business in the early morning, at lunchtime, and during prime-time hours, 5:00 p.m. till 10:00 p.m. On the other hand, movie theaters seldom even bother to open until mid-afternoon, except for special Saturday matinees.

The intermittent nature of this business can cause management difficulties. If the busy and slack periods alternate throughout the day, most facilities will have to keep utilities operating constantly. A constant level of staff, however, could be wasted in slow hours or overwhelmed in busy hours. Some businesses simply forsake the slack period and open only for the peak times. This strategy could give a new competitor the opportunity to gain a foothold in the business by catering to the off-peak periods, if it could be done cost-effectively.

Competitive Climate: A Zero-Sum Market

It is likely that consumers of a commercial recreation or tourism product can choose either an alternative product or an alternative supplier of that product. The commercial environment is a competitive environment, and even if a business has an original idea, it isn't long before another enterprise offers the same, similar, or better idea to the same market base. In a static economy (i.e., one in which no new consumers are being created, and no increase in consumption potential is realized), competition results in a zero sum. The theory of the zero-sum market is as follows: in a static or constant economy, gains of market share (percentage of the market controlled) by any enterprise will be offset by commensurate losses of market share by competing enterprises.

To illustrate this concept, let's assume that the demand for sporting goods in Greenville is relatively constant. Additionally, the overall economic base of the community is neither growing nor declining, and people are spending the same amount for sporting goods each year. Store D decides to expand its product line and compete directly with the three larger stores in town. After three years, Store D has captured 3% of the market from store A and 1% from each of stores B and C. There was no effect on Store E, which specialized in scuba equipment (the only store in town to do so). While a 5% overall market share gain may not sound like much, it represents (in this illustration) a 50% sales increase for Store D (see Figure 3-2).

The zero-sum market theory illustrates the cruel realities of a tough competitive climate. Gains are made only at the expense of one's competitors. This is why a commercial recreation and tourism business must fight so hard to at least retain its market share. In order to retain its core of regular customers and attract new ones, the business must differentiate its product or service from competitors, offer value for the dollar, and provide excellent service.

Figure 3-2
Example of Zero-Sum Market

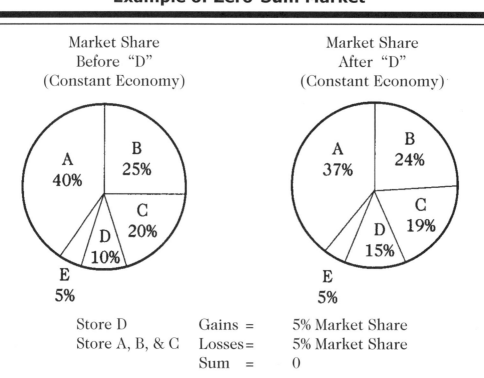

If, however, an economy is growing, the zero-sum market theory is less applicable. All the Stores A-E probably benefit by a growing economy. Growth of discretionary spending in a given area can be the result of increases in population, increases in income, or decreases in taxes or other expenses. In addition, the market for a particular type of product or service can grow due to increased interest. This illustrates the importance of operating a commercial recreation and tourism business in a market where the economy is healthy and growing, and being in an industry that is growing.

ECONOMIC AND POLITICAL CHALLENGES

In addition to the challenges previously discussed, there are economic and political conditions that greatly influence the recreation and tourism industry. These conditions present difficulties for some types of commercial recreation and tourism businesses and opportunities for others. For this reason, it is important that they be well understood.

Inflation and Interest Rates

Inflation results from the natural tendency of goods and service providers in a free market economy to try to maximize financial returns by gradually increasing the prices charged for their goods and services (Brayley and McLean, 1999). Stated as a percentage, the rate of inflation reflects the relative annual increase in prices charged for a particular set of representative products. In the late 1970s and early 1980s, inflation was in the double digits, and these high inflation rates caused certain capital and operational expenses (particularly gasoline, fuel oil, construction materials, and utilities) to increase dramatically. This made it difficult for a manager to project expenses and to set prices that adequately covered those expenses. In the 1990s and the first half-decade of this millennium, the inflation rate in the United States was relatively low and very stable (see Figure 3-3), thus providing a high degree of confidence for price setters. That sense of confidence is especially welcomed in commercial recreation and tourism businesses such as theme parks, ski areas, and resorts that publish their season prices far in advance and have little opportunity to adjust and respond to unforeseen cost increases. Inflation makes advance price setting a risky proposition, and in the first decade of the 21st century, inflation is an economic condition that deserves the careful attention of all entrepreneurs.

Interest is the money charged for the privilege of deferred payment of a debt. It is the direct financial cost of borrowing money and is of great importance to commercial recreation and tourism enterprises built and/or operated with external funding. Interest rates charged by banks and other lending institutions were in the high double digits in the early 1980s, and this made it difficult for consumers to finance major leisure purchases such as an RV, a motor boat, or vacation home. Furthermore, high interest rates made it very expensive to borrow money to start a business or to finance an expansion. It also became very expensive to take out a short-term loan to cover negative cash flow during the off-season. Although interest rates were significantly lower in the following decade, they were still high enough to deter potential investors away from commercial recreation and tourism business into more secure areas of investment. Record low interest rates in the late 1990s and early 2000s have encouraged more risk and investment.

The prime rate of interest charged by banks is always more than the rate of inflation (see Figure 3-4). When the inflation rate is high, the interest rate is higher. When the inflation rate is low, the interest rate is also low, but it still could be as much as two or three times the annual increase of the consumer price index. This means that it is still relatively expensive to borrow money for starting or expanding a business or carrying the business through an off-season.

Figure 3-3
Inflation in the United States (1975–2004)

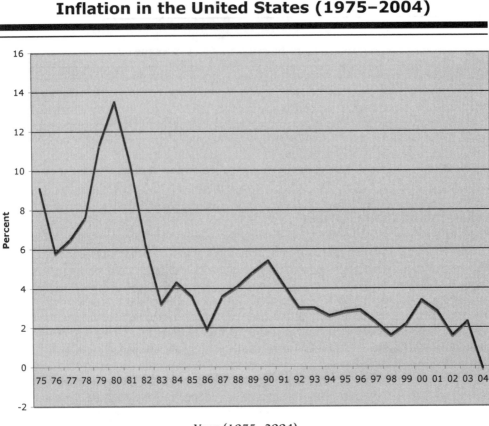

Year (1975–2004)

Source: U.S. Bureau of Labor Statistics (U.S. Census Bureau, 2005b)

Foreign Exchange

Some commercial recreation and tourism enterprises may depend on an international customer base. The relative value of foreign currency is, therefore, relevant to the successful operation of the enterprise. When the U.S. dollar is strong compared to other nations' currencies, American investors and tourists spend more money abroad. When the U.S. dollar is weak compared to other currencies, foreign investors and tourists spend more money in the United States. Even though the manager of a commercial recreation and tourism business is in no position to influence foreign currency exchange rates, he or she can manipulate the impact of those rates on consumer behavior by the way currency exchange is handled. For example, many U.S. businesses close to the Canadian border accept the lower valued Canadian dollar at par in order to attract their northern neighbors as customers.

Stock Markets

During the first three decades of the 1900s, the grandest of all resort hotels in the United States was the West Baden Springs Hotel in south central Indiana. It featured an ornate central atrium under what was, for nearly 70 years, the largest free-standing dome in the world. It was the playground of America's richest people until one day when the guests watched with horror the crash of the world's stock markets. They checked out of

Figure 3-4
Comparison of U.S. Annual Inflation Rates and Average Annual Prime Interest Rates (1992–2004)

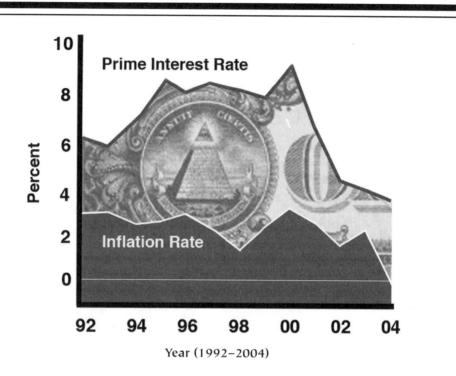

Sources: Federal Reserve Board (2005), U.S. Bureau of Labor Statistics (2005)

the hotel and never returned. This once abandoned and crumbling structure has been saved from ruin and is now an intriguing historical restoration project as well as an eerie monument to the impact of stock market fluctuations on the recreation and tourism industry.

The 20th century ended with a strong U.S. economy, and the activities of the stock market reflected that strength. The Dow Jones Industrial Index (an indicator of the relative value of publicly traded stocks) reached highs that in the early and mid-1990s were thought to be unachievable. The wealth generated by this economic activity is directly relevant to the health of the commercial recreation and tourism industries, due to its impacts upon capital investment and market potential. Entrepreneurs in commercial recreation and tourism need not become stock market experts, but they would be unwise to remain ignorant of daily events and trends on Wall Street and in other major trading centers of the world.

Energy Shortages and Prices

In 1979, the oil-exporting Arab states reacted to a political situation and severely reduced shipments of oil to the United States. This so-called Arab oil embargo resulted in fuel shortages and high energy prices throughout the country and emphasized the dependence of industrialized nations on a limited energy source. That emphasis motivated governments and private industry to increase efficiency and to conserve energy. However, the

The West Baden Springs Hotel as it appeared in the early 20th century.

embargo was eventually lifted, and the increased supplies and reduced demand led to lower and more stable gasoline prices for the remainder of the century.

During a gasoline shortage such as the one in 1979, or when gasoline prices rise dramatically, the biggest losers are the tourist attractions in remote areas. During the Arab oil embargo, attendance at National Park Service areas in Arizona, Colorado, Nevada, Utah, Wyoming, and South Dakota was down by an average of 16.4% (Goeldner & Duea, 1984). On the other hand, some local and regional attractions picked up business from people who substituted local trips for longer vacations. Some recreation enterprises even capitalized on the marketing potential of the fuel shortage. Six Flags Over Texas installed gasoline pumps and promised customers within a certain radius that they could buy enough gas to get home.

When oil prices hit historic highs in 2005, many airlines imposed "fuel surcharges" and sales of gas-guzzling sport utility vehicles declined. While the American public has been somewhat tolerant of the higher oil prices, it is uncertain if this will continue with further price increases.

The Insurance Dilemma

American society seems to be increasingly litigious. That is, people seem to be more likely to sue another person or organization for damages that might, in other times, have been assumed to be the responsibility or shared responsibility of the victim. An abundance of aggressive attorneys and well-publicized multimillion dollar awards or settlements add to the fears of entrepreneurs and their insurers of costly legal action when the inevitable accident occurs.

In response, insurance premiums for commercial recreation and tourism businesses have risen dramatically. For example, Snowbird Ski and Summer Resort in Utah had a 1-year premium increase of 25% with a coverage reduction of 75%. At the same time, Snowbird's deductible amount was raised 300% (Hansell, 1985). Some types of commercial recreation and tourism are even less fortunate and are not able to get insurance at all or have it unilaterally canceled. In 1985, Utah's entire $30 million white-water river tour industry had its insurance canceled. This was a potentially fatal blow to the industry since the National Park Service, the Forest Service, and the Bureau of Land Management all required proof of insurance before river permits could be issued. Only after extensive negotiations, right before the start of the season, was an insurance company found that would underwrite the 16 white-water companies involved.

Terrorism, Crime, and Civil Unrest

Prior to 2001, there was very little terrorist activity in the United States, and the fear of terrorist activity during foreign travel was an important, but relatively small concern for American travelers. The American Society of Travel Agents acknowledged that almost all of its member travel agents believed that terrorism and the fear of terrorism did affect where their clients went. Highly publicized events such as bombings, violent protests, hijackings, and rioting were blamed for a reduction in tourism to the site of an event by as much as 75% for extended periods of time.

The fear of terrorist activity associated with the turn of the millennium significantly reduced travel and participation in a variety of celebratory recreational events at the end of 1999. Fortunately, no such activities occurred, but many otherwise sound financial goals of event planners and tourism operators were not realized.

No other terrorist activity had such an impact on tourism, commercial recreation and other aspects of daily life in America as did the airliner attacks on September 11, 2001. The personal suffering of innocent victims and their families was exacerbated by the wounds inflicted on the national sense of security and on the tourism industry that relied on the instantly shattered confidence of travelers. The legacy of the terrorism murders of September 11, 2001, is ingrained in the tourism industry and will forever change expectations and opportunities.

It should be noted that when people decide not to travel to a given location because of fear of harm at that location or while traveling, they often substitute by engaging in more local recreation or traveling to alternate destinations by alternate means. When terrorism activities hurt European travel, travel within the United States increases, and when American forces are engaged in military conflicts away from this continent, overseas travel increases to the comfortably close Caribbean. Likewise, the perception of New York City and Washington DC as perennial terrorist targets has helped to increase travel to alternate destinations.

CONSTRAINTS TO PARTICIPATION

In addition to the previously discussed challenges to the commercial recreation and tourism industries, there are a variety of more personal conditions that act as barriers to participation. These constraints cause customers to visit a business less often or not at all. Goeldner, Ritchie, and McIntosh (2000) and others identified the following barriers to travel and to recreation in general.

Lack of Money is one of the two most commonly identified barriers to participation in recreation. The lack of money is not only a problem for people in low-income groups, people with large families, and senior citizens on fixed incomes. Lack of money is also identified as a constraint on those persons who have more than average resources but are nonetheless unwilling to part with their dollars in order to participate in recreation. As an expressed constraint, "lack of money" includes having insufficient funds as well as having insufficient willingness to spend.

Lack of Time is the second of the two most common barriers identified by potential consumers. Business persons and other professionals typically declare this as a barrier to their participation. However, others with seemingly fewer time commitments also will point to lack of time as a constraint when there is, more precisely, an unwillingness to preempt their time for that particular choice of recreation.

Physical Condition of the participant can, depending upon the activity, be a significant barrier. This is especially true for persons with disabilities or health problems.

Family Status limits participation by imposing alternative roles, obligations, and priorities. Leisure choices can be quite limited for adults and families with small children. For example, free time for parents declines sharply when school-age children must be chauffeured to community activities and meal times juggled for diverse schedules. Conversely, other barriers are less of a problem during these years. School-age children often are sources of information for parents about community events and recreational opportunities. Additionally, the growing number of single women with children is a trend that brings particular attention to constraints based on family status.

Lack of Interest is a constraint that affects everyone for one recreational pursuit or another. However, some people say that they have a lack of interest when another barrier is actually the real problem.

Lack of Skills restricts many people from attempting an activity that they might otherwise enjoy. Without the required skill, danger and/or embarrassment may be added to the cost of participation.

Lack of Companions, particularly for travel, is a significant barrier for some single people and many senior citizens. There are many recreational pursuits that can be undertaken alone but most require or are enhanced by the company of others.

Lack of Knowledge about what is available is a surprising but common barrier in our complex society. Perhaps this is because so much information is presented to potential consumers (so much that it can not be processed), or because many providers of commercial recreation services are not particularly effective in communication.

Lack of Safety (real or perceived), whether traveling in foreign countries or in your own hometown, will deter people from participation. Even if safety is no longer a problem in a given area, the negative perception and reputation of an area might linger for years.

Lack of Transportation, particularly for day-to-day recreational pursuits, is a barrier to urban and rural people alike. If people have the financial resources and plan properly, this should not be a problem unless there is a deficiency in the transportation network.

Constraints to participation in recreational activities can be classified as either intra-personal, interpersonal, or structural. Intrapersonal constraints such as lack of knowledge, lack of skills, and lack of interest are somewhat internal to the potential participant and must be overcome first. Interpersonal constraints such as lack of companion and family status involve other people or social roles and should be overcome next. Finally, potential participants must overcome structural constraints such as lack of time, lack of money, lack of safety, lack of transportation, and physical condition.

OVERCOMING CHALLENGES AND CONSTRAINTS

It is important for commercial recreation and tourism managers to not only understand the challenges and constraints to participation that their customers face, but they must find ways to overcome them. This section identifies a variety of common constraints that managers might need to overcome. Later chapters focus on specific industries and will examine selected strategies in greater depth, but for now, consider the following constraints and suggested strategies for overcoming them.

Challenges/Constraints and Possible Strategies

Participants Lack of Money
1. Give discounts for youth, senior citizens, families, and off-peak periods.
2. Give group rates.
3. Sell season passes or annual memberships.
4. Allow credit purchases (Visa, American Express, etc.).
5. Emphasize the value of the investment and value/quality for the dollar.

Seasonal, Cyclical, and Intermittent Nature
1. Provide year-round facilities (air-supported structures, snowmaking, indoor stadiums, etc.).
2. Diversify facilities in the off-season.
3. Diversify off-season programs.
4. Have special events in off-peak periods.
5. Seek a different market (conventions, meetings, etc.) for the off-season.
6. Reduce variable expenses.
7. Reduce hours of operation.
8. Close in the off-season.
9. Seek a higher profit margin in the peak season in order to build cash reserves.
10. Obtain short-term loans.
11. Sell unused space or assets.
12. Rent out unused space in the off-season.
13. Diversify the retail product line.

Competition and Substitution of Product or Service
1. Diversify offerings in order to retain clients.
2. Locate in areas of economic health and growth.
3. Differentiate product or service from those of competitors.
4. Emphasize value for the dollar.
5. Provide extraordinary service and personal attention.

Inflation
1. Purchase in advance the supplies and equipment that are most subject to cost increases.
2. Lock in prices from regular vendors through contracts.
3. List your own prices as a range and/or "subject to change."

Transportation Shortage and Energy Crisis
1. Sell group travel packages.
2. Provide fuel for the return trip.
3. Have shuttle buses.
4. Make cooperative agreements with airlines and bus lines.

Insurance Dilemma
1. Plan to pay more.
2. Increase deductible limits.
3. Reduce coverage.
4. Create industry-wide insurance pool.
5. Install risk management program.

Crime, Safety, and Terrorism
1. Promote your good safety record.
2. Increase security.
3. Arrange for insurance that participants can purchase.
4. Make selected security measures "comfortingly" visible.
5. Be vigilant.

Participant's Lack of Time
1. Emphasize closeness and convenience.
2. Increase hours of operation to accommodate people with unusual schedules.
3. Provide time-saving amenities (locker rooms, baby-sitting, eating and lodging facilities on site, etc.).
4. Provide local ground transportation (shuttles, airport pickup, etc.).
5. Develop programs and packages for long weekends.

Participant's Lack of Skills or Physical Ability
1. Improve accessibility for persons with disabilities.
2. Provide beginner-level equipment and facilities.
3. Develop "first time" packages at discount price.
4. Provide group or individual instruction.

Participant's Family Stage
1. Provide a day-care program.
2. Provide special activities for children.
3. Provide programs and facilities that allow the entire family to participate.
4. Give special rates for families.

Participant's Lack of Interest or Knowledge
1. Provide information about the facility and program.
2. Give trial or "first time" packages.
3. Use advertising that stresses attractiveness of area, programs, and so forth.
4. Have personalized contact with prospective participants.

Participant's Lack of Companions
1. Have open houses, mixers, and special events to create social interaction.
2. Provide dorm style or hostel accommodations.
3. Have group travel programs.
4. Give single supplement rates.
5. Provide travel companion matching service.

The above strategies are just a few possibilities. As such, each has advantages and disadvantages. It is up to the commercial recreation and tourism manager to understand the problems and barriers of the particular industry and to adopt and adapt strategies that bring success.

ECONOMIC CONCEPTS RELATED TO COMMERCIAL RECREATION AND TOURISM

The commercial recreation and tourism manager will be more effective with an understanding of general economic concepts related to the business. This section presents a few of these important general concepts. It must be emphasized that these concepts are presented in the context of an introductory overview and this discussion should not replace further study of microeconomics, finance, or management.

Supply and Demand

As defined by economists, *demand* is the quantity of a product or service that consumers will buy at a given price at a given point in time. Factors influencing demand include price, price of related goods, consumer income, tastes and preferences, and advertising. Generally, people will buy more of a product or service at a lower price than at a higher price. Demand for a given product or service may also increase when the price of a competitor's product or service increases significantly. In addition, demand may be stimulated by higher income, by effective advertising, and by social changes that make a product or service more desirable. An example of the latter is the growth of health clubs as a result of society's interest in fitness.

Supply is the quantity of a product or service that is willingly provided by a business for a given price at a given time. Sellers typically are willing to supply larger quantities at higher prices than at lower prices.

Equilibrium is the price at which the market will demand precisely the same quantity that the producer is willing to supply. In a free market, prices tend to drift toward equilibrium because of competition by sellers and because of buyer willingness to substitute if prices are too high.

Price Elasticity of Demand

It was previously suggested that consumers are likely to purchase smaller quantities of a product when the price goes up. The measure of how much a certain segment of consumers changes its purchasing due to price adjustments is expressed as the *price elasticity of demand*. This measure is the ratio of the percentage change in quantity of a product or service demanded in response to a change in price. A particular market segment is labeled relatively elastic if a change in price produces a proportionally greater change in demand. For example, if a 20% increase in facility fees results in 35% fewer users, it is relatively elastic because the user market is obviously quite price sensitive. Another market segment may be less price sensitive and will be labeled relatively inelastic if a change in price produces a proportionally smaller change in demand. For example, a 25% increase in admission fees for a relatively inelastic market may result in a loss of only 8% of the market, but overall revenues will be increased.

The differences between the two market segments is illustrated in Figure 3-5. The relatively elastic market segment for this hypothetical recreation enterprise is the family market. When the family price rose from $10 to $13 (a 30% change), family admissions dropped from 1,200 to 700 (a 42% change). Lost revenue totaled $2,900 ([$13 x 700] - [$10 x 1,200]).

The young adult market for this enterprise is the relatively inelastic segment. When the adult admission price increased from $8 to $10 (a 25% increase), admissions dropped from 1,000 to 900 (a 10% change), and the total revenue from this relatively inelastic market increased by $1,000 ([$10 x 900] - [$8 x 1,000]).

Price sensitivity varies between markets and between products. Markets for "non-essential" or "easily deferred" purchases like recreation products tend to be more price

Figure 3-5
Illustration of Price Elasticity of Demand

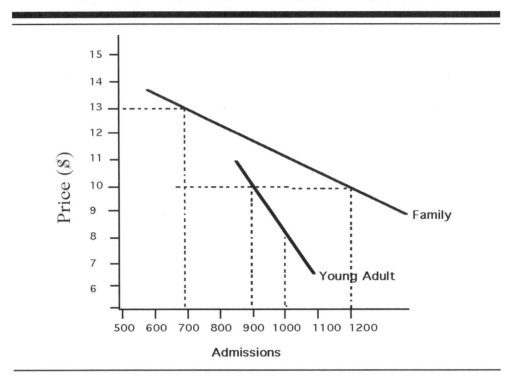

sensitive than markets for products considered to be necessary and urgent consumables. For example, bread is generally recognized as being an essential item. If the price of bread doubled at all retail outlets, it is highly unlikely that grocery stores would report sustained subsequent bread sales of 50% less than previously experienced. Some people will reduce bread consumption, some will begin to make it themselves, and others will substitute other staples for bread, but most will continue to buy it at the higher price. The potential for reduced or deferred consumption, self-service, and substitution is far greater for recreation and tourism products when their prices increase.

The principle of elasticity also applies with respect to price reductions. A relatively elastic market would respond very favorably to a price reduction. For example, a 20% resort room rate reduction during the off-season could generate 50% more guests and, therefore, increase revenues while penetrating the market. This is the objective of discount pricing strategies, but note that such strategies do not work with relatively inelastic markets.

It is critically important for commercial recreation and tourism managers to understand supply, demand, and elasticity. They must know if their industry tends to be relatively elastic or relatively inelastic. They must also know how particular market segments respond. For example, many ski resorts charge premium prices to upscale vacationers during Christmas holidays. Space is limited, demand at the holidays is relatively inelastic, and the resorts fill with upscale customers. On the other hand, weekdays in January and February may have a small number of tourists but have a respectable volume of local skiers using discount passes. For any product or service, demand may be inelastic for one market segment but elastic for another. Commercial recreation and tourism managers must be prepared to do the research necessary and make the effort to understand all aspects of demand for their particular industry and apply that understanding to wise decision making.

System Structure

System structure refers to a variety of systems that provide the basic framework of support for a commercial recreation and tourism enterprise. Elements of system structure include infrastructure (developments on or below ground), superstructure (developments above ground), and other support systems. Although usually associated with resort development, the concept is equally important to all other types of commercial recreation. If the system structure is not in place, the business will not be able to operate properly, if at all. The various components of system structure are detailed below.

Transportation System. Customers, employees, and suppliers must be able to get to the commercial recreation and tourism enterprise. This requires interstate highways, state and local roads, access roads, airports and airlines, bus lines, railroad transportation, taxis, and other ground transfers.

Utility Systems. This includes electricity, gas lines, water and sewage systems, garbage pickup, and telephone service. Increasingly important is the provision of high-speed Internet access.

Public Services. These provide stability and security for the commercial enterprise. Included are police and fire departments, local government management and planning, public schools, and local parks.

Local Services Network. Certain services are necessary to keep the commercial recreation and tourism enterprise operating. These include suppliers and vendors, maintenance and repair shops, trades (electrical, plumbing, etc.), contractors, and a reliable local labor force.

Marketing and Media Network. In order to support the promotional functions of the business, there need to be television and radio stations, newspapers, roadside advertising, printing companies, advertising agencies, and market research companies.

Related Amenities. Certain types of commercial recreation and tourism enterprises need other recreation amenities in order to provide a tourist/customer with a complete experience. These related amenities may include hotels, restaurants, retail shops, tour guides, Internet access, medical services, gasoline service stations, and parking facilities.

In every stage of its development, the recreation and tourism system structure must be in harmony with its natural environment. All development should minimize negative impacts on the land and water resources, the vegetation, and the wildlife of an area.

In addition, system structure must be balanced and compatible with all its elements. If this does not occur, the quality of the experience and/or the local area will suffer. For example, Ocean City, Maryland, has a winter population of about 7,200, but in the summer this swells to over 300,000. Although the city now has hotels and beach houses to accommodate this surge, the roads were once choked, and the water and sanitation systems were overburdened. Using new tax revenue generated after a property reassessment, the Ocean City water and sanitation system was expanded, followed several years later by an inexpensive, expanded public transit system. Low bus fares and "Bus Only" lanes on major thoroughfares encouraged drivers to leave their cars at home, thus greatly reducing traffic congestion and making the transit system more viable.

The cost of developing and maintaining the system structure is not always entirely the responsibility of public agencies. When needed to support a commercial recreation or tourism enterprise, infrastructure and superstructure development may have to be financed in part or entirely by that enterprise. It is not unusual, for example, for a commercial campground developer to spend heavily to bring roads and utilities into a remote location, or for a resort developer to also build housing for seasonal employees.

Critical Mass

A commercial recreation enterprise must achieve a certain "critical mass" at each stage of its development in order to optimize both the experience for the participant and the return on investment for the owners. This ideal size is determined by several characteristics:

- **It is the optimal size for the best recreation experience.** If a facility is too small to meet market demand, it can become overcrowded. On the other hand, if a facility is overbuilt, it will not have an attractive atmosphere. Part of the total experience of a theme park, night club, or health club is the color, noise, and interaction with a crowd. Optimal size, therefore, is achieved when the enterprise is big enough to avoid overcrowding, but small enough to create and sustain the desired social atmosphere. Critical mass is achieved, in part, when the size of the enterprise is such that it can be responsive to market needs.
- **It is large enough to create a desired length of stay for visitors.** Most theme park managers know that if participants stay four or five hours, they are likely to purchase food and beverages. Similarly, vacation resort properties should strive to develop a total package of amenities that will keep visitors entertained and spending money for a week or more. Enterprises with a critical mass have the ability to retain their customers.
- **It is big enough and varied enough to keep participants coming back.** Members of single-purpose aerobic dance studios or racquetball centers often switch memberships when their interest changes. Members of larger, multipurpose sports clubs can simply change activities within the same facility. Similarly, people have forsaken the small water slide facilities in favor of larger water theme parks. Having achieved critical mass, the commercial recreation enterprise is able to engender repeat business.

A water theme park in Bali has gained "Critical Mass" by having numerous slides to keep customers on property for many happy hours. (Photo: J. Crossley)

- **It is balanced in terms of optimal cash flow.** A facility that is overbuilt will have large expenses for buildings and equipment that are underutilized. On the other hand, if a facility is too small, it may not realize its full revenue generation potential, and existing customers may leave due to overcrowding. Critical mass requires the enterprise to be adequately and appropriately resourced.

The major challenge in determining the critical mass of a recreation or tourism enterprise is the seasonal nature of such businesses. A facility may be too small to meet the demands of the peak season, but may also be too large for the off-season demand. The concept of critical mass suggests that there is an optimal capacity that should be developed. Optimal size is determined by consideration of demand fluctuations and operational costs. Figure 3-6 presents average daily occupancy, cost, and profit data from three different-sized resorts. Each is profitable, but the size of the resorts affects the level of profitability they enjoy.

In the preceding illustration, Resort B is closer to having a critical mass than is the smaller Resort A and the larger Resort C. Resort A has a high occupancy rate, but is too small to take full advantage of peak seasons (winter and summer) demand. Resort C does very well in the peak seasons but has far too many unsold rooms in the off-seasons (spring and fall). Resort B loses out on some of the peak season potential because of its medium size, but also keeps its off-season losses down because of its medium size. In this illustration, optimal size was determined by assessing profit potential. Optimal size can also be assessed on the basis of efficiency (per-room profit) and investment return (total profits as a percentage of total investment).

A commercial recreation and tourism enterprise can solve some of its challenges related to critical mass by instituting *phased development*. In its early stages of development, the business may start off at less than its ultimate future size. As participation materializes and profits are generated, the business can expand. Recreation enterprises should plan for phased development by retaining access to additional land or facility areas for future use. Walt Disney World near Orlando, Florida, is an excellent example of a huge resort and entertainment complex that developed in phases over many years.

Gravity Effect

Planners, economists, and tourism researchers have used *gravity models* to predict the amount of travel from a particular origin to a particular destination and to estimate the economic activity involved in that travel experience. A gravity model establishes a mathematical relationship between the location of the population, frequency of visits to a given recreation site, and competing attractions.

The gravity effect, however, is a nonquantitative simplification of the gravity model, which helps to explain the attraction of a major recreation or tourism enterprise. *Gravity*, as the term is used in tourism research, has the same meaning as it does when taught in secondary school science classes; that is, the pull or attraction exerted by a large mass. The greater the mass, the greater the pulling force it exerts. In the context of this discussion, the gravity effect means that larger recreation areas such as New York's Broadway or Orlando's Walt Disney World have a great attraction to millions of visitors from around the world. Smaller attractions have their own significant, yet smaller, gravity effect, which can be enhanced through innovative location and marketing efforts. Major recreation and tourism attractions that exert a gravity effect tend to have all or most of the following characteristics:

Clustering of Similar Businesses. Rather than discouraging competition, an area exerting a gravity effect may encourage the location of similar businesses. Most cities have a major street where numerous auto dealers may be found. Customers gravitate to

Figure 3-6
Critical Mass Comparisons of Three Resorts

	Winter	Spring	Summer	Fall	Average
Market Size	260	75	200	50	
Resort A **(100 rooms)**					
Rooms sold	100	75	100	50	
Occup. rate	100%	75%	100%	50%	
Gross profit*	1,200	900	1,200	600	975
Loss**	0	35	0	500	134
Net profit	1,200	865	1,200	100	**841**
Resort B **(200 rooms)**					
Rooms sold	200	75	200	50	
Occup. rate	100%	38%	100%	25%	
Gross profit*	2,400	900	2,400	600	1,575
Loss**	0	135	0	1,500	409
Net profit	2,400	765	2,400	(900)	**1,166**
Resort C **(300 rooms)**					
Rooms sold	260	75	200	50	
Occup. rate	87%	25%	67%	17%	
Gross profit*	3,120	900	2,400	600	1,755
Loss**	400	235	1,000	2,500	1,034
Net profit	2,720	665	1,400	(1,900)	**721**

*Gross profit=revenue from all rooms sold–costs to provide those rooms. ($12/room in this example)
**Loss=cost to provide all unsold rooms. ($10/room in this example)

this area because of convenience, variety, and quantity. Similarly, many cities have their own entertainment districts and "restaurant rows." People are drawn to these areas because of the collective attraction.

The central Florida area around Walt Disney World has become a primary tourist destination with numerous attractions. People come for 1 or 2 weeks because there are so many different things to do. On a smaller scale, another location, the historic Stockyards area of Fort Worth, Texas, has over a dozen restaurants and saloons. This draws people for an extended evening of dining, barhopping, and Western dancing.

Cooperative Advertising. Once a cluster of recreation attractions has gained a collective reputation, it becomes cost effective to do a certain amount of cooperative advertising. The theory is that if more people are drawn to the overall area, then all the attractions will benefit. Cooperative advertising can be a cost-effective approach for advertising to a larger audience using more expensive media. Ski resorts in Summit County, Colorado, Lake Tahoe, and Utah are active in cooperative promotions with other ski resorts in their destination area and enjoy enhanced visibility and business as a result.

Location of Supporting Amenities. An area that has become a major attraction will be a popular location for related businesses. Most major shopping malls feature a couple of "magnet" or "anchor" stores, such as Sears, J.C. Penney's, or Nordstroms, strategically located at either end of the mall. These stores attract a large volume of customer traffic, upon which smaller specialty shops for clothes, toys, CDs, and books depend for corporate survival. Smaller retail attractions strive to locate near the magnet stores in order to benefit from passing customers. Similarly, fast-food restaurants, gas stations, motels, and souvenir shops are drawn to locations near major recreation and tourism attractions. Often, these small businesses will advertise and emphasize their proximity or connection to the major attraction (e.g., "your launch pad to the Disney adventure").

Location of En Route Attractions. If a manager knows where the primary markets are for a major recreation or tourism attraction, some determination can be made as to the travel routes most frequently used. It becomes a good strategy to locate secondary recreation attractions and amenities along these prime travel routes. Motels, campgrounds, restaurants, roadside attractions, and souvenir stands are common within a day's drive from major attractions. Marketing of these businesses may take advantage of the gravity effect. For example, Wall Drug in Wall, South Dakota, promotes itself as a tourist attraction for people who are en route to Mount Rushmore. The huge drugstore complex includes gift shops, entertainment, and souvenirs, and it advertises all over the world. In fact, its advertising (mostly billboards) has become an important part of the Wall Drug attraction for road-weary travelers seeking scenic diversion while crossing the visually static plains of South Dakota.

In planning for and managing the success of a commercial recreation and tourism enterprise, managers need to understand the principles of market gravitation and be able to create or enhance the attraction exerted by their facilities and programs. In addition to providing an inherently appealing product, managers should enhance the appeal or attraction of their enterprises by appropriate location, marketing, and auxiliary development decisions.

Multiplier Factor

The multiplier factor refers to the number of times an "outside dollar" (or tourist dollar) "turns over" (i.e., is re-spent), in a local economy. For example, a skier purchases a lift ticket for $50, and a portion of that amount goes to pay the wages of the lift operators. The lift operator spends part of her money on groceries, and the grocer uses the money to pay part of his rent. The landlord goes out to dinner and spends it on steaks that were shipped in from Kansas City. The cycle stops here because the money for the steak leaves the local economy. This last transaction is called "leakage" from the economy. Leakage occurs whenever money is spent on goods or services that are imported from outside the local community.

The value of the multiplier factor is in its measurement of how important outside money from industries such as tourism really is to the economic well-being of an area. The higher the multiplier, the higher is the impact of tourism on the local economy. In Las Vegas, for example, the multiplier factor is approximately 1.9. This means that visitor spending of $10 billion in Las Vegas generates $19 billion of economic activity in the community.

Although some communities may claim multiplier factors of 5.0 or higher, it is very unlikely that an economic multiplier can exceed 2.3 (Crompton & Richardson, 1986; Brayley & McLean, 1999). Using multipliers to help understand the actual or potential impacts of tourism is only worthwhile if the multipliers are accurately determined and are realistic.

It is important to realize that communities with low multiplier factors may not benefit from tourism as much as they might like. In such cases, the negative social or ecological aspects of tourism may outweigh the economic benefits. Hawaii, for example, is a popular tourist destination, but due to high import leakage, it has a low multiplier. With tourism-related crowding, high real estate prices, and loss of local culture, many people feel that Hawaii is actually worse off because of tourism.

The communities with the highest multiplier factors are those that are relatively self-sufficient (i.e., those that have local labor, agriculture, manufacturing, food processing, and so on). In such communities, less leakage occurs from buying imported products or services, and the money that is brought into the community from exports (including tourism) circulates more and generates more economic activity. Therein tourism has its most positive economic impacts.

Repeat Visitor Concept (80/20 Principle)

The so-called 80/20 principle is, at best, a rule of thumb. However, there is evidence to support the assertion that it is very applicable to commercial recreation and tourism (Mullins, 1983). Simply stated, the 80/20 principle declares that 80% of business will come from 20% of the customers. In other words, there is great emphasis on the importance of customer loyalty and repeat consumption. Every effort should be made to keep customers satisfied and managers would do well to remember the admonition of McKenzie (1983, p. 10), who stated, "The only reason to be in business is for repeat business; and if you aren't in business for repeat business, pretty soon you won't be in business."

McKenzie observed that in some resorts, it costs four times as much for advertising to bring in a new customer than it does to get a past customer to return. This disproportionate expenditure in advertising for new customers only accounts for the 20% of new customers who did not come from existing or former customer referrals.

Obviously, the best way to get repeat business is to promise a certain quality of experience and then live up to or exceed that promise. For recreation services, when price between competitors is about equal, participants will choose on the basis of friendliness, cleanliness, and service.

The importance of this 80/20 principle lies in its reinforcement of the advice that it is worthwhile to "go the extra mile" for the customer. It is worth it to spend the extra dollars to maintain an attractive atmosphere, provide quality products and services, and be concerned with meeting the customer's expectations. This is critical, particularly in local recreation establishments such as sports clubs, restaurants, night clubs, and retail shops. The local resident is in a position to come back again and again. Similarly, in some resort areas such as Las Vegas, as many as 80% of the visitors have been there previously. With some resorts and theme parks, however, this may not be the case, but word-of-mouth promotion creates the same effect of generating business.

SUMMARY

The entrepreneur must understand the basic nature of commercial recreation and tourism in order to cope with problems to be faced in managing the business. Specifically, the manager must understand that commercial recreation and tourism is dependent upon discretionary income and know who has it and how they spend it. Recreation and tourism is often cyclical, seasonal, and intermittent in nature. Strategies must be devised to overcome these problems in a competitive environment. Additional problems to be faced may include inflation and interest rates, energy shortages, insurance costs, currency exchange rates, stock market fluctuations, terrorism and crime, and personal barriers of participants. Barriers can include intrapersonal, interpersonal, and structural constraints such as expense, transportation, lack of time, health, family status, lack of skills, interests, lack of companion, and safety concerns. Again, the commercial recreation and tourism manager must overcome these barriers in order to operate successfully.

Commercial recreation and tourism managers will probably be more effective if they have an understanding of general economic concepts related to the business. These include supply and demand, price elasticity, system structure development, critical mass concept, gravity effects, multiplier factors, and the 80/20 principle (repeat visitor concept).

SPOTLIGHT ON:

Bill Acker and Manta Ray Bay Hotel

Bill Acker's soft Texas drawl masks his fierce determination to overcome whatever obstacles block his path to success with the Manta Ray Bay Hotel in Yap, Micronesia. Bill first came to Yap in 1976 as a Peace Corps volunteer after earning a degree in marketing at the University of Texas. After leaving this tropical island, located north of the Philippines, Bill earned an MBA at the University of Hawaii and worked as a manager for a men's clothing store. In 1980, friends on Yap invited him back to be the manager of an island transportation company, WAAB.

While Bill managed the transportation company he took up scuba diving, a hobby that would change his life. He explored the reefs around Yap and became certified as a dive instructor in 1982. Bill recognized that Yap had something special that divers would travel the world to see: close-up encounters with manta rays year-round. By 1990 he convinced the WAAB owners to open a 15-room hotel and dive shop. It was fairly successful, and Bill decided he wanted to become the owner and expand the operation. In 1993 Bill put up just $500 of his own money, got a $300,000 loan from his friends/employers at WAAB, and leveraged that to get a $2.6 million bank loan.

Bill's resort, the Manta Ray Bay Hotel, and its dive company, Yap Divers, grew to become a 28-room, award-winning resort. Along the way there have been a series of economic crises and natural disasters that would have caused many people to give up, but not Bill. Here is a list of challenges he has overcome:

With the 1991 Persian Gulf War, he lost many American and Japanese customers due to worries about travel safety. When an investment and banking scandal rocked Japan in 1997, Bill temporarily lost most of his Japanese market, which historically was about half of his customers. With the "Dot Com" stock market crash in 2000 he lost American customers. With the 9/11 terrorist attacks in 2001, he lost 50% of his overall market, including 100% of his Japanese customers. After the Bali terrorist bombing in 2002, he lost the Japanese and American markets. When the SARS scare hit Asia in 2003, he again lost 100% of his Japanese market. In response to these challenges, Bill has expanded his marketing to attract more Europeans, who now represent 50% of his market, while the travel-nervous Japanese market gets less attention. This was a wise strategy, particularly since the increased value of the Euro (compared to the U.S. dollar) has encouraged Europeans to travel more.

Bill's biggest challenge, however, has been to bounce back from the damage caused by typhoons in 2002 and 2004. The last "big one," Typhoon Sudal, brought widespread destruction to Yap, and Bill lost five hotel rooms, his restaurant, and office. With no insurance available on Yap, Bill faced a $750,000 rebuilding project. By this time, he had almost paid off his $2.6 million loan, so he used the equity in his resort to leverage a new loan of $1.75 million. Not only will he rebuild his resort, he will expand to 38 rooms and add a swimming pool. He has 5 years to pay off the loan, which carries a favorable 7% interest rate.

(continued)

Throughout all these challenges, Bill Acker has remained focused and determined while retaining his Southern grace and sense of humor. He has loyal employees, almost like an extended family, and he helped them rebuild their own homes after the typhoons. He has a loyal customer base that appreciates the uniqueness of Yap and the high quality of service that Bill's resort provides. Business is good again, but Bill wonders how nice it would be if world crises and Mother Nature would give him a break!

Source: B. Acker (personal communication, February 12, 2005)

REFERENCES

Brayley, R., & McLean, D. (1999). *Managing financial resources in sport and leisure service organizations.* Champaign, IL: Sagamore Publishing.

Crompton, J., & Richardson, R. (1986, October). The tourism connection. *Parks and Recreation*, pp. 38–44, 67.

Federal Reserve Board. (2005). Prime interest rates (historical) tabulated. http://www.federalreserve.gov/releases/h15/data/Annual/h15prime_NA.txt

Goeldner, C., & Duea, K. (1984). *1984 travel trends in the U.S. and Canada.* Boulder, CO: Travel and Tourism Research Association and the University of Colorado.

Goeldner, C., Ritchie, J. R., and McIntosh, R. (2000). *Tourism principles, practices, philosophies.* New York: John Wiley & Sons, Inc.

Hansell, C. (1985, November 27). Soaring insurance costs mean higher lift rates at ski resorts. *Salt Lake Tribune*, p. D1.

McKenzie, B. (1983, July). Repeat business—New dealing for dollars. *Recreation, Sports, and Leisure*, pp. 10–14.

Mullins, B. (1983). *Sport marketing, promotion and public relations.* Amherst, MA: National Sports Management, Inc.

U.S. Bureau of Labor Statistics (2005). Overview of BLS Statistics on Inflation and Consumer Spending. http://stats.bls.gov/bls/inflation.htm

U.S. Census Bureau. (2005). *National income and product accounts of the United States.* Washington, D.C.: U.S. Government Printing Office

U.S. Census Bureau. (2005). *Statistical abstracts of the United States.* Washington, D.C.: U.S. Government Printing Office

Part•••• 2

INITIATING AND MANAGING COMMERCIAL RECREATION AND TOURISM

Getting into and staying in business is a great adventure. It comes with risk and uncertainty, and it thrives on the promise of great rewards. The next five chapters describe the basics of starting a new commercial recreation or tourism enterprise, managing financial resources, marketing, and the ongoing management of operations and programs.

Chapter ••••

Starting the Commercial Recreation and Tourism Enterprise

There is a great deal of work involved in starting a commercial recreation and tourism business. First, there is the identification of market needs and potential, followed by the development of a product that meets the market needs. Next, a feasibility study should be undertaken that will accurately assess the product's appeal, market demands, utility of distribution systems, competency of management, and viability of financial aspects. Eventually, financing for the venture must be found and an operational plan developed and implemented.

The successful commercial recreation and tourism business can be likened to a four-legged table (Figure 4-1). One leg represents an identifiable market need that is conceptualized and operationalized as an attractive product. Another leg represents the good location from which the product is delivered. The third leg is adequate financing, and the final leg is experienced management. Like the table upon which the fruits of the orchard are served, the business that is supported by these four firm and proven legs will serve to the entrepreneur the fruits of business success. If, for some reason, one of the legs is not as strong as it should be, the business and the table can both stand but will be unstable. Furthermore, the other three legs would be under greater pressure and may reach a fatal level of stress. Moreover, if only two of the legs are firm, neither the table nor the business can stay upright, and it is likely to crash.

This chapter discusses all of the activities involved in getting a new commercial recreation business started. It emphasizes the importance of building the business on a firm base of products, management, location (and/or distribution), and finance.

THE PRODUCT

Success in commercial recreation and tourism begins with a knowledge and understanding of the needs of a meaningful market, followed by the development of products (goods or services) that meet those needs and satisfy the business objectives of the enterprise. Meeting the customers' needs is essential but cannot be done without regard to the need for the business to be profitable. In a sense, the product can really be defined in terms of consumer and producer needs. Meeting consumer needs will be discussed in greater detail in Chapter 6 (Marketing), but this chapter begins with an examination of the needs that entrepreneurs satisfy through starting a commercial recreation business.

Figure 4-1
Four Foundational Legs for a
Successful Recreation Business

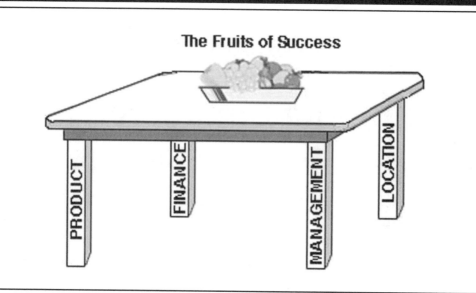

The Fruits of Success

Rewards of Starting a Commercial Recreation and Tourism Enterprise

In starting a commercial recreation and tourism enterprise, an entrepreneur seeks certain rewards and assumes certain risks. The decision to start the business is an indication that the entrepreneur has, through careful research and evaluation, determined that the benefits that come from the enterprise activity will sufficiently meet his or her business-related needs. That determination also includes a probability of success that significantly exceeds the probability of failure.

The benefits of starting a recreation business include:

- **Personal satisfaction**—providing a product or service that is well received.
- **Independence**—being one's own employer.
- **Profits**—leading to a higher standard of living.
- **Power and influence**—proving one's ability.
- **Use of accumulated capital**—making better use of personal assets.
- **Application of skills and background**—testing your training and skills, which may be blocked in other areas of employment.
- **Security**—having the future of employment in one's own hands, rather than at the discretion of others.
- **Getting out of a rut**—escaping boredom, routine, or frustration with the status quo.

Risks in Starting a Commercial Recreation and Tourism Enterprise

Naturally, there are risks associated with starting a new business. Much can be done to reduce the risks, but they will, to some degree, continue to present a challenge to the enthusiasm of the entrepreneur. Risks of starting a business include the following:

- **Financial losses**—if the business fails.
- **Loss of friends and family**—when pressures of the business interfere with personal life.

- **Anguish over uncertainty**—when fluctuations of business conditions are beyond your control.
- **Time and effort**—when constant demands of the business infringe on personal time.
- **Straining of values**—when success may depend on compromise of personal values.
- **Demands above expertise**—when limits of knowledge and experience force guessing or trusting "experts."
- **Growth dilemmas**—as business grows, it may be difficult to stay in touch with all phases of the operation.

The risk of business failure can not be avoided, but it can be reduced. (Photo: R. Brayley)

Risk is inherent in starting a commercial recreation and tourism enterprise, and although many such businesses succeed, more fail. The keys to reducing the risk of failure are to have good (honest) planning and purposeful management.

MANAGEMENT

The most common reason for business failure is lack of management expertise. Many people start a business because of a passionate belief in the profit potential of the enterprise, but they do so without the skills needed to balance the operating budget, hire and supervise employees, schedule inventories, market their products, or respond to changing environmental conditions. All the enthusiasm that they could bring to such a business is not enough to realize success when the financial, temporal, and human resources cannot be efficiently focused on productivity. To be successful, a business must be managed by people who have acquired sophisticated business management skills through education and training and through practical experience.

The second most common reason for business failure is lack of management experience or unbalanced management experience. Management theories and skills learned through study are sharpened on the grindstone of experience, and it is normal for an entrepreneur to have practiced some type of business management in another setting before starting a new business. Perhaps the greatest benefit to this measured development of management competency is the opportunity that the entrepreneur has to make mistakes and learn while someone else takes the risk. This is not meant to offer ethical immunity or to suggest or condone carelessness or impropriety in business dealings, but rather to point out the reality and high potential of error or poor judgment when first operating in the commercial world.

Unbalanced experience can be just as limiting or harmful as lack of experience. An example of unbalanced experience is seen in the accountant who starts a fitness center without a solid knowledge of the fitness industry or a background in marketing. The accountant is strong in financial aspects of the enterprise, but is unable to produce services that generate the revenue that is needed.

While gaining experience, a business manager develops valuable skills but, more importantly, learns to observe and evaluate the market environment and production capability in terms of innovative business concepts.

The Business Concept

One key to promoting business success is to have a sound business concept upon which a strategy for implementation can be based. The eight "sources of innovation" suggested in Chapter 2 contribute to the formulation of the business concept. Beyond the germ of an idea, the entrepreneur needs to engage in a systematic search of the environment in order to discover opportunities. In this search for business concepts, entrepreneurs should consider areas of business in which they have gained past work experience, education, and expertise, as well as carefully examine areas in which the products or services closely relate to their personal leisure interests. Serious consideration should be given to areas of business that serve market segments with which the entrepreneur is already very familiar. According to a study of 3,000 small businesses conducted by American Express and the National Federation of Independent Business, 80% of successful entrepreneurs had worked with the same product or service in their previous jobs (Moore & Golden, 1989). As a cautionary note, management researchers suggest avoiding business concepts that require financial resources that are not currently available or are unlikely to become available due to a lack of proven ability to attract them. Additionally, optimistic business innovators should avoid the temptation to be "crusaders" for a leisure activity or social cause that has a high personal interest, but a low business potential. Further considerations in the development of a business concept include new versus established market entry and the life cycle of the industry.

Established Versus New Market. An important decision in starting a commercial recreation and tourism business is whether the business is to serve an established market or a new market. An established market is one in which participation already exists in the geographic area to be served by the new business. A major advantage of entering an established market is in having a ready-made assessment of the supply-and-demand conditions. A business built on serving an established market hopes that the competition cannot meet all of the demand, or that demand can be further stimulated and the market can be penetrated to a greater extent. Another advantage or opportunity that the new business has is the relative ease with which it can successfully differentiate its product or service and gain a share of the market.

A new market is one that does not currently exist but has the potential to be realized due to the services that the new business hopes to initiate. It is difficult to predict whether the market will materialize, but if the new product or service capitalizes on a latent demand, it could be an excellent opportunity.

Life Cycle of the Industry. Another important consideration for a new business is the life cycle of the product around which the industry is built. Ideally, a new business would enter a market when the product is at the introductory or "takeoff" stages and, thereby, become part of the growth of the industry. While there is a certain amount of risk in working with a relatively new product, the introductory or takeoff stages are the times during which the enterprise has a far better chance to gain loyalty and build a base of satisfied, repeat customers. If, on the other hand, a company enters a market too late, there may be little growth potential left in the industry, and the success of the enterprise would be determined mostly by its ability to take customers away from other businesses.

Competitive Differentiation

The new business must find a way to differentiate its product from that of its competitors. If no practically significant difference can be found, the business enterprise has no competitive advantage and, therefore, no reason to expect to be chosen by the potential customers. It is important that the competitive differentiation is understood and valued by the consumers. It is the consumers who choose, and that choice can be influenced by a number of differentiating conditions, including:

- **Price**—lower or higher. Special prices for children, off-season, etc.
- **Quality**—higher or lower depending upon market preference.
- **Consistency**—reliable quality, time after time.
- **Features**—more or different features and/or amenities and variety of selections.
- **Clientele**—orientation toward a certain type of customer (i.e., senior citizens, singles, sports fans, etc.) in order to draw more of that market.
- **Location**—number of locations, access, convenience, ground transportation to location.
- **Time**—hours of operation, length of season, and so forth.
- **Credit**—availability of credit purchase, credit cards, layaways.
- **Service**—personal attention, repairs, and so on.
- **Packaging and atmosphere**—the physical presentation and atmosphere including appearance, cleanliness, use of color, smell, sounds, and so forth.
- **Awareness**—knowledge that the consumer has of the product and its relationship to consumer needs.
- **Brand recognition and loyalty**—association of the product with the producer and commitment to specifically choose that producer's offerings.

Image and Market Platform

Management of a successful commercial recreation and tourism enterprise includes development, establishment, protection, and enhancement of the image of the enterprise and its products. The way that people think about a business will be influenced by the way it differentiates itself from competitors. Its promotional efforts, physical layout, and courtesy of staff will also affect the image. For example, some sporting goods stores have an image as suppliers to only a few special sports, by offering depth in the product line and expert service. Others have an image as discount stores with a few choices available in a wide array of sports. A business can and must control its image, and that image should be planned from the very outset. In some cases, "instant image" can be purchased by affiliating with a well-known franchise operation. Maintaining a desired company image helps to focus efforts and is very useful in developing a marketing strategy.

The marketing strategy is based on the market platform, which is a concise summary of the key elements of the corporate image and competitive difference. It is the basic business premise and the sales promise to the customer. Often, the market platform is reflected in songs, sales jingles, and other promotions. For example, the Barnum and Bailey Circus promoted itself as the "Greatest Show on Earth," while the Utah Travel Council creatively borrows the well-known circus promotion and promises to provide "the greatest snow on earth" to visitors who ski at Utah resorts. The balmy tropical scenes depicted in Corona Beer advertisements have included a market platform based on the "changes in latitudes, changes in attitude" theme of a Jimmy Buffet song.

LOCATION

In most commercial recreation and tourism enterprises, the product is partly defined by the means through which the good or service is delivered. For this reason, location is a very important consideration in the establishment of a new business. The selection of a business location is a two-step process. The first step is characterized by selection of a general area. In the second step, a specific site within that general area is chosen.

Selection of the general area should be based on assessment of the full market potential of the metropolitan area or the trading area involved. However, some people starting a small business simply decide for personal reasons that they want to live in Tallahassee, Calgary, or Boulder, and they base this business location decision on facts unrelated to business operations. A wiser approach is to make the general area selection based on the following:

- **Overall demographics**—population, growth, income, age, occupations, education, and cultural backgrounds of the desired target market.
- **Community environment**—employee availability, competition, transportation availability, insurance rates, community character, local ordinances, climate.
- **Business environment**—tax rates, real estate costs and availability, business trends, cooperation of government.

Selection of a specific site should be based upon its attractiveness to customers and its cost effectiveness to manage. A checklist of these factors is provided in Figure 4-2.

Figure 4-2
Site Selection Checklist

Auto and pedestrian traffic flow volume	Visibility
Accessibility and turn lanes into location	Signs/storefront design
Proximity to airports, bus lines, and the like.	Community attractions
Nearby business compatibility	Adequate parking
Community attractiveness and safety	Vistas from the site
Access for persons with disabilities	Space for future expansion
Attractiveness of facility and grounds	Proximity to labor source
Utility availability and cost	Zoning regulations
Physical suitability of facilities	Fire and police protection
Proximity to suppliers and vendors	Delivery access
Cost to purchase or lease facilities	Storage facilities
Topography of site—slope and soil types	Vegetation types/tolerance
Risk of floods, landslides, earthquakes	Wildlife

Depending upon the type of business, certain site selection criteria may be more important than others. For example, sports apparel shops, music stores, and many restaurants need sites with high visibility, high pass-by traffic flow, and easy access. On the other hand, specialty businesses such as expedition outfitters, scuba shops, racquet clubs, and travel wholesalers do not need to pay top-dollar rents for locations that draw a pass-by crowd. For other types of businesses, such as cross-country ski touring centers, hunting lodges, and fishing camps, the natural features of the site are of prime importance. The key to site selection, therefore, begins with a realistic analysis of the criteria needed for success.

THE FEASIBILITY STUDY

Any new business needs money to put into place everything that is required to permit an exchange with the customer. It may be that buildings, equipment, licenses, supplies, and personnel are needed for start-up, but these things cost money. Having a sound financial base to facilitate start-up, ongoing operation, and perhaps expansion is, therefore, very important to the enterprise.

It is rare that an individual entrepreneur has sufficient unencumbered personal wealth to apply to start-up costs, therefore money must be borrowed. Often the lender is a group of partners, a bank, or another similar financial institution. To convince the lender to take on the risk associated with the loan, new business owners are almost always expected to prepare a detailed business plan. Part of the business planning process involves conducting a feasibility study.

The feasibility study results in a document that provides a comprehensive analysis to determine if a specific project has potential for reaching its financial goals. The project may be a new product or service at an existing location, a move to a new location, or the creation of a new business. Since the last type mentioned is the most involved, it will be the focus of this section. Feasibility studies for the other types of projects may follow the same process but be shorter in length, since an existing business is involved and many operations are already set in place.

A feasibility study cannot determine the final outcome with total certainty. There are too many variables, assumptions, and unknowns for that to occur. Rather, a feasibility study can help the entrepreneur to see the project in a more objective light. Even with a carefully conducted feasibility study, the entrepreneur will never reach absolute certainty about the success of a proposed enterprise, but can reach "enlightened uncertainty," wherein the risks can be greatly reduced. By conducting a systematic analysis and a reasonable market projection, the entrepreneur may make intelligent decisions about the business. The feasibility study, therefore, acts as a road map to help guide this effort.

There are four important reasons for conducting a feasibility study (Haralson, 1986):

- **To establish feasibility**—deciding whether or not a project will realize a return on the investment.
- **To formulate the optimum concept**—finding the best facilities, location, scale, and market orientation for success; in other words, to serve as a basic form of a business plan.
- **To assist in establishing management and marketing guidelines**—deciding useful operational strategies.
- **To assist in obtaining funding**—creating a document that lenders and investors can study.

The feasibility study may be prepared in-house or by contracting a consulting firm. If the entrepreneur undertakes the in-house approach, it should cost less and be more sensitive to the local market. Counter arguments for this approach are that the in-house researcher may not be qualified, may not be objective, and may not have time to do a thorough job. Another problem is that the results of an in-house study may be viewed with less credibility when a loan is sought. A carefully selected and managed consultant can, on the other hand, bring special expertise and experience to the process and rise above the potentially biased interpretations that are natural to the enthusiastic proponent.

Commercial recreation facilities such as the
Mirage Resort in Las Vegas require extensive feasibility studies and years of planning.
(Photo: Mirage Resorts, Inc.)

It is probably true that the more money that is involved in the project, the more the project is studied. But is the effort really worth it? Hills (1985) surveyed 16 venture capital firms to determine their perspective toward business plans and feasibility studies that were submitted in requests for financing. Overall, the venture capitalists felt that feasibility studies were quite valuable and that new business failure rates could be reduced significantly through feasibility analysis. However, they also believed that the feasibility studies tended to overstate market demand.

Prior to starting the feasibility study, it is necessary to gather a variety of data. Figure 4-3 provides a variety of sources for data, much of which can be found at major libraries, community agency offices, and on the World Wide Web. It is difficult, however, to obtain data for small or specialized industries, such as hang gliding, batting cage operations, and ski rental shops. For such industries, it helps to have inside information gained from past employment in that industry.

Figure 4-3
Sources of Information for Feasibility Studies

General Sources

- Encyclopedia of business information sources—data sources, periodicals, associations, and so on listed by type of business
- Frost and Sullivan Reports—lengthy, in-depth industry reports
- Standard and Poor's Industry Surveys—review of major industries
- Gale's Encyclopedia of Associations—trade association addresses
- Monthly Catalog of U.S. Government Publications
- Funk and Scott Index—covers 750 publications by SIC
- Business Periodicals Index—covers 160 publications
- Wall Street Journal Index
- Trade Publications—check with specific professional associations
- Small Business Administration—a variety of publications plus consulting services

Corporation Data—Information About Specific Corporations

- Standard and Poor's Register of Corporations—by SIC
- Directory of Corporate Affiliations—subsidiary list
- Value Line—corporation reports
- Stock Reports Index—corporation reports
- Moody's Industrial Manual—corporation reports

Industry Financial Data

- Dun & Bradstreet's Key Business Ratios
- Robert Morris Agency Annual Statement Studies
- Almanac of Business and Industrial Financial Ratios
- Dun & Bradstreet's Cost of Doing Business
- Bank of America Small Business Reporter
- Accounting Corporation of America—barometer of small business
- Trade association publications—annual reports, member surveys, and technical aids.
- Financial Survey of Canadian Business Performance—industry averages and ratios compiled by Statistics Canada

Market Information

- Cole's Directory—index of demographics and buying power by local census tracts
- Survey of Buying Power—by Sales Management magazine
- Travel Industry Association of America—travel data
- Statistical Abstract of the U.S.—by the Bureau of the Census
- County and City Data Book—by the Bureau of the Census
- Donnelley Demographics—database file with product usage by types of lifestyles
- Market research consultants—contracted for specific studies

(continued)

Figure 4-3 (continued)
Sources of Information for Feasibility Studies

Other Federal Government Sources

- Small Business Administration—publications and advice
- Internal Revenue Service—tax requirements
- Occupational Health and Safety Administration
- Department of Labor—labor regulations
- Securities and Exchange Commission—stock issue regulations
- U.S. Geological Survey—topographical maps

State/Provincial and Local Government

- Secretary of State—incorporation requirements
- State Tax Commission
- Department of Business Regulations/Consumer and Corporate Affairs
- Industrial Development Office
- State Travel Council or Tourism Office
- State parks, recreation, and/or natural resources—statewide demand surveys
- Department of Transportation—traffic counts
- City and county planning departments—demographic and other data
- City and county regulatory agencies—health, zoning, and so forth.
- Utility companies—demographic data, utility costs, and so forth.

Other Local Sources

- Competitors—check their products, services, prices, and so on
- Local newspapers—marketing department data
- University research centers
- Banks—demographic data
- Chamber of Commerce—local business data
- Present customers—surveys
- Customer data—from license plates, telephone numbers, zip codes, and so on.
- Similar businesses—non-competitors in other cities may provide financial and marketing data

---

It should be noted that there are two schools of thought regarding feasibility studies. One approach is that a feasibility study should be a comprehensive and detailed business plan of sufficient length to cover all aspects of the business. The second approach is that it should be a 20- to 30-page summary business plan giving only the most essential information. This summary plan is used to gain the interest of investors. If interest is generated, then a more complete feasibility study is developed. The remainder of this section will present the elements of a recreation feasibility study based on various formats suggested by several authorities (Brayley & McLean, 1999, Haralson, 1986; Bullaro & Edginton, 1986; Kelsey & Gray, 1985; Fails, 1985). The approach presented here covers the development of a comprehensive feasibility study. Figure 4-4 presents an outline of the feasibility study.

There are several key elements to the feasibility study. They are outlined in Figure 4-4 and described in detail in this section. It should be emphasized here that the feasibility study may be the only source of information used by an investor, supplier, or customer to decide whether or not to support the proposed commercial recreation and tourism enterprise. It must be attractive, accurate, and easy to follow. It does not need to be lengthy, but it does need to be thorough and complete. It should also be kept somewhat confidential (in order to avoid losing a competitive advantage that would have resulted from your concept being first into the marketplace), and it should be introduced to the reader through a formal cover letter.

Figure 4-4
Feasibility Study Outline

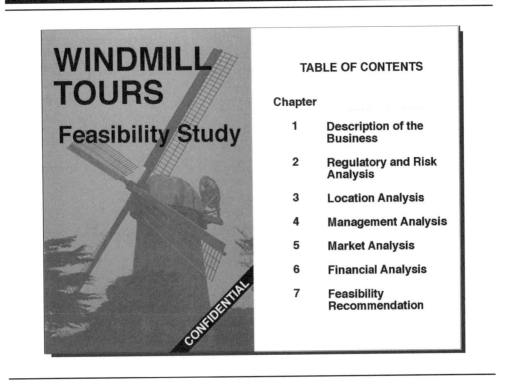

WINDMILL TOURS

Feasibility Study

CONFIDENTIAL

TABLE OF CONTENTS

Chapter

1   Description of the Business

2   Regulatory and Risk Analysis

3   Location Analysis

4   Management Analysis

5   Market Analysis

6   Financial Analysis

7   Feasibility Recommendation

The Cover Letter

In business letter form, a cover letter is delivered with the feasibility study, but is not actually between the covers of the document. The cover letter gives the basic recommendation of the feasibility study and support for that recommendation, including the key items from the market analysis. Also included are any assumptions (the economy, interest rates, energy availability, etc.) that are necessary to support the recommendation.

Chapter I: Description of the Business

The first chapter sets the stage of the feasibility study. It presents the business concept, including a description of the products or services, competitive differentiation, historical background of the industry, and current status of the industry. Also included is an explanation of the legal form of organization of the business.

Each legal form of organization (proprietorship, partnership, limited liability company, or corporation) has its advantages and disadvantages. The one that should be selected depends upon a variety of circumstances, including the entrepreneur's financial condition, type of business, number of employees, risk involved, and tax situation. The following comparison (summarized in Figure 4-5) outlines some of the characteristics of the most popular forms of doing business.

Sole Proprietorship. This is a business enterprise owned and operated by one person. It is the simplest and least costly form for an individual to start. The company name and purpose is simply registered at the county courthouse. The Internal Revenue Service will require forms for employee withholding tax, Social Security, worker's compensation, and so on. As with all other forms of organization, there may also be a city or county business license to purchase, bonds to cover liability on sales tax collection, and special licenses for certain purposes. The owner is personally responsible for all debts, taxes, and legal liabilities but is entitled to all net profits. The business income or loss is reflected on the proprietor's personal tax return. Outside financing for a proprietorship may be difficult to attain, and the owner generally has to rely on his or her own resources and management expertise. Growth is tied exclusively to the owner, who has complete authority over the business. If the owner dies or is incapacitated, this form of business is less likely than other forms to be perpetuated.

General Partnership. This is an association of two or more persons as co-owners. There should be an "Articles of Copartnership" (in writing and filed with the state) that details the financial commitments, distribution of profits or losses, and any other significant agreement. All partners have unlimited liability, as in a proprietorship, and all profits or losses are similarly reflected on the individual's tax return. There is, however, more growth potential in this form due to the combined resources and management abilities of the partners. The partnership may terminate with the death or withdrawal of any partner.

Limited Partnership. This is similar to a general partnership, except that there are two classes of partners. General partners act as officers of the company and have unlimited personal liability. Limited partners invest money or property, but do not share in the management of the company. They are liable only up to the amount of their investment. Amounts invested, distribution of profits, and other agreements must be covered in the written "Articles of Partnership" filed with the state. A limited partnership has more growth potential, since the resources of many limited partners are available. Profits are taxed as individual income. In past years, losses (actual losses or paper losses due to depreciation) could, for income tax purposes, offset ordinary income, so limited partnerships were excellent tax shelters. Now, due to tax law changes, limited partnership losses may be used only to offset gains in other partnerships and may not offset ordinary income.

Corporation. This is a separate legal and taxable entity that usually relieves the owners of liability. It is the most complex legal organization to form and requires "Articles of Incorporation" to be filed with the state, listing the powers of officers, intent of the corporation, classes or types of owners, means of perpetuation, and other aspects. Filing fees and opening taxes are expensive, and the process usually requires help from an attorney. In order to conduct interstate business, the corporation must pay fees, taxes, and filing costs in the other states as well. Stockholders are not individually liable for the firm's debts, but share in the profits or losses according to their proportion of ownership. This is usually the best organizational form for raising large sums of money, since numerous stockholders or "owners" may buy in and sell out with relative ease. Corporate profits are taxed first, and then if the corporation decides to distribute earnings to its stockholders, the dividends are taxed again at the individual level. Managers may be hired and fired by the owners, usually through the corporation's elected board of directors. The corporation lives on when owners or managers die or leave the firm.

Figure 4-5
Summary Comparison of Business Types

	Sole Proprietor	General Partnership	Limited Partnership	Corporation	S Corporation	Limited Liability Company
Ownership	One person	Two or more co-owners	Two or more co-owners (includes general partners [involved in mgmt.] and limited partners [investors only])	Several stockholders (not necessarily involved directly in mgmt.)	Less than 36 stockholders	Several stockholders
Taxing of profits	Business profits taxed as personal ordinary income	Business profits taxed as personal ordinary income	Business profits taxed as personal ordinary income (losses can be used to offset profits only from other partnerships)	Corporate profits taxed first; dividends paid to shareholders taxed as personal ordinary income	Business profits taxed as personal ordinary income	Business profits taxed as personal ordinary income
Liability for corporate debts	Owner entirely liable	All partners have unlimited liability	General partners have unlimited liability; limited partners have limited liability	Stockholders not liable as individuals	Limited stockholder liability	Stockholders not liable as individuals

S Corporation. Once called a "Subchapter S Corporation," this is a regular corporation with limited stockholder liability, but its profits are taxed like a partnership. There is no corporate tax, but stockholders report profits as ordinary income on their taxes. An S Corporation can have no more than 35 stockholders, all holding the same class of stock (no preferred shares). This form of organization has many of the legal advantages of both the corporation and the partnership. The business, however, is restricted to one primary area of endeavor, such as retailing, manufacturing, or land development. This form is very popular among small businesses where the owners desire the legal protection of the corporation but the flexibility and tax treatment of the partnership.

Limited Liability Company. A limited liability company (LLC) is an unincorporated business entity that is really a cross between a corporation and a partnership. Like a corporation, an LLC protects its members from personal liability for the debts and obligations of the company. An LLC is, however, taxed like a partnership (although it may elect to be taxed as a corporation) and is typically formed by filing a "Certificate of Formation" or similar certificate with the Secretary of State. Like a partnership, the members of LLCs typically enter into an operating agreement that establishes how the LLC is managed. Where S Corporations have limits on the number of shareholders who also must be U.S. residents, LLCs have no restrictions in these regards. This makes the LLC a particularly suitable vehicle for non-U.S. citizens. An LLC can have more flexibility in management, because this is controlled by the member's agreement, not by the Business Corporation Act (BCA) of the state.

Chapter II: Regulatory and Risk Analysis

After completing this section of the feasibility study, it will be clearly evident that the United States is no longer a simple place in which to live. As frustrating as it may be, it is essential to find out what regulations must be complied with, what licenses need to be obtained, and what insurance must be purchased. The cost of each must also be reflected when business start-up expenses are estimated. Regulations, taxes, and licenses will vary for different lines of business and from state to state. Agencies such as the Internal Revenue Service and the Small Business Administration, periodically conduct workshops to assist new businesses in meeting their obligations.

Figure 4-6 lists many of the regulations, taxes, and licenses that may be required of a commercial recreation enterprise.

Figure 4-6
Regulations, Taxes, and Licenses

Regulations
- Federal minimum wage laws—Department of Labor
- Worksite safety laws—Occupational Safety and Health Administration (OSHA)
- Worker authorization—U.S. Citizenship and Immigration Service (USCIS)
- Employees identification numbers—Internal Revenue Service (IRS)
- Employee withholding allowance certificates—IRS
- Wage and tax statements—IRS
- Statements of periodic annuities and pensions—IRS
- Equal opportunity laws—Department of Labor
- Land use regulations—Environmental Protection Agency (EPA)
- Employer's withholding tax forms—IRS
- Health regulations—state and county health departments
- Zoning regulations—city and county governments
- Building Codes-State and Local Governments

(continued)

Figure 4-6 (continued)
Regulations, Taxes and Licenses

Taxes
- Franchise and income tax—IRS, state and local governments
- Sales tax—state government
- Property tax—city and county governments
- Self-employment tax—IRS
- Unemployment insurance—IRS
- Workers compensation insurance—state insurance commission
- Employer's share of Social Security (FICA)—IRS

Licenses
- State license fees
- City or county business licenses
- State trade name certificates
- Construction permit fees
- Motor vehicle license and inspection fees

In addition, depending upon the state, special licenses or permits may be required for:

Outdoor advertising signs	Masseurs and masseuses
Amusement devices	Milk vending machines
Beer sales	Musical devices
Billiard and pool tables	Photographer service
Bowling lanes	Private clubs
Burglar alarms	Professional dancers
Card clubs	Public dances
Catering service	Restaurants
Child care center	Rooming house
Cigar and tobacco sale	Service station pumps
Dance halls	Shooting galleries
Dance studios	Vending machines
Fireworks displays	Skating rinks
Golf courses	Soft drink fountains
Ice cream vending machines	Special transportation vehicles
Liquor consumption	Theaters
Live music entertainment	Vehicle rental

Risk Management and Insurance. Adequate insurance coverage is a prerequisite for most loans or other financing, for lease agreements, for purchase of vehicles, and for carrying the retail products of certain suppliers. It is commonplace now to carry policies offering a million dollars or more in coverage. Particularly, if a company engages in any type of risky activity (which, in the opinion of some attorneys, is practically everything) or holds significant assets, it is imperative to be adequately insured. Some common types of insurance are as follows:

- *Fire insurance*—on structure and property within.
- *Liability insurance*—for company, personal coverage, and employees.
- *Automobile insurance*—for all employees and subcontractors.
- *Business interruption insurance*—for fixed expenses if shut down temporarily.

- *Crime insurance*—for burglary, destruction, theft by employees.
- *Glass insurance*—for plate glass windows and displays.
- *Rent insurance*—in case lease property becomes unusable.
- *Group life insurance*—for employees.
- *Group health insurance*—for employees.
- *Disability insurance*—for employees.
- *Key employee insurance*—for loss of a key manager or employee.

The commercial recreation and tourism manager is responsible for identifying the risks inherent in the business and establishing management procedures to minimize those risks. Regular facility inspections, preventive maintenance, crowd control, and adequate supervision are essential steps to take. Insurance should be purchased to cover the largest potential loss exposures, and, as funds are available, lower priority areas should be covered. All insurance programs should be reviewed periodically to be sure that coverage is adequate. Risk management strategies are covered in greater detail in Chapter 7 of this text.

Patents. If the company has invented a product that can be sold for a profit, then it is appropriate to protect the invention through the patent process. This is not an inexpensive proposition; the cost of applying for a simple patent averages over $5,000, with about half of that going for legal expenses. Unfortunately, it is also a long process, taking about 18 months or more. Research for the patent process can begin at major regional libraries or by contacting the Superintendent of Documents, U.S. Government Printing Office, Washington DC 20402, and asking for the publication "General Information Concerning Patents."

Chapter III: Location Analysis

This section addresses the opportunities and challenges associated with the physical location of the business. Discussion should focus on how the location facilitates consumer purchasing and gives a competitive advantage. It should also clearly articulate the drawbacks to the site and outline strategies to minimize their effects on the success and feasibility of the enterprise. Considerations for site location were covered earlier in this chapter.

Chapter IV: Management Analysis

This section is devoted to an explanation of how the project will be managed. The primary components are organization, staffing, and major operational considerations. When the business actually starts, this section should be expanded into a complete policy and procedure manual for the organization.

Organization. Considerations include the following:
- Define the major areas of responsibility in operating the project.
- Decide who in management will be responsible for each area.
- Develop summary job descriptions for key personnel.
- Identify secondary level tasks and duties that must be accomplished in order to carry out the business.
- Determine the number and types of personnel to accomplish the work of the business.
- Develop an organizational chart.

Staffing. After completion of the organizational concept, consider staffing details:
- Specific skills, expertise, and certification required of the various personnel throughout the system.

- Availability of such personnel in the local labor force.
- Compensation and benefits required to draw good personnel.
- Employee housing or transportation if necessary.
- Orientation and training programs.
- Employee incentive programs.

Major Operational Considerations. This includes attention to special areas of the operation, such as follows:

- Particularly significant aspects of programs or services, such as special instructional methods and service philosophy.
- Use of other organizations' facilities through contract, joint-use agreements, trade-offs, and so forth.
- Use of special equipment, backup equipment, and preventive maintenance.
- Use of subcontracted services—what vendors and alternates are available?

Chapter V: Market Analysis

Market analysis is an organized way to find objective answers to the basic questions that every commercial recreation and tourism manager must ask in order to begin to succeed. These questions include the following:

- Who are the customers?
- What are their needs?
- How often and how much do they purchase?
- How can this business differ from its competitors?
- How much market share can be captured? Zero Sum marketing

It should be evident that market analysis is very possibly the most important and the most difficult chapter of the feasibility study.

Market research helps to reduce business risks, to spot problems, and to identify opportunities. Large corporations hire researchers to discover what is going on in the market. Small business managers, on the other hand, are usually closer to their market and have a better "feel" for the market. However, that feel may be biased, so small business managers also need to engage in objective analysis. Market analysis includes segmentation of the market, analysis of competitors, product or service positioning, and projections of market demand.

Market Segmentation. A market segment is a group of people with some common characteristics that make a difference in their purchasing behavior. Market segments can be based on socio-demographic characteristics (age, sex, family stage, income, education, occupation, ethnicity), behavioral characteristics (benefits sought, level of use, level of skill, psychographic profile), or geographic characteristics (place of residence, location of facility).

It is essential that the commercial recreation and tourism manager know what market segments upon which to focus. Otherwise, the efforts of the business will be wasted on people who have little likelihood of becoming customers. The market segment that the business decides to focus on is called the target market and may be a very specific or a very general group. For example, an outdoor adventure tour company may focus on a market that is age 25–40, well educated, upper-middle to upper income, and oriented toward outdoor activities and risk. On the other hand, a water theme park may focus on preteens, teens, and families of middle incomes.

Competition Analysis. Competition in commercial recreation and tourism generally occurs at either the brand level or product level. An example of brand-level competition is that which exists between movie theater chains. All movie theaters essentially offer the same product on the screen, but the consumer may choose between Cinemark, Regal, AMC, Paramount, or any other of a host of theater chains for the movie experience. Brand differentiation usually comes through subtle offerings such as stadium style seating, parking, price structures, or facility cleanliness. Cinema operators must also deal with product-line competition, as some people choose to rent a video movie, bowl, skate, play softball, or go to an amusement park instead of going to the movie theater. Figure 4-7 illustrates these concepts.

Figure 4-7
Two Types of Competition

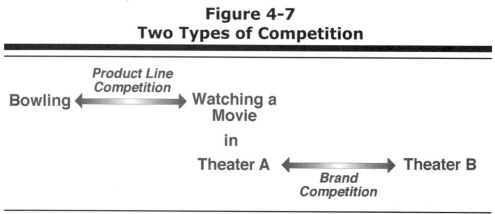

To combat product-line competition, the commercial recreation and tourism manager must promote the superior quality of the product or service, the positive experience that it will provide, and the value received for the dollar spent. Sometimes professional and trade associations help by doing this for an entire industry. For example, the PGA (Professional Golfers' Association) has, in addition to advertising its own tournaments and events, enhanced awareness of and appreciation for the game of golf through a variety of innovative promotions.

In response to brand competition, it may be necessary to undertake a detailed analysis of the competition. Questions to be answered in this analysis are numerous:

- How many competitors are there?
- How big are the competitors?
- How strongly entrenched are they?
- Where is the heaviest competition located?
- What are their successful sales points?
- What are their weaknesses?
- What competitive edge can be developed?

The analysis of competition should lead to the formulation of strategies to exploit the competition's weaknesses and enhance one's own strengths.

Market Positioning. Market positioning is a decision process that helps in deciding the best product or service niche and marketing strategy for a particular business. The process is based on three considerations: internal analysis (including available resources, organizational constraints, and the company's philosophy and values), market segment benefit analysis, and competitive analysis (Wolff, 1986). The most important element may be the market segment benefit analysis. This is an analysis of the benefits that the market segment values most in the particular product or service. The company is then able to position the product or service in an attempt to satisfy the customer's expectation of benefits. The second priority is to differentiate the business on the basis of the competitive analysis.

In Figure 4-8, market positioning for a retail sporting goods store is illustrated. In this case, the most important market considerations were price and variety of selection. Using these criteria, the various stores could be identified as specialty shops versus full-line stores, or as discount marts versus full-price stores. For this situation, it was decided that a discount ski shop would fill a special niche in this community. To further enhance viability, the shop should also develop a good off-season strategy, such as a complementary product line in tennis or water sports.

Demand Projection. Probably the most difficult part of the market analysis and the entire feasibility study is the projection of demand for a given product or service. No matter what method is used to project demand, there are assumptions and weaknesses inherent in the process. There are many different approaches to projecting demand, and some of the most common types are summarized in this section.

Application of standards—This is a simple approach and one that is often suggested by optimistic trade associations. An experience-based criterion is established in which a certain population figure can supposedly support a given type of business. For example, if

Figure 4-8
Market Position for Sporting Goods

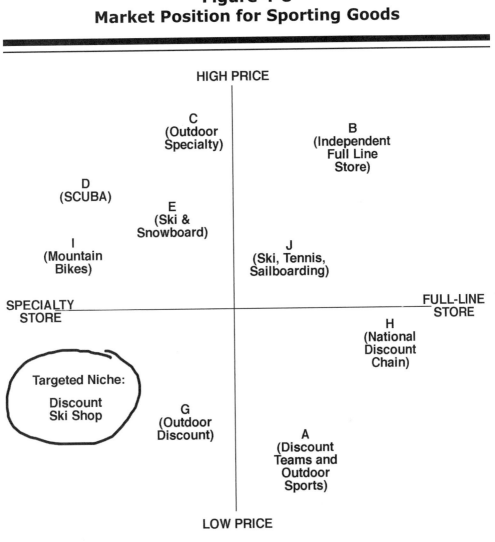

a particular trade association suggested a standard of one golf course per 25,000 in population, then a community of 100,000 should supposedly support four courses. It should be obvious that this approach is a rough approximation that may not work in every locale.

Comparable project methods—An existing recreation business in an area of similar demographics is compared to the project under study. Participation rates and expenditure averages are then transposed to the new location. Although the figures may be adjusted to account for variance in competitors, demographics, and so on, the reliability of this method depends upon how comparable the circumstances are. This method has frequent application among franchisers and large chains with enough outlets to have comparable data for many situations.

Trend analysis or time series analysis—When there is a history of demand data (for example, number of tourist arrivals at a given destination), then demand for future years may be projected. Depending upon the number of variables that have major impact on the demand, a trend line can be extrapolated (using simple or multiple regression techniques) that projects future use. This method is based on the premise that what has happened in the past has some relevance for the future. Be aware of what historical conditions the data reflect, and use caution in extending the trend line too far into the future. Figure 4-9 illustrates this procedure.

Participation rate projection—Surveys are often taken by planning agencies and market research companies to determine the consumer behavior pattern for various products or services. Participation or usage rates can be broken down by various market segment categories such as age, income, residence, and location. It is best when the surveys reflect actual participation rather than anticipated participation. The appropriate participation rates can then be applied to the market population of the project under study to yield expected participation. For example, if a national market survey finds that 5% of adult Americans belong to private tennis clubs, and a certain city has 100,000 adults, then it may be projected that there are 5,000 potential tennis club members in that city. Caution

Figure 4-9
Trend Analysis Example

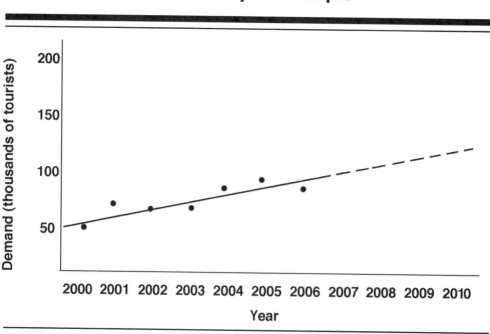

must be exercised, however, when using national or regional participation rates to estimate demand rates for a local business. There could be a huge difference between a data-based projection and local reality. If the new business is a major investment, companies usually find it is worth the expense to contract for market research within the specific market area. The "travel cost model" or "gravity model" approaches to forecasting demand are basically variations of the participation rate approach, in which major considerations are given to the distance factor (distance from origin to destination), cost, and/or alternate opportunities.

Which method should be used to estimate demand? It would be wisest to use more than one method to establish a likely range or average, and it is important to remember that there is a tendency to estimate demand too high.

Determination of Market Share. Once demand for a product or service in a given area is estimated, it cannot be assumed that the new business will capture the market. This would only occur if the business was the first in the area to provide that product or service. It is more likely that the new business will have to fight it out with existing competitors to gain any respectable share of the market. In any case, do not assume that there is infinite potential for growth.

Yesawich (1984) suggested that your "expected market share" can be calculated by dividing your capacity for business by the total capacity in the area. For example, if your resort had 200 rooms and the total of your competitors' was 800 rooms, then your expected share would be 20% of the 1,000-room market.

It is, however, unreasonable to expect a new business to gain its expected market share immediately. Instead, its initial fair share of the market should be estimated by factoring the expected share downward. If the overall market is booming (evidenced by waiting lines, unmet demand, and high prices), and if the new business is truly competitive, then it may not have to factor down very much. On the other hand, if the overall market is saturated or stagnant (evidenced by excess supply, price discounts, and business failures), then the initial fair share may be 50% or less of the expected share.

Chapter VI: Financial Analysis

The financial analysis is based on information presented or considered in all the previous sections of the feasibility study. The concept, product, operating structure, and location of the business will help to determine the costs involved in starting and continuing the enterprise. Revenue projections are based on the market analysis.

The golden rule for the financial analysis section is to be liberal in estimating expenses and be conservative in estimating revenues. Moreover, an analyst may approach the uncertainty of financial outcomes by presenting three scenarios (optimistic, realistic, and pessimistic) for the operating costs and revenue projections. Keeping optimism and pessimism in check and considering a range of alternative outcomes helps to establish a range for the potential profits or losses. In financial analysis, projections need to be developed for the start-up costs, the operating costs, and revenues. The figures must then be organized and displayed on several types of financial statements.

Start-Up Costs include the expense of initiating the business, financing capital facilities and equipment, and covering preopening costs. It is a major mistake to underestimate these expenses, because the business must get off to a solid start. There are, however, some legitimate corners that can be cut. For example, facilities and equipment can be leased instead of purchased. Typical start-up costs include the following:

- *Business initiation expenses*—legal and professional consultants, insurance, incorporation expenses, tax deposits, licenses and permits, cost of obtaining loans.

- *Capital expenses*—land and buildings, equipment, vehicles, machinery, remodeling and decorations, fixtures, displays, signs.
- *Preopening operations*—(for one to three months as necessary) salary for owner/manager, utility deposits and installation, salary for key employees, utilities and telephone, staff training costs, supplies and equipment, initial inventory purchase, maintenance expense, advertising, 10% or more cash reserves.

Operating Costs should be estimated for monthly periods. Most organizations group their expenses into the following categories: cost of goods sold, personnel (including benefits), contractual services (including rent), equipment and supplies, taxes and licenses, debt service (paying on loans) and depreciation (expensing of certain capital assets). There are, of course, many subcategories possible within each of the expense groups. For the feasibility study, it is best to estimate the expenses for at least three years.

In many commercial recreation and tourism businesses, the expenses occur at irregular intervals throughout the year. For example, in a water theme park, certain expenses occur during the off-season, but most of the expenses occur during the months of May to September. Therefore, the manager cannot simply distribute the estimated expenses evenly throughout the 12 months. Again, it should be emphasized that it is safest to estimate expenses liberally.

Revenue Projections also should be made for monthly periods. Categories for revenues are not as standardized as with expenses, because the sources of revenue vary greatly according to the type of businesses. Generally, the bulk of revenues come from the sale of products and/or services, but there may also be income from rents, leases, earned interest, or other sources. The projections of revenue and expense for years two and three are usually based on conservative growth.

Revenue projections can be made by applying the average per capita expenditure of customers as estimated in the demand analysis section. The "per cap" figure may be based on known industry averages, figures from a comparable business, or the experienced judgment of the manager. After 12 months of operation, the "per cap" estimate for the second and third year may be revised. It should be noted that, in certain types of commercial recreation and tourism businesses, there is a high percentage of revenue generated through preseason or advance sales.

Financial Pro-Formas are detailed projections for the future. Four types of pro-formas should be shown in the feasibility study:

- *Pro-forma profit and loss statement*—monthly, for one year; quarterly, for three years.
- *Pro-forma cash flow statement*—monthly for one year, quarterly for three years.
- *Balance sheet*—showing assets, liabilities, and owners' equity at the end of each year.
- *Break-even analysis*—showing the quantity of sales necessary to break even during a period of time, usually monthly.

Examples of these financial forms are included in Chapter 5 of this book.

Chapter VII: Feasibility Recommendation

Based upon the financial analysis and consideration of the risks and assumptions involved, a decision can be made regarding the future of the project. Four basic decisions can be made: (1) to proceed with the project, contingent upon funding, (2) to amend the project and seek funding, (3) to amend the basic concept and conduct a new feasibility study, or (4) to terminate the project. These decisions can be made on the basis of the expected return on investment (net profits divided by equity) to the owners. This is where the three scenarios (optimistic, realistic, pessimistic) come into play. By estimating the return on investment (ROI) in each of the three scenarios, a range of opportunities can be visualized. Figure 4-10 illustrates the comparative opportunity presented by five hypothetical businesses. Based on this comparative analysis, it would appear that the low overhead party-planning service offers the potential for the greatest return (50%). At its best, the fishing guide business is not likely to generate the high level of returns expected for the party-planning service, but it does offer the highest rate of return in the most pessimistic scenario (22.9%). In this example, the bicycle shop would not be deemed feasible because of the potential for loss and the low return expected in the most optimistic circumstances (4.4% is usually lower than could be earned on $800,000 in a relatively no-risk investment such as a certificate of deposit at a chartered bank).

Figure 4-10
Comparative Feasibility Analysis (Using ROI)

Enterprise	$Equity	Pessimistic		Realistic		Optimistic	
		$Net Profits	ROI %	$Net Profits	ROI %	$Net Profits	ROI %
Bicycle shop	800,000	-30,000	-3.8	10,000	1.3	35,000	4.4
Bed and breakfast inn	900,000	45,000	5.0	62,000	6.9	96,000	10.7
Travel agency	220,000	3,000	1.4	10,000	4.5	15,000	6.8
Party planning service	40,000	8,000	20.0	16,000	40.0	20,000	50.0
Fishing guide service	35,000	8,000	22.9	12,000	34.3	16,000	45.7

FINANCING THE VENTURE

After completing the feasibility study, another very important step must be taken in order to actually start the business. The entrepreneur must secure adequate financing for the venture. Occasionally, the entrepreneur will have enough personal resources, but usually, additional funds are needed. Those who provide additional funds will do so at their risk and will first want to know the answers to four key questions:

1. Exactly how much money is needed?
2. How will the money be used?
3. How and when will the investment be repaid?
4. Can you afford the cost of the financing?

In addition to knowing the answers to these questions, the entrepreneur must understand the advantages and disadvantages of using "external funding," which is borrowing and/or using other people's money. Furthermore, the entrepreneur must be creditworthy and know what sources of financing are possible. This section explores those topics.

Advantages and Disadvantages of External Funding

As with everything in business, there are advantages and disadvantages in using external funding rather than depend totally on your own personal financial sources.

Advantages include the following:

- Starting the business now, when the opportunity exists. Five years from now, the entrepreneur may have saved enough to start, but someone else may have already met the market demand.
- Starting with a larger financial base, which could mean opportunity for greater profits and a greater return on the "leveraged" (borrowed) investment.
- Distributing part of the risk to others, particularly to investors.
- People who provide financial assistance want the business to succeed in order to protect their investment. Often, these people will provide expertise, assistance, and contacts that can be very valuable to the success of the business.

Disadvantages include the following:

- There is a cost of financing. Loans must be paid back with interest, and profits must be shared with investors.
- There is personal liability for failure. If the entrepreneur defaults on a loan, personal assets may be taken. If the business fails, co-owners may not be willing to invest with that entrepreneur in the future.
- Some of the advice given by investors may be conflicting, wrong, untimely, or un-wanted.
- One's own business is a commitment that is difficult to walk away from. A salaried employee, on the other hand, can easily change jobs.
- There is pressure to succeed because of the consequences of failure. This pressure can severely harm or destroy a person's personal health and family life.

The Cs of Credit

Lenders and investors consider a wide variety of factors when making a decision regarding the financing of a new venture. These factors can be called the "Cs of credit." Most, if not all of these Cs must be present in order to secure financing (Andrew, 1984):

- **Character**—includes the borrower's integrity, personal background, and desire to fulfill the obligation.
- **Capacity**—the experience and ability to operate the business efficiently and profit-ably.
- **Capital**—the current worth of the business, which could be marshaled to repay the debt.
- **Collateral**—the personal assets that could be converted into cash to repay the debt.
- **Concept**—the overall soundness of the business concept and plan of operation.
- **Conditions**—the overall economic conditions in the area, including interest rates, recent failures, recession versus growth economy, and so on.
- **Contingencies**—alternate plans for utilizing the assets of the business if the initial plan fails.
- **Competition**—likelihood of gaining and retaining an adequate market share from competitors.
- **Circumstances**—any special circumstances that could affect future success of the business; for example, political or social uncertainties.

Financial Sources

There are three primary approaches to financing a new business: personal sources, debt financing, and equity financing. Each has its purposes, advantages, and disadvantages.

Personal Sources include savings, property, and assistance from relatives and friends. In order to secure debt or equity financing, it will probably be necessary to have at least 10% and perhaps as much as 60% of the start-up cost backed by personal sources. It is not uncommon for an entrepreneur to take out a second mortgage on his or her home in order to raise this money.

There is a hidden danger when approaching relatives and friends for money. Will the money be given solely because of the relationship, or because it is a good business proposition? It would be a mistake for relatives or friends to toss away money on a weak project just because of a special relationship. Many friendships and families have been wrecked because of business ventures that have gone sour. Some financial advisers suggest that relatives should not give any money as a loan that they would not otherwise give as a gift.

Debt Financing is the securing of money through a loan. In addition to funding a business start-up, debt financing can also be used to fund an expansion; provide working capital (cash needed to keep the business going); or purchase equipment, supplies, or resale goods. Terms of loans vary according to the type of business involved, but are usually at least 1 to 5% over the prime rate, which is the interest rate that lenders charge their largest corporate accounts or other preferred clients. Sources of debt financing include banks, commercial finance companies, life insurance companies, savings and loan institutions, suppliers and vendors (trade credit), and the government.

- *Banks*—offer all types of loans: short-term loans, inventory financing, equipment loans, and long-term loans. Banks offer some of the best loan rates, usually 1 to 3% over prime, and provide auxiliary services such as cash management advice, credit checking, and deposit services. It is a good idea to arrange in advance for a short-term line of credit to meet unexpected cash flow problems. Unfortunately, banks are the most conservative lending sources and often turn down recreation ventures.
- *Commercial finance companies*—lend money to companies that do not qualify for standard loans made by commercial banks. Finance companies generally make loans against the value of three types of assets: accounts receivable, inventories, and facilities and equipment. Because they accept higher-risk projects, interest rates are usually higher than with a bank.
- *Savings and loan associations*—may provide loans for real estate financing for about 75% of the property's value. Interest rates are similar to commercial finance companies.
- *Insurance companies*—many allow policyholders to borrow against the paid-up cash value of the individual's life insurance. Interest rates are very good, lower than a bank's, because there is less risk involved.
- *Trade credit*—occurs when a supplier of retail goods sends merchandise to a retail store and bills the store at a later date, usually 30–60 days. It may be in the supplier's best interest to encourage the use of its products by allowing no interest or extremely low-interest credit.
- *Equipment financing, rentals, and leases*—are usually available from dealers of major equipment and vehicles. Rental payments can often be applied to the later purchase of the equipment.
- *Government loans*—can be obtained through the U.S. Small Business Administration (SBA), which guarantees up to 80% of certain loans made by a local bank but ap-

proved by SBA. In case of default, the SBA repurchases the loan. Due to this low risk, interest rates are only about 2 to 3% over prime. The maximum SBA loan is for $750,000. In their early years, Apple computers, Nike, and Godfather's Pizza were each assisted by an SBA loan. Another SBA program (Express), introduced in 1999, guarantees 50% of a maximum $150,000 loan but requires less paperwork and fewer steps for approval (Mitchell, 1999). Occasionally, states and cities also provide loans to stimulate business. In Canada, the Federal Business Development Bank makes similar loans through its branches across the country.

- *Small business investment companies (SBIC)*—are privately owned, profit-oriented companies chartered by the state. SBICs are eligible for low-interest federal loans and use these funds to invest in small businesses.
- *Credit cards*—can be an easy way to get cash quickly without having to go through the business planning process. This kind of financing is very expensive, but may be appropriate for small, immediate needs such as a new computer for the office. Tiffany (1999) cautions that

Establishing debt seems to be easier than establishing credit, so before you fill out any of those ubiquitous card offers, plan your expenses and potential cash flow carefully to see whether the downsides of credit cards (interest rates of 18 percent and higher) are worth the upsides.

Equity Financing requires that the entrepreneur give up a portion of ownership in return for the funds to start the business. Sources of equity financing include limited partners, venture capital firms, SBICs, and public stock offerings.

- *Limited partnerships*—allow the entrepreneur, as the general partner, to attract funds for start-up. The contribution of capital by limited partners and the distribution of profits is spelled out in advance in the articles of partnership filed with the state. Limited partnerships can often be arranged through local asset management companies and financial consulting firms.
- *Venture capital firms*—are interested in buying into companies that demonstrate excellent prospects for future earnings growth. Venture capital firms typically look for a return of 30 to 40% a year (Gunn, 1998). Even though many start-up companies will fail to earn this much, the venture capitalists hope that one big winner will make up for several losers. Most venture firms do not seek a position of more than 40% ownership in a company because they want the primary owner to have incentive to keep building the business. Usually, venture capital firms are not interested in projects requiring less than $500,000 because the cost of investigating a proposal could almost equal the profit potential in a very small company.
- *SBICs*—are often interested in an equity position in a new company. The maximum SBIC investment in any single firm cannot exceed 20% of the firm's assets, although several SBICs may join together to finance a company. In Canada, the Federal Business Development Bank has a Venture Capital Division that provides equity financing and becomes a temporary minority shareholder (Canada Yearbook, 1991).
- *Public stock offerings*—allow part of the ownership of a company to be sold to the public. The sale of the stock is arranged through an underwriter/stockbroker who specializes in this service in return for a sales commission. Offerings over $5 million require a myriad of compliances with the Securities and Exchange Commission (SEC). For offerings less than $5 million, the rules and regulations are much less stringent. The success of a small stock offering may depend more on the ability of the underwriter/broker to sell the stock than on the legitimacy of the business concept. The

North American Securities Administrators Association has estimated that 90% of all "pennystock" investors lose money.

- *Private-placement memoranda*—In a PPM, equity in the company is sold to a private pool of investors. This may be arranged by asset management companies or by small groups of business associates. Because PPMs are exempt from expensive, time-consuming securities laws, they are, according to some attorneys, the most cost-effective way for small businesses to raise equity capital.

ALTERNATIVES IN STARTING A NEW BUSINESS

There is more than one way to start a new commercial recreation and tourism business. In fact, there are many alternatives. The previous section presented the three basic financial approaches: personal resources, debt financing, or equity financing. There are, however, several variations that can build upon any of the financial or legal structural approaches. These alternatives are franchises, purchase of an existing business, small business incubators, core product extension at an existing business, and public-commercial cooperative ventures.

Franchises

A franchise agreement permits the buyer/operator (the franchisee) to sell the products or services of the seller or franchisor. In the most popular type of franchise arrangement, the franchisee pays an initial fee (that can range from $1,000 to $1 million) and a continuing royalty, and may be required to purchase the wholesale product from the franchisor. The royalty is typically between 2 and 8% of gross sales. In addition, the franchisee may be required to pay up to 4% of its sales for regional and national advertising expenses (Caminiti, 1991). In return, the franchisor allows the use of the product, trademark, and image and provides management assistance such as market research, marketing strategy development, promotions and national advertising, operating manuals, standards, quality control, and possibly some financing.

Franchising is a good way for an entrepreneur to get started in a business where most of the mistakes have already been made and corrected by the franchisor. Franchising is also an advantage to established companies, because it is a fast, cheap way to expand. There are, of course, some problems with franchising. The franchisor's services may not be of high quality or worth the royalty fees involved. The franchisor could become overly aggressive in awarding franchises and saturate the market. Also, the franchisee/operator may feel somewhat constricted due to the regulations, policies, procedures, and controls required by the franchisor.

Overall, franchising is a very successful concept. Only about 5% of new franchises fail in their first two years. There are over 2,000 different franchise companies in the United States, with about 500,000 outlets. Expansion is very rapid. McDonald's, for example, opens a new outlet (a franchise operation) somewhere in the world every 12 hours and, in 2005, was reported to be the largest private employer in the Washington, DC area. A major portion of all retail sales are made by franchise outlets. One of the key reasons for success of franchises is the consistency of the product. Consumers always know what they are going to get when they eat at a McDonald's or stay at a Sheraton. Franchise opportunity information can be found in the "business opportunities" section of newspaper classified ads and various bookstore and newsstand publications or can be obtained from the SBA.

Some franchise "opportunities" are cleverly disguised scams designed to relieve careless investors of their initial franchise fees. In critically evaluating a franchise opportunity, there are several factors to be considered:

- **The company**—its history, reputation, experience, honesty, net worth, past success, and rate of failures.
- **The product**—quality, market advantages, value for the dollar, availability, durability, purchasing requirements, and so on.
- **Location**—quantity and quality of areas available, protection of exclusive or territory rights, and assistance in selecting a location.
- **Assistance**—quality and value of assistance in training, operational procedures, financial procedures, inventory control, market research, promotion, advertising, and financial help.
- **Control**—exact terms of initial payment and ongoing royalties, restrictions in the conduct of business, product requirements, quotas, and terms for ending the franchise.

Much of the above information can be found in the company's "disclosure circular," a document that the Federal Trade Commission requires of all franchisors.

Buying an Existing Business

The purchase of an existing business is much like the purchase of a used car. Initially, it could look sharp and appear to be running smoothly, but it could turn out to be a lemon. Therefore, it is essential that a thorough feasibility study be conducted, just as with a new business location. There is a difference, however, because with an existing business, there should be plenty of existing records and data to analyze: sales and market data, financial reports, inventory records, and so on. If after careful review it turns out that there are discrepancies or misrepresentations in any of the data, regard them as major warning signs. One way to guard against this is to insist on a "holdback," where part of the purchase price is held back for an agreed period of time to assure that misrepresentations have not taken place. Other aspects to check carefully are as follows: condition of the facility and equipment, employee qualifications and productivity, all contracts and legal aspects (leases, debts, loans, titles, zoning, unsettled lawsuits, etc.), customer relations, and the seller's reasons for leaving the business (Bullaro & Edginton, 1986).

Advantages to buying an existing business include:

- less uncertainty about market demand;
- no "lag time" in receiving returns on investment;
- known capabilities of facilities, equipment, and personnel;
- established sources of supplies;
- easier financing if the business has a good track record;
- less time, effort, and pressure as compared to a start-up; and
- opportunity to purchase the business at a low price.

Disadvantages with this approach include

- compromise of the purchaser's goals to match the existing business;
- existing customers may leave;
- poor selection or quality of goods or services that are currently offered;
- inadequate or deteriorated facilities and/or equipment;
- poor customer relations that linger on from the previous owner;
- questionable policies and practices that may be difficult to change;
- the apparent bargain (business purchase price) could be overpriced; and
- legal problems with property, lease, contracts, or lawsuits.

Small Business Incubators

Another approach to starting a business is to work within the context of a small business incubator. These are facilities and organizations where fledgling businesses share space and office services while receiving management help and, occasionally, financial help. The idea behind the incubator is that the environment will improve the chance of success.

While most small business incubators are for manufacturers or technology firms, there are opportunities for service-based companies. The incubator provides favorable rents, tie-ins with venture capital, secretaries, phone service, computers, copiers, conference rooms, and maintenance. The sharing of services help the small company to lower its operating costs. Not surprisingly, the success rate of incubator-based firms is higher than average. Some types of commercial recreation enterprises that have flourished in the incubator concept include a resort property broker, a party and contract recreation service, and a sportswear importer/wholesaler.

Core Product Extensions at Existing Business

There are many opportunities for an entrepreneur to establish a core product extension at an existing business location. These arrangements are good for small specialty services that can operate with low overhead. In almost every case, there is a contractual agreement between the entrepreneur and the existing business. It is also important that the service be compatible with and complementary to the primary business. Some examples of core product extensions are

- a contracted sailing instructor at a private marina,
- a guide service at a mountain resort,
- a mobile specialty food vendor at an amusement park,
- a ski tune/repair service at a sporting goods store,
- a photography and video service at a ski resort,
- a tour company at a hotel, and
- an entertainment troupe on a cruise ship.

Auxiliary services such as these are attractive to business owners who need to expand their services but lack the knowledge or inclination to do so themselves. It is a good way to expand at little or no risk, and the additional service can be a way to draw new business and further differentiate the company from competitors.

From the entrepreneur's perspective, this approach is a good way to reduce overhead, since the existing business provides the facility and most of the advertising. The core product extension capitalizes upon the customers who are already drawn to the existing business. Of course, the provider of that auxiliary service will probably have to pay a minimum monthly guarantee and usually a percentage of gross sales to the host business.

Public-Commercial Cooperative Venture

In recent years, many public park and recreation agencies have turned to private enterprise in order to continue or expand services. There are many types of public-commercial cooperative ventures, and in most cases the public agency is careful to contract with a proven company. There are, however, opportunities for entrepreneurs to bid successfully for small, but potentially profitable contracted services. For example, many parks provide concessionaire opportunities for paddleboat rentals, tennis instruction, food and beverage service, in-line skate rental, umbrella and beach raft rental, souvenir sales, and pro shops. In some public recreation settings, the private sector is involved in managing and operating the central service or attraction. For example, many state parks in the United States have resort hotels or campgrounds that are developed and owned by the government but are managed, under contract, by private corporations. In the case of concession operations, the private contractor usually has to pay a monthly guarantee fee and a percentage of gross sales.

Further cooperation also exists in the area of infrastructure and facility development. It is becoming quite common for local government to help private ventures such as a theme park, stadium, or hotel by "giving" support services (access roads, parking lots, marinas, trail links, waterways, etc.) to help make a major commercial recreation and tourism enterprise viable. Public-private cooperation can also be seen in the programming of community recreation services. In communities where a private indoor recreation complex is built, there is usually an agreement or understanding that the public agency will use that facility for some of its programs (at a reduced rate) and that the public agency will not use its tax-backed economic advantage to unfairly compete with the private organization. Such agreements are generally very beneficial to all parties involved, especially the consumers.

The advantages of public-commercial cooperative ventures are numerous, and for this reason it is likely to become more common in years to come.

SUMMARY

A new business must begin with a sound concept and a good product. It is critical that any new product or service enter the market at an early growth stage of the life cycle of the industry. Differentiation of the product or service from other competitors is also critical for success. As part of the development of the business concept, careful attention must be given to the desired image, the marketing platform, and the scale or size of the enterprise.

A feasibility study builds upon the initial business concept. Generally, the more money involved in the new business, the more effort will go into the feasibility study. While a feasibility study cannot eliminate all doubt regarding the future of the enterprise, it can illuminate many of the uncertainties. The feasibility study includes a description of the business (including legal organization), a regulatory and risk analysis, a location analysis, a management analysis, a market analysis, a financial analysis, and finally, a recommendation.

The entrepreneur needs to understand the advantages and disadvantages of external financing for the new venture and have a knowledge of various financial sources. In addition to personal resources, the entrepreneur may seek debt financing (loans from banks, finance companies, savings and loan associations, insurance companies, trade suppliers, and the government) or equity financing (limited partnerships, venture capital firms, small business investment companies, and public stock offerings).

There are other ways to get into a new business. These include initiating or assuming a franchise, existing independent business, small business incubator, auxiliary service at an existing business, and cooperative venture with public park and recreation agencies.

SPOTLIGHT ON:

KORY KAPALOSKI and TROUT BUM 2

Kory Kapaloski has always enjoyed outdoor recreation, and fly-fishing is at the top of his list of favorite activities. While Kory attended classes at the University of Utah's Parks, Recreation and Tourism program, he searched for a way to turn his love of fly-fishing into a career. By the time he graduated in 1999, Kory had gained significant practical experience by working for several years as a contracted fishing guide for a local fly shop and by serving an internship during which he learned about the retail side of the business. However, it was his university course on feasibility studies that led to his big break.

As a class project, Kory led a team of three other students in the development of a complete feasibility study for a realistic yet hypothetical fly-fishing shop for the Park City, Utah, area. As the student group project neared completion, Kory's friend and fellow fishing guide, Harley Jackson, introduced Kory to Richard Hansen. Rich was an early retiree from a successful career in the insurance industry and had built a commercial hunting and fishing lodge in Montana. Although operation of the lodge was successful, Rich had also toyed with the idea of opening a fly shop somewhere. Kory showed Rich the feasibility study and Rich was impressed enough to suggest that Kory and Harley join him in starting the shop. The key, of course, was that Rich would fund most of the start-up costs.

The original feasibility study was based on the assumption that the fly shop would be located at a very visible street corner just off historic, Main Street in Park City. It was expected that this site would draw numerous walk-ins from the many tourists who visit the area for its unique shops, restaurants, and bars. However, another opportunity presented itself, and the group rented a larger space for less money in a very rustic looking but new building on the main road leading into town. This turned out to be a fortunate decision, as it placed the shop in a less congested area that appealed more to local, serious fly-fishers.

Trout Bum 2 (an easily remembered name, but not a second shop; the 2 is for "also") opened in May 1999, just 5 months after Kory's student group completed the feasibility study. As is true for most feasibility studies, the actual business start-up costs turned out to be a little underestimated, and the market demand was a little overestimated. However, there was a good reason for both. Rich wanted the shop interior to be of a high quality that would match the top-of-the-line inventory and the atmosphere expected by an upscale market. Also, the larger 2,000-square-foot retail area required more inventory than was expected for the originally planned site. The final start-up costs were about $50,000 plus another $200,000 for inventory.

Projections in the feasibility study for *Trout Bum 2* were reasonably accurate for many of the other aspects of the business. During the first summer tourist season, about 75% of the customers were tourists. In the fall shoulder season, about 80% of the customers were local residents, which was a little higher than anticipated. During that first summer, there were about 15 to 20 customers per day in the summer, and about 70% of them bought something. This was a lower number of customers but a higher "sales capture rate" than originally projected, probably because the new location does not draw upon the heavy street shopper

(continued)

volume of Main Street. In the fall shoulder season, there are about half as many customers per day, and about 50% buy something. The average sale the first year was about $50, just as projected in the feasibility study.

With fewer drop-in browsers, and a higher percentage of serious shoppers, fewer sales staff are needed than originally projected. The shop's first winter season was successful because the winter tourist season in Park City is a proven time for upscale visitors engaging in expensive gift shopping, especially around Christmas.

Trout Bum 2 positions itself as an upscale shop with top-of-the-line equipment and truly expert service. In just a few months they developed a core of loyal customers. The atmosphere is casual and highly personalized, as many customers are known by name, and lengthy fishing talk is an important part of the business. Their computer system allows all sales to be tracked for a perpetual inventory system, for advertising conversion analysis, and for distribution of a store newsletter.

As planned in the feasibility study, *Trout Bum 2* offers inexpensive rental packages, and Kory leads numerous guided fishing trips for individuals and small groups. These both appeal to tourists who have not brought equipment, as well as to highly valued entry-level participants who, once hooked, will make major purchases for equipment and clothing.

Overall, *Trout Bum 2* followed much of the business plan that was laid out in Kory's feasibility study. Over the next 5 years, the business grew. They now have 11 guides to lead a variety of fishing trips. There is an attractive Web site, which Kory says is by far the most worthwhile use of his marketing dollars. The shop now averages about 50 sales per day (including sales of guided trips), and the average sale is up to about $90. There was, however, an ownership change, as Richard Hansen sold both his Montana lodge and his majority share of the shop. The new owner initiated an employee health insurance plan and paid vacations and increased the shop's insurance coverage. These enhancements cost money, but are good signs of the owner's long-term commitment to the business. *Trout Bum 2* is not a highly profitable investment yet, but it is becoming a more mature and stable business where the lifestyle is the major attraction for Kory and his crew.

Source: K. Kapaloski: (personal communication, April, 2000, and May, 2005)

REFERENCES

Andrew, W. (1984, February). Lender's perspective: The key to successful borrowing. *The Cornel Hotel and Restaurant Administration Quarterly*, pp. 37–43.

Brayley, R., & McLean, D. (1999). *Managing financial resources in sport and leisure service organizations*. Champaign, IL: Sagamore Publishing.

Bullaro, J., & Edginton, C. (1986). *Commercial leisure services*. New York: Macmillan Publishing Company.

Caminiti, S. (1991, September 23). Look who likes franchising now. *Fortune*, pp.125–130.

Canada Yearbook 1992. (1991). Ottawa, Canada: Statistics Canada, Ministry of Industry, Science and Technology.

Fails, B. (1985, January). *The feasibility study process*. Presentation at the annual conference of the Resort and Commercial Recreation Association, Phoenix, AZ.

Gunn, E. (1998, March 16). Would you please take my money. *Fortune*. p.165.

Haralson, W. (1986). The economic feasibility study. In A. Epperson (Ed.), *Private and commercial recreation* (pp. 155–198). State College, PA: Venture Publishing, Inc.

Hills, G. (1985, January). Market analysis in the business plan: Venture capitalist's perceptions. *Journal of Small Business Management*, pp. 38–46.

Kelsey, C., & Gray, H. (1985). *The feasibility study process for parks and recreation*. Reston, VA: The American Alliance for Leisure and Recreation.

Mitchell, L. (1999, February 10). SBA program boosts small-business loans. *Salt Lake Tribune*. p. D-6.

Moore, L., & Golden, S. (1989, October 23). The 1990 guide to small business. *U.S. News & World Report*, pp. 72–77.

Tiffany, L. (1999, May). Plastic players. *Business Start-Ups*, pp. 6.

Wolff, R. (1986). Effective marketing. In A. Epperson (Ed.), *Private and commercial recreation* (pp. 199–263). State College, PA: Venture Publishing, Inc.

Yesawich, P. (1984, November). A market-based approach to forecasting. *The Cornell Hotel and Restaurant Administration Quarterly*, pp. 47–53.

Chapter•••• 5

Financial Management

Once a new commercial recreation and tourism enterprise has been started, it must be managed *efficiently* and *effectively*. The two terms should not be confused or used interchangeably, because a business can easily fail if it is managed efficiently but not effectively. By the same token, it can also fail if managed effectively but not efficiently.

Effective management is management to create an effect. In other words, all that is done is done to achieve a goal. If, for example, the goal of a resort recreation department is to have 90% of the guests participating in its programs, this could be achieved by eliminating participation fees and providing free on-call transportation and meals to the participants. These incentives would contribute significantly to the desired effect of 90% participation, but they may reduce the overall profits of the resort. Efficient management, on the other hand, implies that all actions be taken with an economy of resources for optimal results. The resort recreation department in the preceding example might more efficiently achieve 90% participation by a well-designed and executed promotional campaign and a reasonable fee schedule.

Naturally, the manager should strive for a realistic and workable combination of efficiency and effectiveness. This chapter is concerned with the efficient and effective management of the financial aspects of the commercial recreation and tourism business. This discussion of financial management includes a review of financial records, financial planning, maximizing profits, and other financial issues. Other aspects of management (including marketing, facility and personnel management, and programming) will be covered in Chapters 6, 7, and 8.

FINANCIAL OBJECTIVES

The first step to successful financial management is to determine and articulate clear objectives. Objectives serve as reference points to help the manager determine whether the company is on course toward financial success. By definition, objectives must be measurable and achievable within a specific period of time. The objectives that are most important to the commercial recreation and tourism enterprise are those that deal with *liquidity* and *profitability*. All secondary objectives should ultimately relate to the primary objectives of liquidity and profitability.

Liquidity

Liquidity is the ability that the enterprise has to generate enough cash to pay the bills. This can be measured each month by comparing the total revenues with the total expenses. For a retail operation, any returned merchandise and the cost of all goods sold must be subtracted from the revenues. Expenses comprise all current operating expenses (labor, utilities, advertising, depreciation, property taxes, etc.) including debt service (mortgage and loan payments). A company is considered to be liquid if it can pay all of its currently due invoices with its currently accessible cash resources. Figure 5-1 shows the basic determination of liquidity.

Figure 5-1
Liquidity Determination Example
(For a Retail Store for 1 Month)

Sales of merchandise	$22,500
Less: returned merchandise	-$300
Net sales	$22,200
Less: cost of goods sold	-$10,200
margin on sales	$12,000
Less: operating expenses	-$5,500
Less: debt service	-$2,500
Profit before income taxes	$4,000

Obviously, the objective is to have more revenue than expenses, but this can be very difficult for a new company or an existing company in a new location. This is why it is necessary to have an adequate cash reserve when starting the business. That cash reserve is to cover expenses during the initial months when the business is not otherwise liquid. The topic of liquidity will be discussed further in the section concerning cash flow.

Profitability

Short-term liquidity is just the first part of a company's financial objective. Ultimately, the commercial recreation and tourism enterprise must achieve long-term profitability. Without profit, there would be no capital to expand the business or to provide a cushion in times of financial emergency or market demand fluctuation. Most importantly, if there are no profits, there would be no one interested in investing in the business.

How much profit is considered to be sufficient? The answer to that question really depends on the amount of risk involved in the profit-generating activity. The greater the risk, the more profit will be expected. At the very least, a new business must return several percent more than is available through relatively secure investments, such as U.S. Treasury bills or money market funds. On the other hand, a venture that involves significant risk or that has a short life cycle may be expected to earn an annual profit that has as much as a 30–50% return on investment.

In the case of nonprofit recreation organizations, profit may not be an objective. Usually, it is sufficient that a nonprofit enterprise breaks even. It is wise, however, for nonprofit organizations to strive for some excess revenue (profit) to use as seed funds to start future projects or to hold in reserve as a cushion for financial exigencies.

Other Financial and Operational Objectives

Depending upon the organization, there may be other objectives that ultimately relate to liquidity and profitability. Some of these objectives include the following:

- **Market share**—the percentage of the overall market for a particular product or service that the business hopes to gain.
- **Occupancy rate, use rate, or load factor**—the percentage of available rooms, court times, or airline seats filled by paying customers.
- **Labor factor, food factor, or fuel factor**—the percentage of total costs attributable to specific items such as labor, food, fuel, and the like. Some businesses consider these costs to be somewhat controllable and set targets below which they strive to hold expenses.

FINANCIAL RECORDS

One of the most important aspects of financial management is the keeping of accurate records. Without accurate financial records, many management decisions would have to be made in a barrage of misinformation. Additionally, many legal requirements for operating a business would not be met if appropriate records are not maintained. For most people, financial record keeping is not a very exciting aspect of management, and many managers prefer to spend their time on other tasks. Nevertheless, the commercial recreation and tourism manager must understand why financial record keeping is important, know what records to keep, and understand the accounting process.

Reasons to Keep Financial Records

The general reasons for keeping financial records (as well as other types of records) can be categorized into three areas: (1) to meet legal requirements, (2) to safeguard assets, and (3) to help plan and control operations. These reasons are not mutually exclusive. For example, keeping records for tax purposes is a legal requirement, but it is also important in planning and controlling the business. Specific reasons for keeping records are

- to meet requirements for government reports, tax returns, and licenses;
- to determine the current status of the business;
- to measure profitability and performance;
- to provide data upon which to base forecasts of future performance;
- to provide evidence in lawsuits;
- to provide information to present to creditors when seeking a loan;
- to inform potential investors or buyers about the company;
- to inform partners, stockholders, board members, or governing authorities;
- to evaluate the results of responsibilities that have been delegated to others and monitor employee performance; and
- to monitor facilities and equipment for preventive maintenance.

Records to Keep

A commercial recreation or tourism business should keep records relating to a variety of financial and operational functions. As illustrated in Figure 5-2, records to be kept include the following:

Figure 5-2
Business Records to Keep and Manage

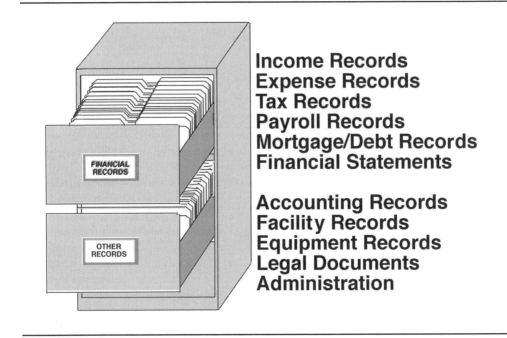

Income Records
Expense Records
Tax Records
Payroll Records
Mortgage/Debt Records
Financial Statements

Accounting Records
Facility Records
Equipment Records
Legal Documents
Administration

Income records—documentation from all original transactions whereby revenue comes to the business. Examples include sales slips, cash register tapes, or ticket stubs.

Expense records—evidence of all current and periodic expenses whether paid by cash or check. Documents include invoices, bills, cancelled checks, and receipts.

Tax records—documentation of the liability for and payment of income taxes, sales taxes, and property taxes, as well as records of withholding employee income taxes, social security payments, unemployment insurance, and workers' compensation.

Payroll records—including employee timecards and payroll ledgers; commission records (if applicable); and annual leave, sick leave, and compensatory time records.

Mortgage and debt records—including payment certification and records of balance for mortgages, bonds, or other loans.

Regular financial statements—including monthly, quarterly and annual profit and loss statements, balance sheets, and cash flow statements.

Other accounting records—including accounts receivable ledgers, bank deposits, bank statements, and asset depreciation records.

Personnel records—including employee contracts, accident reports, injury claims, critical incident reports, and evaluations.

Facility and equipment records—including inventory records, lease contracts, and preventive maintenance records.

Legal records—including trademarks, patents and copyrights, contracts, and any legal claims or suits.

Other administrative records—including audits, annual reports, board minutes, executive correspondence, and bid documents.

The Accounting Process

The system of financial record keeping is called an accounting system, and its purpose is to allow the commercial recreation and tourism manager to find and easily understand information about the history of transactions and about the current financial condition of the business (Brayley & McLean, 1999). The process of accounting involves organizing and summarizing a multitude of business data into a form that is usable to a manager. If a commercial recreation and tourism manager asks to look at this year's revenues, it does not do much good to bring a shoebox full of cash register tapes. If the information from those tapes can be organized, summarized, and reported as monthly totals, then the revenue effort can be evaluated. Therein lies the value of accounting. However, accounting alone is not enough; what is needed is timely accounting. A wise manager does not wait long periods before organizing the relevant business data. Instead, the accounting process is considered as a constant and ongoing process, just as is the process of making decisions for the good of the enterprise. Figure 5-3 illustrates this process.

Figure 5-3
The Accounting Process

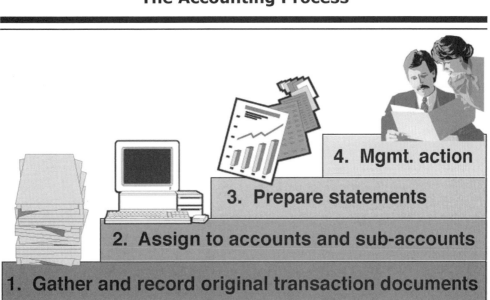

Large commercial recreation and tourism firms often have in-house account management offices with people who are trained in the principles and practices of accounting. Some companies hire an independent accounting firm to manage their records, and in many smaller enterprises, the task of accounting is just one part of the manager's job. Even though there is a variety of accounting software packages available to help manage financial data and present them in standard reporting formats, the first step of the accounting process is an elementary and somewhat unchanging task. The first step of the accounting process is the daily entry into the record of information from original transaction documents.

Original transaction documents (sometimes called documents of original entry) include such items as sales slips, ticket stubs, cash register tapes, check stubs, invoices, and the like. The second step in the accounting process is to record all receipts and expenditures to accounts and sub-accounts. Each account and sub-account provides a running balance for that allocation. The third step in accounting is the preparation of appropriate financial statements and reports. Primary financial statements include the income statement (also called the profit and loss statement or operating statement), the cash flow statement, the balance sheet, and the budget statement. The final step in the accounting process is management response. Accounting does not exist for its own sake. Accounting exists for the benefit of the manager by providing information that is needed for sound business decision making.

Financial Statements

Financial statements are the documents or reports that bring together all the data in the accounting process. Typically, financial statements are developed annually, quarterly, and monthly in order to describe the financial condition of the organization.

The **income statement** summarizes the financial activity of the organization over a specific period of time (usually a month, a quarter, or a year). An example of an income statement is shown in Figure 5-4. It shows all the revenue sources and total revenue received, as well as all the operating expenses, total expenses, pretax income, taxes (or tax reserve), and net income during a specified 6 month period. The income statement allows the commercial recreation manager to monitor the firm's performance and compare that performance with corporate objectives and with performance in previous months.

Figure 5-4
Example Income Statement

Mid-West Sports Center
Income Statement (Jan. 1–June 30)

		Amount
Revenue		
	Pro shop profits	15,500
	Memberships	100,500
	Court fees	20,200
	Class fees	24,800
	Vending concession	2,500
	Total revenues	$163,500
Operating expenses		
	Salaries, wages, and benefits	80,300
	Utilities	12,200
	Advertising	8,500
	Insurance	6,400
	Rent	18,000
	Equipment and supplies	1,200
	Depreciation	4,000
	Debt service	3,600
	Miscellaneous	800
	Total operating expenses	$135,000
Pre tax income		28,500
	Less tax reserve	-6,400
Net income		$22,100

The *cash flow statement* is an important planning and control tool for the commercial recreation and tourism manager. It shows the difference between revenues and expenses for the monthly (or quarterly) period. The positive or negative cash flow is also shown cumulatively through the statement. This in turn allows the manager to know if it is necessary to borrow additional cash to remain operationally solvent or whether to invest excess cash. All of the data used for the cash flow statement come directly from the income statement, with one exception. Depreciation is not considered a cash expenditure on the cash flow statement. Figure 5-5 shows a monthly cash flow statement in which a $10,000 cash balance was available at the beginning of the 6-month period. This cushion allows the company to remain liquid through the first several months when the operation actually lost money.

Figure 5-5
Example Cash Flow Statement

Mid-West Sports Center
6-Month Cash Flow Statement

	Jul.	Aug.	Sep.	Oct.	Nov.	Dec.	Total
Net revenues	13,000	18,100	27,200	32,800	35,500	36,900	163,500
Expenses	18,800	18,600	21,200	23,000	24,200	25,200	131,000
Monthly cash flow	(5,800)	(500)	6,000	9,800	11,300	11,700	
Cumulative cash flow	(5,800)	(6,300)	(300)	9,500	20,800	32,500	
Cash at beginning of month	10,000	4,200	3,700	9,700	19,500	30,800	
Cash position at end of month	4,200	3,700	9,700	19,500	30,800	42,500	

cushion money

The *balance sheet* shows the financial condition of the organization at a specific point in time, usually the end of the month, quarter, or year. This information also helps the manager to monitor the firm's progress by allowing comparisons with statistics at other milestone dates or by facilitating comparisons with targets established in the goal and objective setting process. Several important numbers from the balance sheet (as well as the income statement) can be compared to industry norms to see how the company is operating relative to others in the commercial recreation industry. Figure 5-6 shows a balance sheet for a sports club that does not own its building or land. Notice how the bottom line figure on the right side of the sheet is equal to, or "balances," that shown on the left side. The balance sheet always presents the total value of assets as being equal to the total value of liabilities plus owner's equity or net worth. The balance is achieved by adjusting the total net worth to reflect the remaining value "owed" to the owner(s) of the enterprise. Hence, total net worth (or equity) is shown as a liability, not an asset.

Figure 5-6
Example Balance Sheet

Mid-West Sports Center
Balance Sheet (December 31, 2005)

Assets		Liabilities and net worth	
Cash	16,300	Accounts payable	$13,100
Merchandise inventory	7,000	Taxes payable	400
Accounts receivable	17,500	Total current liabilities	$13,500
Total current assets	$40,800		
		Bank loan balance	28,000
Pro shop fixtures	1,000	Total long-term	
Fitness equipment	45,000	liabilities	$28,000
Office equipment	4,000	Total liabilities	$41,500
Total fixed assets	$50,000		
Less accumulated			
depreciation	-8,000	Total net worth	$41,300
		↳ Total Assets −	
		Total liabilities	
Net fixed assets	42,000		
Total assets	**$82,800**	Total liabilities + net worth	**$82,800**

Some of the terms used on the balance sheet are defined as follows:

- **Current assets**—cash and those assets that can be turned into cash in the near future.
- **Accounts receivable**—amounts not yet collected from customers that are currently due.
- **Fixed assets**—the assets not intended for sale that are used to create, display, or transport the product or service. This includes land, buildings, machinery, and equipment.
- **Depreciation**—an accounting method used to expense the decline in useful value of a fixed asset due to normal wear, tear, and obsolescence.
- **Accounts payable**—the amount the company owes to its suppliers and service providers from whom it has bought goods or services on credit and to employees for salaries.
- **Current liabilities**—debts for regular business operations that will come due in the near future, usually the coming month.
- **Long-term liabilities**—debts that are due after 1 year from the date of the financial report, typically mortgages, bonds, and other major loans.
- **Net worth (or owner's equity)**—the portion of the business that is owned free and clear of all debts (Merrill Lynch, 1984).

The *budget statement* is a useful tool that allows the commercial recreation manager to review the financial activity of the enterprise with respect to the planned program of income and expenditure (i.e., the budget). It shows how much of a budgeted amount has been spent or received at a given point in the fiscal term. The budget statement (see

Figure 5-7) shows only how much *has* been spent or received, not how much *should have been* spent or received at that time. Seasonal fluctuations in demand and other conditions that affect the even distribution of income and expenditure should be considered when making judgments based on the budget statement (Brayley & McLean, 1999).

Figure 5-7
Example Budget Statement

Sandy Point Resort
Recreation Services Department

Budget Statement
June 30, 2006 (50% of budget period)

	Budget	Actual	Committed	%	Balance
REVENUE					
Guest service assessment	120,000	60,000	0	50.0	60,000
Bike rentals	18,000	5,920	0	32.9	12,080
Supply fees	2,000	831	0	41.6	1,169
Total revenue	140,000	66,751	0	47.7	73,249
EXPENSES					
Personnel	108,000	42,000	2,000	40.7	64,000
Equipment maintenance	9,000	6,850	0	76.1	2,150
Program supplies	1,500	988	0	65.9	512
Transportation	4,500	2,123	1,200	73.8	1,177
Promotion	2,000	1,112	400	75.6	488
Administration	12,000	5,857	0	48.8	6,143
Contingency/enterprise	3,000	800	500	43.3	1,700
Total expenses	140,000	59,730	4,100	45.6	76,170

Issues in Accounting

Unless an entrepreneur is particularly well versed in accounting practices and current tax laws, there are some issues relative to business accounting that should be discussed with a qualified financial and accounting adviser. Good decisions in these areas could improve the company's operation and profitability. For example, a good accounting advisor could explain:

- The tax advantages of different methods of business organization, accounting, depreciation, inventory evaluation, borrowing, and so forth.
- The advantages of early payment of bills if substantial discounts are involved. (The advisor will also explain that, in periods of high inflation, it may not be cost effective to pay bills early even if there is a small discount).
- Which accounting system will meet the data processing requirements of the company as it grows or expands its technological capabilities.

FINANCIAL PLANNING

One of the main purposes of financial records is to provide the commercial recreation and tourism manager with information that can be used in planning and decision making. Due to the seasonal, intermittent, and competitive nature of recreation and tourism, financial planning is essential. The manager must know the current status of the business and have a plan to take the business in a direction that will make achievement of financial goals possible and probable. Some of the tools that are used in financial planning are *break-even analysis, financial comparative analysis, cash flow management, tax planning,* and *budgeting.*

Break-Even Analysis

Break-even analysis is a management control device that helps determine how much of a product or service must be sold at a given price in order to exactly cover costs. Profit is realized with the sale of each unit after the break-even point. To calculate the break-even point, fixed costs must first be separated from the variable costs.

Fixed costs are those expenses that, regardless of how many customers purchase the product or service, must be paid in full. Depending upon the type of business operation, fixed costs typically include management salaries, property taxes, operating licenses and permits, office equipment, basic telephone, regular maintenance, some utilities, insurance, rent or mortgage, legal fees, accounting fees, advertising, vehicles, and major equipment.

Variable costs are those expenses that increase or decrease depending upon how many customers use the product or service. Typically, a ratio can be established between the number of customers and the item of expense. For example, a river rafting company may order food on a basis of $5.00 per person per trip. Therefore, a group of ten customers would cost $50 per trip for food, five customers would cost $25, and so on. The total cost for food for each half-day trip varies according to the number of customers. Management tries to control variable expenses by scheduling or committing only enough resources to meet the needs of the customers. Depending upon the type of business, variable expenses may include seasonal and part-time labor, additional maintenance, additional utilities, food, and program supplies.

Figure 5-8 illustrates the break-even point for a river rafting company offering half-day float trips on a western river. The company's fixed costs are $2,500 per week during its operating season. Its total variable cost is $75 per boat per trip. Depending upon demand, the company can schedule more staff, order more food, and so on.

Notice that the line representing fixed costs is horizontal. This illustrates the fact that fixed costs are relatively constant over a wide range of activity. The line representing total costs begins at the level of fixed costs (there are only fixed costs but no variable costs when there are no customers) and is plotted on a slope to illustrate the variable cost ratio of $75 per boat per trip. The difference between total cost and fixed cost for a given level of activity is the variable cost. The line representing revenue is plotted from the zero point (zero customers means zero revenue) and rises to reflect the $200 per boat (four customers @ $50 each)s that the company charges. The point at which the revenue line and the total cost line intersect is called the break-even point at this price. It appears that 20 boats at $200 per boat per week will result in no losses but also no profits for the company. Obviously, the purpose for calculating the break-even point is to know what level of activity must be exceeded in order for the enterprise to be profitable.

A more precise determination of the break-even point can be made using the "contribution method" formula. The "contribution" refers to the difference between the revenue received from each customer and variable cost associated with serving that customer. This difference is an amount that can be "contributed" toward offsetting the fixed costs. The contribution method formula is

Figure 5-8
Break-Even Analysis

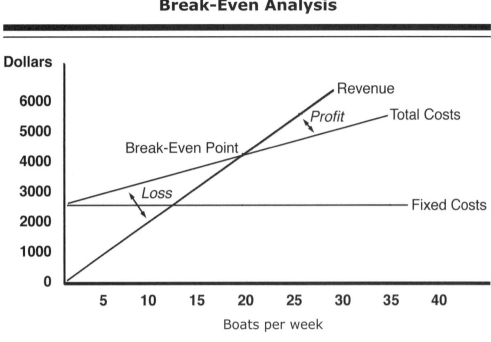

BE point = total fixed costs / (revenue per unit - variable costs per unit)

Thus, for the preceding example,

BE point = $2,500 / ($200 - $75) = $2,500 / $125 = 20 boats per week.

Using Financial Indicators to Analyze the Business

In the broadest sense, the primary financial indicator that one needs to use in evaluating the commercial recreation or tourism business is the *return on investment*. This is the profit (return) divided by the owner's investment (owner's equity). The actual return should be calculated and then compared with the target established by the owner(s). If the target is reached or exceeded, then the management of the enterprise has been effective. But has it also been efficient? To determine efficiency, there are several financial comparative analyses that can be conducted. They include *ratio analysis, year-to-date (YTD) comparisons, 12-month trend analysis,* and a number of other industry performance indicators.

Ratio Analysis is one of the best ways to measure the relative efficiency of the business. Meaningful ratios can be created from a variety of data included in both the income statement and the balance sheet. These ratios can be compared with similar ratios from past months or years or with industry averages. Financial ratios for a large number of industries can be found in Standard and Poor's *Industry Surveys*, Dun and Bradstreet's *Industry Norms and Key Business Ratios, RMA Annual Statement Studies,* and other sources. In Canada, ratios can be found in the Financial Survey of Canadian Business Performance.

Financial ratios can be classified as liquidity ratios, activity ratios, profitability ratios, or debt/coverage/leverage ratios (Brayley & McLean, 1999). Liquidity ratios (also called solvency ratios) indicate the ability of a business to meet its short-term obligations.

Activity ratios (also called efficiency ratios) are quantitative indicators of the ability of the business to expediently and efficiently exchange its products for financial resources. Profitability ratios show how successful the business has been during a certain period of time (usually a year) in terms of investment returns. Debt/coverage/leverage ratios measure the long-term solvency of the business. Examples of the commonly used ratios are as follows:

Liquidity Ratios

Quick ratio—Used to estimate the ability of a business to meet its short-term financial obligations without selling off its inventory.

Quick = (current assets - inventories)/current liabilities

Current ratio—Used to estimate the ability of a business to meet its short-term financial obligations (assuming ability to dispose of inventory at full value). Sometimes called the banker's ratio. A liquid company has a current ratio greater than 1.0.

Current = current assets/current liabilities

Debt-to-net worth—Used to compare the total financial obligations of the business to the investment of its owners. This is used by lenders as a measure of risk involved in extending credit to the business.

Debt to net worth = current and long-term liabilities/net worth

Activity Ratios

Average collection period—This is not a true ratio but is often included in the ratio analysis. It shows the average time (in days) to receive payment for products delivered.

Average collection period = (accounts receivables/sales) × 365 days

Sales-to-inventory ratio—Used to indicate the inventory turnover rate. Low numbers may indicate an overstock situation, or low sales.

Sales to inventory = cost of goods sold/average inventory value

Assets-to-sales ratio—This ratio is used in determinations of how well the assets are being utilized to generate sales.

Assets to sales = total assets/total sales

Profitability Ratios

Return-on-sales—This ratio is used only when comparing with similar businesses or with performance over a period of time. It indicates ability to generate profits from sales.

Return on Sales = net income/net sales

Return-on-assets—Sometimes called the productive ratio, this index is useful for comparisons with other enterprises and with gauging the effectiveness of asset utilization.

Return on assets = net profit after taxes/total assets

Return-on-equity—This ratio measures the ultimate profitability of the enterprise from the perspective of stockholders/owners. It indicates ability to earn adequate profits and should be greater than safe investment rates.

Return on net worth = net profits after taxes/owner's equity

Debt/Coverage/Leverage Ratios

Equity ratio—This ratio indicates the extent of the owner's investment in the enterprise.

Equity = owner's equity/total assets

Debt-to-total asset ratio—This ratio indicates the extent of the enterprise's borrowing.

Debt to total asset = total liabilities / total assets

An Example of Ratio Analysis. Figure 5-9 illustrates how financial ratios can vary between different classes of leisure industries. Three figures are shown for each ratio for each industry. These figures represent the ratio of a business at the upper quartile, the median, and the lower quartile of performance in that industry.

Figure 5-9
Example of Leisure Industry Ratios (2003)

Ratio	Fitness centers	Amuse. parks	Hotel/ motels	Eating places	Travel agencies	RV dealers
Current	1.7	1.1	1.8	1.7	2.5	1.7
(times)	1.2	0.7	0.9	0.9	1.3	1.3
	0.7	0.3	0.5	0.5	0.9	1.1
Sales to inventory	196.3	43.2	158.7	137.6	999.9	4.5
(times)	98.7	39.0	81.9	91.5	999.9	3.4
	76.8	33.5	42.6	45.7	696.3	2.7
Return on Equity	28.8	93.0	119.6	43.9	41.5	34.2
(%)	12.8	23.0	4.7	13.7	4.4	13.0
	6.3	6.2	(3.0)	(0.1)	(10.6)	4.9

Source: Dun's Analytical Services, 2004

Looking at the reported quick ratios, it can be seen that the typical (median) business in three of the industry classifications presented is able to cover its current liabilities from its current assets (1.0 or higher). The amusement park industry is the laggard, but its median return on equity is still a very good 23%. For RV dealers, the median inventory turnover rate of 3.4 (sales-to-inventory ratio) is much lower than it is for the other industries presented, but the return on investment is still a very respectable 13%. The "problem" of a low inventory turnover rate is less critical when the price and profit margin of each RV unit sold is quite high.

These ratios are most valuable in comparing the financial performance of a particular business with the figures for other businesses in the same industry. A certain amount of judgment and caution needs to be exercised in making such comparisons, as local conditions may be very atypical, or the industry classification may not be specific enough to account for the special operating conditions of the unique enterprise. For example, large sports and fitness clubs and small aerobics studios are both classified as fitness centers and averaged into one industrial classification (U.S. Census Bureau, 1998), but they operate very differently and serve different markets.

Year-to-Date Comparisons. A less complicated but similarly useful analysis of business performance can be made by comparing actual totals in budget categories with anticipated totals or with totals recorded at the same point in time in previous years. If, for example, expenses are far above the expense total for the previous YTD, then the manager can be alerted to the potential problem and examine the circumstances that have contributed to the situation. If necessary, appropriate remedial action can then be initiated.

12-Month Trend Analysis. As noted earlier, the demand for most commercial recreation and tourism businesses is highly seasonal. Fluctuations in demand are manifested in income and expenditure patterns that, if plotted on a trend chart, would render the chart difficult, if not impossible, to interpret. Figure 5-10 shows the actual monthly utility

Figure 5-10
Area Chart and 12-Month Trend Line Example

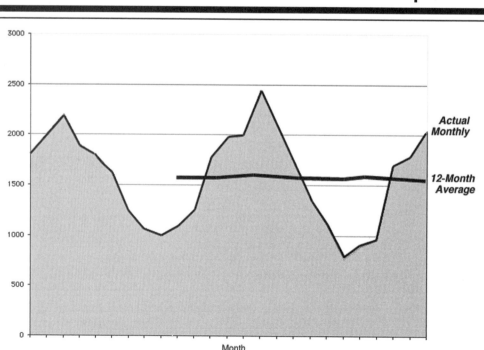

costs of a recreation enterprise represented on an area chart. Note that representation of the seasonal demands for the utility generates peaks and dips in the chart. Note also how difficult it is to use that part of the chart to determine if utility costs are going up, down, or remaining stable. In contrast, the 12-month average trend is much more instructive.

Each point on the 12-month average trend line is calculated by dividing the sum of the previous 12 months' utility costs by 12. This process minimizes the distraction created by the variability in seasonal spending, but it does somewhat mask small but significant changes until they are firmly entrenched.

Other Industry Performance Standards. Depending upon the type of recreation or tourism enterprise being evaluated, there may be established performance indicators or standards that the manager can use in determining how efficiently the business is operating. For example, national or regional occupancy rates are important standards for comparison in the resort or lodging industry. Standards or published reports of membership retention rates are of value to commercial recreation enterprises that rely on a membership base, and conversion rates are the index against which a sports marketing company will determine the relative success of a particular promotional campaign.

Cash Flow Management

Most commercial recreation and tourism businesses have periods during their peak season when revenues generate more cash than is needed to meet expenses. Conversely, during off-seasons, expenses usually demand much more cash than revenues can generate. The primary objective of cash flow management is to smooth out these uneven combinations of revenue and expenses. Businesses are putting increased emphasis on cash flow as a measure of financial health, because cash is an immediate indicator of liquidity.

There are two primary strategies used in the management of cash flow. The first is to emphasize transactions that increase or accelerate cash inflow, and the second is to

Cash flow analysis can help companies determine how much money they need to get through the off-season. (Photo: J. Crossley)

engage in transactions that economize or delay cash payments. Specific strategies applied to cash flow management include

- tightening customer credit by requiring cash payment or major credit cards,
- accelerating billing of credit sales and requiring prompt payment,
- selling of aging account receivables to collection agencies,
- depositing revenue the same day that money is received,
- delaying payment of bills until the last possible date that they are due,
- paying bills within the discount period only if the invoices offer attractive discounts,
- minimizing inventory buildup, and
- reducing investments in idle assets by selling them or leasing them.

Note that each of these strategies, if carried too far, can backfire. For example, restricting customer credit too much can result in lost sales, or minimizing inventory could lead to an unexpected shortage. The key to successful cash flow management is to find an optimal balance in the application of these strategies. In periods when there is excess cash, the common strategy is to invest idle funds. This requires the manager to make accurate projections of expenditures in order to know how much cash is available to invest. The manager must also be familiar with short-term money markets such as bank savings, certificates of deposit, and treasury bills. It is important to consider risk versus yield, and high-risk speculative investments are not recommended as part of cash flow management.

In periods when cash flow is short, the common strategy is to operate off the reserve fund generated in better times or, if that is nonexistent, to take out a short-term loan. The commercial recreation and tourism manager needs to keep good relations with a bank or other financial institution in order to have loans available on short notice. Of course, another major strategy is to cut back on operational expenses, particularly in the off-season. In these circumstances, the flexibility of a part-time or seasonal labor force is advantageous. Some commercial recreation and tourism businesses even close down completely in the off-season.

Tax Planning

In the early 1980s when tax rates were high, some business decisions were made primarily to realize a tax advantage. For example, if a company knew that it was going to finish the year with a $100,000 profit, it might spend the money for new vehicles rather than pay tax on the profits. In this way, the expenditure might yield a $10,000 investment tax credit, and, in later years, the accelerated depreciation of these assets would yield further tax reductions.

Since the mid 1980s, top corporate tax rates have dropped significantly, investment tax credits have been repealed, and there are longer periods required for many asset depreciation write-offs. As a result of these tax law changes, most business decisions today tend to be made on the basis of the merits of the case, not because of potential tax angles. The commercial recreation and tourism manager should, of course, be sure to take whatever legitimate tax deductions are available, but business success must be built on quality products, customer service, and careful management. Further, when trying to raise money through limited partnerships, the enterprise must show its potential for earning income, because limited partnerships are no longer tax shelters for losses and huge tax write-offs. A manager must be alert to every presidential and congressional election, because tax policies could change again. For example, if investment tax credits were allowed again, or if capital gains taxes were lowered, this could stimulate a new round of business expenditures for facilities, equipment, and expansion.

Another important tax issue is the trend toward "taxation without representation" in the travel industry (Baker, 1992). State and local governments, with voters weary of additional taxes, are seeking new revenue sources. Unfortunately, out-of-town travelers have become the non-voting target of some tremendous tax hikes. At some Florida airports, for example, an auto rental customer can pay as much as an extra 43% due to surcharges and taxes. Many American cities impose a hefty (sometimes nearly 20%) hotel tax (alternatively called a "bed tax" or "transient occupancy tax") on top of the state sales tax. Other cities have adopted or are considering similar taxes.

The implications of taxation directed at the traditional commercial recreation and tourism markets are of major significance to the industry. It is reasonable to expect that overtaxed, frustrated travelers will decide to go to a different destination. If tourist volume slows, the effects on all businesses, not just the hotels and rental car companies, could be devastating. Commercial recreation and tourism managers need to monitor their state and local governments and exercise their democratic right and voice in ensuring that tax laws support the development and protection of the industry.

Budgeting

A budget is simply a plan of action with price tags attached. It shows everything that is expected to occur in the coming year, with the associated revenues and costs. In this way, it is a very important financial planning tool. When the budget is established, it is a mechanism used to monitor and control expenditures.

The budget process begins with establishing goals and objectives for all units of the organization. Next, it is determined what programs, projects, and tasks will accomplish those objectives. Revenues are then estimated based upon the projected demand for the products or services. Finally, costs are calculated for the labor, equipment, supplies, and services that are necessary to accomplish the programs, projects, and tasks.

The commercial recreation and tourism manager needs to guard against the following problems that can occur in budgeting:

- **Over-budgeting**—too-complex and overly detailed budgets can stymie the flexibility needed to operate the enterprise.
- **Budgeting based only on precedent**—budgets should reflect current market conditions, not ancient history.
- **Overestimating revenue by overestimating demand**—managers should be cautiously conservative and keep an eye on competitors.
- **Underestimating expenses**—some managers underestimate inflation or fail to establish and maintain a reserve fund to cover unexpected costs.
- **Regarding budgets as a straitjacket**—budgets are a tool, not an end in themselves; during the year when conditions change, budgets can be changed, too.

HOW TO INCREASE PROFITS

Every entrepreneur or manager of a commercial recreation or tourism business wants to increase its profits. The income statement (profit and loss statement) identifies the area of activity that contributes to increased or declining profits. It becomes clear that profits will increase when sales revenue increases, costs of goods or services sold decrease, and operating expenses decrease. This section will consider each opportunity identified in the income statement and suggest a number of strategies for increasing profits.

Price Increases will improve the margin on sales, provided that the cost of goods remains constant. The increase, however, could be offset by a decrease in sales volume.

Increased Sales Volume can lead to increased profits under several circumstances. First, if the margin on sales and expenses can be held constant, increased sales will always yield greater profits. Second, even if the margin is reduced a little (through discount prices), a large increase in volume can more than compensate. Lastly, increased volume could result in "economies of scale." This means that the expenses to sell a large volume are proportionally lower due to more efficient use of available facilities and labor.

So how is sales volume increased? One place to start is to improve the product or service so it better meets the needs of the customer. Another approach is through more effective marketing to bring in more customers and/or by reducing the price. Finally, increased demand might be realized due to demographic changes, the loss of competitors, or changes in public interest.

Improved Purchasing can result in significant savings that, in turn, yield greater profits. Unfortunately, some commercial recreation and tourism managers overlook the many ways in which purchasing may be improved. First, and most important, is to make smart purchases. In a retail situation, this means to purchase the types of products that customers want and in a quantity that will not be left unsold, occupying valuable sales space. For a tour operator, this means "blocking out," or committing to, just the right number of rooms in a resort that people want to visit. Obviously, smart purchasing requires a good knowledge of the market, its preferences, and its ability to pay.

Volume Purchasing can also save money. One danger, however, is that storage space may cost more than the amount that is saved by virtue of the volume purchase. Another risk with some types of products is spoilage. Once an airline seat, tour bus seat, hotel room, or aerobics class space goes unused, its value is lost forever, just as certainly as old food can spoil. One approach to volume purchasing is to form a cooperative purchasing group. Here, several companies, even competitors, pool their purchasing needs in order to get the volume necessary for a price reduction. A bonus advantage is that each company may attain the savings and not risk having unused product.

Consignment. It may be possible to get some products on consignment from the manufacturers. This means that the business is billed only for what it sells, and any unsold products can be returned without penalty. This approach reduces the assumed risk for unsold merchandise. Consignment agreements are often available from small manufacturers who are just starting out with a product line and are eager to find outlets.

Inventory Control can help a company to increase its sales and save money. As much as 25% of potential sales are lost by businesses with inadequate stock, and as much as 15–25% of the cost of goods sold is incurred in storage and static inventory. Obviously, improvements in either area can increase profits significantly. Ideally, stock received would go directly onto the sales floor, thus eliminating the need for extensive storage. Some businesses find it to be less expensive to pay for rush shipping from regional warehouses than to maintain storage facilities. However inventory storage or delivery is handled, the manager must be sensitive to the normal fluctuations in market demand and be sure that the customer can get the product. Computer-linked sales registers, barcode scanning, and other technological advances make inventory control easier than in years gone by, but its importance in a demanding marketplace is in no way diminished.

Yield Management is a combination of pricing strategy and inventory control that is increasingly used in service industries such as hotels, airlines, cruises, tours, and fitness clubs. A computer model, programmed with past market trends, monitors the inventory of reservations and sales for each day. Then pricing schemes are tailored to maximize profits. If for example, hotel reservations in the group discount class exceed 30% of all bookings within 60 days of arrival, then all remaining discount rooms are shifted to a higher rate. This is in anticipation that the remaining rooms will be needed to meet historically expected volume that occurs on shorter notice. The yield management model might also call for the discounting of room inventory for days when expected demand is not materializing. Some hotels claim that yield management programs have added hundreds of thousands of dollars in annual revenues.

Reduced Labor Costs can result in great savings for the commercial recreation and tourism business. In many service organizations, labor represents 80% of the budget. Any savings here would be almost a dollar for dollar improvement in profits. Unfortunately, reducing labor cost is easier said than done, and sometimes labor reductions can come back to haunt in terms of safety or customer satisfaction. If this is the chosen strategy, there are several approaches to reducing labor costs:

- *Use of Part-Time and Seasonal Labor*—Many jobs can be performed by nonprofessional labor hired on a part-time or seasonal basis. It is relatively easy to increase or decrease the hourly schedules of this labor force in order to meet fluctuations of the business.
- *Below Minimum Wage Rates*—It is justifiable to pay below the minimum wage in certain circumstances. Camp counselors, for example, may be given a small weekly salary plus food and lodging. Bellboys, valet parking attendants, tour guides, and waitresses may also receive low wages because of the amount they make in tips.
- *Hire Generalists*—Employees who can do several jobs can be scheduled where they are needed most. This allows a business to be flexible and responsive to the market.
- *Contract Out For Specialists*—If tasks requiring specialists (electricians, accountants, lawyers, draftsmen, etc.) do not absolutely justify full-time, year-round workloads, then do not hire for these positions. Instead, contract out for these specialists, but only when regular staff cannot do the job.
- *"Union Busting"*—Some companies have been restructured under bankruptcy laws and, in the process, avoided costly union contracts. New employees are then hired at more reasonable and competitive pay scales.

Reduced Overhead Costs can greatly reduce overall expenses and thereby contribute to profitability. There are several possible strategies:

- *Lease facilities and equipment*—This could be less expensive than purchasing them, especially if there are high interest payments for a mortgage or other loan.
- *Share certain capital assets and overhead expenses with other businesses*—As mentioned previously, some small businesses share office space, secretarial services, and copy machines with other enterprises in a small business complex or "incubator."
- *Sell off nonproductive assets*—such as land, buildings, or equipment if they do not contribute profits in proportion to their costs.
- *Reduce other overhead costs*—such as utilities, telephones, maintenance, and advertising by aggressively monitoring those costs. Again, this is easier said than done. One executive who spends a million dollars a year on advertising is absolutely positive that half the money is wasted. The problem is, he does not know which half!
- *Add telecommuting options*—Rather than pay for expensive office space in premier locations, set up satellite work centers or facilitate employees working from home.

Financial Controls can help an organization to avoid losing money through employee error or dishonesty. It is sad but true that this type of loss occurs much too often. The most important factor in financial control is to assure that there is a division of duties so that no individual handles a transaction from beginning to end. Gray (1986) suggested 10 steps that will increase financial control:

- Assign someone other than the bookkeeper to receive bank statements and reconcile them.
- The person who records disbursements should not be authorized to sign checks. Two signatures should be required for all checks.
- The person signing checks should review, approve, and cancel invoices or other disbursement documents.
- Disbursements (except for petty cash) should be made by serially numbered checks.
- Someone other than the bookkeeper should open the mail and list incoming checks.
- The person opening mail should endorse all checks "for deposit only" upon receipt.
- Someone other than the bookkeeper should authorize write-offs of non-recoverable accounts receivable.
- Detailed records of fixed assets should be maintained and periodic inventories taken.
- Carry fidelity insurance against loss from embezzlement.
- Monthly financial statements should be prepared in sufficient detail to disclose significant variances from prior months and years.

OTHER FINANCIAL MANAGEMENT ISSUES

Several financial management topics that deserve examination have not previously been covered in this chapter. These topics include auxiliary revenue sources and consumer credit.

Auxiliary Revenue Sources

Most commercial recreation and tourism businesses have a primary line of products or services. It is very possible, however, to have secondary or auxiliary revenue sources that contribute significantly to the overall profit of the business. Often these auxiliary efforts can be conducted with existing personnel or managed contractually. Examples of some common auxiliary sources are provided here.

Core Product Extensions can complement a company's primary business, particularly in the off-season. Examples include

- alpine slides and summer concerts at ski resorts;
- snowmobile sales at a motorcycle dealer;
- tennis, sailing, or bicycle lines at a ski shop;
- autumn hunting guide services and lodging at a summer camp; and
- racquetball and fitness activities at a golf or tennis club.

Recreation Programs can generate additional revenue and, just as importantly, bring in additional clients. Programs can be conducted by virtually any type of business. Examples are

- knitting, painting, or ceramics classes conducted at an arts and crafts shop;
- trips and tours offered at a resort hotel;
- fun runs sponsored by a sporting goods store; and
- climbing clubs sponsored by outdoor specialty shops.

Equipment Rental Programs can be convenient and major revenue producers. Bicycle rentals at Kiawah Island Resort in South Carolina, generated almost half a million dollars in just one year. Other examples include video machine and movie rentals at hotels, sports equipment and game rentals at resorts, and equipment "demo" rentals at sporting goods stores.

Repair Services can be an auxiliary revenue source and are particularly appropriate for certain types of retail stores, including those selling bicycles, boats, cameras, recreational vehicles, and ski equipment.

Food and Beverage Concessions can be made available to clients in several ways. The organization can self-operate the service and gain potentially good revenue. However, this can be a risk and a management headache. Another approach is to contract out the space to a food and beverage concessionaire. This can reduce risk and still yield decent revenue. Finally, a very popular approach is to use vending machines. Again, these can be owned and self-operated or contractually operated by a vendor.

Retail Product Sales, even on a small scale, can be a profitable addition to many service businesses. Almost any business that has a sales register and staff on duty could have retail products for sale. At a small sports club, for example, front desk staff who greet members and make court reservations could also sell rackets, balls, sports clothing, health foods, and fitness videos. Other examples includes

- T-shirts and postcards at a tourist attraction;
- clubs, shoes, and clothing at a golf course; and
- travel guidebooks at a travel agency.

Video Games have become more sophisticated and have maintained their popularity. Renting video games can bring in some extra revenue with very little risk. Most video game companies will provide the machines, rotate them periodically, service them, and provide 30 to 50% of the gross revenue to the host location.

Leased Space can provide revenue for a business that does not want to self-operate a given service. Examples include

- pro shops at sports and racquet clubs,
- small restaurants and retail shops at resorts,
- travel agency desks at large sporting goods stores, and
- souvenir stands at sports arenas.

*A coffee shop is a good source of alternative revenue at
this commercial ceramics studio. (Photo: R. Brayley)*

Consumer Credit

Credit purchases are an important part of many commercial recreation and tourism enterprises. For some types of businesses, such as travel agencies and resort hotels, credit purchases may be the bulk of the sales. There are five types of consumer credit:

- **Open (or charge) account**—Purchases are billed on a regular cycle, usually the first of the month, and the entire amount is due within 10 days of billing.
- **Revolving account**—Customers are allowed a fixed amount of credit and each month pay a minimum percentage of the unpaid balance, plus interest. Consumer credit cards can be included in this classification.
- **Budget account**—Used for somewhat costly items, an account is established for a set number of months, typically three to six. A down payment is made, followed by monthly installments plus interest.
- **Installment account**—Used for high-cost items, a down payment is made, and the balance plus interest is paid monthly over one to five years.
- **Bank Debit Card**—This is an account access card by which the purchase is immediately charged against an existing deposit balance in a bank or money market account.

Advantages of Extending Consumer Credit. There are many advantages of allowing customers to make purchases using one of the five types of credit.

- Credit reduces buying resistance and can lead to increased volume of business.
- Certain types of credit, especially credit cards, make it possible to accept orders by phone, mail, or Internet.
- Charge customers typically buy higher quality merchandise and have less tendency to wait until there are discount sales.
- Allowing credit can help improve customer loyalty.
- Lists of credit customers are good mailing lists for advertising.
- Significant revenue can be earned from the interest charged on the credit purchases of "big ticket" items.
- No actual cash exchanges hands (thus reducing theft potential).

Disadvantages of Extending Consumer Credit. There are also disadvantages of extending credit:

- The receipt of payment is delayed.
- It costs money to investigate the creditworthiness of customers.
- There are risks in extending credit, as some customers do not pay up.
- There is extra paperwork for billing and bookkeeping.
- There are service charges involved with some types of credit. Fees for credit card sales average about 3%.

SUMMARY

A commercial recreation and tourism enterprise must be managed effectively and efficiently. This means that the right things are done to further the objectives of the company and are done with an economy of resources for a maximum of results. The key objectives are liquidity and long-term profitability. Other more specific objectives may include market share, occupancy rate, management overhead percentage, and labor cost ratios.

The business must keep records in order to meet legal requirements, to safeguard assets, and to plan and control operations. Important records to keep include those for income, expenses, taxes, payroll, long-term debts, personnel, facilities and equipment, legal aspects, and regular financial statements.

Accounting is a process in which business data are organized and summarized into a form that is useful to a manager. It is a staged process in which documents of original entry are consolidated, recorded, reported, and then acted upon. The primary financial statements are the income statement, the cash flow statement, and the balance sheet. These financial statements are important aids in managerial decision making.

Various financial planning tools help the manager to know the current status of the business and to plan for its future. Break-even analysis determines how much product or service must be sold in a given period of time to cover fixed and variable costs. Ratio analysis permits comparison of different aspects of the business with past periods and with industry standards. There are numerous ratios for analyzing debt, liquidity, activity, and profitability. Cash flow management helps determine when excess cash may be invested, or when a loan is needed to cover expenses. Although tax rates are lower than in past years, it is still important to take advantage of all strategies to reduce tax liability. Finally, budgeting is simply a plan of action with price tags attached. A well-planned budget will help the organization meet its objectives and control its expenses.

Every commercial recreation and tourism business wants to increase its profits, and there are a variety of ways to do this: increase prices, increase sales volume, reduce purchasing costs, reduce inventory costs, reduce labor costs, reduce overhead costs, improve financial controls, and various combinations of the above. There is, however, the potential for strategies to backfire due to inaccurate assessments of market demand or due to improper management.

Auxiliary revenue sources can supplement a company's business and/or diversify the business in the off-season. Types of auxiliary sources include alternative products or services, recreation programs, equipment rentals, repair services, food and beverage concessions, retail sales, video games, and leased space.

The availability of consumer credit can be the difference in making a sale or not. Although there are advantages and disadvantages to each type of consumer credit (open account, revolving account, budget account, installment account, and bank debit card), most commercial recreation businesses would probably benefit by allowing some type of credit, especially the use of credit cards.

SPOTLIGHT ON:

THE HEART OF A BAD INVESTMENT

Nolan Bushnell was known as the inventor of *Pong*, the first computerized arcade video game. Bushnell then developed a very successful video game company, Atari, and became a millionaire in the process. He next teamed up with Joseph Keenan to start a chain of pizza restaurants that featured dozens of video games and a variety of stage shows performed by computerized robotic animals. The first opened in 1977 and was named "Chuck E. Cheese's Pizza Time Theatre."

Pizza Time Theatre was an innovative concept because of the emphasis on recreation rather than food. They had full-time special event coordinators to develop dozens of program ideas, including overnight slumber parties, sports team video service (filmed at local parks and shown on the screen at the restaurant), and, of course, birthday parties. Adults, teens, and children flocked to Chuck E. Cheese's, and some restaurants would have 20 different parties and events every weekend. They were more than restaurants; they were "fun centers" with food! It seemed like a beautiful marriage of recreation programming and restaurant business. It also seemed, on the surface, to be a great idea with tremendous financial opportunity for investors.

In April 1981, Pizza Time Theatre completed a public stock offering at about $20 per share. One investor, named here as "Sammy" (to protect the identity of the individual), was able to visit a few of the restaurants and was captivated by the concept. In 1982, Sammy rushed to a stockbroker to buy a bundle of Pizza Time shares, confident that they would yield great profits in coming years. What Sammy did NOT do was read the company's financial statements very carefully. This was an investment made by Sammy's heart rather than by Sammy's head.

Chuck E. Cheese's Pizza Time Theatre had grown from 25 "centers" in 1980 to 88 in 1981 and then to 204 centers in 1982 (and later to over 300 centers). Expansion was rampant, and some cities had numerous Pizza Time centers. However, a careful analysis of the financial statements would have revealed a number of the key financial ratios were in dangerous territory. The 1982 Annual Report for Pizza Time Theatre showed that key figures such as total liabilities to net worth, return on assets, and return on net worth were at levels below the industry average. Sales revenue compared to total assets was very low, and, most troubling, the company was extremely "cash poor" compared to other restaurant chains.

Unfortunately, the novelty of Pizza Time Theatre soon wore off, and adults tired of the mediocre-tasting pizza. The tremendous cost of overexpansion caught up to the cash-poor company, and debts piled up. In 1984, Chuck E. Cheese's went into bankruptcy. Now Sammy wished he had read and analyzed the financial statement in the stock prospectus, but it was too late. The stock was worthless, and Sammy lost every cent of his investment.

In later years, Chuck E. Cheese's would be reborn and merge with Showbiz Pizza Place, Inc., improve the quality of their food, and follow a more conservative growth strategy. They also decided to focus less on teenagers and more on young children. With these changes came a moderate level of success.

Meanwhile, Sammy learned the importance of reading and analyzing financial statements!

Sources: Pizza Time Theatre, 1983; Labate, 1993.   *(continued)*

REFERENCES

Baker, L. (1992, January 6). Taxation without representation. *Travel Weekly*, p. 32.

Brayley, R., & McLean, D. (1999). *Managing financial resources in sport and leisure service organizations*. Champaign, IL: Sagamore Publishing.

Dun's Analytical Services. (2004). *Industry norms and key business ratios*. Murray Hills, NJ: Dun & Bradstreet Information Services.

Gray, R. (1986). How to prevent fraud in a small association. In Bullaro & Edginton (Eds), *Commercial Leisure Services*. New York: MacMillan Publishing Company.

Labate, J. (1993, May 17). Showbiz pizza time. *Fortune*, p. 102.

Merrill Lynch. (1984). *How to read a financial report*. New York: Merrill Lynch, Pierce, Fenner, & Smith.

Pizza Time Theatre, Inc. (1983). *Pizza Time Theatre, Inc.* 1982 Annual Report. Sunnyvale, CA: Pizza Time Theatre, Inc.

U.S. Census Bureau. (1998). *North American Industrial Classifications*. Washington, DC.

Chapter •••• 6

Marketing in Commercial Recreation and Tourism

The primary focus of any successful commercial recreation or tourism enterprise must be the stimulation of a desired exchange between customers and the enterprise. The exchange will only occur if consumer needs are met *and* if the business can thereby achieve its corporate objectives. The attitude and activities associated with the concurrent satisfaction of consumer and corporate needs is called *marketing*.

Marketing is often considered to be synonymous with advertising and promotion. Perhaps this is because promotional efforts are the most visible and glamorous elements of marketing, but it must be understood that promotion is only a small part of the complete process. *Promotion* is like icing, which, if disproportionately applied on the marketing cake, does attract initial interest but fails to fully satisfy. Those other elements of marketing include *product, price,* and *place (distribution and allocation)*.

These four elements of the marketing mix (see Figure 6-1) are usually referred to as "the 4 Ps of marketing" and are as relevant to marketing commercial recreation and tourism as they are to any other product or industry. Each is discussed and illustrated in this chapter.

PRODUCT

The product is that which the consumer receives from the business transaction or exchange. Sometimes the product is packaged as a tangible good (e.g., a tennis racket), and sometimes it is packaged as an intangible service (e.g., tennis lessons). Ultimately, however, the product is defined by the consumer as a certain kind of experience from which he or she derives specific benefits. In purchasing the tennis racket, the consumer experiences the satisfaction of having thoroughly researched different brands and product lines, interacted with a sales representative, showed off the racket to friends, and served an "ace" while using the new racket. In taking the tennis lessons, the consumer defines the product as an experience through which benefits such as being encouraged by a pro, escaping housework, getting exercise, socializing with other participants, or developing a new skill are enjoyed.

Until the commercial recreation and tourism manager begins to view products as bundles of benefits that meet consumer needs, the success of the enterprise will be limited, and the insensitivity and lack of response to market demands will increasingly impact the financial bottom line. Figure 6-2 identifies some common benefits that consumers seek from commercial recreation and tourism products.

Figure 6-1
The Elements of the Marketing Mix

Product development involves arranging activities or attributes such that the consumer will get from the product specific benefits that he or she needs or wants. If a young professional is looking for an opportunity to get away from city life (escape daily routines), overcome new challenges (feeling of success), be aggressive, and reinforce friendships, then a product that may provide those benefits is available at the paintball battlefield. A very different product form, Jet-Ski racing, also offers a similar bundle of benefits, as do rock climbing, rugby, and white-water kayaking. With respect to benefit-driven decision making, these different activities are essentially the same product. They are differentiated more by consumer constraints (time, money, equipment, skill, etc.) than they are by consumer definition.

The Differences Between Goods and Services

In general, products are classified as either goods or services. *Goods* are tangible items or devices that the consumer uses. Examples are sports equipment, maps, clothing and footwear, souvenirs, and literature. The consumer is rarely involved in the production of goods, especially since the goods can be made well in advance and far away from the time and place of purchase. The quality of goods is relatively easy to control through production specifications and standardization, and the deliverer of the good is not usually its manufacturer. *Services*, on the other hand, are intangible endowments, deeds, performances, or efforts. Examples are theatrical productions, housekeeping service, massage, recreation program leadership, tours, and bicycle rental. Production and consumption of services occur simultaneously, and the consumer plays an important and active role in production. Because services are somewhat customized and dependent on the variable abilities of human service providers and consumers, it is very difficult to control quality and to standardize production. Services are produced by the person who delivers it.

In most respects, marketing services is more difficult than marketing goods. The service product is less clearly defined, and the system of delivery has fewer elements but is far more complex.

Figure 6-2
Benefits Sought in
Recreation and Tourism Products

Escape from daily routine—sometimes the only appeal of a commercial recreation product is its novel setting, schedule, or social context.

Improved health—participation in exercise programs or activities that require physical activity are of interest to those who want to develop or maintain a healthy lifestyle.

Improved looks—some activities are demanded because they can help customers to lose weight or develop a tan and, thereby, potentially improve their physical appearance.

Social interaction—recreation activities provide many opportunities to associate with friends and strangers.

Skill development—consumers often hope to develop a new skill or improve an existing skill as a means of reinforcing their feelings of competency and utility or for other practical reasons.

Stress relief—rest and relaxation or active diversion can be very effective means of avoiding and reducing harmful stress.

Education—travel and other experiences offered in commercial recreation often expand the knowledge and understanding of the participants, especially those who participate with that expectation.

Ego enhancement—sometimes people do things like sky dive or travel to Siberia just to be able to say they did it. They choose their activities as much for the bragging rights as for any other benefit.

Aggression release—many recreation activities provide the only socially acceptable way of displaying aggressive behavior.

Authentication—travel experiences allow people to verify or discount the perceptions of the world that they have developed from reading or watching television.

Centering—through certain types of travel (e.g., pilgrimage) or recreational activities, it is possible to ponder and develop an understanding of one's place in the universe and purpose for life.

Product Development

New products represent a repackaging of benefits that consumers may be receiving elsewhere or are not being provided through any existing products. They are developed in response to the expressed or anticipated need of a market with which the business desires to have a commercial exchange. New products may be developed to replace less efficient products or to provide a more appealing mix of offerings in the marketplace. New products help to maintain interest in a market where variety and novelty are considered highly desirable, and such is the case in commercial recreation and tourism.

The satisfaction of consumer needs should be the primary motivation for product modification or new product development. Obviously, the new product should also improve the business's profitability. That improvement and the response of the market may not be readily apparent when the new product is released.

Product Diffusion

Product diffusion is the process by which innovations (new or different goods or services) are spread to members of a social system. A diffusion curve, shown in Figure 6-3, illustrates how innovations are adopted by various types of people over time. The time period could be very short, or it could be many years. Consumer behavior researchers (Hawkins, Coney, & Best, 1980) have described the characteristics of the various classifications of adopters.

Figure 6-3
The Diffusion Curve

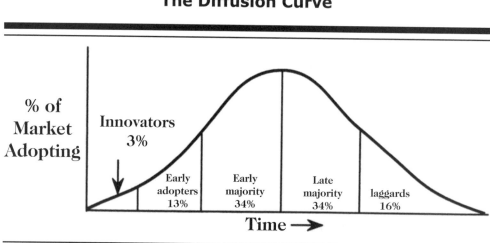

Innovators are adventuresome risk takers. They are typically younger, better educated, and more socially mobile than the other groups. Innovators make extensive use of commercial media in making their purchase decisions. They are also capable of absorbing the financial and/or social costs (e.g., embarrassment about an unwise purchase) if the new product is unsuccessful.

Early adopters are opinion leaders in local reference groups; they are also successful, well educated, and somewhat younger than other groups except innovators. The early adopters are willing to take calculated risks on products, but they are also concerned with failure.

The *early majority* are cautious. They adopt a product earlier than most of the market, but only after it has proven to be successful. These persons are socially active, but seldom opinion leaders. They are somewhat older, somewhat less educated, and less socially mobile than the two previous groups. The early majority rely more on interpersonal sources of information.

The *late majority* are skeptical about new products. They tend to respond more to social pressures than to advertising in adopting an innovation. They try new products when there is a decrease in availability of their previous choice of products. The late majority are typically older, with less social status and less mobility.

Laggards are locally oriented persons who engage in limited social interaction. They are relatively dogmatic and oriented toward the past. They are the last to buy the product.

It is important to note that these characteristics are generalizations for the entire spectrum of commercial recreation and tourism goods and services. The market for any particular product might, in reality, comprise only consumers from the first three categories. For example, some people will never be in the market for bungee jumping, parasailing, or vacations to Margaritaville. A modified diffusion curve could be developed for any particular product or service for any given target market.

Product Life Course

Most new products follow a similar pattern of development and decline from introduction to abandonment. This pattern is called the *product life course*, and it has several distinct stages during which the marketer must respond to the market in different ways.

Introduction Stage. It takes time for consumers to change their consumption patterns or abandon corporate loyalties. The introduction stage of the product's life course is characterized by gradual adoption and, hopefully, steady increases in consumption. A disproportionate amount of management attention is required at this stage due to extensive promotion and the need to quickly deal with unforeseen product defects.

Takeoff Stage. Once the product has proven itself, and a significant number of people are experienced enough to tell others about it, the product usually begins to enjoy a sharp increase in popularity. Rapid growth in the customer base is a signal that the business is figuratively taking off like a jet plane or rocket. This success, however, does not go unnoticed by competing businesses. During this stage, it is not uncommon to see the product being offered elsewhere and, perhaps, at a lower price or with added features.

Maturity Stage. There comes a time when most of the market is aware of the product and has decided to consume or not to consume. At this mature stage of the product life course, the market is stable, loyal, and about as large as it can be. This is a stage that the entrepreneur should try to prolong as much as possible.

Decline Stage. Eventually, new products will be developed to take customers away from the product in its maturity stage. Additionally, consumer characteristics or environmental conditions (e.g., the economy, security, etc.) may change sufficiently to cause customers to reduce or cease consuming the mature recreation or tourism product. Its popularity begins to decline, and unless appropriate actions are taken, the product will be abandoned by the consumers and the producer. Ideally, the marketer waits a long time for the product to enter this stage, but once it is there, there is no value in delaying its rejuvenation or demise.

Product Withdrawal

Withdrawing a failing product from the company's offerings is not always as simple as putting up a sign that says "Program Cancelled." Even though most consumers have given up on the product, there will always be a small and intensely loyal segment of the market that will resist any attempt to abandon a service or product. Additionally, the product may be tied to a facility or equipment investment, for which sufficient returns have not yet been realized. Other barriers to withdrawal include irrevocable contractual commitments to staff and suppliers, political pressures from within the company, and fear of how the product's demise might reflect on its manager's professional reputation.

Products should be withdrawn according to a carefully formulated retrenchment strategy. That strategy is developed and implemented with consideration to the needs of consumers, the requirements of law, the constraints of operation, and the personal feelings of staff.

Product withdrawal is not necessarily a negative action. Products can be withdrawn simply because they are no longer needed (e.g., wooden tennis rackets, certain aspects of travel arrangement), or because they use company resources that might more efficiently be employed in a product area with greater growth or profit potential. If, however, the product is essential to the business's identity or operations, then strategies should be developed to rejuvenate it.

Product Rejuvenation

There are four ways that new life can be given to a product entering the decline stage. The first is *market penetration*. Market penetration does not involve a change in the product or the market, but rather a change in the way the product is presented to the market in order to increase the intensity and frequency of consumption. For example, new advertising or discount pricing can get more of the same market to purchase a particular recreation service. The second approach to product rejuvenation is *market development*. This involves offering the same product to a much wider market. A struggling resort recreation program might, for example, achieve a critical mass of participants by being made accessible to residents of adjacent communities. The third product rejuvenation strategy is to serve the same market with a modified product. This is called *product development*. An example of product development is the addition of small sailboats or kayaks to the canoe rental program. *Diversification* is the fourth product rejuvenation strategy. It involves modifying both the product and the market. When a commercial sports club adds banquet and party facilities and services to its restaurant and café operations, it has diversified its products and extended its market.

PRICE

Price plays an important role in the exchange between consumers and producers of commercial recreation and tourism products. Price is the cost to the consumer of acquiring the product. It goes beyond the monetary "sticker price" to include time and opportunity costs, psychological costs, personal effort costs, and indirect financial costs. To some extent, price is a product attribute since it articulates the financial value benefit of consumption.

The *sticker price* of a product is the direct dollar amount required of the consumer by the producer for that recreation or tourism product. In order to participate in a white-water rafting trip, a consumer might have to pay the sticker price of $200 to the commercial outfitter.

The *time and opportunity costs* that the white-water rafter pays are the 12 hours of travel to and from the activity site, the 6 hours on the river, 3 hours at the base camp, and the opportunity to be earning income or building family relationships during that time.

Psychological costs include the guilt associated with using $200, 21 hours, and other opportunities in exchange for a personal thrill, the embarrassment of having to wear an extra-bulky life jacket because of being a slightly overweight nonswimmer, and the discomfort associated with spending the whole day in close quarters with a dozen total strangers.

Participation in the activity will incur *personal effort costs* as the rafter does his or her share of the work to steer and handle the heavy watercraft. He or she will also expend physical and mental effort in driving to and from the site.

Indirect financial costs include all cash outlays required for full participation, except activity fees and charges. Transportation, lodging, clothing, insurance, equipment, and food are some of the indirect costs that a white-water rafting participant might have to add into the total price for that participation. Figure 6-4 illustrates the impact of these extra costs on the total cost for a family of four to spend a day at some of America's major theme parks. On average, just the cost of parking and food adds nearly 20% of the admission price to the direct cost of participation.

Figure 6-4
Direct and Indirect Costs of Theme Park Attendance

	Admission	Hamburger	Soft Drink	Parking	*Total
Paramount King's Island	$130.50	$2.50	$1.75	$6.00	$153.50
Six Flags Kentucky Kingdom	$117.50	$3.50	$2.00	$3.00	$142.50
Universal Studios Hollywood	$168.50	$4.00	$2.00	$7.00	$199.50
Dollywood	$135.50	$4.00	$1.50	$4.00	$161.50

*Total for survey of 2 adults and 2 children.
Source: Amusement Business, 1999

It is important that the commercial recreation and tourism manager recognizes the total price that consumers will have to pay. It is the total price that influences the purchase decision, not just the sticker price.

Setting Price

The sticker price is set by the producer at a level that is expected to accommodate and encourage purchasing and satisfy business objectives. The basic business objective is to generate a profit, which means that the money paid by consumers (price) must be more than the money paid by the producer (cost). If there is no difference between the amounts, the business has recovered costs without losing money or generating profits. Straight cost recovery is, for the entire enterprise, unacceptable, so consumer prices must be set higher than producer costs. In order to do that, the producer costs must be known, and the cost recovery ratio should be specified. Figure 6-5 illustrates the application of cost recovery ratios in determining consumer prices.

Figure 6-5
Pricing Schedule Using Cost Recovery Ratios

Product		Unit cost ($)	Cost recovery ratio (%)	Consumer price ($)
Goods	Beach towels	1.90	160%	3.00
	Sunscreen	.49	300%	1.50
	Soft drinks (cans)	.26	400%	1.00
Services				
	Umbrella rental	.30	250%	.75
	Villa shuttle	1.50	0%	Free
	Surfboard rental	.35	300%	1.00
	Towel laundry	.50	100%	.50

Special care should be exercised when setting the price for a new product or for an existing product in a new market. The introductory price, unless clearly identified as being unusually low, tends to become the consumer's reference price for that product, and future price increases are met with resistance that results in a loss of sales (see the discussion on price-demand elasticity in Chapter 3). One pricing strategy that uses a low introductory price is called *price penetration*. A different strategy that uses a high introductory price is called *price skimming*. There are a few appropriate circumstances and, occasionally, some advantages to introducing a product with a higher-than-usual price. Some managers of commercial recreation or tourism enterprises base their prices on existing market reference points and closely mirror the fee levels used by their competitors. This strategy is called *going-rate pricing*. A fourth strategy involves the conscious application of different price schedules in different circumstances. This is called *variable-cost pricing*.

Price Penetration

A price penetration strategy initially sets the price of a product or service at or below cost in order to capture customers away from the competition. Penetration pricing is based on the assumptions that (1) consumers perceive few differences among the competing alternatives; (2) low prices will generate sales quickly; (3) low prices will expand the market; (4) the competition will respond slowly to the pricing strategy; and (5) once established in the marketplace, the entrepreneur can raise prices to going-rate levels.

A price penetration strategy should be used only for a brief introductory period. If the strategy is used for too long, demand may drastically suffer when price increases are attempted. Furthermore, price cutting in an overbuilt market will inevitably bring out similar or deeper discounts from competitors. Trade publications for airlines, hotels, and restaurants routinely report on the effects of price wars undermining the bottom lines of businesses. Extended use of penetration pricing will force other competitors to scramble to maintain their market share. When overt price competition breaks out, all businesses suffer a loss per transaction. If price competition continues, the market over time may condition consumers to postpone purchases until discounts are available and prices may never be brought back to normal. Where price discounts are the norm, non-price dimensions of the products and services decline in importance (Crotts, 1997).

Price Skimming

The basic idea of price skimming is to set a relatively high initial price for a new product or service and then gradually reduce the price over time as the market becomes more competitive. By starting with a high price, the business can determine what customers are willing to pay while retaining the ability to reduce prices when competitive conditions make this necessary. If the business mistakenly sets a price too high, it can always be reduced, whereas a price that is too low cannot easily be raised without an effect on demand.

The price-skimming policy is designed to skim off that segment of the market that responds to innovative high-quality products and services and is not overly sensitive to high prices. When the product is relatively new and there are few alternatives, the price-skimming policy can generate greater profits per transaction, which in turn can be used to repay start-up costs or to finance expansion opportunities into larger and different markets. It can also help generate quick profits at a time when a start-up business may be unable to keep up with a large volume of orders. When the entrepreneur is able to increase production capacity, prices can be slowly lowered to increase demand.

Price is one of the 4-Ps of marketing and a popular way to differentiate one business from another. (Photo: J. Crossley)

Going-Rate Pricing

Using the going-rate pricing strategy, a business simply matches the price charged by the other companies for the same product and then competes for customers on non-price variables. The selection of this approach is based on the assumption that the competition will quickly respond to any price penetration strategy, thereby negating any potential advantages. This passive approach to pricing can be successful when non-price elements of the marketing mix are effective. Superior service, a convenient and appealing location, availability of customer credit, and a more efficient production and distribution system may generate sales without a price inducement.

Going-rate prices are less likely to solicit immediate and overt responses from competitors. This is comforting to managers of new businesses, because their start-up costs are high, and they may not have the financial strength to survive an extended price war.

Variable-Cost Pricing

Variable-cost pricing (also called differential pricing) is based on the idea that a single, unchanging price is not always necessary to produce profits for the business. This pricing strategy is often used in situations where fixed costs comprise a large proportion of cost per unit of sales. A golf course that charges higher greens fees during the weekend when demand is high and discounts during the weekdays when demand is low is using variable-cost pricing. Cruise ships, hotels, and airlines also make effective use of this strategy by offering discounts to increase demand from price-sensitive customers. Variable-cost pricing is an acceptable option because, as many believe, it is better to make a sale at a rate that contributes incremental profits to the enterprise than to not have the business at all. Furthermore, variable pricing may stimulate off-peak sales by (1) generating demand from price-sensitive customers and (2) shifting demand from periods when demand exceeds capacity.

A variable-cost pricing strategy is not a panacea for all commercial recreation and tourism businesses. This approach to pricing can lead to higher revenues and profits only for those sophisticated businesses that understand its potentials and limitations. Price wars can occur when competing firms use variable-cost pricing. The danger is that increased demand during nonpeak times may not be sufficient to offset the loss of revenue from the decreased profit margins. Moreover, other businesses competing for the same limited number of customers may match or exceed the discounts, thus negating any possible effects of improving a business's bottom line.

PLACE (DISTRIBUTION AND ALLOCATION)

A well-designed product offered at the right price needs to be distributed to the market in order for the desired exchange to occur. To be successful, the commercial recreation and tourism entrepreneur must know where the market is and the best way to reach it. The following discussion examines the nature of markets and the type of business decisions that need to be made in order to deliver products to target consumer populations.

Target Markets

A target market is a relatively homogeneous group of consumers who have similar needs and product preferences and with whom the entrepreneur wishes to have a business exchange. A target market is a smaller group than the entire market of potential consumers, and it is the focus of particular marketing efforts. For example, the market for a tour company may be defined by nationality and geography (e.g., Americans living in the northeast and traveling in Europe), but segments of the market may be targeted for special product packages or seasonal pricing incentives. Target markets may include military personnel, diplomatic corps, students, families, or retired couples.

Individual consumers may belong to more than one market segment and be targeted through different promotional campaigns. Shown in Figure 6-6 is a market that was segmented by gender, municipal residency, student status, and type of vehicle driven. Clearly, the largest market segment is made up of women who do not live in the county, are not students, and do not drive a truck. However, if the product is a monster truck show at the fairgrounds, the target market is more likely to be the much smaller group of male county residents who are not students and who do drive trucks.

Market segmentation is done for several reasons:

- Larger markets may exhibit a great deal of heterogeneity. Averaging attribute values is not only of little utility, but it may be counterproductive.
- Market segments respond differently to different marketing mixes.
- Market segmentation is philosophically consistent with the marketing concept (i.e., it recognizes that consumers have different wants and needs). (Crompton & Lamb, 1986)

Markets should be segmented using only those criteria that are relevant to the product and its delivery. It makes no sense to segment a market using gender as a criterion if both men and women need and can obtain the same benefits from the product, receive information about the product through the same medium, respond to the same message, and are equally willing and able to pay for the recreation experience. Similarly, there is little value in segmenting the market for cheap souvenirs on the basis of household income. People from all income classes can afford the product. It does make sense to segment the market for a fitness center using household makeup as the criterion, because some programs offer childcare as an auxiliary service, and some are designed to include family members of all ages in the activity.

Figure 6-6
Target Market Segments Within the Total Market

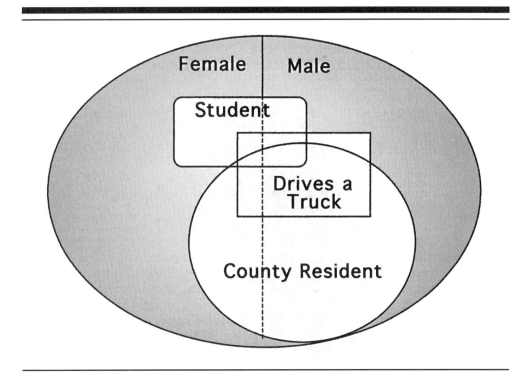

Some of the more common segmentation criteria used in commercial recreation and tourism marketing include geographic (place of residence, distance from site, accessibility, etc.), socio-demographic (age, income, gender, education, marital status, ethnicity, etc.), behavioral (usage patterns, skill levels, purchase propensity, brand loyalty, etc.), and psychographic (values, opinions, lifestyles, and beliefs). Geographic, demographic, and behavioral characteristics are relatively easy to measure and are very useful in describing the external nature of consumers, but psychographic profiles of market segments are most useful in understanding their choices and behaviors (Brayley, 1990).

Through market segmentation, the commercial recreation and tourism manager can identify the benefits sought by the homogeneous group of consumers and design products that meet those needs. The shared economic conditions of the target market can be reflected in prices, and the location or scheduling of the activity can respond to the segment's time and travel constraints. Promotional efforts are much more efficient and effective when they are focused on a specific audience whose information search behaviors are well understood.

Delivery of the Product

Location of the product outlet or service site is one of the most important business decisions to be made. It is through the consumer-producer point of contact that delivery of the product is achieved. The discussion on this topic in Chapter 4 emphasized attributes of the physical location that are essential to success. This discussion will cover other aspects of product delivery such as intensity, scheduling, and channels of distribution. Also discussed will be the important subjects of allocation and group sales.

Intensity

It is important for the commercial recreation and tourism business to be located in the right place. However many locations a business may have, each one needs to be in the right location.

There are advantages and disadvantages to *intensive distribution* (i.e., multiple business locations). For example, a company may decide to build several neighborhood sports centers with a basketball court, a few racquetball courts, and an exercise room in each. This intensity of distribution offers ready access to a greater share of the market and a sense of community attachment. Programs offered at the centers can be more responsive to the communities in which they are located. Unfortunately, the centers are individually too small to host any tournaments or major revenue-producing events and collectively are inadequate because they are too dispersed for efficient management of a major sporting event.

Some economies of scale issues can be addressed through *selective distribution* (i.e., few business locations) or *exclusive distribution* (i.e., only one business location). For many years, Disneyland in Anaheim, California, was an exclusively distributed product, but then Walt Disney World was established and continues to grow in Florida, Euro Disney opened in France, and new Disney theme parks were introduced in Japan and Hong Kong. The Disneyland experience is now selectively experienced. Disney retailing, however, has become an intensively distributed opportunity as hundreds of shopping malls and airports now include The Disney Store. You no longer have to go to California to "get your ears"!

Scheduling

Marketing revolves around the goal of satisfying consumer wants and needs. In distributing commercial recreation and tourism products, careful consideration needs to be given to the temporal circumstances, wants, and needs of customers. Obviously, people cannot participate in a recreation activity or purchase a good whenever they feel like so doing. They have many demands on their time, and discretionary purchases and involvements must be fit in whenever possible. One simple rule to follow when scheduling product delivery is: "The best time to offer a service is when the consumer is able and willing to receive it." While this may seem almost ridiculously obvious, the commercial recreation and tourism industries are constantly bidding farewell to failed business enterprises that could not or would not respond to consumers' temporal needs through market-oriented scheduling.

Channels of Distribution

There are several channels through which recreation and tourism products can be distributed to consumers. It was earlier noted that services are simultaneously produced and consumed, that is, they are delivered directly to the consumer. Goods, on the other hand, can be delivered directly or through a distribution channel that involves one or more intermediaries. Figure 6-7 illustrates several possible distribution channels.

To further illustrate the concept of distribution channels, the producer represented in Figure 6-7 might be an airline company. The passenger (consumer) can purchase his or her ticket directly from the airline by logging on to the Internet and booking online or by visiting the ticket counter at any airport served by that airline. The passenger could also buy his or her ticket from a charter company (retailer) that has purchased a block of seats and is reselling them. That charter company may have purchased the seats either directly from the airline or through a travel company that acts as an agent (wholesaler) of the airline. Occasionally, the traveler may find a travel arranger or travel consolidator that can sell tickets directly to him or her at the wholesale price.

If intermediaries are involved in a distribution channel, the producer of any recreation or tourism product should monitor the treatment of the product on its way to the consumer. That treatment includes handling, packaging (e.g., bundling), pricing, and promotion.

Figure 6-7
Distribution Channels for Recreation and Tourism Products

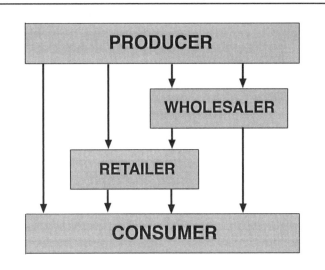

Allocation

Allocation differs from distribution in that it involves the determination and use of merit as a criterion upon which product delivery decisions are made. Merit refers to the deservingness of a market and may be measured in social or economic terms. Merit is used in deciding which, if any, market segment will receive a disproportionate share of the product. For example, one particular market segment receives a disproportionate share of the opportunity to buy a lifetime membership at a commercial sports club. That segment is defined as those who paid the membership fee. They have merit based on the fact that they were able to pay the very high amount. In a public governmental recreational setting, merit may have more to do with social resources. Those who have fewer social resources (education, employability, etc.) may receive a disproportionate share of services like scholarships, training programs, and family support services.

Typically, commercial recreation and tourism enterprises allocate products on the basis of economic merit. They do, however, also demonstrate some social merit features in giving discounts to seniors, children, and other socially disadvantaged market segments, but that social goodwill is often motivated by the realization that such considerations are also an important part of smart business.

Group Sales

One market that displays particular economic merit is the group market. Groups represent a major source of revenue for many types of commercial recreation and tourism. Theme parks, resorts, airlines, cruise ships, bus tour lines, white-water rafting companies, convention centers, and tour wholesalers are among the businesses that count heavily on group sales. It is very common for such businesses to employ one or more group sales coordinators. These employees typically work on a commission basis or salary plus commission.

Some commercial recreation businesses such as theme and amusement parks seek group sales but prefer that they not exceed 25–30% of gate revenue. This is because too much group discounting can undermine the integrity of the basic price structure. Some of the most common types of group discount methods are presented next.

Regular Group Discounts are the foundation of group sales. Small groups of friends, family reunions, scout groups, singles clubs, day camps, and other groups prearrange to attend a recreation attraction on a specific day. In return, the groups are given discounts ranging from half a dollar to half price. There is always a minimum number of participants required to qualify for the discount. Minimums are typically 15, 20, or 25.

Industrial Group Discounts are provided to company employee groups. The minimum might be higher (50 to 100), but the discounts are usually deeper than for the regular groups.

Consignment Tickets are commonly issued to large companies, college student unions, military bases, or other major organizations. A set of prenumbered tickets is issued to the organization with the written agreement that they will be sold at a certain price or returned by a certain date. Some organizations take a small percentage of the sales price in order to cover their cost of staffing the ticket outlets. Figure 6-8 illustrates a typical consignment ticket agreement for a hypothetical tourist attraction.

Discount Cards are prenumbered cards issued to individuals in an organization. The individual receives a predetermined discount whenever they present the card at the ticket window of the given attraction.

Group Buyouts are also called group parties, group exclusives, or charters. In any case, a group contracts for the exclusive use of a recreational facility or transportation carrier (plane, bus, etc.). This, of course, has to be scheduled to avoid conflict with regular users. Early- or late-season evenings are excellent times for group buyouts. The minimum number of participants for a buyout may be quite substantial; for example, 1,000 persons in the case of a water theme park. Sometimes two or more compatible groups are allowed to combine their numbers to have enough participation to meet the minimum number.

Cooperative Packages can be developed between two or more noncompetitive businesses. Individuals or groups buying into one facility or service are given a discount for a second attraction. An example would be a tour operator who puts together an attractively priced group package that includes transportation, hotel accommodations, and admission to a sports event, world's fair, expo, or other special event.

Figure 6-8
Consignment Agreement

The Seminole Sports Hall of Fame (SSHF), subject to the terms and conditions hereof, agrees to consign to _____ (consignee, company name)

___ adult tickets to SSHF
___ child tickets to SSHF

from _____ to _____.

1. The consignee agrees to remit on or prior to _____ (final settlement date) to SSHF $ _____ per adult ticket, $ _____ per child ticket unreturned on or prior to final settlement date (less any payments made on interim dates).
2. On reorder (interim payment dates), consignee agrees to remit to SSHF $ _____ per adult ticket, $ _____ per child ticket for each sold to date.
3. Should the consignee fail to meet any of the interim payments, SSHF may, at its own option, cancel this agreement by written notice to consignee, and, in such event, consignee shall immediately deliver all tickets in its possession to SSHF and/or its authorized representative. All funds due for tickets unreturned shall be immediately payable in accordance with the above schedule upon demand.
4. Consignee assumes full responsibility for tickets received and agrees to pay SSHF (upon final settlement date, unless prior arrangements have been made) in accordance with the prices set forth herein for tickets unreturned, regardless of reason for said non-return and agrees to reimburse SSHF for all legal fees and court costs relevant to the execution of this consignment agreement dated _____.
5. All payments due hereunder are to be paid by check payable to the Seminole Sports Hall of Fame to an authorized representative of Seminole Sports Hall of Fame or forwarded to the attention of Accounting, 401 East Tait Drive, Tallahassee, Florida. All payments must refer to the document number at the top of this agreement or a copy of this agreement may be returned with the payment.

_____   _____
Representative of SSHF   Representative of consignee (date)

_____   _____
Title   Title

_____   _____
Date   Company name and address
                                     _____

The following ideas are suggested to make group sales more effective:

- Try to get group business for off-peak periods when you need the volume most.
- Try to get up-front payment or at least a deposit. This may be relaxed for proven groups that have been reliable clients.
- Have a well-organized mailing list of all prospective groups in your area with over 100 members.
- Promote group rates at least six weeks before the season opening.
- As soon as a group order comes in, assign them the best unsold seats (or rooms) available at that time (within the given rate structure).
- Check back with the group to confirm their attendance.
- Provide tickets to the group leader in advance by personal delivery, insured mail, or alone at the facility entrance or ticket window. Group members should wait in a designated area away from the entrance congestion.
- Groups should utilize a separate entrance if available.
- Make the group feel welcome by announcing their presence, providing a personal greeting, or even surprising them with special programs, refreshments, meal discount coupons, and so forth.
- Contact the group after their visit to make sure everything went well.

PROMOTION

By definition, promotion is the advancement or appreciation of the status, position, or value of a product or idea. It is an important part of marketing, but promotion cannot be successful if there are shortcomings in the product, price, and/or place. Promotional activities are for making good products known to the market, preferred by the market, and remembered by experienced customers.

In making the product known, the promotional message *educates* potential consumers about the benefits to be derived from the product and about how to get the product. Through education, promotional messages create an awareness of the commercial recreation or tourism product.

In making the product preferred by the market, promotional activities have a distinctly *persuasive* tone to them. The messages are designed to convince the consumers that the particular product and supplier are superior to any alternatives.

Through *reminding* messages, promotions strive to keep customers loyal by restoring awareness of the benefits they receive from the product. Because of the wide range of alternative activities and producers in commercial recreation and tourism, reminder promotions are just as important as educational or persuasive promotions.

The Promotions Mix

Effective promotions involve an appropriate mix of activities and media that efficiently deliver the educational, persuasive, or reminding message to the consumer. Ideally, the company's promotional plan includes public relations, personal selling, sales promotions, publicity, and advertising.

Public Relations

Public relations are simply the way the producer relates to the consumer public. One way in which the commercial recreation entrepreneur relates to the public is through face-to-face interaction. Good public relations develop if, through *face-to-face interaction*, the corporate representatives exude genuine delight in the opportunity to serve the customers. This can be established by hiring the right people and providing them with appro-

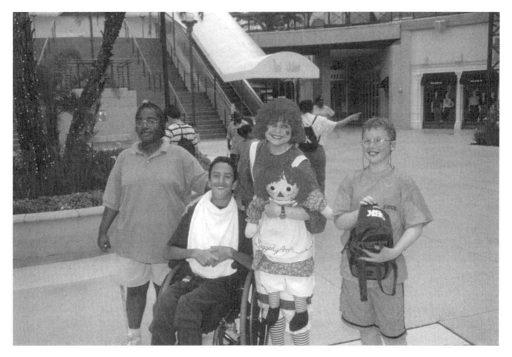

A guest relations specialist is employed by FAO Schwarz toy store to interact with customers.
(Photo: J. Crossley)

priate customer service training. Standards of dress, grooming, and conduct may be established in order to at least appear and sound to be every bit as good as the product was proclaimed to be.

Another way in which public relations develop is through *written communications* with the consumers. All distributed materials, including business correspondence, e-mail memoranda, and corporate Web pages, should be well planned, accurate, and clear and should reflect positively on the sponsoring organization. Public relations are also affected by the way *telephone* inquiries and calls are handled. Procedures should be established and training provided to assist all who operate a company telephone to know

- the desired greeting,
- the answers to the basic questions about operations,
- when to transfer a call or take a message,
- how to transfer calls, and
- what information should not be released over the telephone.

Finally, public relations include the *visual presentation* of the product. Physical facilities should be in good condition and be clean and accessible. Even the selection of paint color and other decorative features communicate a message to the consumer about the type of relationship to be maintained.

Customer Service

One of the greatest opportunities to develop good public relations is through the ongoing service that is provided to customers. The notion of service quality is by no means an outdated idea, and its application is increasingly the difference between successful and failing businesses.

How important is quality customer service? Consider this example provided by Mike Hurst, former president of the National Restaurant Association. Suppose a customer spends $50 in a restaurant in one year. If she has a pleasant experience, she is likely to spread the word. As a result, two of her friends come to the restaurant and spend $50 the next year. Suppose this chain continues with each new customer resulting in two additional customers. After 10 years, this sequence of satisfied customers will spend $1,476,150 at the restaurant, and this may be conservative, since some customers influence more than two friends. On the other hand, dissatisfied customers often influence as many as eight friends! Can it be assumed that guests who do not complain are "satisfied customers?" Absolutely not! A study by the U.S. Office of Consumer Affairs reported that 37 to 45% of all service industry customers are dissatisfied but don't complain (Hurst, 1991). Therefore, it should be considered imperative that all commercial recreation and tourism businesses should have a proactive customer service or guest relations training program.

The following ideas are useful principles for providing outstanding customer service (Fasching, 1992):

- **Smile and speak to people**—be the first to speak by greeting people as soon as they arrive.
- **Recognize your guests**—learn your guests' names and use them.
- **Learn your guests' preferences**—especially for repeat guests, learn what they like and do not like.
- **Make a positive first impression**—have a well-lighted parking lot, an attractive entrance, a clean and orderly front desk or reception area, and well-groomed staff in appropriate attire.
- **Show genuine interest**—listen to what people say and look at them while talking and listening.
- **Be helpful and friendly**—go out of your way to do the "little extras."
- **Be knowledgeable**—not only about your job, but about your entire facility. Keep reference material about nearby attractions.
- **Fulfill your guests' expectations**—deliver the product or service at least as well as promised in your advertising.
- **Reduce the effort required of the customer**—minimize waiting lines and maximize conveniences such as child strollers, off-site transportation, express check-in, and so on.
- **Focus on the customers' perception**—reality is in the eye of the customer; if they think conditions are dirty and service is slow, then management should do something to improve the customers' perception.
- **Be thoughtful and considerate**—respect the opinions and customs of others.
- **Be generous with praise and cautious with criticism**—this includes your interactions with staff in front of the public.
- **Be flexible and have a sense of humor**—things don't always go your way, so be prepared to deal with customers' problems in a pleasant manner.
- **Have enthusiasm and pride in your own work**—if you do not, how can you expect the customer to have confidence in you?
- **Never tell a guest something will take "a minute"** if you know it will take longer. Be more accurate and do not string guests along.
- **Be specific when giving information and directions.**

Although good customer service is the responsibility of every employee, the following functions may be included in a specific guest services department:

- switchboard
- concierge
- customer complaint department
- gift/package wrapping
- shuttle/transportation
- day care program
- lost and found

- reservations
- room service
- valet service
- coat check
- greeters
- information service
- first aid station

Excellent customer service is an essential part of marketing. (Photo: J. Crossley)

Some commercial recreation and tourism businesses are large enough to have separate staff for each of these functions or a combination of two or three. Some organizations such as hotels may place several of these responsibilities under the auspices of the concierge service. The expanding role of the concierge service is examined in greater detail in Chapter 8.

One particular task that guest relations staff (and all other employees to some degree) must be competent in is the fine art of handling guest/customer complaints. Figure 6-9 provides some general guidelines for handling complaints.

Figure 6-9
Checklist for Handling
Guest/Customer Complaints

1. Stop whatever you are doing and face the guest. Identify yourself and your position.
2. Listen to your guest's problem without interrupting. Allowing them to let off steam helps diffuse the situation. Don't take it personally.
3. Do not treat the problem as insignificant. Do not say "No problem" when you mean to say "We can take care of that."
4. Be an understanding and pleasant recipient of their comments.
5. You do not have to agree with everything. Get all the facts, taking notes if necessary.
6. Evaluate the problem and explain the proper policy or procedure to the guest.
7. Tell the guest what can be done, not what can't be done.
8. Invite the guest to choose between some logical and helpful alternatives.
9. Never argue with or talk down to a guest or make them feel stupid.
10. Try to use the customer's name in your conversation.
11. Let the guest see you record his or her complaints, especially if it needs to be referred to higher management.
12. If the guest is not satisfied, serve as his or her link to higher management, and present the guest (and his or her problem) with due dignity.
13. If you are the higher management, again present alternatives (room change, merchandise exchange, refund, etc.) and let the guest choose.
14. Invite the customer to call back regarding the resolution of the problem or, in some instances, initiate the follow-up contact yourself.
15. If the guest becomes abusive or physically belligerent, summon authorities who are trained and equipped to handle such problems.

Adapted from Cagle, 1992; Marriott Hotels, 1990)

Personal Selling

Personal selling is face-to-face communication between the corporate sales force and a customer. It is designed to influence the customer to purchase. Personal selling is a powerful element of the promotional mix, because the salesperson can assess the customer's needs, develop a sales message, evaluate the customer's reaction, and make adjustments accordingly. Even if a sales contact does not immediately result in a sale, it can be beneficial in establishing rapport with the customer and is therefore likely to at least generate a degree of trust and confidence that may lead to a sale in the future.

Personal selling is the backbone of many effective businesses such as convention centers, meeting planners, and hotel group sales departments. The sales process involves two initial steps. First, there is the identification of prospects. Individuals who respond to advertisements by coming to the place of business (or respond by letter, e-mail, phone, etc.) are generally good prospects. Another approach is to research for prospects among the membership of relevant professional associations, hobby clubs, special interest affiliations, and from prospect lists that have been purchased from other businesses having similar customer profiles. The second step in the personal selling process is to contact the prospect in person or by telephone. At that point of personal contact, the sales person can determine the customer's interest in the product or service, assess the benefits the customer seeks, and communicate an individualized message to explain how the product or service will satisfy the customer.

The major advantage of personal selling is that one can research the prospects' needs and requirements and offer the appropriate inducements for them to buy. A disadvantage of personal selling is that it is expensive. A personal visit to every sales prospect is costly in both time and money. Therefore, the approach is generally used by manufacturers, large hotels, and convention bureaus, where one sale is associated with a large volume. In these settings, a sales person may interact with a prospect for quite some time before a sale occurs. In such a setting, the ultimate payoff occurs, for example, when the national conference rotates back to the same hotel conference facility every 3 to 5 years.

Sales Promotions

In contrast to long-term promotional campaigns such as advertising, sales promotions are short-term inducements of value to consumers that are designed to persuade them to buy. Sales promotions commonly utilize tools such as discount coupons or sweepstakes opportunities. There are two main reasons that a sales promotion might be implemented: to influence nonconsumers to try a product or service (in hopes that they will make repeated purchases in the future) and to motivate existing customers to purchase more frequently or at different times.

Using sales promotions to entice new customers is usually appropriate and often very effective. In some cases, however, customers who respond to special promotions switch back to their regular brand once the promotional deal is off.

There are several dangers associated with sales promotions. One is the potential of promotional packages and prices becoming the reference set for the consumer. In other words, when a product is frequently advertised with a low promotional price, customers get used to that price, and the regular price seems expensive in comparison. Another danger lies in the possibility that those who respond to a particular sales promotion might be the consumers of a different product of the same enterprise. No net gain of consumers will be realized, and revenues may be negatively affected. Care must be taken to ensure that sales promotions don't just enhance substitution within the already-captured market. A third danger is in the likelihood that current consumers who are loyal will feel unjustly treated because new customers are paying less for the same product. Finally, there is a possibility that the too-frequent use of sales promotions will cause the market to wonder what is so wrong with the product that it needs to be continually or frequently discounted.

Publicity

Many businesses try to supplement their sponsored promotional efforts with publicity, which is unpaid communication about the business or its products or services in the mass media. Because the business does not pay for the communication or manage its content, publicity comes with a certain amount of risk. It could be complimentary or condemning, thorough or cursory, correct or incorrect. Fortunately, there are a few things that the entrepreneur can do to increase the chances of receiving good publicity:

- **Have a good product.** To some degree, let the product speak for itself.
- **Actively manage the evaluation of the product.** Help consumers to focus on and articulate the benefits that they receive from the recreation or tourism experience.
- **Prepare the medium.** Describe to the news medium the relevance of the story, the interest it would have to the audience, and the reporting format to which the event is

most suited. Additionally, intelligent, interesting, and informed spokespeople should be provided, and detailed press kits with press releases should be prepared and distributed.

The major advantages of publicity are its credibility and its cost. When information about a product appears as a news item in an objective medium such as a television news broadcast, it is more likely to be believed than when it comes directly from the producer in the form of an advertisement. Most people would believe that a new model of a mountain bike is preferable if *Bicycling Magazine* rates it as superior to all others in their annual consumer guide. The cost of publicity is lower than the cost of advertising, but it is not free. It takes financial, temporal, and human resources to develop and maintain the kind of relationship with the media that will generate positive publicity.

Advertising

Advertising is any paid form of nonpersonal presentation of ideas, goods, or services by an identified sponsor. An advantage of advertising is that the sponsoring corporation has complete control over the content and nature of the message, and, therefore, it is always a favorable communication. Furthermore, the advertiser selects the market, timing, and medium to be used.

An advertisement doesn't just happen. It is the result of a carefully planned and executed campaign in which the market is clearly identified and analyzed, advertising objectives and themes are set, substantial financial resources are committed, media are utilized, and results are measured.

Various elements of the advertising campaign will address the state of the market with respect to the product. If the product is new to the target market, the advertising message will be *pioneering*. It will introduce the product and extol its virtues. If the product has been in the market for a while and alternative products have been developed, then the advertising message will be *competitive*. This message will emphasize the superior qualities of the product. For loyal markets of established products, the third type of advertising message will be *retentive*. It will emphasize the wisdom of the consumer in staying loyal to the product.

The coincidental evolution of an advertising campaign with the life course of a product is referred to as the advertising spiral (Kleppner, 1979) (see Figure 6-10). If product revitalization or life course extension strategies are employed, then the revised product and/or market would become the focus of *new pioneering* advertising, followed by *new competitive* advertising, and so on. Thus, the advertising campaign continually changes to respond to the developing product and dynamic market.

The major disadvantages of advertising are its cost and the dilution of impact as consumers are flooded with hundreds of advertising messages daily. To be effective, an advertisement must cut through the clutter to gain the attention of potential customers. This takes a level of investment that many small businesses cannot afford, especially in such media as national television and magazines. Local cable television and newspapers provide affordable alternatives for entrepreneurs wanting to invest in an advertising campaign.

It is beyond the scope of this text to present content about each of the many types of advertising that can be used: newspaper, magazine, mail, flyers, posters, roadside billboards, radio, television, and so on. That material should be part of a separate course in marketing and advertising. However, since advertising through the Internet has grown so much in the last 10 years and may not be part of some marketing texts, a few tips for using a Web page and the Internet are provided here.

Figure 6-10
The Advertising Spiral

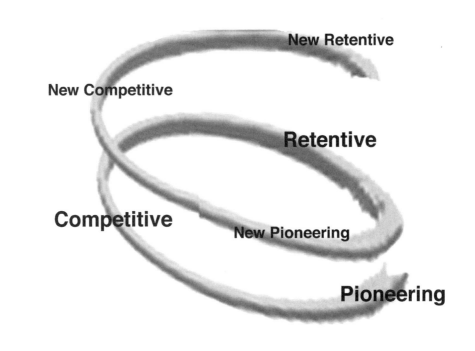

Web Pages are now used by most successful businesses, and some business managers consider it their most cost-effective advertising method. Regardless of the level of sophistication used in a business Web site, it is essential not to get lost in the visually creative effects and neglect the essential elements. Be sure that your Web page includes (adapted from Moore, 2005):

- market platform
- operating hours
- contact phone numbers
- program schedule
- admission fees and costs
- newsletter and sign-up form
- program or product details
- location and directions
- e-mail contact
- facility features
- comment form
- online reservation or purchase form

E-mail Messages swamp customers' computers, and many advertisements get deleted by a spam filter. However, since the cost of production and distribution is so low, e-mail advertising is still a good promotional tool to consider. Below are some tips for using e-mail advertising that were originally created for advertising water theme parks (Bitterman, 2005). However, the tips are logical for other applications as well.

- *Grab attention.* The subject line of the e-mail is the first thing the customer sees and often makes the difference in whether the e-mail gets opened or not. It must grab attention.
- *Make it easy to read.* People tend to skim e-mails, so keep line length short and use bullet points.

- *Keep it personal*. Most people prefer personal e-mail, so try to use the recipient's name and other specific information you might have collected such as a past visit or past purchase.
- *Time it right: send e-mails out on Tuesdays*. This avoids the weekend buildup of other e-mails. Later in the week, a person's plans for the weekend may already be set, or they may be focused on the following week.
- *Make contact easy*. Have a link so the reader can go directly to your Web site. Provide your phone number, location, and e-mail address.
- *Don't make inflated claims*. People are wary of e-mails that promise too much.
- *Reply promptly*. Get back to that customer within the same day, even if it is an automatic response that buys you time to personally answer within a day or two.
- *Add value to bring customers back*. Offer something that will bring the customer to your facility or at least to your Web site. This could include a contest, special discount, or e-mail-only offer.
- *Use newsletters to keep customers interested*. Create a monthly newsletter with features about recent events, new facilities, programs, special offers, staff news, and even customer "spotlights." A good newsletter might get forwarded from one current customer to a potential new customer.
- *Maintain contact*. Once you have established a relationship with a customer, keep it going with future e-mails.
- *Make it easy to un-subscribe*. If a customer just isn't interested in your e-mails, make it easy to get off your mailing list. You don't want to build ill will with people who might still be customers but don't want the e-mails.

SUMMARY

Marketing is focused on satisfying consumer and corporate needs through a desired exchange. That exchange is more likely to occur if proper attention is given to the four Ps of marketing: product, price, place, and promotion. The product is, from the consumer's perspective, a bundle of desired benefits. That bundle may take many forms, which accounts for substitutability.

Recreation and tourism products may be goods or services. Diffusion of the well-designed, consumer-responsive product begins relatively slowly, but the majority of consumers usually adopt it within a reasonable period of time. The product has a life course, as determined by its appeal to and support from the market. The life of a product can be extended by revitalization strategies such as market penetration, product development, market development, and diversification.

The price of a product is the total cost to the consumer for its purchase and use. Price is more than the sticker price—it includes other financial, temporal, opportunity, effort, and psychological costs. The basis of pricing in commercial recreation and tourism is cost-recovery. Final determination of the price may be influenced by competitors' prices, consumer willingness to pay, and variable cost advantages.

Markets may be segmented on the basis of relevant characteristics. Homogeneous groups of consumers with whom the enterprise desires to do business are called target markets. Products can be delivered to target markets through distribution systems of varying intensity, at different times, and through different distribution channels. Allocation of products to markets is done on the basis of merit, primarily economic merit.

The promotion mix includes public relations, personal selling, sales promotions, publicity, and advertising. Promotion can only be effective if it deals with a good product that is priced correctly and distributed efficiently. Marketing is much more than advertising and promotion. It is a way of viewing the producer-consumer relationship and a set of activities designed to meet the needs of both producer and consumer.

RED DEER RECREATION DEPARTMENT "CATCH THE LEISURE BUG" MARKETING CAMPAIGN

In an effort to promote diverse recreational activity in the community, the Recreation Department of the City of Red Deer, Alberta, solicited support from all local commercial recreation establishments, leisure-related retail stores and most community service agencies for an innovative marketing concept based on the theme "Catch the Leisure Bug." A project steering committee was formed and funds committed. The provincial government became a partner in the project and gave full rights to the use of its Leisure Bug character, logos, and themes. Because of the exceptional cooperation exhibited by the community for this project, the government also assigned a community recreation consultant to assist the city department. The Optimist Club added funds to hire a local part-time project coordinator.

After several weeks of advance publicity and advertising, the city newspaper distributed several thousand "Leisure Passports" to every home in the city. The passport contained several blank pages in five different sections. Each section represented a type of recreational activity (such as physically active, outdoor, cultural/ arts, social, and family oriented). Recipients were encouraged to carry their passports and present them to an identified leisure customs officer (staff member or volunteer) whenever they participated in an activity at any leisure service or leisure goods outlet in the city. The leisure customs officer would stamp the visa-like image of the Leisure Bug in the appropriate section of the passport. If, during the program period, the passport holder collected a designated number of stamps in all activity categories, a personalized Leisure Visa Card was issued. With the Leisure Visa Card, the individual could get special discounts at local sporting goods or department stores (on leisure/recreation items only), free admission to public swimming or skating on Friday evenings, and preferred parking at the games of the popular local Junior A hockey team. Other occasional privileges and discounts were added throughout the program.

The Leisure Passport initiative was evaluated and shown to have had a significant impact on the leisure activity of local residents for the short time since the program began and, hopefully, would improve lifestyles in the long term.

The program is an example of community cooperation and mutual support. Government, commercial, private, and nonprofit organizations worked together with one goal in mind—to make the project succeed. The Leisure Bug Passport Program was also an example of extensive marketing (especially promotion) and creative programming. It involved advertising, publicity, sales promotion, personal selling, and a great deal of very effective public relations. The special mix of promotional strategies and the effective use of media helped make the program a success.

Why doesn't the Red Deer Recreation Department run the Leisure Passport program any more? It simply ran its course, and it was time to set it aside. It did not fail; it is just time to use a different approach to motivate, excite, and help the members of the community to stay active and enjoy varied leisure experiences.

REFERENCES

Amusement Business (1999, July). Cost of going to amusement park decreases. *Sunday Herald Times*.

Bitterman, K. (2005, June). Getting results. *Aquatics International*, p. S-56.

Brayley, R. (1990). Psychographics. In M. Khan, M. Olsen, and T. Var, (Eds.), *The encyclopedia of hospitality and tourism*. New York: Van Nostrand Reinhold.

Cagle, R. (1992, January). Dealing with the irate customer. *Fitness Management*, p. 42.

Crompton, J., & Lamb, C., Jr. (1986). *Marketing government and social services*. New York: John Wiley & Sons.

Crotts, J. (1997). Marketing a commercial recreation and tourism enterprise. In J. Crossley, & L. Jamieson, *Introduction to commercial and entrepreneurial recreation* (revised ed.). Champaign, IL: Sagamore Publishing.

Fasching, D. (1992, July). Customer service: A company is known by the customer it keeps. *Resort and Commercial Recreation Association Journal*, p. 5.

Hawkins, D., Coney, K., & Best, R. (1980). *Consumer behavior: Implications for marketing strategy*. Dallas, TX: Business Publications, Inc.

Hurst, M. (1991, Summer). The importance of quality service in restaurants. *Arizona Hospitality Trends*, pp. 1, 11.

Kleppner, O. (1979). *Advertising procedures* (7th ed.). Englewood Cliffs: Prentice-Hall.

Marriott Hotels. (1990). *Front desk operations manual*. Unpublished document.

Moore, M. (2005, June). Back to basics. *Aquatics International*, p. S-4.

Chapter•••• 7

Operations Management

OVERVIEW OF MANAGEMENT

The operation of any commercial recreation or tourism enterprise is initially mapped out in a feasibility study or business plan that sets forth the components of the business concept. These components are used as an estimate of the long-term profitability of the enterprise and therefore compose an operational road map for business success. Indeed, if great care has been taken in the business planning process, the road map for operations is readily available to structure and refine the business as it is started and maintained over time. Entrepreneurs often fail to link the initial plan to the ongoing operation of the business due to shortsightedness or other reasons. Frank, Plaschka, and Roessl et al. (1989) alluded to this in a planning "behavior" study that points to the value of an effective business plan. The more successful ventures focused on key elements of the business plan and became more profitable than those who abandoned these elements and focused on secondary, less important elements. The importance of this is underscored in a *Fortune* article ("What Makes a Company Great?" 1998) that notes, "The Disney system pits strong division managers against a strategic planning unit that acts as a check on their power" (p. 29). The Disney philosophy has been successful over the years due to the valiant adherence to Disney values and consistent planning components. People know what to expect in a Disney operation, and if it is not successful, then customer service principles are employed to correct the mistake. One of the authors of this text shares this personal example: "We were seated in a Disneyland (Anaheim) restaurant. Some wait staff were rushing about, and one dropped a bowl of salsa. The trajectory of salsa was approximately 15 feet, and it spattered me on one side of my clothes and hair. *None of the wait staff initially noticed* what happened. We reported it immediately and were presented with a free meal, and they covered the cleaning bill for the clothing as well. We enjoyed the meal on the house."

The preceding example is shared to underscore the constant effort that is necessary to provide a positive visitor experience. It illustrates a commitment to a positive approach to operations management. In the hurried and dynamic environment of a commercial recreation or tourism business operation, managers command the most information and resources to deliver a positive leisure experience, and through the force of leadership, must give positive direction to the organization. The manager of a commercial recreation or tourism enterprise will demonstrate the following characteristics that will improve business success (Lancaster, 1999):

1. Managers will treat their employees well as "one main strategy."
2. Managers will adjust their enterprise to improve as the corporate standard dictates.
3. Managers will address as many full-service components as are feasible to accommodate customer needs.

4. Managers will watch pricing and rising operational fees as indicators that fewer clients will participate.
5. Managers will provide "inspiring leadership."
6. Managers will provide "knockout facilities" in terms of atmosphere and cleanliness.

In summary, "Managers will focus on customers, teamwork, fair treatment of employees, initiative, and innovation" ("What Makes a Company Great?" 1998). These characteristics may be considered essential in making a company great, and it is the intent of this chapter to focus on the factors of the fundamentals of success, facility operation, and risk management as key indicators of business success. Operations management, as defined in most commercial recreation and tourism enterprises, involves the day-to-day management of human resources, facilities and programs, supervision of frontline personnel (employees who interact with the public), and maintenance of positive customer service, which was covered in Chapter 6 as part of marketing. In this chapter we will also examine the role of technology needed to deliver service more efficiently and effectively. This chapter will present an overview of operations management as it directly applies to maximizing effectiveness and efficiency of the enterprise, and the chapter will cover select topics that are deserving of special attention in commercial recreation and tourism.

NEW FUNDAMENTALS OF SUCCESS

A business can be viewed through the hard, cold analysis of financial data. However, it can also be viewed in terms of how it treats its employees, customers, and other publics. This should be of great concern to any business entrepreneur. Taking a look at success factors, in general, may provide an important start in the study of a successful business operation.

Today's customers are increasingly sophisticated. They are exposed to more information than ever before, and they are the subjects of intense competition for their money. Now, most customers feel that value for the dollar is more important than finding the cheapest price. In this environment, commercial recreation and tourism businesses need guidelines for the future. The U.S. Chamber of Commerce (Pollan & Levine, 1992) has suggested a dozen "new fundamentals of small business success."

- **Plan for unexpected change**—Be willing to sacrifice some short-term efficiency to institute a company culture of change. Managers should make occasional changes, whether they are necessary or not, simply to get people used to the idea of change.
- **Focus on the process**—A business can use technological advances to cut expenses while keeping revenue steady. Getting smarter is often easier and cheaper than getting bigger.
- **Pursue equity financing**—Businesses should shift their financing emphasis from debt to equity sources. The debt levels of the past were excessive and dangerous.
- **Strive for uniqueness**—If you cannot differentiate your product or service from others, then why will customers buy from you? Since price discounting requires economies of scale that are beyond the means of most small businesses, a better strategy is to differentiate on the basis of better value, service, or unique features.
- **Concentrate on the core**—Companies need to realize what business they are really in and concentrate on that core business. Contract out or "outsource" ancillary or staff functions to specialty firms. For example, a small amusement park could outsource its legal services, park security, local transportation, landscaping, and some maintenance.
- **Think and act globally**—Thanks to technology and the globalization of the media, customers are influenced by international trends and fashions more often than most

managers realize. You need to know what is happening overseas, because tomorrow it could be happening next door.

- **Develop relationships with your customers**—Almost any company can copy your product or service, beat your price, or imitate your marketing. It is much more difficult to replace an emotional bond developed between a business and a satisfied customer.
- **Be fair and flexible with employees**—It is important to hold on to skilled workers once they have been found and trained. Employees want a variety of flexible choices in their workplace and their benefits.
- **Address expanded constituencies**—A business's constituents include its owners, employees, customers, suppliers, and the community. All these constituencies need to be taken seriously, and companies need to respond to their concerns.
- **Address and use environmental concerns**—It can be difficult to afford compliance with environmental regulations, even though we may agree that the regulations are worthwhile. However, when environmental obstacles are dealt with successfully, they present an exceptional publicity and marketing opportunity.
- **Establish and maintain solid business partnerships**—In an age of networking, contracting, cooperative marketing, and long-distance suppliers, it is essential to have reliable business partnerships. There should be mutual commitment to basic objectives, values, and ways of doing business.

A FEW WORDS ABOUT BUSINESS ETHICS

Before endeavoring to address specific topics regarding the operations of an enterprise, it is important to establish a basic sense of business ethics. The development of a sound business ethical environment has been increasingly the focus of many concerned entrepreneurs as well as investors and the public at large. Recent scandals involving Enron, WorldCom, and other corporations have caused thousands of employees, investors, and creditors to lose billions of dollars. Although the perpetrators temporarily made millions though their unethical and illegal acts, they were eventually caught and jailed, but meanwhile their companies were ruined. By addressing business ethics and operating honestly, not only may entrepreneurs improve the profit margin, but also they may be viewed more positively by employees, customers, and an increasingly sophisticated public.

In any business and/or governmental operation, ethics plays an important role in managerial success. Each day, the media reports another case of "white collar" crime associated with breaches of honesty and integrity in business. Further, the degree to which surveillance technology has been developed to identify employee theft and other issues shows the pervasiveness of the level of dishonesty that prevails in even the smallest business operation. In pursuit of profit, some entrepreneurs find themselves in a position to circumvent what is right, rather than take the honest, more difficult route. However, in the long-term perspective, honest and ethical operations will pay off, as employees, customers, suppliers, and the community will develop a trusting relationship that they will want to continue. Below are some ethical principles that should be fundamental to every business (adapted from Pegg, 2005).

1. Strive to create sustainable long-term prosperity, not just short-term profit, and share that prosperity with everyone in the organization (owners, managers, and employees), and with the community through appropriate service projects and charity.
2. Sustain the environment in which your company operates. This includes the physical and natural environment, plus the community's social and cultural environment.
3. Practice equity and justice in operations. This includes hiring practices, contract negotiations, delivery of promised services, paying of bills on time, and so forth.

4. Practice accountability and disclosure in financial operations by following accepted accounting and tax liability practices and appropriately disclosing information to employees, stockholders, and the public.
5. Respect people and other businesses and organizations. This includes fairness and good faith in all transactions, being honest and sincere at all times, and dealing fairly with complaints.

HUMAN RESOURCES MANAGEMENT

Most commercial recreation and tourism businesses involve more than one employee. Therefore, the manager must devote time to human resources management. According to traditional management theory, the work of the organization would be divided into various tasks and specialties, procedures would be written for the "best way" to do each task, and people would be hired and trained to perform each task/slot of the formal organization chart. Communication would flow down from the top, and workers would perform rather mechanically to achieve the previously agreed goals of the organization.

We now know that the traditional theories of management did not account for the worker's individuality. In reality, human resources management is possibly the most difficult area of management. Service industries such as recreation and tourism are very labor intensive, and employees should not be treated too simplistically, according to traditional management theory. It is important to recognize that each employee is an individual with his or her own needs, goals, abilities, and weaknesses.

The success of most recreation and tourism businesses depends on the interaction of their personnel with the public. Customers will judge the enterprise on the friendliness, alertness, and performance of its staff. A good manager can make a difference in this area by influencing the attitude and behavior of employees. This section will examine several key aspects of human resources management in commercial recreation and tourism settings.

Creating Culture and Climate

An operations framework must include a positive environment for customers and employees. This climate takes into account the organizational culture, comprising common goals, diversity, and personality. The manager creates a positive climate by investing in employees who in turn deliver a positive impression to customers. According to Herb Kelleher, CEO for Southwest Airlines, one strategy exists to "treat employees well" (Lancaster, 1999, p. D1). In an interview regarding the tight-knit family culture, Herb indicates:

> I've tried to create a culture of caring for people in the totality of their lives, not just at work. There's no magic formula. It's like building a giant mosaic—it takes thousands of little pieces.

Further, in creating a positive organizational culture, great managers do the following, according to Robinson (1999):

- Select for talent.
- Don't micromanage.
- Allow employees to navigate their own course.
- Help employees find roles that allow them to best express what they are.

In fact, according to *Fortune* magazine, the corporate culture was the most significant factor in gauging what makes a good company great ("What Makes a Company

Great?," 1998). It is further suggested that a happy employee can contribute to improving profitability, although that is not always the case. In any instance, an improved work environment cannot help but positively reflect on a business enterprise, especially one concerned with providing leisure satisfaction either directly or indirectly.

Hiring, Training, and Compensating Staff

Successful sports coaches know that game strategy is not the only key to winning championships. The keys to winning begin with recruiting talent and developing that talent into the best players they can be. Similarly, any business that finds talented people with good attitudes and develops their potential should be a winner. This is easy to say but so difficult to do! Even in times of economic prosperity and high employment rates, companies are finding it more difficult to hire, train, and retain quality employees. Labor shortages increase the likelihood that employees are hired with fewer qualifications, and businesses have to rely on improved methods of recruitment, retention, and compensation packages. The hotel/motel, attraction, and local commercial recreation enterprise segments are frequently affected by employee shortages, as are seasonal operations that compete for the same employees. It is therefore highly important to employ sophisticated strategies to hire, train, and retain employees rather than have high employee turnover rates.

Rather than wait for talent to come to us, we can go out and find it. Recruiting trips to high schools, trade schools, colleges, and professional conferences can generate a large number of interviews where the best candidates can be screened for further consideration. Some employers do not give much consideration to academic grades, but this could be an error. Good grades are earned through intelligence, aptitude, effort, the ability to get along with "the system," or a combination of these characteristics. In virtually any job, these characteristics are an asset.

It is, of course, standard procedure to examine work experience, references, professional/trade affiliations, and certifications when assessing a prospective employee. But what about a person's attitude and personality? References may or may not yield accurate information. Elaborate tests are available but are too expensive for many commercial recreation and tourism businesses.

In *Management Strategy* ("The Ten Commandments of Hiring," 1998), it was noted that there are 10 commandments for hiring employees for golf shop operations. These "commandments" may also be well worthwhile in many other operations, especially those with the need for positive face-to-face customer service:

- Make the time commitment to do this process right.
- Familiarize yourself with the legal implications.
- Get a clear fix on the job.
- Be realistic in your expectations for the job.
- Choose your recruiting sources carefully.
- Monitor your screening procedures.
- Become a better interviewer.
- Do the reference checking yourself.
- Do your best to be objective.
- Don't delay the decision.

Hiring. Occasionally, a person with "superstar" potential will apply for employment when no positions are open at the time. If you do not hire this person, he or she will leave and find employment elsewhere, possibly with a competitor. If, however, there are a number of part-time personnel in your labor force, their schedules can be adjusted and space found for the superstar. Later, this person can be worked in to a regular position. The bottom line is: Find a way to hire the superstars when they walk in.

Orientation and Training. Employee orientation programs should be based upon written job descriptions, company policies, and operating procedures. It is important that the employee understand the overall mission of the organization and how his or her position is important to the success of the organization. Specific orientation topics should include the history and philosophy of the organization; details regarding the specific job responsibilities, equipment used, and employee benefits; and key operational policies regarding emergencies, rain days, guest relations, and so on.

Training of employees can be accomplished through a combination of written materials, workbooks, audiovisual media, and personal instruction by staff. One popular method of personal instruction, especially for part-time and seasonal employees, is called "shadowing." The new employee basically follows around, or "shadows," an experienced employee and learns the job through firsthand observation and trial.

It is a good idea for the manager to have some part in the training process of all employees. This allows some rapport to be established between management and new employees at the very start. It is also an opportunity for the new employee to be exposed to the service philosophy, energy, and drive of the manager.

Employees need to be taught the importance of generating repeat business. They need to understand that the satisfied customer is always the backbone of any organization's success. For example, in order to respond to common customer problems and situations, some theme parks develop standard responses for employees to use in given situations. Employees may be encouraged to take part in "scripting sessions" where these responses are created.

Compensation. Fair compensation is generally determined by three factors: federal regulations, market conditions, and company philosophy. The Fair Labor Standards Act requires that employees be paid at least the minimum wage for the first 40 hours of work per week. For employees other than management professionals, time-and-a-half wages must be paid for work over 40 hours. There are exceptions for some small businesses, for public agencies, seasonal businesses, and certain jobs that pay tips and/or employee lodging. Consideration may also be given to the provision of a bonus, profit sharing, or company stock when the company has a great year. "Employees are investing in an enterprise and should yield a positive return on the investment" (Stewart, 1998, p.169).

Competition for skilled labor will help determine prevailing local wage rates. Further, some companies may desire to take a leadership role in offering higher wages in order to attract the best employees.

Another consideration related to employee compensation is the provision of employee benefits, which may include the following:

Health care programs	Insurance programs
Employee discounts	Retirement fund contributions
Child care	Employee recreation programs
Employee fitness programs	Travel discounts
Sick leave	Educational reimbursements
Vacation leave	Uniform reimbursements
Sales commission	Professional expenses
Maternity leave	Employee housing and meals

Retention. Today, it is not enough to hire and train employees. A commercial recreation and tourism enterprise has to focus on the retention of personnel. In this competitive job market, the benefits beyond the monetary gain may keep employees loyal to the organization. For example, in a study about the reasons that employees love their companies, Lieber (1998, pp. 72–73) notes that employees' comments include:

- *Everyone, from the highest executive to the maintenance staff, lives the corporate philosophy.*
- *People are dying to work here, and I like being at a company that is sought out like that.*
- *I'm absolutely tied to my benefits here, and I also feel that what I'm doing is good in some larger sense.*
- *This is a company that understands that positive emotions are good for the soul.*

Retention is very challenging in commercial recreation and tourism. For example, in mountain resort towns, the "equity gap" refers to the prevalence of millionaires and billionaires and the difficulty in keeping workers. The inability to live in these environments causes turnover, the need for constant training, and cultural clashes (Rademan, 2003).

Staff Supervision and Motivation

There are many theories regarding employee management and motivation. Textbooks in management and in parks and recreation administration typically examine Maslow's hierarchy of needs, Herzberg's motivation/hygiene theory, and other theories. Rather than duplicate such content, this section will present a variety of specific suggestions regarding employee supervision, motivation, morale, and incentives:

- Learn employees' names and treat them as individuals.
- Do not be afraid to do an employee a favor.
- Remember that employees live up or down to expectations.
- Recognize that employee needs and goals exist outside the workplace, and, if possible, help them achieve these goals as well as work-related goals.
- Eliminate dull jobs, or combine them with good jobs and learning experiences.
- Do not be afraid of high employee turnover if the people are moving up to better jobs, even outside the organization.
- Develop career paths within the organization.
- Provide opportunities for recognition, praise, achievement, responsibility, and social prestige.
- Show employees that their welfare is closely related to the success of the organization.
- Give employees a true opportunity to contribute to the decisions within the organization.
- In a small organization, let key employees take major responsibilities and grow with the job. Then when the company grows, you have the base for a management team, rather than having to import new managers.
- Be more flexible in offering options such as flex-time, job sharing, and part-time scheduling.
- Offer a smorgasbord of choices for employee benefits, including child care and varieties of health care coverage.
- Implement training and development programs targeted at career mobility.

Part-Time and Seasonal Labor

Almost every commercial recreation and tourism business uses numerous part-time and/or seasonal personnel. There are good reasons for this. Many businesses are seasonal in nature, and it is impractical to hire many year-round employees. There is flexibility in using part-time and seasonal employees whose hours can be increased or decreased as operating conditions warrant. In addition, wages and benefits typically cost less if the work can be performed by less-experienced employees.

The use of part-time and seasonal employees presents several distinct problems for the commercial recreation and tourism manager. Do the school vacation schedules coincide with the business's peak seasons and labor needs? Are there enough employees in the local community, or does a labor force have to be imported? Do the employees have the maturity, skills, and experience to do an adequate job? Will they burn out by season's end and/or quit early? Many resorts, theme parks, and summer camps face labor shortages in late August and early September when summer employees quit to take time off before returning to school.

There are a number of strategies to help combat these problems:

- Have a higher pay level for returning employees who completed their full season the previous year.
- Have a bonus for employees who complete the full season.
- Hire extra employees to start the season so you have the flexibility to fire those who don't perform up to standards.
- Provide a thorough orientation and training program.
- Utilize supervisors who understand and can communicate with the part-time and seasonal employees.
- Diversify the jobs so that the boredom factor is reduced.
- Provide employee housing if labor must be imported from outside the local community.
- Provide employee transportation if labor must be imported from adjacent communities.
- Provide recreation programs for employees in their off-duty hours.
- Plan on "creative scheduling" late in the season when labor is short. Use supervisors, and give overtime pay to the best employees remaining.

Unions

In some commercial recreation and tourism industries, part of the labor force may be unionized. Managers should be aware of unfair labor practices that are contrary to the National Labor Relations Act. Under this law, employers cannot interfere with, restrain, or coerce employees in the exercise of their rights as union members or induce employees to resist unions by offering higher pay, more benefits, or a better job. Neither can an employer allow union membership to influence any personnel decisions including hiring, promotions, and firings. The employer must bargain in good faith with representatives of the employees and provide the union with information it needs to bargain intelligently.

Summary of Human Resources Management

In summary, the factors associated with human resources management are key to any business operation; however, it is even more crucial in a leisure service operation to have employees who are happy and well compensated. A positive leisure experience is most important to ensure repeat business, a positive image, and continued success of the business operation. The recruitment, hiring, training, and retaining of employees are the first steps to ensure continuous customer satisfaction with the leisure product being delivered.

FACILITY MANAGEMENT

Many commercial recreation and tourism enterprises have facilities that are worth hundreds of thousands if not millions of dollars. This is particularly true of resort hotels, theme parks, sports clubs, campgrounds, golf and country clubs, and other businesses where the facility is part of the recreational experience. The management of these facilities should therefore be a high priority. This section will examine various aspects of facility management, including maintenance, operations, and security, that are of special interest and/or importance in commercial recreation and tourism.

Overview of Facility Management

The details involved in managing a first-class facility are staggering. It is imperative that the commercial recreation and tourism manager take into account the many details associated with such management. For example, the University of Texas at Austin facility usage guidelines cover a variety of policies that address rules and regulations designed to provide equal access and protection to the participants. Each policy represents a part of a total system of management and involves rules on the following topics:

ID cards	Conduct	Entrance/exit
Food and drink	Smoking	Alcohol/drugs
Bicycles	Pets	Attire
Stereos	Facility closures	Posted rules
Personal belongings	Children	Informal recreation
Organized activities		

Sales floor layout, lighting, cleanliness, and attractive display of merchandise are characteristics for successful retail operations. (Photo: J. Crossley)

What makes a facility superior, adequate, or inadequate? It basically boils down to two elements (assuming the location is good): facility design and facility maintenance/management. Some guidelines in this area include the following:

- The facility should be of sufficient size for the people who are expected to attend, and it should have room for expansion. It is probably less expensive to add on than to relocate.
- The facility should be designed to serve the needs of the programs and services that will be offered. Too often we see facilities shortchanged in storage areas, dressing rooms, sound systems, buffer zones, and so forth.
- The facility should be designed to be flexible. Mobile staging, room dividers, and changeable floor surfaces can increase flexibility.
- The facility should be designed for safety, ease of maintenance, and resistance to vandalism. This includes provision of fire escapes; sprinkler system; durable furnishings and equipment; choice of floors and floor coverings; types of paint; and access to electrical, plumbing, and other utility systems.
- Facilities should provide the aesthetics and amenities that the participants want. This includes attractive lounges, furnishings, color, decor, adequate parking, areas for food and beverage, spectator viewing facilities, and locker rooms.
- Facilities must be maintained in a safe and attractive manner. Participants value safety and cleanliness above most other aspects of their recreational experience.

Facility Maintenance

The ultimate objective of maintenance is to provide a facility that is as close to original condition as possible. This, of course, is difficult to achieve due to normal wear and tear, participant traffic, and environmental conditions. Realistically then, the objectives should be to do the following:

- Provide safe, clean, and attractive facilities.
- Minimize "downtime" (unplanned shutdowns) of equipment and facilities by preventive maintenance.
- Minimize normal deterioration of facilities.
- Renovate, replace, or rejuvenate facilities before conditions deteriorate.

The importance of good facility maintenance must not be underestimated. Customers will take their business elsewhere if they perceive facilities to be unsafe or unclean compared to competitors. Industry leaders such as Disney have recognized this and made maintenance a keystone of their philosophy.

Unfortunately, some commercial recreation and tourism managers and a large number of college students underestimate the sophistication of modern maintenance. Good maintenance today requires employees who can operate sophisticated equipment, become certified in handling certain chemicals, understand basic landscaping, have fundamental skills in the "trades" (painting, carpentry, plumbing, etc.), be able to supervise seasonal employees, and be competent in public relations.

Due to the importance of safety and public relations, several aspects of maintenance deserve special attention in the commercial recreation setting. These practical ideas include the following:

- Schedule maintenance tasks during off-peak or closed hours so as to minimize conflicts with participants.
- Routine maintenance tasks conducted during operating hours should be performed by staff who have public relations training.
- Preventive maintenance should be the number one priority, especially for equipment that participants come in contact with, such as amusement park rides, ski lifts, and elevators.

- Maintenance supervisors may not necessarily be the best technically skilled employees. Rather, they should have an adequate general background in most maintenance areas and be skilled supervisors of employees, including numerous seasonal employees.

- Special care must be taken when closing a facility for the off-season. The objective is to protect the facility and make it easy to open again next season. Interiors should be put in order and cleaned, inventory taken, water pipes bled dry, windows and doors secured, and so on.

Operating Procedures

Every commercial recreation or tourism facility needs a complete set of operating procedures. These procedures could be organized according to physical area (front desk area, retail area, food stands, rides and attractions, etc.), by functional responsibility (cash register operations, food handling, opening and closing, etc.), or a combination of the two. Figure 7-1 illustrates the opening procedures for the ticket office/guest relations division of an amusement park.

Operating procedures should be written and in some cases illustrated by diagrams or photos. During training sessions, employees should be provided with copies of all procedures that are relevant to their particular jobs. The employees may be tested on their knowledge of the procedures and/or be required to acknowledge their understanding of the procedures by signing the procedure sheet. It is advisable to have regular and periodic reviews of all procedures. The input of seasoned employees should be solicited for these reviews, and the employees should also have input on any changes that are made.

Figure 7-1
Amusement Park Ticket Office/Guest Relations Office Opening Procedures

1.	Sign in at operations office.
2.	Turn on lights in guest relations office and ticket booths.
3.	Take out and raise flags.
4.	Sweep carpet corners.
5.	Vacuum floors and stairs.
6.	Set up toll turnstiles.
7.	Check daily sales projection to see how many tickets will be needed.
8.	Check out change drawers and tickets from controllers.
9.	Set up I.D. camera and laminating machine.
10.	Record items from previous day's lost and found.
11.	Log ticket numbers.
12.	Clean ticket booth windows inside and out.
13.	Clean tape player heads.
14.	Turn on background music to proper level.
15.	Check cashiers into ticket booths.
16.	Open front gate.

Security

The commercial recreation and tourism manager must recognize the importance of security. Substantial losses and lawsuits can occur if there are problems with guest safety, guest security, and/or security of financial operations. General areas of concern include crowd control and safety, hours of operation, emergency procedures, and facility security.

Each topic may warrant extensive written procedures and training of employees. Professional consultants are available to help develop security procedures and to provide security service on a contractual basis.

Crowd Control Procedures are essential at amusement parks, sports events, concerts, or any other event that draws a large number of people. Some specific suggestions for crowd control include the following:

- Know your facility and its capacity, blind spots, traffic bottlenecks, emergency exits, and so on.
- Have special entrances for preformed groups.
- Be ready to accommodate groups with special needs such as preschoolers, people with disabilities, older persons, international visitors, and so forth.
- Keep track of sales and admissions to avoid overselling/overcrowding the facility.
- If sold out, station staff out front to tell people.
- Have special parking areas for buses.
- Channel vehicle traffic in one direction.
- Have uniformed attendants in the parking lots at all times.
- Be prepared for emergencies and disasters by anticipating problems and planning responses to them.
- Use "peer group" security staff, not police in uniform, to monitor crowds.
- Have security staff trained in nonconfrontational public relations.
- Resort to police intervention only when a situation is beyond the control of the security staff.
- Check all areas after closing, including every corner and every restroom stall.

Hours of Operation. Determining the hours of operation and the related staff scheduling requirements are the direct result of the elements present in the feasibility study or business plan. Within this plan, projections of customer demand help determine how the overall business should function in periods of peak demand, normal operations, and slack demand. This serves as a basis for establishing hours of operation that reflect the market intended for the business. From there, shifts may be scheduled to fulfill staffing needs to adequately handle the influx of clients. At peak periods, additional staff is needed, not only for customer service, but also for safety and security. In slack periods, little-used areas may attract illicit behaviors from customers, so security staff must continue to monitor these areas or shut the areas down.

Emergency Procedures should be developed for all possible problem scenarios and rehearsed on a periodic basis. In some cases, proper preparation may require a large expense. A major stadium concert, for example, may require a staff of 100 EMTs, nurses, and doctors, plus a couple of ambulances on duty. Some cities have volunteer organizations to assist in these functions. Specific emergency procedures should be developed for fire, serious illness or injury to a guest, disappearance of a guest, power failure, severe weather, natural disaster, vandalism, bomb threats, and terrorist activities. Procedures for all of these should be coordinated with appropriate authorities such as police, hospitals, fire departments, and civil defense. Procedures should be practiced by employees periodically.

Facility Security has benefited from a number of technical innovations in the last 20 years. Communication between staff has been greatly improved by the use of cell phones and pagers. Closed-circuit TVs can be used to monitor entrances, hallways, money vaults, ticket booths, or any other important area. Microwave and infrared intrusion-sensing systems provide "night eyes" to guard against trespassers. Photo ID cards help identify staff and can be used for season pass holders. In many situations, however, employees stationed in key areas are the best way to accomplish facility security. It is also a good idea to keep facilities attractive and well maintained. Such facilities are more likely to be appreciated and are less likely to be abused. Night lighting also may reduce trespassing and vandalism. If facilities or equipment are vandalized, they should be repaired immediately.

What if the Facility Has a Long Way to Go?

Even with all the procedural requirements for ensuring operational management success, it is possible that problems will still arise. In looking at ways to evaluate and improve the operation, note the five principles for a turnaround (Bethune & Huler, 1998):

- Two rules for managers: Get your job done, and work together.
- Tell employees what's going on, fully and honestly.
- Remember that customers want dependability and predictability.
- If you're the top manager, every problem is your problem.
- It's a lot harder to keep things going great than to get them going great in the first place.

Another way to become a successful facility is to assess the "fun factor" that is provided to guests and add technological innovations where appropriate. For example, Wild River Country in North Little Rock, Arkansas, added a new ride called the Vortex. It was an enclosed, dark ride, and customer excitement picked up significantly. As a result, the new season was highly profitable (Berger, 2000).

On the other hand, visitors will often be the best judges of promising enterprises. A tour of the silver mines underneath the ski mountain in Park City, Utah, was closed due to low visitation. The main problem was identified as the difficulty of getting people away from skiing. A solution might have been to operate it only during the off-season and market it to summer tourists who are looking for a truly cool pursuit.

Often, a profitable business may improve due to the ability of that business to carve out a niche of extended services. For example, the Downtown Atlanta Ritz Carlton provides room service to solve computer glitches suffered by its many business guests. By offering this service, business travelers can count on technical support while away from the office and improve their own profit margins while working remotely (Templin, 1999).

Facility Arrangements for Meetings

Meeting rooms and meeting-related services are frequently requested at commercial recreation and tourism facilities. This includes the obvious need for meeting rooms and services at hotels, but also at restaurants, theme/amusement parks, sports and fitness centers, bowling lanes, movie theaters, cruise ships, camps, and many other types of facilities. The meetings may be directly related to the primary purpose of the facility (nutrition workshop at a fitness club), or not related at all (scuba club meeting held in the back room of a restaurant).

Some of the facility arrangements to be considered are listed in Figure 7-2.

RISK MANAGEMENT

A commercial recreation and tourism enterprise must provide a process for assuring that risks are avoided and, if they cannot be avoided, they must be addressed properly. Even in the most carefully monitored operations, harm or injury may occasionally come to a customer or employee. Therefore, a sound risk management plan must be in place.

There is evidence that the liability and insurance crisis that plagues the country has at last moderated a little. After receiving tens of thousands of formal complaints, numerous states have passed legislation adopting legal reform in varying degrees: by putting

Figure 7-2
Check list of Facility Arrangements for Meetings

___ Cleanliness
___ Ventilation
___ Acoustics
___ Lighting and controls
___ Lectern with light
___ Water pitchers and glasses
___ Floral arrangements and plants
___ Banners, balloons, and the like
___ Flags (national flag on audience left)
___ Food arrangements
___ Registration area
___ Adequate parking
___ Data projection equipment
___ Head table
___ Emergency exits

___ Checkroom operation
___ Seating plan (for group type and size)
___ Room temperature (start cool, people warm rooms)
___ Visual obstructions
___ Accessibility for persons with disabilities
___ Decorations
___ Restroom accessibility
___ Proximity to kitchen
___ Microphones
___ Table covers
___ Blackboard, white board, projection screen
___ Overhead, video, and slide projectors
___ Name cards for head table
___ Pre-meeting control of area
___ Directional signs to meeting

Source: "M & C Checklist," 1994).

---

limits on awards, by creating stricter definitions of "pain and suffering," by limiting "joint and several liability" damages (wherein a wealthy "deep pockets" company pays the majority of a liability claim even though they were found to be less at fault than another defendant in the case), by imposing penalties for filing frivolous suits, and by setting limits on contingency fees. A number of states have also adopted a new legal ethics code, endorsed by the American Bar Association.

The main goal in risk management is loss prevention. In addition to the cost of implementing a sound risk management program, provision must be made for the business to survive the costs associated with legal claims. These include tort and contractual claims as well as other aspects of business risk. Therefore, risk management involves providing for the identification and analysis of risks and the implementation of risk strategies. Each step of the process is subsequently described.

Identify All Risks

This can be accomplished by analysis of past accident records, through facility and program inspection, and by staff input. It is very likely that experienced staff have better ability to foresee potential dangers than inexperienced staff do. However, it is also possible that some experienced staff may have become complacent and are blind to risks that might be more obvious to a new employee with a fresh perspective. Therefore, it is suggested that all employees, regardless of experience, can contribute to the identification of potential risks. Also, risk management specialists from professional associations and from insurance companies can provide this service.

Analyze Every Risk

Analyze and classify every risk according to the Risk Management Strategy Grid presented in Figure 7-3. Each risk is classified according to its expected frequency of occurrence and severity of injury when it does occur. It is important to note that some

Figure 7-3
Risk Management Strategy Grid

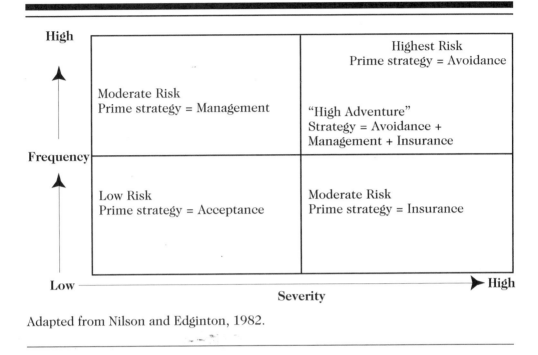

Adapted from Nilson and Edginton, 1982.

organizations will be very conservative at this step because of their service philosophy, their past history, and their insurance rates. Using the grid and other methods of analysis, the company may design a plan that addresses all risk factors associated with operating the business. This involves developing strategies that best mitigate or eliminate risk in a typical commercial recreation or tourism operation.

Implement Risk Strategies

According to frequency and severity, different action is suggested by the Risk Management Strategy Grid. Each quadrant is discussed below.

Low Risk: Acceptance. Certain accidents happen infrequently and with minor injury. For example, a participant might cut a finger on a piece of paper in an arts and crafts class. Such injuries are very difficult to anticipate or prevent. Many organizations and their participants accept these minor risks as a natural part of engaging in the activity. Typically, the cost of any such accident falls below the deductible limits of the organization's insurance policy. Therefore, if there is any expense involved, it is picked up directly by the organization or by the participant.

Moderate Risk: Insurance. On rare occasions, there are accidents with very major injury and/or property loss. Usually their occurrences are also very difficult to anticipate or prevent. An example would be a hotel fire caused by an angered guest. In such instances, adequate insurance coverage is the best remedy. Although rates are very high, insurance purchased through major carriers is the most common approach. Some organizations join together with peer organizations and contribute to cooperative insurance pools to collectively insure themselves.

Moderate Risk: Management. There are many recreation activities in which minor injuries are relatively common: slips on the deck of a water theme park, sprained ankles and broken bones in sports competition, and so on. While insurance is advised to back up the organization in these instances, the best strategy is to manage the activity better. As related to the accidents mentioned above, this means training lifeguards to prevent running at the water theme park and providing safety-conscious supervisors for sports competition. A number of other risk management guidelines are presented in Figure 7-4.

Highest Risk: Avoidance. There are some recreational activities that have relatively frequent accidents with rather severe consequences. Examples include competitive boxing, mountain climbing, and hang gliding. Some conservative managers also put rugby, tackle football, skydiving, backcountry skiing, scuba diving, and other popular activities into the highest-risk category. The best strategy for highest-risk activities is to avoid offering them to the public. However, some types of businesses specialize in these activities: helicopter ski tours, wilderness challenge schools, Amazon jungle tours, and others. These providers of high-risk/high-adventure recreation must combine the strategies of management, insurance, and avoidance. For example, the skydiving service operator must be well insured, be extremely professional in all aspects of the operation, and avoid going up during bad weather conditions.

Figure 7-4
Risk Management Guidelines

General Guidelines
1. Have clear objectives.
2. Corporate charter, bylaws, etc., must be up-to-date with all legal regulations.
3. Review the security of office files and safe.
4. Have all contracts in writing.
5. Do not advertise facilities, equipment, or programs you cannot provide at an appropriately high level of quality.
6. Have a public information officer to be the spokesperson regarding any accidents.
7. Develop safety policies and procedures.
8. Practice the emergency procedures.
9. Conduct analysis of all accidents.
10. Provide notice and/or post signs regarding any hazards or damages involving facilities, equipment, or programs.
11. Adhere to advertised time schedules for facilities and programs.
12. Provide transportation of participants only by insured, qualified operators with a chauffeur's license, and use appropriate, insured vehicles.

Personnel Guidelines (for employees and volunteers)
1. Carefully screen all applicants.
2. Provide appropriate orientation and training.
3. Be sure staff have appropriate licenses, certificates, or other requirements for the work.
4. Monitor job performances.
5. Do not go beyond the scope of the job.
6. Provide emergency training to all staff.
7. Staff should not make statements regarding accidents.
8. Never tell participants not to seek medical attention.
9. Keep supervisors informed of any problem.
10. Staff must stay active in the profession and up-to-date in competency areas.

(continued)

Figure 7-4 (continued)
Risk Management Guidelines

Facility and Equipment Guidelines
1. Facilities should comply with all design standards.
2. Use only approved equipment that meets all appropriate industry standards.
3. Avoid using unsafe and/or damaged equipment.
4. Have proper security systems, especially smoke detectors, fire alarms, and sprinklers.
5. Provide security and lighting for parking area.
6. Inspect facilities and equipment regularly.
7. Perform preventive maintenance in accordance with standards.
8. Repair damaged facilities/equipment immediately, or remove them from service.
9. Train employees regarding proper use of all equipment.
10. Do not allow the use of hazardous facilities and equipment (guns, horses, chainsaws, boats, etc.) by employees unless they have proper training.
11. Know facility capacities and avoid overcrowding.
12. Have appropriate emergency equipment available.
13. Post emergency numbers next to telephones.

Program Guidelines
1. Be sure that leaders have proper qualifications.
2. Design programs for safety—use buddy system, rest periods, and so on.
3. Instruct participants in safety practices.
4. Keep activities within the ability of participants.
5. Adhere to proper ratios of staff to participants.
6. Comply with recognized program standards, procedures, rules, and so forth.
7. Instruct participants in program skills prior to their participation.
8. Know the health status of participants when appropriate to activity.
9. Have consent forms and release forms for participants.
10. Monitor activities, including warm-ups.
11. Strive to match competitors and provide balanced team competition.
12. Place participants in appropriate age group, ability level, or weight class in competitive activities.
13. Provide equipment and clothing lists for trip participants.

Special Guidelines for Release Forms
1. Realize that release forms do not absolve you from all liability.
2. Explain all potential hazards and risks.
3. Explain participation procedures, rules, and so on.
4. Explain participation in the activity as voluntary.
5. Urge participants to purchase insurance.
6. Be sure participants are aware that they cannot collect damages if they sign "consent" or liability release forms. (Note: this may not hold up in court.)
7. Have information in conspicuous print so that participants have fair notice of what they are signing.

Overall Risk Management Guidelines

Liability claims against commercial recreation and tourism businesses generally fall into the following categories:

- **Equipment.** Faulty equipment can cause injury and increase liability.
- **Personnel.** Acts of omission or commission by personnel, including suppliers, contractual employees, service personnel, and day-to-day staff, can develop into lawsuits that claim harm to the customer.
- **Policy and procedure.** Failure to have safe policies and procedures, and/or failure to carry them out may increase the risk of injury or other problems.
- **Design.** Errors in facility and program design may cause constant problems that result in claims.

All of these factors need to be addressed to adequately plan for the reality of lawsuits and other claims. How does a business develop an ongoing strategy for managing risk? The following are ways to continually assess an operation so that risk factors are constantly at the forefront:

- Designate an in-house safety team to conduct regular walk-throughs, inspect and log equipment, develop maintenance procedures, and conduct training programs.
- Assign a "high-risk" team to be responsible for program safety, responsible marketing, facility use restrictions, and the posting of disclaimers.
- Assign a crisis team to implement all emergency procedures and document all details. These can include emergency drills. Documentation includes every detail: time, place, weather conditions, indoor conditions, witnesses, and other pertinent information.
- Assign a dispute avoidance team to work with injured parties and expedite settlement.

These strategies can serve to mitigate, but not totally avoid all risk in an operation. The main factor to note is that risk cannot be totally eliminated and to try to do so is too costly. However, liability can be greatly reduced and accommodated if there is a sound plan in operation. What is possible is the reduction of risk, and the aforementioned process helps that to occur.

Some businesses assign the roles mentioned above to a single "safety manager." However, a single individual cannot address all the variables associated with risk reduction in a dynamic leisure service operation. In fact, all employees have a stake in contributing to the avoidance of injury and other claims. The greater the number of employees serving on a "team," the greater the "buy-in" to providing an increasingly safe and risk-reduced operation.

INFORMATION TECHNOLOGY

Access to the World Wide Web can provide important linkages to marketing, financing, and customers. An increasing number of commercial recreation and tourism enterprises are becoming linked to various information technology innovations to ensure that customers receive updated marketing information about their services, assess leisure opportunities and plan for them on their own, and book reservations or purchase products online.

In addition, many office and operational functions have become computerized, and sophisticated software packages can link initial inquiries of potential customers with full service management. The following packages enable the businesses to thrive in an increasingly automated environment.

- **Accounting and financial functions**—payroll, accounts payable, accounts receivable, general ledger, financial statements, ratio analysis, break-even analysis, sales and cash flow forecasts, budgeting, material and labor forecasts, profit-sharing tabulations.
- **Sales and inventory functions**—cash register sales, inventory tracking and control, inventory valuation, automatic inventory ordering, and status tracking of ordered merchandise.
- **Marketing functions**—mailing lists, production of flyers, target market profiles, market analysis and demand forecasts, ticket printing, ticket/seating inventory, reservations, storage and access of press releases and advertising copy, Web site display of information, and interactive content with online customers.
- **Program management**—program registration, team roster maintenance, league and tournament scheduling, membership list maintenance, tour scheduling, class and facility scheduling, progress reports for individual fitness/skill programs.
- **Graphic programs**—headlines, clip art, original art, bar graphs, line graphs, pie charts, color features, shading.
- **Personnel administration functions**—employee records, benefit calculation, absence and leave records, accidents, insurance claims, keys and property checkout records, employee orientation material, employee training programs.
- **Environmental management**—programs to control heating, cooling, lights, irrigation, pool chemicals, and facility special effects.
- **Maintenance management**—including inspection records, preventive maintenance records, preventive maintenance requirements, work-order tracking and tabulation, material and labor forecasts, project scheduling, project progress reports.
- **E-marketing/sales**—Programs designed to connect directly with customers.

SUMMARY

Successful operations management relies heavily upon sound administrative practices in the areas of human resources, facilities, risk management, and information technology Human resources management takes into account the hiring, training, and compensation of staff, the development of staff morale, the handling of part-time and seasonal labor, and interaction with unions. Facility management deals with maintenance, development of sound operating procedures, security, safety, and accident prevention.

Every commercial recreation and tourism enterprise can benefit from a comprehensive risk management program that includes insurance, preventive management, and, if necessary, avoidance of certain activities. Finally, information technology can help any company manage its operations more efficiently, especially in the area of accounting, sales and inventory, marketing, communications, and maintenance.

SPOTLIGHT ON:

SUNSCAPE PUERTO AVENTURAS

All-inclusive resorts are becoming more and more prevalent as tourists seek a hassle-free vacation. One example of an all-inclusive resort is Sunscape Puerto Aventuras located near Cancun, Mexico. From the moment that a plane takes off from any part of the world till the visitor returns home, the vacation has been pre-paid, and nearly all amenities are part of the experience. This all-inclusive resort provides excellent accommodations, cuisine, entertainment, and services 24 hours per day with no reservations or hassle. This particular resort is located on a beautiful section of what has come to be known as the Mayan Riviera.

The Mexican Caribbean is a region of great historical and natural beauty with a range of accommodations, pristine ecological areas, historical sites of ancient Mayan ruins, lagoons, rare species of flora and fauna, and many other attractive features. Close in proximity to Cancun, known as "the tourist gem of the region," this area features 24 miles of beach where many tourist resorts exist.

One of these resorts is Sunscape. Amenities include three "strategically placed pools, including one pool adjacent to a private beach. In addition, 304 guest rooms each have an excellent view of either the ocean or the bay area. Activities are numerous on-site and convenient to other area attractions. Regularly scheduled events include many land and water sports, use of bicycles, use of kayaks and other watercraft, fitness classes, kids' programs, and special tours and arranged events.

There are five restaurants on-site that require no reservations, and the cuisine ranges from casual to haute. Entertainment is varied throughout one's stay, with a special emphasis on local cultural exposure. Staff are plentiful and include activity leaders and directors, a five-person concierge operation, and numerous service personnel. Many of the staff hold degrees in tourism management, and they are equipped for managing a dynamic, international bevy of guests year-round.

Managerial challenges include the ability to compete with the many other resorts in the region. The market niche that this resort provides is its location in one of the most diverse locations, combining ocean and marina inlets. In addition, the amenities are unique in their reliance on cultural and historic events that provide education to all guests.

Source: DreamDays.com, 2005

REFERENCES

Berger, J. T. (2000, January/February). When riders take a plunge, profits rocket upward. *Resort Management*, p. 19.

Bethune, G., & Huler, S. (1998). *From worst to first: Behind the scenes of continental's remarkable comeback*. New York: Wiley & Sons.

DreamDays.com. (2005, May 26). Sunscape Puerto Aventuras. http://dreamdays.com/Sunscape-Puerto-Aventuras/index.asp

Frank, H., Plaschka, G., & Roessl, D. (1989). Planning behavior of successful and unsuccessful founders of new ventures. *Entrepreneurship and Regional Development*, pp. 191–206.

Lancaster, U. (1999, August 31). Herb Kelleher has one main strategy: Treat employees well. *Wall Street Journal*, p. B1.

Lieber, R. B. (1998, January 12). Why employees love these companies. *Fortune*, pp.72–73.

"M & C checklist: Meeting rooms." (1994, February). *Meetings and Conventions*, p.153.

Nilson, R., & Edginton, C. (1982, August). Risk management: A tool for park and recreation administrators. *Parks and Recreation*, pp.34–37.

Pegg, S. (2005). *Ethical issues related to operations*. Unpublished document course notes for TALM 2303 Commercial Recreation. The University of Queensland, Brisbane, Australia.

Pollan, S., & Levine, M. (1992, October 13). The 12 new fundamentals of small business success. *U.S. News and World Report*, pp. 67–80.

Rademan, M. C. (2003). Change comes to the mountains. *Planning*, pp. 48–51

Robinson, A. (1999, June). Great expectations: How to be a great manager. *Continental*, p.75.

Stewart, T. A. (1998, April 13). A new way to think about employees. *Fortune*, pp.169–170.

Templin, N. (1999, August 30). For hotel guests with glitches: Hi-tech room service. *Wall Street Journal*, pp. B1, B8.

What makes a company great? (1998, October 26). *Fortune*, p. 218.

Chapter ●●●● 8

Commercial Recreation and Tourism Programming

Traditionally, university recreation curricula prepared students to become activity leaders, program supervisors, and administrators of governmental and nonprofit community recreation agencies. Students typically received an activity skill background in sports, arts, outdoor recreation, social recreation, and so on. There were usually several courses in leadership techniques, program supervision, and program development. In short, programming and leadership were the heart of the curriculum.

Today, many recreation curricula have become more management oriented, and others have dropped the heavy core of activity classes. Still, most curricula have a small core of program-related classes, and many recreation majors have a relatively rich personal background in recreational activities. Thus, programming remains one of the key elements in the preparation of the recreation professional.

Many of the pioneers in commercial recreation and tourism did not gain this background in programming because they did not come from recreation curricula. They came from curricula in business, hotel management, communications, and so forth, or from the school of hard knocks. These people managed transportation systems, sold retail products, maintained lodging and dining facilities, and occasionally offered recreation via "amenity" facilities.

In recent years, however, many of these traditional managers have come to learn what the recreation professionals have known all along: that programming can make a big difference in the success of a business. There are many ways that this can happen. When a city's convention and visitor's bureau creates a special event, it draws tourists to the area and fills hotels. When a sporting goods store sponsors a 10-kilometer run, the event can be a very cost-effective marketing tool that puts the store's name in front of the public. When a bowling lane conducts low-cost instructional classes for children, it is building future clientele. When a campground offers square dance and live entertainment, it is probably building a base of repeat customers. When a hotel offers bicycle rentals, it may discover a popular new "profit center." Recreation programming does not have to be a costly frill for a commercial business. Instead, recreation programming can be a very important part of the business concept, and it can often pay for itself.

Programming is probably the single most important skill that recreation professionals have to differentiate themselves from people with other academic backgrounds. Theoretically, the recreation professional should be the person who is best equipped to understand the leisure interests of guests/customers, to visualize opportunities for programs, and to conduct successful programs without making structural or logistical errors.

There is no doubt that programming has become a viable part of the commercial recreation and tourism industry. Most of the major resorts in the Southeastern states now have recreation program professionals on staff year-round. Many hotels, retail stores, theme restaurants, tour operators, and other enterprises are finding that recreation programs can improve business. This chapter will examine various types and purposes of recreation programs, review the programming process, and consider several special types of programs in commercial recreation and tourism.

TYPES AND PURPOSES OF RECREATION PROGRAMS

Not all recreation programs are the same, nor do all programs have the same purposes. In some cases, the recreation program serves as the primary way to provide benefits that customers seek. In other cases, recreation programs primarily embellish the overall experiences and benefits that customers gain at a resort, a restaurant, theme park, or other facility. Programs can be structured as the primary service, as a revenue-generating amenity, or as a supporting amenity. Further, commercial recreation and tourism businesses that do not directly conduct programs can benefit by facilitating programs. Note, however, that these categories are not mutually exclusive. For example, a resort may have a golf course that generates revenues greater than its costs, while the resort's children's programs are provided as a supporting amenity, and the front desk staff and concierge service facilitate other types of recreation through referral and information service.

Recreation Programs as the Primary Service

In many commercial recreation and tourism industries, the provision of a specific recreational activity or several activities is the primary focus of the business. Common examples include tennis clubs, bowling lanes, ballet schools, summer camps, party services, and guided tour companies. In every case, the facilities, equipment, and staff exist in order to facilitate the activity. As an example of programming in one industry, Figure 8-1 illustrates the variety of programs offered at several different sport and fitness centers.

Almost any activity may be offered in a *structured* or *nonstructured format*. Tournaments, leagues, instructional classes, and guided tours are examples of the structured format. The structure is provided by a combination of an established schedule, procedures or rules, and staff who take an active role in leading the participants. Individuals skating on their own at an ice rink, playing pool at a billiard hall, or working out on exercise equipment at a fitness club are involved in nonstructured activity. Some programmers call this "free play" or "open use." Staff supervision in nonstructured programs may be present for general safety and order, but not actively and regularly engaging with the participants.

Entertainment activities have characteristics of both formats. The performers at a concert are certainly leading an activity that has an established agenda, but the customer is basically a spectator. Any spectator can come or go, eat, drink, talk to friends, daydream, or doze off while the activity is in progress. On the other hand, some people would argue that their emotional and intellectual involvement can be extremely high while watching a concert, a play, or a sporting event.

Generally speaking, it is easier for a commercial recreation or tourism business to provide a nonstructured activity than a structured activity. In a nonstructured activity, the customers must be provided with an attractive "opportunity setting" (facility, equipment, support personnel, etc.). The customers enter the opportunity setting and participate pretty much at their own discretion. They lift the weights, volley the tennis ball, or swim in the pool according to whatever agenda they wish. In a structured activity, the manager must provide the opportunity setting plus the additional staff to instruct, officiate, or lead people in the activity. In addition, there may be special rules, methods, or procedures that have to be followed during the activity.

Figure 8-1
Sport and Fitness Center Programs

Aerobic dance	Pool parties
Basketball league	Private party service
Bike race	Racquetball classes
Body sculpting class	Racquetball tournament
Boxercise	Racquetball video clinic
Children's ballet and tap classes	Scuba diving classes
Children's karate tournament	Ski trip
Climbing wall instruction	Spinning classes
Dancercise	Swim classes
Fitness assessment	Swimnastics
Fitness for expectant mothers	Swim teams
Group caribbean trip	Tai chi class
Infant swim class	10-K run
Jr. tennis league	Tennis camp
Karate class	Tennis clinic
Kid's field trips	TGIF exercise social
Las Vegas trip	3 on 3 basketball tournament
Member/guest tennis tournament	Triathlon club
New member social	Wallyball tournament
Parent-child tennis tournament	Weight lifting contest
Pilates	Western barbeque
Pizza social	Yoga class

Some commercial recreation and tourism managers do not have the basic under-standing of recreational needs to establish an attractive opportunity setting. Other managers may be able to establish the opportunity setting but do not have the programming background to provide a high-quality, structured activity. It is not unusual to hear these managers rationalize their lack of programming background: "Our customers don't want any fancy programs," or "They just want to do their own thing." This view is indeed unfortunate because the managers may be missing certain customers who desire the benefits that a structured program can provide.

The key to good recreation programming is to realize that different people seek different benefits and to know how to provide these benefits and assess the outcomes. This is the essence of the "Benefits Based Programming" approach, which will be discussed in a later section of this chapter. A successful programmer manipulates the choice of activity, the type of setting, and the type of activity structure to create the blend of benefits that customers seek.

Recreation Programs as a Supporting Amenity

Whereas some commercial recreation and tourism businesses use recreation programming as a primary service, other businesses see recreation as an amenity to their main mission. That mission might be to sell rooms in a hotel, meals in a restaurant, supplies in a crafts store, spaces in a campground, or equipment in a sporting goods shop. Figure 8-2 illustrates some of the types of recreation programs that can complement a variety of businesses. These businesses are in the commercial recreation and tourism industry, but their primary revenue comes from selling a product and/or service that is not actually a planned recreation program.

Figure 8-2
Recreation Programs as Supporting Amenities

Type of Business	Program Examples
Sporting goods store	Races, sports teams, tournaments
Outdoor specialty shops	Climbing clubs, rafting trips
Hunting and fishing shop	Hunter safety course, fishing tournament
Arts & crafts store	Ceramics classes, crafts shows
Hobby, toy, and game store	Hobby show, card collection swap meet
Video arcades	Video games contests
Nightclubs	Dance classes, New Year's eve party
Casinos	Slots tournament
Boat dealers	Boating safety classes, boat shows
Restaurants	Theme parties, birthday programs
Hotels	Entertainment events, children's programs
Music stores	Instrument classes, music writing contest
Campgrounds	Square dances, nightly entertainment
Water theme parks	Concerts, slide contests, tan contests
Photography store	Photo contests, digital imaging class
Travel agency	Vacation open house, travel shows

Why do such businesses occasionally offer recreation programs and amenities? The answer is that recreation is good for business. In general, recreation programs and amenities can help differentiate one business from another and be a key factor in generating repeat business. For example, recreation programs can be the difference in a family's selection of one hotel over another. Many parents choose a particular resort because that is where their kids want to stay (Milligan, 2005).

Some of the specific benefits that supporting amenity programs can provide are as follows:

- People are introduced to new activities.
- Activity skills instruction may increase future participation.
- Social interaction increases contacts for future participation.
- Length of stay may be increased.
- Additional equipment and supplies may be purchased.
- Children can be meaningfully occupied, freeing parents to play.
- Programs improve relations between employees and customers.
- The overall experience is diversified and enriched.

These benefits translate into increased sales, diversification of sales, and repeat customers. This is the ultimate benefit of recreation programs as a supporting amenity to the commercial recreation and tourism business. Recreation programs can contribute to the overall success of the business even when they are not the primary product or service of the enterprise. Therefore, many resorts, retail stores, and other businesses find that recreation programs are worthwhile amenities to offer their customers.

Recreational amenities may or may not bring in revenue of their own. The recreation facilities and programs may be relatively inexpensive to offer or they may represent a large financial commitment. The key to their justification is how strongly they contribute to the overall objective of the business. The commercial recreation and tourism business that believes in recreation programs evidently feels that there is a positive cost-benefit ratio.

An example of this attitude is illustrated with the efforts of numerous businesses in the Phoenix area. A series of 50 special events are conducted in association with the Tostitos Fiesta Bowl football game. Some of the special event programs make enough money to pay for themselves, but the big payoff is the economic impact to the area. The Fiesta Bowl and its many events bring over 70,000 out-of-state tourists to town to stay in hotels, eat at restaurants, play golf, and make purchases in the many unique shops. They spend well over $150 million. Visitors coming for the bowl game typically buy an entire package of lodging, meal events, recreation, and special events for 3 or 4 days. They also spend a lot of time shopping, partying, and touring the area, including trips to the Grand Canyon. Many of the visitors make repeat trips and tell their friends about the many things to do. Figure 8-3 illustrates some of the 50 events held as part of the 2005 Tostitos Fiesta Bowl. Note also that many of the events are for local residents and for people who may not even attend the football game (T. Taylor, Personal Communication, 2005)!

Figure 8-3
Tostitos Fiesta Bowl Related Programs

NAU Volleyball Tournament
RC Cola, Charter Funding Golf
Wells Fargo Million Dollar Hole-In-One
Quick Mart Middle School Spot Shot
Senior Open Tennis Tournament
Gila River Casino Week
Fiesta Bowl Ladies Luncheon
    Presented by Bank One
Fiesta Bowl Media Day
Blue Cross, Blue Shield National
    Band Championship
Fort McDowell Fiesta Bowl Parade
VIP Reception
Youth Football Clinic
Fiesta Bowl Women's Gymnastics
APS Fiesta Bowl Pre-Game Party
Fiesta Bowl Art Walk
Fort McDowell Fiesta Bowl Parade
Fiesta Bowl Team Dinners
College Football's Biggest Party
Ball Park Fiesta Bowl Stadium Club
Fiesta Bowl Ball

34th Annual Tostitos Fiesta Bowl
Fiesta Bowl Queens Coronation Challenge
Sparkle Cleaners Quarterback Invitational
Twirl, Pom, Cheer, Flag, and Dance Cham-
    pionships
Fiesta Bowl Coaches Dinner
Honeywell Aerospace Challenge
Runner's Den Distance Classic
Fiesta Bowl Soccer Classic
Fiesta Bowl Women's Basketball Classic
Desert Diamond Casino Western Classic
Youth Gridiron Day
Fellowship of Christian Athletes Breakfast
Fiesta Bowl Player Event
Children's Day Presented by Arizona
    Science Center
Fort McDowell Fiesta Bowl Parade Awards
    Breakfast
Ladies Day Presented by Nordstrom
Fiesta Bowl Media Golf Challenge
Tempe Block Party

Recreation Programs as a Revenue-Generating Amenity

Some commercial recreation and tourism facilities have taken the idea of the recreation amenity to a higher level. Not only is recreation used to draw new customers and repeat customers, the recreation program is expected to generate a profit.

To be a revenue-generating amenity, the recreation program must be totally responsive to the interests of the customers. Otherwise, they will not participate, and the program will result in a loss. The successful recreation manager must be up-to-date with recreation interests and fads, be alert to customers' comments and suggestions, understand the full program potential (and limitations) of the facility, know what support staff can be counted on, and be able to execute the details and logistics of a program. Ideas alone are not enough. A poorly planned or executed program can do more harm than good.

It is interesting to note that many of the most successful revenue-generating recreation amenity programs are at resorts in Florida and along the southern Atlantic coast. The recreation managers and staff at these resorts are usually members of the Resort and Commercial Recreation Association (RCRA). This association has been extremely instrumental in spreading the practice of professional quality recreation programming in resorts, campgrounds, cruise lines, and other commercial recreation and tourism settings.

A great example of revenue-generating recreation programs is Amelia Island Plantation, in Florida. Some of their most financially successful programs are listed below (W. Lees, personal communication, 1999).

- **Recreation packages**—Depending upon the type of room package guests book, a small fee is included in the room price to cover the cost of basic recreational amenities and services. This yields about $190,000 a year.
- **Conference group recreation**—Conference groups can have private recreation programs provided just for their members. Programs include various "Adventure Recreation" activities such as paintball and Jet Ski riding; "Instructive Recreation" such as chili cooking; and "Spirited Recreation" activities such as a challenge course, beach Olympics, and other competitive events. The Conference Recreation program brings in about $145,000 a year.
- **Youth recreation programs**—These include a Kids Camp that can serve up to 85 children a day. Revenues are about $80,000 a year.
- **Social activities**—These include the various teen programs and adult and family evening programs. Revenues are about $80,000 a year.
- **Group trips**—Trips to nature areas, tours of the local Anheuser-Busch plant, shopping trips, and others. Trips bring in about $30,000 a year.
- **Nature center**—This is a new facility that offers a variety of nature-based classes, special events, and trips. The facility essentially breaks even with about $100,000 a year in revenue.
- **"Wheels and keels"**—This is the retail and rental program that offers 450 bicycles, 80 "Island Hopper" four-seat golf carts (for local transportation, not golf), paddle boats, and some snack food sales. This program has revenues of about $440,000 and expenses of just $120,000. Obviously, this program is a big cash cow.

If you have been keeping score, the above total revenue is $1,065,000! That is a major revenue operation that generates an overall profit of about $428,000 above its operating costs. However, an aquatics division, not included in the above, costs about $400,000 a year to operate pools and beaches.

It should also be noted that golf, tennis, and a fitness center are not included in the recreation division programs listed above. These would add substantially more revenue as well as profit to the overall resort.

Facilitating Recreation

Many commercial recreation and tourism businesses are not in the business of directly providing recreational amenities or programs. They might not have the facilities, staff expertise, financial resources, or philosophical orientation to do so. This would not mean, however, that they only sell hotel rooms, meals, sports equipment, or craft supplies. These businesses exist to satisfy customers, and one way to help do this is by "facilitating" recreation. This means to act as an information resource, an encourager, a catalyst, or an enabler. It really does not take much time, effort, or resources to do this. What facilitating does, however, is to improve the business image with its customers. The key idea is that the manager should help customers find the benefits they seek, even if it is not something that the business directly offers. This makes a positive impression on the customer, and a satisfied customer leads to repeat business.

 Some of the ways to facilitate recreation are listed below:

- **Keep a calendar of community events**—Help your guests and customers know what is going on in the community. For example, a sporting goods store should keep listings of bicycle races, fun runs, tennis tournaments, and the like.
- **Serve as a referral service**—Refer guests to community agencies and businesses that have the programs they desire. For example, a hotel should know where a guest can go for a fitness workout or cultural activity.
- **Provide "how to" information**—Have game rules, skills information, equipment use guides, and so on. A hotel might have maps of local jogging trails, and a sports shop might have books and videos for sports skills.
- **Provide loan or rental equipment**—To make it easy to participate, a theme park might have baby strollers available. A condominium resort might have table games and books on loan.
- **Publicize other programs**—Have posters, flyers, and brochures of other community programs and attractions. Similarly, your business promotional literature should be available at those other locations.
- **Provide day care**—To enable parents more time to shop or recreate, provide a day care service. This has been done successfully in hotels, health clubs, and shopping malls.
- **Employees should be interested and informed**—Employees should be trained to show interest and help facilitate a positive experience for their guests and customers. Therefore, employees need to be informed of the opportunities and resources available. Another subcategory of recreation programming, the concierge service, is an expansion of this concept.

Concierge Services

Long a hallmark of better European hotels, a concierge provides services limited only by human ability and resourcefulness. A hotel/resort guest is likely to ask for anything, and the concierge's job is to make it happen. In this way, a concierge is almost a personal recreation programmer for a guest.

A concierge service may exist in different organizational structures and under a variety of names in the United States. Some of the higher quality hotels do in fact call it a concierge service, while others have a "guest services director" or a "guest relations director." Bell captains at other hotels provide many of the same duties.

A concierge service can be a competitive advantage for a hotel and is viewed as a "necessary extra" for service-oriented hotels. Guests at some upscale hotels say that they return to a hotel because of such service, not because of physical amenities at similarly priced properties.

Front desk and concierge service are key elements in the operation of hotels.
(Photo: J. Crossley)

Most concierge duties can be considered as either information or services. Information requests typically concern dining, shopping, hotel amenities, entertainment, recreational activities, transportation, or general information about the city. The range of services offered varies greatly from one hotel to another, but may include any of the following: arrangement of local tours; tickets to concerts and sporting events; express check-in/checkout; and flight, hotel, and restaurant reservations.

Under an expanded concept of "guest services" (that may be seen more in the future), the services may include babysitting, youth recreation, exercise classes, and tour programs.

To be a good concierge or guest services director, a person must be friendly, polite, polished, and resourceful. The ability to speak foreign languages is highly valued in some hotels. There is a prestigious professional fraternity for concierges, Les Clefs d'Or, and its presence now in the United States marks the emergence of concierge service as a major trend in the hospitality industry.

THE PROGRAM PROCESS

Whether a recreation program is a primary service or an amenity, the program must be planned and carried out effectively. There are numerous textbooks devoted to this topic: the recreation programming process. Figure 8-4 illustrates a composite of the programming process as described in several of these textbooks.

Recreation programming occurs within a framework that is created by a combination of the organization's philosophy, the organization's goals, the social environment, and the economic environment. Within the limits imposed by this framework, recreation programming is a process that completes a cycle of events and starts over again.

The programming cycle begins with an understanding and assessment of the participants' needs and interests and the benefits they expect to receive. Next, program ob-

Figure 8-4
Recreation Programming Traditional Planning Process

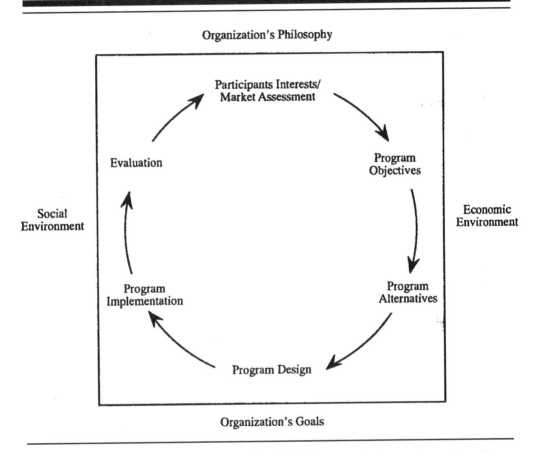

Organization's Philosophy

Participants Interests/
Market Assessment

Program
Objectives

Evaluation

Social
Environment

Economic
Environment

Program
Implementation

Program
Alternatives

Program Design

Organization's Goals

jectives are established that are designed to fulfill those needs, interests, and benefit expectations. Different types of program alternatives are then considered, and a determination is made as to what type of program can best fulfill the objectives. Next is the program design phase, where the logistics of the program are planned. The program is then implemented according to the design.

Finally, the program is evaluated. This evaluation provides feedback regarding the outcomes of the programs from both the participants' perspectives and the program provider's objectives. This confirms or amends the organization's perception of the participants' needs, interest, and benefit expectations. Thus, the cycle begins anew.

This traditional concept of program planning is taught in most recreation curricula. From a practical standpoint, however, one strong criticism of the traditional concept can be made. This criticism concerns the unrealistically low emphasis on the design and implementation phases of the program cycle. These phases represent one third of the theoretical process but are often given about one tenth of the consideration in text literature. In reality, the recreation programmer often spends 80% of the time on "nuts and bolts" work of program design and implementation. Therefore, a more realistic recreation program process is proposed here. It is a process that emphasizes the many tasks that must be done to successfully conduct a program. It is also a process that is well suited for the commercial recreation and tourism manager who may not have much background in recreation programming, thus needing a more practical approach. This approach, for lack of a better description, will be called the "nuts and bolts" programming process.

The "Nuts and Bolts" Programming Process

Although the steps presented in this program process are listed in a numerical order, that order could change under certain circumstances. For example, if it typically takes an organization more time to recruit and train staff than to order equipment, then the time sequencing of the two steps could be reversed. Some commercial recreation and tourism businesses need to generate advertising for an event as much as a year in advance. Therefore, certain aspects of Step 7, promotion, could occur any time after Step 1, initial planning. The promotional effort could continue right up to the start of the program. With these timing considerations in mind, the steps in the "nuts and bolts" approach to programming are presented below:

1. **Initial planning**—Several tasks are essential from the outset:
   a. Assess the interests, needs, and benefit expectations of the target market.
   b. Determine objectives, both from the participants' and organization's standpoints. Be sure that your objectives are consistent with your organization's mission and service philosophy.
   c. Analyze the program alternatives that could accomplish the objectives and select the best alternative.
   d. Design the program structure, considering program format, frequency, duration, skill level, number of participants, etc.
   e. Establish a budget for the program, considering both the direct costs and the overhead costs. Be conservative in estimating revenues.
   f. Coordinate the initial plan with other divisions within the organization, particularly maintenance, security, finance, and legal departments.
2. **Arrange for the facility**—If the organization manages the facility that is needed for the program, then scheduling arrangements may be simple. Otherwise, it is necessary to lease or contract the facility from another organization.
3. **Obtain equipment and supplies**—This may involve writing specifications for equipment and going through a lengthy purchasing process. Equipment might also be borrowed, leased, solicited for donation, or repaired or reconditioned.
4. **Staff recruitment and training**—New employees may have to be hired or existing employees may have to be reassigned. In either case, some degree of training may be needed. Volunteers may also need to be recruited and trained.
5. **Make special arrangements**—Depending upon the program, there may be a variety of special arrangements required, including:

Bus use	Sponsors
Lodging and meals	Prizes and awards
Special maintenance	Medical assistance
Permits	Traffic control
Portable toilets	Concessions
Entertainment	Insurance

6. **Develop specific procedures/operating manuals**—Depending upon the complexity of the program, it may be necessary to develop specific time schedules, rules, activity procedures, program information, emergency procedures, and so forth.
7. **Program promotion**—A variety of promotional methods may be utilized: advertising, publicity, special promotions, Web site info, and so on.
8. **Program Registration**—If registration is necessary, will it be in advance or on-site, by phone, mail, e-mail, online, or in person? What form of payment will be accepted? Is a deposit required? When the participants register, it may be appropriate to provide them with information sheets, schedules, and waivers as previously developed in Step 6.

9. **Program setup**—This step involves the physical setup of the facility for the program: seating, trash cans, sports field preparation, equipment distribution, sets, props, lighting, sound systems, and so on.

10. **Final safety check**—Prior to starting the program, make a final check of the area and equipment to be sure safety standards are met.

11. **Conduct the program**—Finally! Most people only see this phase and do not realize all the preparation that went into it.

12. **Program wrap-up**—Schedule staff for this or they will disappear when the program ends. Tasks include some of the following:

Cleanup	Various report forms
Equipment return	Financial forms
Payrolls	Post-event publicity
Sponsor thank-yous	Volunteer recognition

13. **Evaluate results**—Consider if the program results, attendance, revenue, and expenses met the objectives originally established. Evaluate how well the participants' benefit expectations were met. This step leads back to initial planning for the next program.

Compatibility with the Benefits Based Programming Model

Is the "nuts and bolts" programming process presented above compatible with the popular concept of benefits based programming (BBP) as advocated by Allen (1999), Rudick (1998), and others? Theoretically, the answer is "absolutely!" However, some of the key elements of BBP are too often given limited attention, especially by commercial recreation and tourism businesses that deal with large numbers of different clientele every day. Areas where we typically need to do better include identifying participant needs and benefit expectations, developing objectives and strategies that specifically address those needs and benefits, and measuring the outcomes in light of those benefit expectations. These steps may be more difficult to achieve in commercial recreation and tourism compared to therapeutic recreation, for example, where individualized assessment, treatment, and evaluation is common. The answer in commercial recreation may be to have better needs and benefits assessments and outcome evaluations through the use of cost-effective methods such as representative participant samples and focus groups that are completed periodically rather than with every program.

An Approach to Programming

One mistake that many recreation programmers make is to fall into the "stereotype trap." That means to program a certain type of activity in the same way, repeatedly. For example, basketball is usually offered at a sports club as free play or as a competitive league. As such, it provides certain benefits to the participant, primarily physical activity, competition, and some social interaction. However, a good programmer would see how a variety of other program structures would provide different benefits to additional sports club members. Alternative approaches could include the following:

"Slam Dunk" league with lower baskets	3 on 3 leagues and tournaments
"Slow Break" league for ages 40 +	1 on 1 contest
Father and son, 2 on 2 tournament	"Hot Shot" contest
Demonstration/exhibit by pro or college players	Half-court league
Booster club for local college or pro team	Coed league or tournament
Group outings to local college or pro games	Skill instructional classes
Trips/excursions to national tournaments	Basketball films
Exhibit of basketball memorabilia	Fantasy basketball league

Basketball photography exhibit/contest   Basketball officiating class
Under 6 ft (player) league   League awards party

As stated previously, the key to good recreation programming is to provide the benefits people seek. This is done by manipulating and blending the choice of activity, the program format, and the program structure that best brings out the particular benefits sought by participants. Program formats include leagues, tournaments, instructional classes, clinics, exhibits, demonstrations, clubs, trips, special events, and free play. Program structure variations include frequency of program, duration of program, skill level, and number of participants. For any given activity, there may be some participants who want the program offered in one way, while other participants desire it differently. As long as the participation volume allows it, why not offer activities in two or three different ways so that participants can choose the program with the benefits they want most?

SPECIAL TYPES OF COMMERCIAL PROGRAMS

Most conventional textbooks about recreation programming give attention to the planning of games, tournaments, leagues, and instructional classes. Since many commercial recreation programs utilize these program formats, the traditional text content is generally of value. However, certain other types of recreation programs are sometimes overlooked in program textbooks. Examples are special/promotional events, food and beverage events, entertainment events, resort programs, and trips and tours. Since these types of programs are important in commercial recreation and tourism, some extra attention should be devoted to them. This section will focus on these special types of programs and examine some practical operational strategies for each.

Special/Promotional Events

Special/promotional events are a great way to announce the start of a new season, kick off a new product or service, spice up the old program, provide a change of pace, and attract new customers. Staff as well as participants can get charged up for a special event. Many special/promotional events can be based around a holiday theme. Examples include a Valentine's Day dance at a resort, Fourth of July fireworks party at an amusement park, or a Turkey Trot 10-K race sponsored by a sporting goods store.

In order to generate the most promotional value, it is very common to cosponsor an event with a radio or TV station or a newspaper. An example would be a "Beach Party" at a water theme park. A radio station could sponsor the event and broadcast live from the park throughout the day. Activities could include fitness contests; water slide relays; volleyball games; CD giveaways; and bands playing reggae, calypso, and music from the Beach Boys or Jimmy Buffett.

Ideas and operational strategies for special/promotional events can come from many sources, including customers, staff, media, and product representatives. Professional associations such as the International Festivals and Events Association (IFEA) and the International Special Events Society (ISES), as well as state associations such as "CalFest" (California & Nevada Festivals & Events Association), now have services such as training programs, seminars, and conferences for professional development and sponsor contacts. Some specific strategies for special/promotional events include the following:

- **Have a fun concept**—No amount of publicity can offset a dull concept, and it must be a good program to get repeat visitors.
- **Have a central theme**—Make it easy to promote.
- **Target large crowds**—Sporting events and concerts get visibility and crowds.

- **Tie in to the market**—Plan events that capture the target audience of the business and the sponsors.
- **Get community involvement**—Involve community groups in the event to expand the base of support.
- **Recognize cosponsors and contributors**—Provide recognition in all brochures, during the event, and with follow-up after the event.
- **Involve the media in planning**—Invite the media to planning meetings in order to build interest and anticipation for the event.
- **Maintain events**—Keep the ball rolling to the next year so you can build on past success.
- **Avoid staleness**—Although the main theme may remain the same, have some variety from one year to the next in specific activities.
- **Have different activities each day**—For a multiday event, have a variety of activities so people will want to come back each day.
- **Utilize celebrities**—Media personalities, sports and music stars, politicians, beauty pageant winners, and the like., all draw more visitors.
- **Control spending**—Limit the number of individuals who have authority to spend funds and stick as closely as possible to budget plans.
- **Have a broad base of funding**—Do not rely too heavily on a single financial source. Seek resources and revenues from ticket sales, concessions, donations, advertising, cosponsors, and so forth.

An important idea is to develop a *special event checklist* that serves as a reminder during the planning process. Rather than forget a topic, review the list every time an event is planned. Figure 8-5 illustrates a generic special event checklist. It should also be noted that many of these ideas can be adapted to other programs in this section. It is a good idea to modify this list for each different type of special event and update the list each year with additional topics. Not everyone is well suited to organize and manage special events. It takes a person who "sees the big picture," takes a multidimensional view of the tasks, and can juggle several tasks at once.

FOOD AND BEVERAGE EVENTS

Throughout history, some of humankind's merriest moments have occurred around a full table of food and drink. Consider the feasts that are associated with the ancient Chinese, Greeks, Romans, medieval kings, and even some of the pioneers and settlers in the United States. Today, food and beverage events are a major service of hotels, restaurants, and resorts. Typically, the leadership in this area of recreation has been assumed by convention and meeting managers and banquet or catering departments of hotels. However, recreation staff can also generate an idea that can become a successful event with the help of a food service professional.

There are many types of food and beverage events, and they range from the relatively simple to the very complex: wine and cheese parties, open house socials, receptions, Western-style barbecues, beach party clambakes, and complete theme parties.

Many major resort hotels have complete sets of stage props, background sets, costumes for all personnel, and entertainment programs for a variety of food and beverage theme parties. These may include: Wild West, Hawaiian Luau, Star Wars, and Mexican Fiesta. Consider for example a "Bedouin Party on the Red Sea." Guests would be encouraged to wear robes and are provided with Keffiyehs (Arab headdresses) to get them in the spirit. The event would take place in a large Bedouin tent with low tables, comfortable sitting cushions, Bedouin music, costumed waiters, and belly dancers for entertainment. Dinner would consist of Oriental lamb on a bed of rice garnished with salads, followed by sweet meats, strong Bedouin coffee, pita breads, and cinnamon tea.

Figure 8-5
Special Event Checklist

Site Suitability and Impact on
  Neighborhood and community
  Facility
  Turf and vegetation

Facility
  Accessibility
  Parking
  Traffic flow
  Road signs
  Information/direction signs
  Information booth

Maintenance
  Water availability
  Trash cans
  Electric demands
  Electric outlets
  Reserve generator
  On-site maintenance
  Setup crew
  Cleanup crew

Extra Equipment
  Projector bulbs
  Tools, batteries
  Magic markers, pens
  Tape, string
  Trash Bags

Notice of Event to
  Fire department
  Hospital
  Police/highway patrol

Safety/Security
  First aid station
  Ambulance (large crowds)
  Fire extinguisher
  Two-way radios, telephone
  Security personnel

Amenities
  Restroom or portable toilets
  Shade and rest area
  Tents/umbrellas
  On-site transportation
  Concessions
  Food and beverage service
  Drinking water
  Entertainment
  Background music
  Special effects displays

Other
  Insurance
  Theme
  Schedule
  Press package
  Announcer
  PA system
  Backup PA
  Change fund
  Revenue security
  Lost and found department
  Alternate/extra activities
  Site supervision
  Publicity
  Registration forms
  Staff break area
  VIP area
  Display of contributors

To manage a successful food and beverage event, consider the following strategies and planning tips:

- Realize that theme parties require some risk.
- If appropriate entertainment is not available in the local market, change the theme.
- Anticipate problems posed by colorful themes and locations that may be difficult to replicate.
- For unique buildings and scenic outdoor areas, minimize the amount of decoration.
- For outdoor events, anticipate changes in weather; have alternatives.
- Be familiar with local customs and cuisine; avoid local holidays if staff will be off duty.
- Work closely with the caterer; be sure to have accurate estimates of attendance.
- Develop menus that are sent along with the promotions and/or invitations.
- If you need background sets, build small modules that can be used in different layouts.
- Be honest and open about your budget capabilities.
- Know your customers. Some groups today are very health-food conscious.

- Have balance in meals; avoid "pasta shock," high-starch meals that make people drowsy.
- The last night banquet should be the most extravagant, except on a cruise, tour, or other occasion requiring early morning departure.
- Service and ambiance can count as much as food quality.
- Create variety with different foods, decorations, tablecloths, centerpieces, costumes, and entertainment.
- Use buffet service carefully—it takes longer and people eat more.
- Keep close control over cocktail parties; do not schedule them for more than 1 hour.
- Use foreign and exotic dishes sparingly, especially at a U.S. location.
- Structure theme events around history, literature, movies, sports, cultures, or countries.

Figure 8-6 illustrates a separate planning checklist that can be devised for food and beverage events.

Entertainment Events

Entertainment events can take many forms, such as nightclub acts, dances, concerts, entertainment at receptions, or shows at fairs and carnivals. Proper planning and management can make these events enjoyable experiences for all people involved. On the other hand, a poorly managed event can be a nightmare. Some of the important planning and management considerations for an entertainment event are as follows:

- **Allow Adequate Time in Planning the Event**—Local entertainers usually require at least a month's notice, while regionally or nationally known entertainers may need to be booked three months to a year in advance.
- **Match Entertainment to the Clientele**—If the theme is "Western Days," do not schedule a rap or hip-hop band.
- **Consider the Clientele When Arranging Security**—Some entertainers have a following that requires tight security.
- **Utilize Booking Agents**—Agents have access to numerous entertainers at various prices.
- **Determine the Method of Payment**—Typically plan on a minimum guarantee to the performer, a fixed or cost-based amount to the presenter, and a percentage split after both these costs are covered. Be aware that cancellations may cost half of the guarantee.
- **Reach Agreement on Expenses**—Travel, lodging, food, etc., for entertainers and support crew.
- **Contact Music Recording Companies**—for major national entertainers. Their tours are usually booked a year in advance to coincide with the release of a new CD or video.
- **Get Names of Individual Performers Written into the Contract**—Personnel changes can be disastrous for ticket sales.

Resort Programs

Increasingly, resorts are offering special programs for parents who want to take children on vacation but not have them constantly underfoot. The idea is to provide quality recreation for the kids, not just babysit them. Meanwhile, the parents have time to spend with each other without worrying about their children's activity and supervision.

Club Med is among the resort chains that have taken a leadership role in providing youth programs by designating certain clubs as "Mini Club" locations. These mini clubs

Figure 8-6
Check List for Food and Beverage Functions

☐ Breakfast/Lunch/Brunch/
Dinner/Buffets/Coffee Break

___ Location
___ Number of each
___ Number to be served
___ Menu/cuisine
___ Wine/liquor/champagne
___ Cost
___ Gratuities
___ Guaranteed minimum
___ Serving time

☐ Room

___ Size
___ Seating capacity
___ Air-conditioning
___ Lighting
___ Acoustics
___ Decor/decoration
___ Diagram of set-up

☐ Tables

___ Shape (oval, round,
rectangular, etc.)
___ Number
___ Number seated at each
___ Table covering:
     Cloth
     Place mats
     Other covering
     Color
___ Chairs:
     Number
     Type
___ Reserved seating:
     Alphabetical seating list
___ Table numbers/reserved
signs
___ Place cards
___ Floral arrangements
___ Other table decorations

☐ Dance Floors

___ Permanent or portable

☐ Check Rooms

☐ Restrooms

☐ Telephones

☐ Music

☐ Speakers

☐ Entertainment

___ Program timetable

☐ Photographers

☐ Gifts & Souvenirs

☐ Printed Menu & Program

☐ Deadline for Confirmation
and Attendance

☐ Cocktail Receptions and
Happy Hours
___ Location
___ Location of bars:
     Public
     Private
     Full bar
     Limited bar
     Hosted bar
     Cash bar
___ Brands:
     Liquor
     Wine
     Champagne
     Mixers
___ Hors d'oeuvres:
     Hot
     Cold

☐ Cocktail Receptions
and Happy Hours (cont.)
___ Service:
___ Bartenders
___ Waiters
___ Attendants
     (door, check-
     room, other)
___ Decoration
___ Guaranteed minimum
___ Corkage charges
___ Gratuities
     included/at will
___ Attendance expected
___ Estimated cost
     per event

☐ Head Table

___ Location
___ Configuration
___ Level:
     Floor level
     Raised
___ Floor covering
___ Dias covering:
     Number to be seated
     Seating arrangements
     Place cards
___ Lectern
___ Microphones
___ PA system
___ AV facilities
___ Floral & other
     decoration

☐ Buffet Table:

___ Size
___ Number
___ Table cover
___ Decoration
___ Service/self-
     service

Adapted from Hosansky, 1985

have full programs, much like a day camp. There are sports, games, aquatic activities, music, crafts, meals, and snacks. A U.S. company, MeriStar Hotels and Resorts, offers its "Fun Factory" program at 13 different resorts and manufactures "funology," with a variety of creative and enriching activities.

In the United States, some of the best summer programs for kids are offered at major resorts in Florida, Georgia, and South Carolina. Figure 8-7 illustrates programs that are available at three of these resorts: Kiawah Island Resort in South Carolina; Amelia Island Plantation in Florida; and the Westin Innisbrook Golf Resort, also in Florida.

Figure 8-7
Examples of Resort Recreation Activities:
Kiawah Island Resort, Amelia Island Plantation, and
Westin Innisbrook Golf Resort

Children

Nature boardwalk tour	Golf/tennis clinic	Crafts fun shop
Chefs-for-an-hour	Splatter art	Film fiesta
Tales for tots	Capture the flag	Junk food bingo
Sand candle crafting	Baseball clinic	Field soccer
Junior naturalist	Sand castle fun	Ocean seining
Marine life discovery	Crabbing excursion	Nature crafts
Pond life exploration	Aquatic crafts	Recycled art
Creepy crawly hayride	Pirate bonfire	African safari
Ghosts and goblins	Myths and legends	Scavenger hunt
Pirate adventure day	Color me crazy	Park parade
Children's acting workshop	Shell collecting	Mini bowling
Superstars contest	Ice cream making	Cartoon party
Fossil Fun	Wildlife discovery	Beach combing

Teens

IMAX trip	Tye dye and pizza	Night volleyball
Three-point shoot-out	Pool pizza party	Sound wave
Photo scavenger hunt	2 on 2 volleyball	Frisbee golf
Light up the night	Flag football	Beads and bracelets
Teen kayaking	Teen TV workshop	Video tournament
Boogie boards	Horseback riding	Miniature golf

Families

Ice cream social	Bingo family fun	Family movies
Poolside trivia	Family jeopardy	Nature bike hike
Edible plant ramble	Nature photography	Bird watching
Family feast bonfire	Critter talk	Crab grab
Jet stream boat races	Raging raft race	Sand sculpture
Poolside games	Family kayaking	Stargazing

Among hotel chains, the Marriott Resorts and the Hyatt Hotels and Resorts may have the most comprehensive programs for children. The "Camp Hyatt" program is available year-round at about 16 resorts and is available at over 80 other properties in summer and on holidays and weekends. Hyatt lists their priorities as safety, fun, and learning.

The value of recreation programming at resorts is gaining recognition throughout the world, particularly at ski resorts and beach resorts. For example, the Plantation Bay Resort and Spa in Cebu, Philippines, offers over 30 different recreation programs each week. These include: hobie cat sailing lessons, lei making, guitar lessons, sand castle building, slide and glide contest, fish feeding, wall climbing, archery instruction, aqua aerobics, card and palm reading, and many others (Plantation Bay, 2005).

A survey of resorts with recreation programs (Linden, 1999) revealed some interesting trends in children's programming at resorts:

- Most resorts (90%) offer programs for both mornings and afternoons.
- Only 50% offer evening programs year-round.
- Most (70%) have daily theme activities.
- Only a few (30%) provide beepers for parents, and most of those charge for the services.
- Most (80%) charge for the children's recreation program and most also provide lunch, although it is an extra charge in 30% of the programs.
- Half offer either specialty classes or specialty camps.
- About 30% have computer activities (games, e-mail, Web, etc.) as part of their programs.

In developing a resort summer program, many of the activities are similar to those offered at day camps and playgrounds under the auspices of YMCAs and city recreation departments. There are some major differences, however. Parents and children often expect a better program at a resort and are quite sophisticated in those expectations. They are willing to pay for a good program, and the program should be priced accordingly. Finally, the children typically attend for only a few days to a week, so the staff cannot really get to know the kids as well as they would at a community day camp. Some other important planning considerations for organizers are as follows:

- Be sure that all state and county regulations for day care programs are met.
- Consider carefully the ages to be served. Some resorts have found it difficult to work with children under five, while other resorts develop programs for five and over and provide day care for younger children.
- Have an adequate ratio of staff to children; at least one staff member for every seven to 15 children of elementary school age and one staff member for every four or five preschoolers.
- Be sure that meals and snacks meet all applicable health codes.
- Restrict access to certain areas such as the ocean beach.
- Be flexible enough to accommodate variable numbers of children from day to day.
- Develop the programs around the character of the resort.
- A full-time, salaried, professional staff person should manage the program.
- Utilize the talents of staff in other departments: the chef for kitchen tours and cooking classes, the boutique manager for fashion shows and makeup demonstrations, and so on.
- Be prepared to supervise children with different languages, religions, and cultures. Having some multilingual staff is essential at international resorts.

There is also a definite trend toward the provision of programs for adults at resorts. For many years, Club Med resorts have offered a variety of aquatic and sports instructional programs. Today, however, we are seeing the emergence of many programs in "wellness" (fitness, health, nutrition, stress reduction, etc.), cultural arts, local history, and environmental activity. Frequent leisure travelers are now more sophisticated and are more interested in enriching experiences (culture, history, natural environment) than in the traditional escapism of sun, sand, nightlife, and shopping.

Craft activities are an excellent way to balance sports and games in resort recreation programs. (Photo: Wintergreen Resort)

Trips and Tours

Several thousand outfitters, tour guide companies, and specialty travel agencies offer or arrange adventure tours. Samples include an 18-day bicycle tour of China, a two-week safari through Africa, an Alaskan glacier skiing trip, and a fishing trip on the Amazon River. Although these adventure trips seem quite glamorous, such trips are in the minority. For most Americans, a group tour is a five-to-15 day motor coach trip with overnight stops at hotels. Typical destinations are to festivals, historical sites, cultural events, major cities, or scenic attractions. These tours are not only conducted by commercial operators, but by many municipal park and recreation departments and nonprofit recreation agencies. All of these tours should be directed and led in a professional manner.

In conducting a tour, all the responsibilities may be handled by one organization or by several organizations working together through contracts. The possible parties involved include the following:

- **Tour operator/wholesaler**—develops the overall tour itinerary, prices it, and markets it to travel agencies, and sometimes directly to the public.
- **Retail travel agencies**—sells the tour to the public and preformed groups. In some cases, may also be a tour operator.

- **Tour manager**—Employed by the tour operator; operates the day-to-day aspects of the tour and supervises the tour director, escorts, and/or guides.
- **Tour director**—goes with the group, represents the company, directs day-to-day events, and provides narration to the group.
- **Tour escorts**—similar to tour director, but do not provide tour narration.
- **Step-on tour guides**—joins the group at a specific location and provides expert narration.
- **Local suppliers**—hotels, restaurants, attractions, and so on who sell their services to the tour.
- **Transportation carriers**—charter buses, planes, cruise ships, and so forth.

The tour manager and director have the most contact with the group and generally coordinate everything once the tour is in progress. They are consumer advocates, troubleshooters, quality control persons, social directors, public relation specialists, and ambassadors of goodwill. They must enjoy working with people and have common sense.

Tour Itinerary

The basic idea in planning a tour is to provide an interesting itinerary without wearing the participants out. One way to do this is to build in several optional tours or events. Participants can choose to go along on the optional tours or have free time on their own. Figure 8-8 illustrates a typical itinerary for an eight-day tour with a single primary destination and side tours emanating from that hub location.

Figure 8-8
8-Day Tour Itinerary Format

Day	Morning	Afternoon	Evening
Sunday	Travel	Travel and check-in	Rest/on own
Monday	Half-day tour	Optional tour	Group meal
Tuesday	All-day tour	All-day tour	On own
Wednesday	Optional tour and entertainment	Half-day tour	Group meal
Thursday	All-day tour	All-day tour	On own
Friday	Half-day tour	Optional tour	Major evening event
Saturday	Half-day tour	Open for shopping, packing, and so forth	Short meeting re: return, free time
Sunday	Checkout/travel	Travel home	

Note: All-day and half-day tours may be sightseeing tours, shopping tours, or scheduled activities (round of golf, chartered fishing trip, sporting event, theme park visit, etc.).

Further Suggestions for Planning Trips and Tours

The remainder of this section will examine some specific suggestions for working with hotels and motor coach operations, for leading the group, and for handling emergencies (Novak, 1989; Goldsmith & Waigand, 1990; Kwortnik & Mancini, 1997).

Tips for Working With Hotels

Start your contact of hotels you wish to book with by talking with the hotel sales manager. Some large hotels may even have a specialist to work with tour groups. See Figure 8.9 to understand the paperwork flow in booking hotels. Also, consider the following tips:

- Work with hotels with significantly more than enough size to handle your group.
- Pick a strategic location central to the attractions you plan to visit.
- Pick a hotel with on-site dining, especially for breakfast.
- Pick a hotel with adequate support facilities: lobby, meeting room, bus parking.
- Know the published rates (rack rate) and competitors' rates.
- Talk to the highest-ranking decision maker and ask for better rates.
- Expect better rates with higher volume at the same hotel or same chain.
- Get the best rate for volume business (net-net rate) from the hotel's national sales representative, not the local sales director.
- Strive for savings in related areas such as hotel restaurants.
- Know the peak seasons of the hotel.
- Know currency exchange rates if foreign hotels are involved.
- Make realistic room blocks (number of reservations).
- Compare what you are getting for the price.
- Be prepared to make a deposit unless you are a proven customer.
- Payment in full upon arrival will give you leverage in negotiations with the hotel.
- Be aware that the hotel's cancellation policy is usually nonnegotiable. Most require at least 10 days' written notice but prefer 30 or 60 days' notice.
- Major hotels and chains offer consistency of product but have difficulty making quick decisions.
- Independent hotels may have more character and can make quicker decisions, but quality may not be known until arrival.
- Provide the hotel with a rooming list 14 days in advance.
- Call the hotel the day before arrival to verify room lists, special requests (handicapped, adjoining rooms, medication storage, number of beds in each room, etc.), arrival time, number of luggage, food and beverage arrangements, driver's room, activities and events planned.
- Upon arrival at the hotel:
  - If the rooms are not ready, arrange a quick sightseeing tour.
  - Keep people on the bus or in a comfortable reception area while you pre-register the group.
  - Bring the room keys back for distribution to the group.
  - Find out about bag pull time (collection of luggage from rooms) and the location to meet for the departure.
  - Get special luggage tags for the group.
  - Get to know the bell captain.
  - Be in the lobby for half an hour to give information and answer questions.
  - Remind the group when and where to meet next.
  - Arrange wake-up calls.
  - Call ahead to reconfirm the next day's itinerary.

- Upon departure from the hotel:
    - — Confirm the bag pull.
    - — Check with accounting office to be sure guests paid incidental charges (phone, room service, movies, etc.).
    - — Tell the hotel where you are going next.
    - — Count the luggage and check the tags.
    - — Thank the bell captain.
    - — Collect room keys on the bus and count the passengers.
    - — Ask clients if they have everything, especially passports, tickets, vouchers, etc.

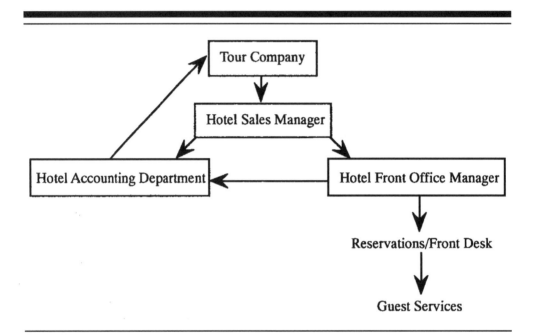

Figure 8-9 Illustrates the paperwork flow when booking a hotel.

Figure 8-9
Paperwork Flow when Booking a Hotel

Tips for Motor Coach Procedures

- Check out the PA system upon boarding.
- Introduce the driver at the start.
- Start each day by reviewing the program with the group.
- If there are four points of interest within 100 yards, stop the bus.
- If you are running late, do not cut out an advertised stop; cut out an unscheduled site stop.
- Pass out maps showing where the group is going.
- Have written quizzes, puzzles, and other travel activities during less interesting parts of the ride.
- Have frequent rest stops—do not encourage use of the bus restroom.
- Encourage passengers to use the trash can.
- Do not block the driver's mirror or lean against the door.

- Designate a loading/unloading procedure such as first on/first off.
- Plan seat rotation twice a day. More than two creates a problem with personal items in the overhead racks.
- Plan rest stops before and after lunch.
- When stopping for the day, tell the group about the departure time and location; baggage pickup time and location; restaurant location and hours; how to dress the next day; and information about shopping, entertainment, and safes for valuables.
- Count people every time they load and unload.
- Ask group members if they have special requests or desire picture stops.

Tips for Tour Directors and Guides

- Talk loud enough.
- Stand where you can make visual contact, but don't block the driver's view of mirrors.
- Do not dispense drugs or medication.
- Help people get on and off a bus (or boat).
- Point out hazards when the group is walking.
- Be sincere no matter how difficult it is.
- Avoid political, religious, and personal views.
- Do not bring up negative things.
- Use firsthand experiences.
- Relate to the participants' generation.
- Relate everything (including questions) to the group.
- Use humor when appropriate, but not off-color or degrading humor.
- Be topical to the area and know current events.
- Let the group know the rules at the start.
- Ask participants to write down all key information about arrivals, departures, or other procedures.
- Hand out your business card with cell phone and central office numbers so you can be reached if there is an emergency when you are not present.
- Try to discover the tour members' expectations.
- Tell people about local customs, laws, and the like.
- Cover the information listed in the tour itinerary.
- If your group talks a lot, cluster your key information when you have their attention.
- Point out things your group may like to go back to on their own.
- Strive to provide accurate information.
- Remember that the job itself is entertainment.

Handling Emergencies

There is no set way to handle emergencies. Each situation requires calmness, visibility, assertiveness, and common sense. Some general suggestions are as follows:

- Do not try to diagnose illness or dispense drugs—seek medical attention if possible.
- For detours or bus problems, notify the hotel and the home office of the problem and delay.
- If bumped ("walked") from a hotel due to overbooking, get the hotel to provide alternate accommodations and a refund—if the group is split up, make sure everyone knows where you are.
- If there is a death, report it to authorities and inform tour members of the situation—phone the tour company, take care of the spouse/friend/family, and continue the tour.

SUMMARY

Recreation programming is becoming an important part of the commercial recreation and tourism industry. Even the industries that are retail or hospitality oriented have found that recreation programs can help them differentiate their product or service from competitors and, in the process, gain repeat customers. Programs may be offered as a primary service, as a supporting amenity, or as a revenue-generating amenity, although these categories are not mutually exclusive. Recreation may also be provided through a "facilitating" approach and through concierge service in the hotel industry.

The programming process consists of an assessment of market segment interests and expected benefits, the establishment of program objectives, consideration of program alternatives, the design of the program, implementation of the program, and, finally, evaluation and measurement of program outcomes. Much of the actual time that is spent in programming occurs at the design and implementation stage. Tasks to be accomplished at this time include arrangement for facilities, equipment, and staff; training of staff; development of a procedure manual; program promotion; activity registration; safety check; program "showtime", and various wrap-up tasks. Certain types of programs are more common to commercial recreation settings than to public or nonprofit agencies. These programs include special/promotional events, food and beverage events, resort programs, entertainment events, and trips and tours. Each type requires strict attention to details, many of which are suggested in this chapter.

SPOTLIGHT ON:

NANCY DONNELLY: A MEMORY MAKER

Nancy Donnelly is the Children's Program Manager for Wintergreen Resort, but she is really much more: she is a "memory maker." It is her responsibility, and the official mission of her department, to provide programs that will be truly memorable experiences for their guests. At one time or other, over 20 years of service to Wintergreen, Nancy developed most of the programs that are now offered though other divisions of the resort. Her many creative programs are both innovative and educational as well as fun and safe.

A sample of Wintergreen's weekend special events in recent years illustrates the range of creative themes:

- Spring Wildflower Symposium
- Women's Luxury
- "Voices of Virginia" Performing Arts
- Memorial Day Country Fair
- Performing Arts Gala Fundraiser
- Annual Summer Music Festival
- 4th of July Jubilee
- Annual Festival of Virginia Wines
- Performing Arts Jazz Fest
- Nature Foundation's Annual Golf and Tennis Classic
- Virginia's Natural History Retreat Weekend
- Mountain Heritage Weekend

(continued)

- Fall Foliage Festival
- Blue Ridge Mountain Christmas
- Wintergreen Film Festival

Each of the above special events includes a variety of interesting programs. For example, the Spring Wildflower Symposium includes numerous hikes, workshops, and lectures on native plant families, nature-related folklore, wildflower sketching, nature photography, and more. Other major programs at Wintergreen Resort include an all-day children's program, over 20 different teen programs, a birthday party service, the Wintergreen Nature Foundation programs, the Out-of-Bounds Adventure Center, craft workshops, a series of family programs, group theme parties, children's theme parties, a performing arts series, and "Owls," a complete Outdoor Wilderness Leadership School for individuals or groups.

How has Nancy Donnelly developed such a great program in her 15 years as Director of Recreation at Wintergreen? There are several keys to her success:

1. Nancy brings a rich personal background of talents and skills to the job. She worked 6 years as an art teacher and has skills in painting, folk art, quilting, papermaking, and many other crafts. She also has expertise in swimming, hiking, nature activities, and scuba. Similarly, Nancy's staff have a rich blend of their own personal expertise in many other recreation, activities. This forms the foundation for high-quality leadership in each program.
2. Nancy nurtures creativity in her staff. She challenges them to constantly be on the lookout for new ideas from improbable sources such as toy stores, literature from other professional fields, store windows, and life in general. When a creative idea pops up, it is written down and placed in an "idea file," even if she has no idea how to use it at that moment. Eventually, many of these ideas find a creative use.
3. Program quality is monitored closely. Programs are expected to be balanced to meet the interests of guests and be accurately and enthusiastically conducted (seamless execution). Participant input is sought via questionnaires, comment cards, and direct discussion. Programs do not just fill space on the resort calendar. Each one must be a worthwhile activity that leads to positive outcomes that support the mission statement.

Nancy Donnelly is recognized by her peers in the Resort and Commercial Recreation Association as one of the very best recreation programmers in the industry. Because of her efforts, Wintergreen Resort offers an outstanding program for its guests, who invariably head home with memories of rich and rewarding experiences (N. Donnelly, personal communication, 2000; Wintergreen Resort, 2005).

REFERENCES

Allen, L. (1999, February). Just what is BBP? Seminar at the University of Utah, Salt Lake City.

Goldsmith, C., & Waigand, A. (1990). *Building profits with group travel.* San Francisco: Dendrobium Books.

Hosansky, M. (1985, August). The way to a meeting planner's heart. *Meetings and Conventions,* pp. 37–40.

Kwortnik, R., & Mancini, M. (1997). *Essentials of travel packaging.* Lexington, KY: National Tour Association.

Linden, L. (1999, November 13). Global recreation tips & trends. Resort and Commercial Recreation Association, 1999 National Conference, Hilton Head, SC.

Milligan, M. (2005, May 16). Family ties: Hotels discover it's a kids world. *Travel Weekly*, pp. 1, 20–22.

Novak, V. (1989). *Step-up to step-on guiding*. Salt Lake City: Vera Novak Publisher.

Plantation Bay. (2005). *Plantation bay schedule of activities*. Cebu, Philippines.

Rudick, J. (1998, May). Benefits-based programming—You can do it. *Parks and Recreation*, pp. 20–24.

Wintergreen Resort. (2005, September 19). *Activities*. http://www.wintergreenresort.com/activities/activities.cfm

Part 3

INDUSTRY PROFILES

Part I (Chapters 1–3) of this text established an introduction to the basic nature of commercial recreation and tourism. Part II (Chapters 4–8) examined the initiation and management of the commercial recreation and tourism enterprise. The content in all of these chapters is oriented to the overall commercial recreation and tourism industry. Therefore, the content was rather "industry generic" in order to cover a wide range of concepts having some degree of universal allocation to the field. Part III (Chapters 9–12) reverses this approach and examines specific commercial recreation and tourism industries.

As explained in Chapter I, commercial recreation and tourism includes three major industry groups: travel, hospitality, and local commercial recreation. These groups overlap in many instances. For example, cruise ships may be considered as part of both the travel industry and the hospitality industry. Rather than present the many overlapping "hybrid" industries in a separate chapter, they will be presented within just one of the major industry groups to which they belong.

There are hundreds of commercial recreation and tourism industries that could be examined in this text, some very large industries and some very small. The industries that will be presented in Chapters 9–11 each meet one or more of the following criteria:

- An industry that presents significant career opportunities for students in recreation, tourism, or hospitality curricula.
- An industry that is a major component of the overall commercial recreation and tourism industry and essential to the "big picture" of commercial recreation and tourism.
- An industry that has an important supporting relationship to any of the industries covered by the previous two criteria. For example, campground managers need to understand the recreation vehicle (RV) industry.

It should also be noted that each chapter will include one or more profiles of "facilitator" type industries as defined in Chapter 1. These will be covered in the chapters for the industries that they tend to facilitate most. For example, travel agencies will be covered in Chapter 9, "The Travel Industry."

It must be noted that there are numerous professional and trade associations and publications affiliated with each industry. Rather than use many pages listing these resources, it is suggested that readers conduct a Web search for associations and publications in the industry of their interest. Another great source is to talk with industry professionals and find out what associations they belong to and what professional publications they receive.

Chapter•••• 9

The Travel Industry

Consider the following data regarding the U.S. travel industry (Travel Industry Association of America, 2004, 2005):

- It involves about $571 billion of direct expenditures.
- Its total economic impact from both domestic and international travelers in the United States is over $1.23 trillion.
- It involves over 1.2 billion trips away from home by Americans.
- It directly generates about 7.2 million jobs in the United States.
- It generates about $95 billion in tax revenue for local, state, and federal governments.
- It is one of the top three industries in almost every state.

BACKGROUND OF THE INDUSTRY

This section will present definitions and sales and distribution characteristics of the travel industry.

Definitions

There are many definitions used by different organizations and authorities. After many years of debate, the following definitions were recommended by the World Tourism Organization (WTO) and were adopted by the United Nations.

Tourism—the activities of persons traveling to and staying in places outside their usual environment for not more than one consecutive year for leisure, business, and other purposes. *Domestic tourism* involves residents of a country traveling only within that country. *International tourism* consists of inbound and outbound tourism of a given country.
Overnight visitor—visitors who stay at least one night in a collective or private accommodation in the place visited. This may include passengers on a cruise ship, yacht, or train.
Same-day visitor—visitors who do not spend the night in a collective or private accommodation in the place visited.

In addition to the WTO definitions, the following are definitions used for this text:

Tourism industry—the broad industry comprising a loose network of businesses that serve tourists/travelers. According to this definition, the industry would include transportation carriers, travel agencies, and tour companies, plus most of the hospitality industry and whatever part of the local commercial recreation industry that also serves tourists.

Tour—a combination of services, including transportation and one or more of the following: accommodations, meals, recreational activities, entertainment, or sightseeing, which are provided to individual or group pleasure travelers.

In some situations, the word *tourist* has assumed a somewhat negative connotation. This might occur when local residents resent the negative impact that some tourists cause. Therefore, it is also becoming popular to use the word *traveler*, which includes the subclassifications of *business traveler* and *pleasure traveler*. Other terms such as *international guest* are used sometimes and imply a positive tone. For practical purposes, it must be realized that some terms are used almost interchangeably, including the basic terms *tourism* and *travel industry*. It is also important to realize that the industry does not function in isolation; it intermingles with the natural, physical, social, and political environments. More specifically, the components of the tourism industry include (Goeldner, Ritchie, & McIntosh, 2000; Gunn, 1979).

- the traveler who seeks psychic and physical experiences and satisfaction;
- the businesses providing transportation, lodging, products, and other services to the traveler;
- the government of the host country, region, or community;
- the host community, including the residents' cultural background; and
- the natural resource base and physical environment.

This is indeed an industry of complex interactions. The complexity should be apparent throughout the rest of this chapter. Although several sections of conceptual content about the overall tourism industry are key parts of this chapter, the industry profiles in this chapter will be limited to the types of businesses that specifically involve the transportation of tourists.

Travel Industry Sales and Distribution System

Today, travel and transportation is a huge industry with thousands of businesses competing for the travel dollar, yet working together in many instances. Because the industry is so large, complex, and interrelated, there is no single process by which sales are made to the consumer. Instead, there is a distribution system in which sales occur through a variety of methods. Figure 9-1 illustrates the travel industry sales distribution system as adapted from Gee (1984).

In a one-stage sale, the supplier sells directly to the consumer. The consumer may make several purchases separately in order to arrange a vacation, including air transportation, rental car, lodging, and activities. This has become increasingly easy because of Internet sites that have reservation/sales capabilities. In a two-stage system, the transaction goes through a travel agent, tour operator, or specialty channeler who makes all the arrangements. A specialty channeler could be a travel coordinator for an organization such as a nonprofit agency, corporation, ski shop, scuba retail shop, or club. In a three-stage sales system, a travel wholesaler may also be used. Wholesalers contract for large blocks of space with airlines, cruise ships, hotels, and resorts at a substantial discount. Then they market the space through travel agents or directly to the consumer. A four-stage system can bring all these middlemen into play. It would seem logical that the more complex transactions would wind up costing the consumer more, but such is not necessarily the case. Whenever middlemen exist, you can be assured that they are purchasing the product at a low enough cost to make a profit while they pass a reasonable value on to the consumer. In addition, the various wholesalers, tour operators, and travel agents also provide services such as travel counseling and itinerary coordination.

Figure 9-1
Travel Sales Distribution System

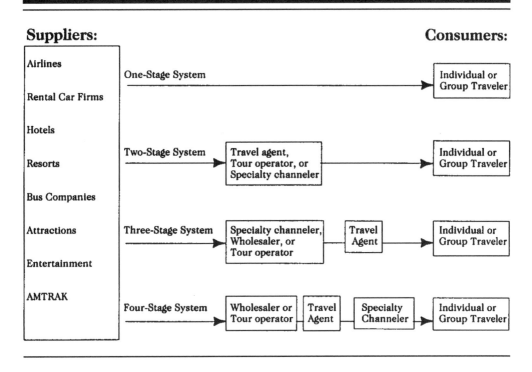

In recent years, however, due to commission cutbacks from the airlines, many travel agencies and wholesalers have been adding a service fee. This fee could result in a higher price than a consumer might find in a "one-stage" transaction, particularly though a Web site sale. Further, some international tour companies have found that they can charge a higher price because of the convenience services that are provided to their customers.

TRAVEL TRENDS AND EXPENDITURES

As mentioned previously, the travel business is a huge industry in the United States, serving over 1.2 billion "persons-trips" and having an economic impact of over 1 trillion. This industry grew an average of about 4% a year from 1984 to 2000. That was faster than the overall growth of the gross national product. Meanwhile, travel prices typically lagged behind the rise of the consumer price index, meaning that travel was a relative bargain. This travel boom of the '80s and '90s was influenced by several factors:

- With a few short-term exceptions, oil prices remained fairly stable, thus keeping fuel prices stable.
- Deregulation of airlines and competition within the industry kept prices down (except in areas with little competition).
- Hotel and motel construction led to overcapacity in the lodging industry, resulting in competition and stable prices.
- Tax reforms in the United States gave Americans more discretionary income in the 1980s. The tendency is to spend the extra money first for a home mortgage or a vehicle, then for travel.

- The 1990s featured a remarkable period of financial gain for millions of Americans who had investments in the U.S. stock market. Again, financial well-being leads to a willingness to spend for travel.

Unfortunately, the travel boom of the 1980s and '90s was not sustained into the new century. Stock market declines in 2000 and terrorist attacks by Muslim extremists in the United States (9/11/2001) and Bali (2002) combined to influence a significant decline of travel. Worldwide tourism receipts dropped 2.9% (World Tourism Organization, 2004), and international travel to the United States dropped 22% through 2003 (Miller & Associates, 2005). However, worldwide tourism recovered from 2003 to 2005 even though terrorism acts continued (Spain, London, etc.), the United States engaged in the Iraq conflict, and a severe acute respiratory syndrome (SARS) scare shook Asian markets. In spite of these problems, international tourism rebounded 10% (*Travel Weekly*, 2005).

About three fourths of all United States residents take at least one trip per year of 50 miles or more. Most of this travel (78%) occurs by car, truck, or recreation vehicle (RV) (Travel Industry Association of America, 2005). This travel can be analyzed from several perspectives: domestic travel, international travel, pleasure versus business travel, and short trips and weekend travel.

Domestic Travel

Within the United States, domestic travel accounts for most of the overall American travel industry. Some of the characteristics of domestic travel are reviewed below (Travel Industry Association of America, 2004, 2005; Miller & Associates, 2005):

- The most popular destinations for domestic travel are California, Florida, Texas, Pennsylvania, and New York.
- The National Park System areas (includes national parks, memorials, recreation areas, etc.) are also major destinations, with about 414 million visits in 2003.
- The average adult leisure trip lasts 6 nights and costs about $1,459 per party.
- Fifty-five percent of U.S. travelers stay overnight in hotels and motels, while 39% stay in private homes with friends or relatives.
- The average spending on a leisure trip is 36% for transportation, 25% for food, 18% for lodging, 12% for entertainment, and 8% for general retail purchases.
- June, July, and August are the most popular travel months, accounting for 33% of annual trips.
- Leisure travel accounts for 82% of trips, with 12% for business or convention, and 6% combined leisure and business.
- Half of all business and leisure trips are for 2 nights or less.

International Travel

International travel has seen major changes in recent years. In addition to the problems with terrorism, war, stock markets, and disease, there has been a change in the buying power of the "Euro" dollar. In 2000, the Euro was worth only about 82 U.S. cents, but by 2005, the Euro was worth around $1.20. This appreciation of European buying power has helped fuel the travel recovery. Although this has made it more expensive for Americans to travel, pent-up demand has influenced a 12% increase of American travel to Europe (Kiesnoski, 2005). In order to understand the international travel industry, the following data and trends are presented (Miller & Associates, 2005; Office of Travel & Tourism Industries, 2005; Travel Industry Association of America, 2004, 2005; World Tourism Organization, 2004).

- International travel arrivals to the United States come from the following locations: Canada, 31%; Mexico, 26%; United Kingdom, 10%; Japan, 8%; Germany, 3%; France, 2%; South Korea, 2%; Austria, 1%; Italy, 1%; and the Netherlands, 1%.
- Asian, European, and South American visitors to the United States spend proportionately more per day than do Canadians and Mexicans, who both tend to come for frequent, short visits and for shopping.
- The fastest-growing individual markets for travel to the United States are Mexico, India, Ireland, and South Korea.
- U.S. resident trips to foreign countries are to Europe, 33.6%; Mexico, 14.3%; The Caribbean, 14.2%; Asia, 12%; Canada, 24%; Central America, 5.7%; South America, 5.4%; Oceania, 2.1%; the Middle East, 1.3%; and Africa, 0.6%. Among European countries, the rank order is: United Kingdom, France, Italy, and Germany.
- The U.S. travel deficit of $10 billion in 1985 balanced out by 1989 and grew to a travel surplus of $26.3 billion by 1996, before dropping to $2.6 billion in 2004 (Shields, 1991; Travel Industry Association of America, 2000, 2005).
- The top 10 leading destinations for worldwide travel, as measured by the number of tourists are, in order: France, Spain, United States, Italy, China, the United Kingdom, Austria, Mexico, Germany, and Canada.
- U.S. destinations for international travelers are, in order: Florida, New York, California, Hawaii, and Nevada.

Business Versus Pleasure Travel

It is difficult to determine what portion of the overall travel industry should be attributed to pleasure travel and what portion should be considered as business travel. About 82% of all trips are for pleasure (Travel Industry Association of America, 2005), but it should be noted that "pleasure travel" includes visits to friends and relatives, which for some Americans is more of an obligation than a form of recreation. It is also important to note that the 82% pleasure travel rate is a major increase from the 50% rate that was commonly reported 30 years ago.

There is also an important trend in combining business with pleasure. About 34% of business travelers add a leisure portion to their trip. On international trips, leisure extensions are even more common, and often the business traveler brings a spouse.

There are several important differences between business and pleasure travelers (Travel Industry Association of America, 2000, 2005; Lenhart, 2005; Office of Travel & Tourism Industries, 2005; Pfenning, 2005). Business travelers are more likely to be male (70% male to 30% female), travel solo, be more educated, and have higher incomes than leisure travelers. Business travelers are more likely than pleasure travelers to travel by airplane, use rental cars, and stay in hotels and motels. Pleasure travelers, however, take longer trips. Pleasure travelers also plan their trips much more in advance, but spend much less per day. These differences can be extremely important in tourism management and marketing decisions. For example, airline frequent flyer programs and hotel frequent stay programs might be promoted more aggressively to business travelers, particularly those with patterns of repeat trips to certain destinations.

Short Trips and Weekend Travel

One of the major social trends of the last 25 years is the increase in the number of women who enter the workforce. This has led to a dramatic increase in the number of "two-career families." Many of these families find it difficult to coordinate their work schedules to allow time for long vacations. As a result, mini-vacations have become one of the significant travel trends of recent years. Weekend and long weekend trips now account for 50% of American vacation trips. Among two-career families, this rate is even higher. Another study (Travel Industry Association of America, 2005) reported that 57% of Americans actually prefer to take several short trips rather than one long vacation. This trend is in sharp contrast to the European tradition of long (3-plus weeks) vacation trips.

The mini-vacation market differs somewhat from the overall travel market. Obviously, the duration of stay is shorter and use of the auto or RV is higher. This market is also more likely to visit cities and visit friends and relatives than other travel segments are.

TRAVEL PSYCHOLOGY AND BEHAVIOR

Some of the most interesting aspects of any study of the travel industry are the underlying psychological and behavioral aspects. These include motives and attractions for travel, barriers to travel, allocentric and psychocentric travelers, and market segmentation. Each of these aspects is considered in this section. The importance of these topics lies in the implications they have for marketing and managing a travel-related enterprise.

Motives and Attractions for Travel

Motives and attractions for travel have been identified by a variety of researchers. Often, the reasons for travel are identified as either "push" factors or "pull" attractions. Push factors are those forces within us that motivate us to travel.

Typical push-motivators include the following:

- health pursuits
- curiosity
- escape
- rest and relaxation
- prestige/ego
- cultural interest
- pleasure seeking
  (entertainment, gambling, shopping, etc.)
- physical activity
- friends and relatives

- novelty/change
- adventure
- challenge
- spiritual/religious
- search for roots/family heritage
- social interaction
- professional development
- business
- learn new skills

Pull factors are those attractions that draw people once they have the urge to travel. Typical pull-attractions include:

- natural scenic areas
- historical areas
- cultural events and attractions
- religious shrines
- entertainment events

- sports participation facilities
- educational events and meetings
- wildlife
- sporting events
- comfortable climates

Periodically, studies are conducted to assess why people travel and what they like to do. Figure 9-2 illustrates the findings of three such studies. Note that there is not uniformity in the answers; some are push-motivators and some are pull-attractions. This is not really a fault; it just reflects the different research orientations that may be taken. There are some similarities in the results, however. Notice that "visits to friends and relatives" is consistently highly ranked.

It must be realized that the studies in Figure 9-2 represent a very broad market segment, the general public. In realistic application, each particular travel-related company and destination resort needs to analyze the travel motives of their own particular market segments.

Figure 9-2
Three Travel Studies

Trends in Motivation for Leisure Travel
(TNS-Plog, 2004) Rated 1–10 scale
8.2 Chance to relax and get rid of stress
7.7 Do what I want, when I want
7.5 Spend more time with spouse/family
7.4 See new things, gain new experiences
7.0 Renew mind, body, and soul
6.2 Feel alive and energetic
5.9 Enriches my perspective on life
5.2 Gain knowledge about history and cultures
5.2 Nice to have others wait on me
5.0 Spend more time with friends

Motivation for Leisure Travel
(Yesawich, Pepperdine, Brown, & Russell, 2005)
* multiple responses possible
87% Rest and relax
81% Spend time with spouse
80% Experience new places
53% Experience new cultures
52% Experience an adventure
33% Spend time with children
28% Spend time with friends
24% Meet new people

Top 10 Activities of U.S. Resident Travelers
(Travel Industry Association of America, 2004)
* multiple responses possible
30% Shopping
27% Attend a social/family event
11% Outdoor recreation
10% City/urban sightseeing
10% Rural sightseeing
10% Beach activities
8% Historical places, sites, and museums
7% Gambling
7% Theme/Amusement park
7% National/State park

Barriers to Travel

Just as there are motives for travel, there are also reasons why people do not travel or travel less frequently. Different market segments may face different barriers. For example, the expense of travel may be the greatest barrier for many students. On the other hand, a corporate executive with a spouse who works may find that lack of time is the most significant barrier. Overall, the major barriers are as follows:

- **Expense**—Travel can be expensive compared to other forms of recreation. In one study, 63% of the people reported that expense is a barrier.
- **Lack of time**—This may actually reflect a lack of priority.
- **Health**—Poor health can be a major problem, particularly among senior citizens.
- **Lack of skills**—Children and many adults may lack skills to engage in certain outdoor activities at travel destinations.
- **Lack of interest**—Some people would simply rather stay home.
- **Family stage**—Families with young children are often limited in their travel.
- **Lack of information**—It may be surprising, but many people are not aware of the range of travel opportunities and values.
- **Lack of travel companion**—About 31% of all Americans travel alone on leisure trips, and the percentage has increased due to delayed marriages and divorce.
- **Security**—More than ever, Americans are concerned with crime and terrorism.

Each travel industry business must determine what barriers are relevant to their particular market segments. Next, strategies must be developed to combat the relevant barriers. Examples are reduced fares for infants on airlines, clubs for single travelers, and marketing programs that emphasize the ease and convenience of cruise travel.

Allocentric and Psychocentric Travelers: Venturesomeness

Motives for travel are a key aspect of a classic psychographic model developed by Dr. Stanley Plog (1974). This model classified destinations that were favored by two types of travelers: allocentrics and psychocentrics. Plog found that the U.S. population was normally distributed along a continuum between these two types. Figure 9-3 illustrates the allocentric-psychocentric curve. Note that the majority of the population is "mid-centric," sharing some characteristics of both types.

An allocentric traveler is a person who seeks new experiences and adventure in a variety of activities. This person is outgoing and self-confident in behavior, with higher income and more educational/cultural interests. An allocentric person prefers to fly and to explore non-touristy areas before others have visited the area. Allocentrics enjoy meeting people from foreign or different cultures. While they prefer good hotels and food, modern chain-type hotels are not necessarily sought. For a tour package, a "near-allocentric" would like to have the basics arranged (transportation and lodging) but not be committed to a structured agenda. They would rather have the freedom to explore an area, making their own arrangements and choosing a variety of activities. The more extreme allocentrics would seek the most undeveloped and/or adventurous destinations.

Psychocentrics, on the other hand, are more conservatively oriented. They prefer to return to familiar travel destinations where they can relax and know what types of food and activity to expect. Psychocentrics prefer to drive to destinations, stay in typical tourist accommodations, and eat at family-type restaurants. Not surprisingly, psychocentrics are a lower-income group than allocentrics or even mid-centrics. When arranging a package tour, psychocentrics would prefer a structured agenda, so that they know what to expect. Safety and security are very important to this group.

Figure 9-3
The Allocentric-Psychocentric Curve

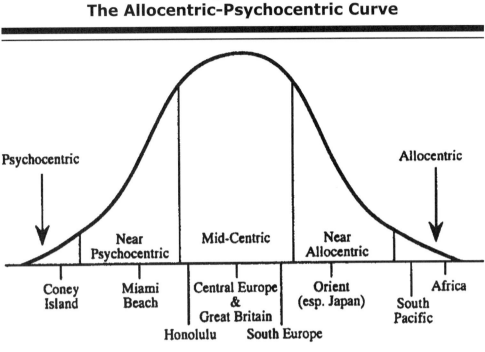

While Plog's model was developed many years ago, it has been conceptually accepted by many in the tourism industry. Occasionally, a tourism researcher may present data that fail to support Plog's model, but, generally, the model has more advocates than detractors. In recent years, Plog has updated the model and now uses the term *Venturesomeness* as the key concept. Now terms such as *dependables* (psychocentrics), *centrics* (mid-centrics), and *venturers* are used to describe the market segments (Plog, 2002).

Some groups of people, such as college students and young professional couples with infants, may be allocentrics or venturers by nature but not be able to afford an allocentric-type vacation. Therefore, they demonstrate mid-centric or near-psychocentric travel patterns or save up for a less frequent allocentric-type trip.

Plog's model has many implications for travel marketing. For example, a tour company might promote to allocentrics the adventure of flying to Malaysia for a jungle excursion to see the native orangutans "before the jungle is tamed forever." On the other hand, a destination that appeals to the psychocentric/dependables market should promote the comforts, reliability, and security found in a familiar resort. A scenario such as "an easy drive to your own time-share cabin by the lake, where you can fish with old friends," might catch the eye of the psychocentric traveler.

A refinement of Plog's model was proposed by Nickerson and Ellis (1991), who suggested that activation levels also played a part in the model of travel personality. For example, high-activation type people would be drawn to a destination that could provide a broad range of activities and a non-touristy atmosphere. These tourists could be the typical allocentric, outgoing, experimental travelers, or they could be more introverted, culturally oriented travelers who are active mentally, rather than physically. On the other hand, low-activation type people could be more private, low-key people who travel to visit family or friends.

Travel Market Segmentation and Lifestyles

Many businesses in the travel industry are interested in market segmentation. Travel businesses typically want to know demographic characteristics such as area of residence, age, income, family stage, and transportation mode. It is also helpful to know behavioral characteristics such as those related to Plog's allocentric-psychocentric model, as well as VALs: values, attitudes, and lifestyles, which help to group people into different lifestyle segments. If travel businesses understand their market segments, they will do a better job in providing the product or service that the market seeks and in communicating the message to the target market.

Travel businesses often develop market segment profiles to help characterize and understand their own specific clientele. One example is the vacation market segmentation developed for the Cruise Lines International Association (Travel & Tourism Executive Report, 1999):

- **Family folks** represent about 31% of their market. They are relatively young (average age of 40), married, parents of children under 18, budget-minded, practical and more concerned with their children's entertainment than their own. They look for vacations and cruises with a wide array of children's activities.
- **Want-it-alls** are about 17% of their market. These are workaholics with high expectations for their professional and personal lives. On vacation they demand a tremendous amount of pampering and relaxation.
- **Adventurers** are 12% of their market. They are sophisticated, well educated, and like exotic, remote, and romantic destinations such as the Far East, Antarctica, and Africa.
- **Comfortable spenders** are 25% of their market. They are well-off 40-somethings who are well traveled and active. They are big fans of resort vacations and are good prospects for a cruise vacation as well.
- **Cautious travelers** are about 15% of the market. These are 50-somethings who prefer the simple things in life and opt for family experiences. Few are good prospects for a cruise unless it is a short cruise.

Another interesting typology of leisure travelers was suggested by Yiannakis and Gibson (1992) and included the following types, which are pretty self-explanatory by their titles: sun lover, action seeker, anthropologist, archaeologist, organized mass tourist, thrill seeker, explorer, jetsetter, spiritual seeker, independent mass tourist, high class tourist, drifter, and escapist.

Other Travel and Tourism Patterns

There are a number of other interesting patterns in tourism participation and spending that deserve mention and consideration. Each could have implications for tourism managers and marketers (Milligan, 2005; McDonald, 2004; TNS-Plog, 2004; Travel Industry Association of America, 2000, 2005):

- Friends and relatives are the number-one source of travel information, followed by travel agency advice and then advertising by airlines, hotels, and rental car companies. In terms of travel media used, the newspaper travel section is used most, followed by the Internet, TV shows travel magazines, and consumer lifestyle magazines, in that order.
- People under the age of 35 are almost twice as likely to use the Internet to book travel.
- More travel occurs in the summer (33%), but other seasons still account for significant travel: winter—21%, spring—22%, and fall—24%.

- More travelers (46%) stay overnight in hotels and motels, but many travelers (35%) stay at homes of friends and relatives.
- Compared to the average traveler, mature travelers (age 55 and up) spend more time away from home on trips, travel greater distances, and spend more money, but are least likely to use the Internet for travel information.
- The majority (61%) of American family vacations include children under the age of 18, and only 25% of families decide on their destinations more than three months in advance.
- Fifteen percent of Americans spend over $5,000 per year on travel, 31% spend between $2,000 and $4,999, 20% spend between $1,000 and $1,999, 19% spend between $500 and $999, and 15% spend less than $500 per year.
- Tax refunds are used by 19% of Americans to pay for trips.
- When adults bring pets on leisure trips, they are more likely to stay overnight with friends and relatives than at hotels, but 29% of leisure travelers share a hotel room with a pet.

IMPORTANT ISSUES IN THE TRAVEL INDUSTRY

Before examining specific types of travel businesses, it is appropriate to consider several important issues in the travel industry. These topics include the role of government; rural tourism development; tourism trade associations; terrorism, crime, and safety; and ecotourism.

The Role of Government in Travel and Tourism

In many foreign countries, the national government takes a very active role in the travel and tourism industry. Airlines, railroads, and even some resorts are owned and operated by many foreign governments. They also coordinate travel and tourism planning and financially stimulate development of tourism destinations. Almost every major country spends more to promote inbound tourism than the United States does. In fact, of the 41 largest industrial nations, the United States is the only nation that does not have a dedicated and ongoing federal government budget to promote tourism. It should be noted, however, that many U.S. cities and states spend considerable sums to promote tourism, although most of the money is used to promote domestic tourism.

Overall, state governments spend about $603 million for travel and tourism development and promotion. The average budget for state travel offices is $12.8 million, and Hawaii leads the list, spending $69 million, followed by Illinois at $48 million (Travel Weekly, 2005). This funding goes toward media advertising, the operation of visitor welcome centers, and other functions to promote the states as tourism destinations. It is also important to note that many cities spend more than their state governments on tourism promotion (Miller & Associates, 2005). These cities include Las Vegas ($125 million), Orlando ($35 million), Los Angeles ($29 million), and Reno ($29 million).

At the federal level, the United States is a poor example of how to promote tourism. In 1995, the Clinton administration held the first-ever White House Conference on Travel and Tourism, yet the following year they eliminated the U.S. Travel and Tourism Administration (USTTA). In its place, the U.S. Congress passed the United States Tourism Organization Act of 1996. This act designated the U.S. National Tourism Organization (USNTO) as the official organization responsible for marketing the country abroad. USNTO was to be privately funded and led by a board composed of representatives from the major national trade organizations in the tourism industry. However, the USNTO board disbanded the organization and suspended operations when the federal government failed to provide any money for tourism promotion.

In 2003, Congress approved the establishment of the United States Travel and Tourism Promotion Board with $50 million for promoting international tourism. However, a subsequent congressional bill cut the funding to just $6 million for 2005 and $10 million for 2006 (American Hotel and Lodging Association, 2005; De Lollis, 2005). As a result, the United States has no effective organization or budget for promoting itself to international tourists.

Several other U.S. agencies are involved in other aspects related to tourism. These include the Federal Aviation Administration (FAA), which controls airspace, sets safety standards, and controls airport operations. The U.S. Customs Service monitors international travel, the Bureau of Transportation Statistics compiles travel statistics, the Interstate Commerce Commission regulates bus transportation, and the Federal Highway Administration helps provide the National Scenic Byways and numerous transportation enhancements. Of course, the National Park Service, the Forest Service, the Bureau of Land Management, the Army Corps of Engineers, the Fish and Wildlife Service, and the Bureau of Reclamation administer a large number of natural resources and recreational areas that have tourism appeal. A section of Chapter 10 will address the provision of these areas by government.

Federal, state, and local governments also fulfill other important functions related to tourism. One of the most important is the provision of infrastructure, such as roads and utilities. Government also has a role in the stimulation of the free enterprise system, the regulation of land development, and the regulation of business. It is also important to note that the various levels of government in the United States raise over $95 billion per year in revenues through tourism-related taxes. These include taxes on airline flights, gasoline, hotel rooms, restaurant meals, highway tolls, and auto rentals. Much of this tax revenue is dedicated to the construction and operation of airports, roads, convention centers, visitor bureaus, and other travel-related facilities and services.

Public beach parks such as Hanauma Bay in Hawaii draw thousands of visitors and put local government in the tourism business. (Photo: J. Crossley)

Rural Tourism Development

Compared to most other "industrialized nations," the United States is relatively rural. In fact, 96% of the population lives on 4% of the land, so the other 4% of the population is spread out over 96% of the landmass. It is also well documented that agriculture, mining, and other such natural resource industries are no longer the leading economic sectors of the nation's overall economy. As a result, many people living in small towns and rural areas have faced hardships in recent years as they struggle to maintain their economic stability and rural lifestyles. In many cases, rural communities have turned to tourism development as a tool for stimulation of their economies. Unfortunately, rural community leaders often lack the understanding of the process of tourism development, and, therefore, it becomes difficult to generate tourism (Lewis, 1998).

Tourism has the potential to rejuvenate a rural community's economic vitality through the infusion of tourists' dollars, the creation of new jobs, and the generation of tourism-dedicated taxes. Further, tourism can be a major factor in helping to conserve natural areas and encourage the preservation of unique cultural practices. However, if not managed properly, tourism can bring overdevelopment, abuse of natural resources, traffic congestion, real estate inflation, uneven economic cycles, crime, and loss of local culture. This is why rural tourism development must proceed slowly, carefully, and according to a sound plan.

Lewis (1998) suggests that rural tourism development typically occurs in four stages:

Stage 1: **The evolution of tourism** occurs when an individual or an organization believes that there is a resource in the community that would be of interest to tourists. A few tourists may already be visiting, but there are few services to support them.

Stage 2: **Formalization** occurs when formal organizations such as a local merchants association get involved by starting to market tourism and enhance tourism attractions.

Stage 3: **Development** occurs when development and marketing are in full swing. There is cooperative marketing to promote the area, and special events are developed.

Stage 4: **Centralization** occurs when a formal tourism organization, such as a convention and visitors bureau, is created. Dedicated tourism taxes are initiated, and the agency takes the lead in tourism planning and promotion.

Careful analysis of the rural tourism development model above should lead to the conclusion that Stages 1 through 3 probably occur without a formal plan through the leadership of well-intended local individuals. During these stages, negative consequences of tourism can simply begin to evolve in the absence of comprehensive planning and professional tourism leadership. Hopefully, by the time the fourth stage occurs, it is not too late for the area's natural resources, culture, and quality of life.

It is fortunate that many states have state tourism agencies, university extension services, and/or regional tourism councils with individuals who possess expertise in rural tourism development. These individuals and agencies can develop statewide or regional plans for tourism development, and provide expertise to guide rural communities through the first three of Lewis's four stages. In this way, a rural community can optimize its tourism potential, while reducing the risks of negative impacts generated by unplanned or unwise development. Some areas of the country have embraced rural tourism development in a big way. New York state alone has over 2,500 agrotourism operators who generate over $210 million in revenue. California has more than 500 agrotourism businesses scattered throughout the state, and some generate as much as 60% of their revenue from tourism rather than crop harvest (Rodriguez, 2004).

Tourism Trade Associations

Almost every segment of the tourism industry has a trade association to unite its members and advance its interests. Examples include the National Tour Association (NTA), the American Society of Travel Agents (ASTA), the Cruise Line Industry of America (CLIA), the American Hotel and Motel Association (AHMA), the International Association of Amusement Parks and Attractions (IAAPA), and the Air Transport Association of America (ATA). These associations monitor industry trends, conduct research, facilitate communication among members, conduct industry conferences and educational programs, and lobby for their industry's interests in the political arena.

One association, the Travel Industry Association of America (TIA), deserves particular attention, because this nonprofit association is the unifying organization for all the components of the U.S. travel industry. TIA's mission is to promote and facilitate increased travel to and within the United States. TIA also has taken a leadership role in organizing industry councils to address legislative issues relative to the tourism industry. Another TIA function is its role as the leading organization in travel industry research, analysis, and forecasting. TIA's Web site is www.tia.org.

Terrorism, Crime, and Safety in the Travel Industry

Terrorism is an age-old political weapon, and in recent years it has become an all too common occurrence, with several thousand incidents occurring every year. Many of these attacks have involved the travel industry. One of the first big shocks to the tourism industry came in 1997 when Islamic fundamentalists, posing as tourists and police, opened fire on visitors at one of the ancient temples at Luxor, Egypt. Sixty tourists and 10 other people were killed. American and European travel to that region withered immediately. In the next few years, other tourists were kidnapped and/or killed in Uganda, Jamaica, Malaysia, Indonesia, Israel, Columbia, Ecuador, the Philippines, and the former Yugoslavian states.

The worst terrorism incident occurred when Arab Muslim terrorists hijacked four U.S. airliners on 9/11/01 and murdered over 2,000 people in the resulting crashes. As mentioned previously, world tourism dropped immediately, and over the next 2 years, international tourism to the United States fell 22%. In 2003, a survey revealed that 84% of Americans said that concerns over terrorism were having at least some effect on their travel (Pfenning, 2003a). Continued terrorism attacks in Spain, London, and twice in Bali (2002 and 2005), renewed fears across the world.

Crime is another concern for tourism. Even in the United States, many urban areas, such as New York, Detroit, and Miami, periodically have their reputations stained by crimes against tourists. Riots have followed events such as the Rodney King trial in California, World Series and NBA championships, and rock concerts such as Woodstock II.

Finally, natural disasters have caused devastation to residents and tourists alike in recent years. These include the tsunami in December 2004 that killed over 200,000 people in Indonesia, Thailand, and Sri Lanka, and the hurricanes that hit the U.S. Gulf Coast states in September, 2005.

What does the tourism industry do to recover from terrorism, crime, and natural disasters? The first priority is usually given to rescue, then restoration of law and order, victims' aid, health services, and communications. Rebuilding comes next, though some areas never fully recover. Some areas are remarkably resilient, however. For example, Phuket, Thailand, had 90% of its rooms ready for tourists again just 2 weeks after the tsunami hit. However, it lost about $10 million a day in tourism revenue during its peak season because many tourists canceled their trips and others stopped making reservations (Sidron, 2005). In order to counter these declines in tourism, most destinations initiate aggressive marketing campaigns once the areas are safe. Tourism destinations also give additional "familiarization tours" to travel agents in hopes of influencing the agents to promote their areas again. Another approach is to offer deeply discounted packages to lure tourists back. In the case of crime-plagued areas, great efforts are taken to warn tourists about crime-ridden areas; erect directional signs to resort areas; and provide maps, brochures, and other materials to educate tourists about how to reduce their risks.

Ecotourism

One of the most significant trends in the tourism industry is the rise of ecotourism, which has also been called "green tourism," "nature tourism," and recently, "geotourism." *Ecotourism* is defined as "responsible travel to natural areas that conserves the environment and improves the well-being of local people" (International Ecotourism Society, 2005). Similarly, *geotourism* has been defined as "tourism that sustains or enhances the geographical character of the place being visited—its environment, culture, aesthetics, heritage, and well-being of its residents" (National Geographic Traveler, 2002). The presence of this tourism brings money into an area and provides an economic incentive to stop uncontrolled development, logging, slash-and-burn farming, poaching, and overfishing. For most practical purposes, the terms *ecotourism* and *geotourism* can be used interchangeably.

Ecotourists/geotourists are more likely than other tourists to travel internationally and be middle-aged, highly educated, and affluent. They want to experience a natural environment and learn about the history and indigenous culture as well. They typically stay longer at a destination and are willing to spend more money on a trip that guarantees responsible travel practices. (Travel Weekly, 2005; *National Geographic Traveler*, 2002; Crossley & Lee, 1994). Further, their money makes a deeper impact on the local economy, because the ecotourist spends for locally produced food, crafts, and services and locally owned lodging. Some countries such as Belize and Costa Rica have made ecotourism the central theme of their tourism industries.

Close encounters with wildlife at rehabilitation parks are one of the main ecotourism attractions at destinations such as Kangaroo Island, Australia. (Photo: J. Crossley)

The rapid increase in ecotourism popularity has created a definite danger, expressed by Jean Michel Cousteau: "I see ecotourists loving nature to death" (Bartlet, 1991). Indeed, there have been instances where tour operators and resorts have abused an area by bringing in more "ecotour" groups than the destination can sustain and/or failed to practice responsible ecological methods. Loss of local culture is another possible negative impact.

Another problem is that some ecotours have become victim to an "eco-sell" marketing mentality where any tour that includes nature is called ecotourism. As many as 5,000 companies offer some type of outdoor adventure tours and ecotours within the United States and abroad, and too many fail to maintain an environmental ethic. For example, some tour boats in the Galapagos Islands dump raw sewage directly into the ocean, and timber along Nepal's Himalayan trails has been cut to heat water for tea-sipping trekkers. In response to the need to regulate ecotourism and to curb possible abuses, The Ecotourism Society has developed detailed guidelines for ecotours. Web sites to explore further are www.ecotourism.org and www.adventuretravel.com.

INDUSTRY PROFILE: AIRLINES

How many commercial recreation and tourism graduates are going to own or manage an airline? The answer is probably none, but this does not mean that there are not opportunities within the industry. Most airlines require that employees start at entry-level positions and work their way up. Flight attendants can become senior attendants, supervisors, and trainers. Reservationists and customer service staff may move up through ticket counter work to supervisory and management positions. Both career paths can build upon the leadership skills, public relations skills, business skills, and knowledge of the travel industry that are gained by a commercial recreation and tourism major.

It is also important for students who are interested in tour companies, the hotel industry, and other travel services to understand the airline industry. Much of the travel business is interrelated, and career-minded students must understand airlines in order to understand the overall travel environment.

Airlines Industry Overview

Air travel is the preferred transportation mode of the upscale tourist. The typical air traveler covers three times the distance of an auto trip, stays longer, and spends more money. About 80% of adults in the United States have flown on commercial airlines, and about 40% take an airplane trip at least once a year.

A milestone in the history of the airlines industry occurred with deregulation in 1978. This change allowed airlines to set their own routes, schedules, and fares. In a Darwinian struggle of the fittest, route systems expanded to meet new opportunities, and unprofitable routes were eliminated. Within 6 years, the number of certified airlines quadrupled, but there were also 161 companies that went broke or merged with other airlines.

The airline industry was generally profitable from 1995 through 2000. This was due to several reasons: a stable U.S. economy, stable fuel prices—at least until early 2000, record load factors (percentage of seats sold) averaging around 70% a year, and various cost controls. However, with the SARS scare, terrorism concerns, and economic recessions, the outlook for airlines has been very gloomy since 2000. In fact, the airline industry lost $10 billion from 2000 to 2004, and four major airlines declared Chapter 11 bankruptcy (Weber & Freed, 2005).

It is important to note that the success of airline companies is a concern to the overall tourism industry. When an airline fails, it can create a domino effect of trouble for travel agencies, tour companies, and entire destination areas until another airline can pick up the lost routes.

The remainder of this section will examine the types of airlines and major trends that affect their operation: the hub and spoke concept, cost controls, discount fares, and other trends.

Types of Airlines

There are two major classifications of airline flights: international and domestic. Airlines operating internationally must have their routes, schedules, and fares approved by the governments of the countries involved. There are particular problems inherent with international flights: time zone differences, baggage handling difficulties, passports and visas, custom regulations, and foreign currencies. International airlines may also operate domestically within their own country. The U.S. Department of Transportation classifies airlines as one of three types, according to revenues. Each is presented below, plus a fourth category containing charter airlines.

Major Carriers have at least $1 billion in annual revenue. Ten major airlines qualify for this rating and account for 87% of all passenger miles in the United States. The top three, United, American, and Delta, account for about 48% of all U.S. air travel (Corridore, 2004). These dominant carriers each have a national route system, based on hubs in several key cities, and sophisticated computer reservation systems. However United and Delta have lost billions of dollars in recent years, much of it due to having some of the highest union-driven wages in the industry.

The most consistently profitable major carrier has been Southwest Airlines, an airline that built a short-haul, point-to-point system characterized by no frills, low costs, and cheap fares. Some of these strategies have also been adopted by other airlines. In recent years, however, Southwest has expanded its route system to include long-haul routes between several eastern and western U.S. cities.

Major carriers typically operate jet aircraft with 130–400 seats and have average flight lengths of about 1,000 miles. Many major carriers have developed strategic alliances and code-sharing agreements with foreign airlines to serve international markets, and with other major carriers and regional carriers to serve smaller U.S. markets.

National Carriers have revenues between $100 million and $1 billion. Some of these carriers limit their service to regional markets, while others offer some international service. Their aircraft average 100–150 seats and operate more short-haul flights on a point-to-point service.

Regional Airlines (including commuter airlines) have revenues under $100 million and provide service between small cities and major hubs. For this reason, many of the regional/commuter airlines form alliances with major airlines, and some are being taken over by the majors. Most of the regional/commuter lines are low fare, no frills, and have nonunion labor. These aggressively managed airlines exemplify the deregulated free market, but failure rate is high.

Charter Airlines are often linked with tour operators who can come close to filling every seat by putting together bulk-purchased hotel and rental car packages. Most airlines will provide some charter service on a contract basis, but few specialize in this. With high load factors and lower operating costs, the charters can usually undercut scheduled airline prices by a significant amount.

The Hub and Spoke Concept

The hub and spoke concept (see Appendix for travel definitions) has become the most popular routing system among the major airlines. The concept has numerous advantages:

- A large number of destinations are connected with fewer total flights.
- Aircraft and personnel are used more efficiently.
- Load factors (seat occupancy percentage) are higher.
- Passengers stay with the same airline to make connecting flights.
- Average revenue per passenger is higher.
- Enables a major airline to coordinate schedules with feeder airlines (regionals and commuters).

There are now about 30 principal hub cities, and some of these airports operate above their design capacity. The increased congestion of the hubs has caused chaos at some locations. It is not unusual for one airline company to schedule 40 or more flights to arrive at a hub within a 50-minute period. While the planes refuel and baggage is transferred, passengers scramble to make their connecting flights. About 40 minutes later, the "bank" of 40 planes is scheduled to take off again to the next destination.

The lack of airport congestion has become so unusual that it has become part of the marketing campaign for some destination areas. For example, the Utah ski resorts emphasize their accessibility through Salt Lake International Airport where tourists can take early morning flights from eastern cities and be skiing by midday.

Some major airlines, including Southwest and many of the regional airlines, do not base their operations on the hub and spoke concept. They have found that the point-to-point routing system works better for the short-haul routes that have enough volume to fly several times a day. Using this system, and flying the fuel-efficient 737s, Southwest flies its jets more hours per day than American, United, or Delta.

Airline Cost Controls

To be successful, airlines need to control their costs, most of which are fixed costs such as labor, fuel, advertising, facilities, and, of course, the planes. Whether a plane carries one passenger or a full load, these expenses must be covered. Several of the key elements in cost control are:

- **Fuel costs**—For United Airlines, every penny per gallon increase in fuel costs the airline $2.2 million over a year. Other airlines face similar pressures, as fuel costs have increased greatly in recent years. Therefore, worldwide stability of the oil market is essential for the airlines' success. Newer planes tend to be more fuel efficient, so the age of an airline's fleet also helps fuel cost control (Manor, 2004; Corridore, 2004).
- **Labor costs**—Labor, at 40% of overall costs, is the largest single expense. Airlines that reduce corporate overhead jobs and keep their unions in check can save millions.
- **Reservations and ticketing**—In 2002, most of the major airlines eliminated the payment of commissions, once as high as 10%, to travel agencies. This saved the airlines several billion dollars a year, as travel agencies still book about 70% of passenger flights. Another innovation, electronic tickets (e-tickets), reduces processing costs from $8 per ticket to 50 cents, and this saves hundreds of millions, too. About 95% of domestic tickets are now e-tickets. Finally, about 30% of airline reservations are now made directly online with the airlines, saving millions more (Corridore, 2004).

Discount Fares

One of the major outgrowths of deregulation is the competition that has led to a variety of airfare discounts. Now, about 95% of all passengers fly on some type of discount, but the cheaper the fare, the more restrictions apply. Occasionally, an airline initiates a radical discount, usually for specific markets, other airlines counter and expand the discount, and soon a fare war breaks out. This can greatly stimulate leisure travel during slow periods and/or to weak markets. It is great for passengers and the resorts they go to, but, overall, the airlines often lose money in the cutthroat action.

Other Important Trends

There are several other trends in the airline industry that deserve mention here:

- **Load factors** grew from 50% in the 1970s to 74% in 2004, and some airlines are around 80%. However, part of this improvement reflects the fact that many airlines have cut back on their number of flights, particularly since 2001. Because of significant cost increases of fuel and union labor, the margin between success and failure is still very thin.
- **Alliances** between airlines help them to serve more destinations including international cities, stimulate business, and save operation costs. Meanwhile, customers may save money, experience smoother connections, and benefit from shared frequent flyer programs. Most major airlines are seeking to participate in such alliances. For example, the "Star Alliance" includes United, Lufthansa, SAS, Air Canada, Varig, Thai Airways, Singapore Airlines, All Nippon Airways, Austrian Airlines, Spanair, and Air New Zealand.
- **The Legacy of 9/11** lingers in many ways. While airlines have almost recovered to the level of passengers in 2000, many other issues remain. The losses of 2001 through 2004 depleted the cash reserves of most airlines, making it difficult to cope with cost increases such as fuel, new airport fees, and the costs of increased airport security. Taxes and fees now constitute about 26% of the cost of a domestic flight, which is double the rate from a decade ago (Milligan, 2004).

Several other problems lurk on the horizon for the airline industry. First, it is a cyclical business that can change rapidly with economic conditions, especially recessions or increases of oil prices. Next, terrorism could reduce travel demand to certain destinations, thus hurting the airlines that fly those routes. Finally, the consolidation and mergers of airlines could ruin the competition that has kept prices low enough to stimulate travel, but, on the other hand, if the competition causes too much discounting, then the airline will continue to lose money.

INDUSTRY PROFILE: CRUISE LINES

In 1970, only about 500,000 Americans went on cruises, but during the mid-1970s, a successful television show, *Love Boat*, introduced the concept of cruising to millions of viewers. This TV show has been given credit for broadening the cruise market and lowering the average passenger age (Beekhuis, 1984). By 2005, the North American cruise industry was expected to serve over 11 million passengers, and growth rates have averaged about 8% a year over the last 10 years (Tobin, 2005a). This rate is over double the growth rate of the overall travel industry. To serve this booming industry, there are over 184 cruise vessels in North America, and many of these are new or refurbished. Some of the newest ships carry as many as 3,800 passengers, while others, capable of sailing to smaller and more exotic ports, carry only 100. Cruise customers enjoy this form of vacation, because most cruises are all-inclusive packages that include room, meals, snacks, entertainment, and shore excursions to a variety of interesting ports of call.

Major cruise ships have taken advantage of modern technologies including stabilizers, lighter materials, modular construction, fuel-efficient design with gas turbine engines, and satellite-assisted navigation. The newest ships may have several different types of swimming pools, theme restaurants, high-tech nightclubs, extensive health spas, grand theaters, ice rinks, in-line skating tracks, rock-climbing walls, full jogging tracks and basketball courts, and youth centers. These facilities complement the usual sun decks, casinos, libraries, shops, lounges, and showrooms.

In addition to the major cruise lines, there are about 600 passenger vessels that serve large cities bordering major lakes, rivers, bays, and inland waterways. These include dinner cruise operators, excursion vessels, passenger ferries, and riverboats devoted to gambling. The riverboats have proven to be very successful and have helped to rejuvenate the economies of several cities along the Mississippi River.

Major Trends

The United States is the largest cruise market in the world. Even so, only 12% of the U.S. population has ever cruised. Interest in cruising is much higher, however, as research shows that about half of the population is interested in taking a cruise. Indeed, great changes in the market have occurred. Once, cruise passengers were primarily wealthy senior citizens. This has changed; now only 25% of cruisers are retired, and 30% are under age 40. Most of these passengers are first-timers, but once they go, most want to repeat (International Council of Cruise Lines, 2005; Miller & Associates, 2005). Another major market change is the length of cruises. The industry average is seven days, but the three-to-four-day cruise is the fastest-growing area of business. These are typically low-cost excursions to relatively close destinations. Examples include Port Everglades, Florida, to the Bahamas, and Long Beach, California, to Ensenada, Mexico.

A second major trend is the use of discounts and incentives to attract new markets. Some cruise lines discount for early bookings, while others discount more as a given sailing date approaches. There are also changes in pricing for single passengers. Instead of charging single passengers at double rate, some cruise lines are building more single cabins into the ships or creating room-share programs for single travelers. Other incentives include "free" airfare and package deals linked to land-based attractions. For example, 34% of cruise passengers departing from Miami area ports stay extra days to see the South Florida area and spend an extra $177 (International Council of Cruise Lines, 2005).

A third trend is the increased diversity in the cruises, destinations, and activities. Most cruises in North America depart from Florida ports and visit destinations in the Caribbean. West Coast cruises typically go to Alaska or to the Mexican beaches of Mazatlan, Puerto Vallarta, and Acapulco. Newer port cities include New Orleans, Tampa, Galveston, Vancouver, New York, Honolulu, and Boston. In Asia, Singapore is positioning itself to be the cruise center for the Pacific region. More adventure cruises, however, are gaining great popularity. Destinations include the Nile, Amazon, and Yangtze rivers, plus numerous exotic islands.

Many cruises have a variety of programs available, such as golf, skeet shooting, exercise classes, shore excursions, and talent shows. Theme cruises take the programming one step further with a variety of themed entertainment, classes, or other activities. Theme cruises include NASCAR, big band, country-western days, jazz festival, NFL football, murder mystery, great American food and wine, and fitness.

Opportunities in the Cruise Industry

While there are opportunities for employment in the cruise industry, students should not be deceived by perceptions of glamour. Ships' officers are almost always non-Americans from the cruise line's home country: often Italy, Holland, or Norway. With the exception of NCL, crew members on large ships are primarily non-Americans (Indonesia, Philippines, Portugal, etc.) who fill low-paying, nonprofessional positions. The primary opportunities, therefore, are for positions in the entertainment department or with the onshore offices.

A ship's entertainment department is headed by the cruise director, who as a professional entertainer must host shows, sing, dance, and be a comic. The assistant or deputy cruise director also entertains and helps the cruise director supervise the ship's recreational programs. Social hosts, front desk staff, tour directors, sports directors, and youth activity coordinators are hired by most cruise lines, but the positions do not pay high salaries. Some cruise lines also contract specialists for golf, tennis, snorkeling/diving, adult arts and crafts, bridge, and other activities. Most major cruise lines also hire certified fitness trainers who organize and carry out a variety of activities such as aerobics, weight training, stretching, relaxation, and jogging/walking. These social staff members get shared cabins, meals, and airfare to the port cities. Employment may be contracted for eight months or as little as two weeks.

Cruise line offices also hire reservationists, personnel specialists, public relations specialists, corporate level recreation planners, sales and marketing staff, and office managers. Students wishing to apply with cruise lines should first get the correct addresses from the Steamship Directory or the CLIA Cruise Manual, which are available at many travel agencies. Another possibility for cruise-related employment is to work as a tour group escort. Alumni groups, singles travel clubs, travel agencies, and tour operators may all occasionally employ tour escorts.

INDUSTRY PROFILE: TRAVEL AGENCIES

Travel agencies are a high-tech industry where young people with management skills can begin a career in the travel industry. Every major city has several travel schools where students can learn the computer reservation skills needed to become a travel agent. While travel agency managers make salaries of about $40,000 a year, the average compensation for agents is just a little over $31,000, though agents in large companies make more (Pfenning, 2003). The work can be stressful, as agents must try to please all cus-

Exotic destinations such as Tahiti make cruise vacations one of the fastest-growing segments of the travel industry. (Photo: J. Crossley)

tomers, some of whom can be obnoxious. Benefits are good, however, since agents get free or discounted airfares and hotel accommodations. Agents also go on occasional "Fam Tours" (familiarization tours), which are mini-vacations to inspect hotels and resorts.

The mark of a professional agent is the achievement of "Certified Travel Counselor" status. This certification requires five years' experience and additional training. The next step is to become an agency manager. At this level, skills gained in a college degree program become more important. Some agents and managers go on to become travel agency owners, where agency profits can add significant income. However, this can be a very risky proposition, because numerous travel agencies have gone out of business in recent years.

Another career track for an experienced agent is to become a travel coordinator for a major corporation or manager with a tour company, travel council, or convention/visitor bureau. In all these positions, it is important to have good interpersonal and communication skills plus knowledge of geography, travel interests, computers, and business.

Travel agencies were not a major industry until air travel began to flourish. In 1978, the airline deregulation act led to many changes in routes, schedules, and fares, causing people to begin to seek help in finding the best airfares. The number of travel agencies more than doubled to 32,238 in 1995. However, as airline companies initiated severe cuts in the commissions paid to travel agencies, many agencies were forced to close, and the number of agencies dropped to 20,875 in 2005 (Compart, 2005).

Services of a Travel Agency

The primary duty of a travel agency is to arrange transportation and lodging for its clients. An agent should first become knowledgeable about the suppliers of transportation and lodging. A good agent will then help match the traveler's expectations and financial ability with the appropriate travel options. The agent also has a duty to provide necessary information about the trip (visas, currency, civil unrest, etc.). Reservations for transportation, accommodations, and other services must be made, and, at a later date, confirmed if necessary. Ticketing and the processing of payments must also be completed.

A second major service is the retailing of tour packages. In some cases, the agency may develop the tour package and even provide escorts. It is more common, however, to purchase the tour package through a tour operator or wholesaler and then to retail the package to the client.

The provision of auxiliary services is the third major responsibility of the travel agency. Services include arranging for passports, traveler's checks, videos, maps, guidebooks, and tourist convenience items.

In exchange for its services, the travel agency receives commissions from the various travel suppliers. The industry standard used to be 10% for airline bookings. However, in the mid 1990s airlines started to cut back on that rate. In 2002, Delta became the first airline to eliminate base commissions for domestic routes, and most other U.S. airlines followed suit. This is the reason that most travel agencies now charge a service fee that averages $27 per booking (Sidron, 2004). U.S. hotels, rental car agencies, and other suppliers still typically pay commissions, and airlines still pay commissions for international flights and tours. Many agencies try to sell bookings for "preferred" airlines, resorts, cruises, and tours that offer "overrides" or extra commissions to agencies that book a high volume of business with them. These overrides can range from 2% to an occasional 10%.

Travel Agency Markets

An agency's total sales volume comes from two different markets: business travel and leisure travel. Even though leisure travel represents 80% of all U.S. trips, it accounts for only 55% of travel agency revenue. This difference exists because leisure travelers are less likely to use travel agents, are less likely to fly, and tend to stay in less expensive hotels (Chipkin, 2000).

Air travel is still the biggest revenue area, accounting for 36% of agency bookings. This is followed by cruise bookings (26%), tours (18%), and hotels (12%) (Travel Weekly, 2004).

Most travel agencies serve both the business and leisure markets. The best markets appear to be the following: business executives, high-income groups, married couples (old or young) without children at home, upscale singles, families with teenage children, and more highly educated individuals. People seeking cruises, package tours, or international travel are very likely to use an agency's services. As with many commercial recreation and tourism industries, repeat business is critical for success; most travel agency bookings are made by repeat customers.

Travel Agency Operations

There are very few federal, state, or city requirements specifically oriented to travel agencies, and it is relatively inexpensive to open a business. One of the first expenses in starting an agency is to post a performance bond to guarantee that all accounts between the agency and suppliers will be settled. The Airlines Reporting Corporation requires this bond, plus proof of adequate cash reserves. Another key expense is to allow about $700 per month to lease a computer reservation system (CRS) from an airline. Once a significant volume of business (200 or more flight segments per month) is established, the CRS lease price is discounted, and many high volume agencies pay less than $100 per month. Altogether, it should take at least $60,000 to start an agency, but another $50,000 or more per year could be lost until a solid customer base is developed. Banks and other conventional lending sources are reluctant to loan this amount for travel agency start-ups, so personal resources or partnerships are typically the financial sources used.

Areas such as shopping centers are good locations to attract leisure travelers, while city business centers are better for the corporate travel market. Both locations need to be on the ground floor with easy access for walk-in business. Professionally operated travel agencies are usually members of ASTA, the American Society of Travel Agents.

Seventy-five percent of travel agencies have five or fewer employees, and only 7% have more than 25 employees. The small agencies average less than $58,000 in sales per week, while the largest agencies average more than $384,000 a week in sales (Travel Weekly, 2004).

Travel agencies are trying a variety of strategies to hold their own at a time when more people are using the Internet to make their own arrangements. Among people under the age of 35, about 53% use the Internet to book at least some of their travel (McDonald, 2004). Travel agency survival strategies now emphasize the personal service that can be given to customers. This includes counseling customers about their choice of destination, type of accommodation, activities available, and development of complex itineraries. Adventure travel, cruises, and international travel typically fit this profile. These services require the travel agent to devote more time to the customer, but the overall package price is usually higher, as are the commission rates. A related strategy is to specialize in certain travel niches (by destination or activity) and develop a reputation for being experts in that area. Finally, many travel agencies are joining the Internet wars and marketing via Web sites.

Agency Alternatives

Discount agencies and travel consolidators are designed to serve a special niche in an effective manner and draw customers by offering discounted tickets.

A discount travel agency may make reservations at the regular fare but charge a lower sales fee or rebate part of its commission to the customer. The discount agency could also contract with the travel supplier for a discounted rate and pass part of that savings on to the customer. Either way, it is a high-volume, low-margin approach in order to save the customer a few dollars. The catch is that there is no travel consulting and no changing of itineraries. Many discount agencies make extensive use of the Internet for their business.

Travel consolidators offer "distressed merchandise" or potentially unsold space on flights, cruises, and tours. This approach works best for travelers who can decide on a trip a couple weeks or a few days before its departure. Discounts range from 20 to 70%, yet the consolidator still makes a good profit, because they buy the unsold space at deep discounts. Consolidators also may contract with scheduled airlines 6 months in advance for bulk discounted rates and pass on savings of 20 to 30% to customers.

INDUSTRY PROFILE: TOUR COMPANIES

Packaged travel is a $166 billion industry, with about half the business coming from group tours and half from packaged travel without an escort (National Tour Association, 2005b). About 630 specialty travel and tour operators belong to the top professional association, the National Tour Association, but there are about 3,000 tour operators who are not members.

Most of the NTA-affiliated companies operate "intermodel" tours that incorporate motor coach travel with planes, cruises, river runners, or rail carriers. Less than one third of NTA tour operators own their own motor coaches. The majority contract space with various carriers or charter the transportation necessary for the tour.

Tour patrons come from all across the United States, and markets vary from company to company. However, the largest segments for group tours are the well-educated segments of the "leading edge baby boomers" (20%, age 50–59) and "future seniors/ seniors" (46%, age 60 and over). Clients for international tours and adventure tours tend to be younger and mostly college educated (National Tour Association, 2005a).

Advantages and Disadvantages of Group Travel

Why do people go on group tours? There are numerous advantages and disadvantages. For some travelers, the *advantages* are as follows:

- Financial savings of group rates.
- Economic simplification—travelers know what they will spend.
- Solves the problem of what to see—inexperienced travelers appreciate this most. The best sights and activities are usually included.
- A shared experience—group interaction increases the trip value, and people make new friends.
- A convenient and carefree experience—the traveler is released from the work of planning and executing the trip.
- Greater security with group travel and a tour guide to act as a buffer to the foreign environment.

Disadvantages of group travel can exist in the opinions of some people:

- It may be too regimented or too slow for some adventurous travelers.
- It may move too fast for the person who seeks depth and quality of experience.

- Passive sightseeing, the heart of most tours, is still important, but more travelers now seek activity and adventure.
- A sick, hurt, lost, or obnoxious group member can ruin the experience for many people on the tour.

Types of Tour Companies

There are several different types of tour companies: tour wholesalers, motor coach companies, receptive operators, and outdoor adventure services. Each type may provide all the elements of a tour (make arrangements, market tour, lead tour), or they may specialize in one or two elements while contracting out the other aspects. Travel agencies may also perform any of the functions.

Tour Wholesalers specialize in putting tours together and selling the package to travel agencies, who retail the tour to the public. Some tour wholesalers also market the package directly to the public. Because wholesalers "block out," or reserve, thousands of hotel rooms, cruise berths, motor coach tour seats, and so on, they can command great discounts from the suppliers. These discounts can be built into an attractively priced tour package and still leave room for a healthy profit. Many tour wholesalers do most of their business creating and selling "independent vacation packages" rather than "escorted tours." With an independent package, vacationers get the discounts of group airfare, lodging, and activities, but they are not tied to an escorted tour group's structured daily itinerary.

Some wholesalers work with a variety of destinations, markets, tour lengths, prices, and activities. They continuously evaluate the tours, adding, dropping, or changing the tour to meet market interests. This approach has strength in its diversity and is less seasonal. On the other hand, there are also many specialty tour wholesalers who concentrate on a particular market segment or destination.

Motor Coach Companies provide regularly scheduled intercity (between cities) transportation and/or chartered bus service. In the mid-1990s, intercity bus travel stabilized after many years of decline that had left many small cities and towns without bus terminals. Low airfares are blamed for most of this decline. On the other hand, the charter and tour segment of the industry has increased dramatically, in part due to the improved image of the modern luxury coach. Today, a modern motor coach can cost $300,000 new, or as much as $200,000 for a 5-year-old used coach. They are air-conditioned with plush reclining seats and extra large windows for sightseeing. Some motor coaches show movies and have enlarged restrooms, tables, and concessions for food and drinks.

Receptive Operators are businesses based at a destination area that offer services to incoming groups of travelers. These businesses specialize in knowing a particular local area and provide many types of services:

- Planning and arrangements for tours coming into their area, including arrangements for lodging, meals, sports events, theme parks, and so on.
- "Step-on guides" for incoming motor coach tour groups.
- Motor coaches for tour groups who fly into the area. The motor coach may be owned by the receptive operator or leased from a separate company.
- Guided tours for local residents or for tourists who are traveling on their own. Horse-drawn carriages, tour vans, tour boats, or motor coaches may be used.

Because they know an area so well, receptive operators are often contracted by tour wholesalers to provide all the local arrangements for a particular geographic segment of a wholesaler's package. This saves the wholesaler valuable time. One 15-minute phone call can set up arrangements that would otherwise take hours to complete. It can also save money because receptive operators may get better rates by dealing frequently with their local market. Perhaps more importantly, the receptive operator should improve the quality of any tour, since they know the best places to go and the best way to present their local area. Keith Griffall, president of Western Leisure Inc., reports that receptive tour operators also work on partnership opportunities with suppliers such as convention and visitor bureaus (CVBs) and help package a destination that completes the sales cycle of the CVB. It is not surprising, therefore, that business for receptive operators is one of the fastest-growing segments of the group travel business.

Outdoor Adventure Tours and Ecotour Companies are a booming segment of the travel industry. The boom has coincided with three other growth areas: the fitness industry, environmental awareness, and air travel. Active, physically oriented baby boomers can easily afford the airfare to numerous origination points for adventure tours. In addition, active senior citizens are an important market for less challenging, "soft adventure" tours.

Many people choose the group adventure tour approach because the necessary equipment, guides, instructors, and permits are supplied in one complete package. Popular types of tours include white-water river rafting, ski touring, hiking/backpacking trips, bicycle tours, scuba dive excursions, helicopter ski weeks, jungle treks, guided fishing/hunting trips, mountain climbing, archaeological digs, and wilderness challenge outings. Adventure tours can also vary by length, from one to 30 days, and by price. For example, backpacking trips where participants supply their own equipment can be relatively inexpensive. On the other hand, heli-ski weeks are high-priced due to the use of helicopters, expensive ski lodges, and fine restaurants.

Many outdoor adventure companies start on a limited basis with only a small investment. Banks, however, are reluctant to loan money for such start-ups, so personal resources or partners are the typical funding sources. While the company's office location may be in a city for marketing purposes, a base location is needed close to rivers, mountains, deserts, or other appropriate natural resources.

One of the major barriers to starting an outdoor adventure company is the acquisition of permits for use of those natural resources. The Bureau of Land Management, the National Park Service, and the Forest Service limit the number of commercial users. Once the permit ceiling is reached, no new permits are issued. Some aggressive new companies try to buy out the older or marginal companies in order to secure their permits. Some international ecotours may require negotiations with chiefs of indigenous native tribes in order to gain access to the traditional coral reefs and forests that serve as sacred fishing and hunting grounds.

For an outdoor adventure tour company to be successful, it must offer exciting activities in a picturesque environment. Tours should have some variety: some short, some long, some easy, some challenging. Food, equipment, and tour guides must be of the highest caliber, and safety must not be compromised. It is essential that adventure and ecotour companies follow "responsible tourism" practices related to cultural and environmental issues. Almost 93% of adventure travelers say this is very important and they are willing to pay, on average, 10% more for a tour that meets this expectation (Travel Weekly, 2005).

Tour Company Operations

A tour company is a low margin business where volume of business is essential for success. Therefore, tour companies try to package into each tour as many products or services a customer is likely to buy. There are also great risks, since most tours are created as much as a year in advance. During that period the destination could experience natural disasters, terrorism attacks, political changes, and/or currency fluctuations (Cogswell, (2001b).

The typical tour company is a small business. Sixty-eight percent have 10 employees or less, and 66% have less than $3 million per year in sales. Only 17% of companies have more than $7 million in sales per year. Almost half of the NTA tour companies offer receptive services, while 67% offer outbound tours; therefore, some companies do both. The typical NTA tour company offers an average of 201 tours per year, of which 63% are multiday (average of 4.4 nights) and the rest are one-day tours. Tour companies rely heavily on marketing to previous customers. Eighty-four percent of tour companies use direct mail, 73% use the Internet for both marketing and booking, and 70% use print advertising such as newspapers, and magazines. Although 59% of customers book their tours at least 3 months in advance, there is a growing trend for people to book tours on shorter notice (National Tour Association, 2004a, 2004b, 2005a).

Trends in the Tour Industry

In addition to trends in the various types of tour companies as explained above, there are several other trends that deserve to be mentioned here. In all of these, a marketing key is to reach some type of group leader. This could be the president of an alumni group or hobby club; a church, company, or school leader; or simply the key decision maker in a family. If the tour company can sell the concept to the group leader, then these groups are essentially "preformed" by virtue of their common interest.

Family Tours are one of the fastest-growing segments of the industry. These could include soft adventure tours, family reunion tours, and traditional packages to resorts, national parks, and theme parks. One of the leading companies serving this niche is Ambercrombie and Kent, Inc., who developed tours such as the "Kenya and Tanzania Family Safari," "A Family Adventure in Alaska," and "Family Barge Cruising in Europe."

Sports and Event Tours are another major growth segment. These include tours by sports fans to university and professional sports events and trips to music concerts and special events such as spring break, New Year's events, and large conferences and conventions.

Special Niche Tours are being developed by many small tour companies and destinations to serve distinct interests. Although these tour packages may serve relatively small markets, they can have significant impact if enough are created. A good example is a series of travel packages created for the St. Johns Interactive Institute in St. Augustine, Florida. Packages for seminars include: "Backyard Elegance, Cooking in the Great Outdoors," "Florida Ecosystems," and "Antique Institute."

Opportunities with Tour Companies

There are numerous opportunities for employment with different types of tour companies. Operators of local, overland, international, and adventure tour companies all prefer clean-cut, outgoing people with good communication skills to work as tour guides and tour directors. Some companies like their tour staff to have a collegiate appearance, others prefer a business look, and others want retired people, so their older clients will identify with them. In some cases, specific skills in river rafting, horsemanship, bicycle touring, and so on may also be needed. Wages for tour guides are not high, averaging about $100 per day for NTA member companies (National Tour Association, 2004a), but tip income can substantially supplement the salary. Since many tour staff positions are seasonal, an off-season strategy is important. Options include guide work in other seasonal tours, return to school, or seasonal work in other occupations.

It is not unusual for experienced tour guides to move up to management positions such as general manager, operations manager, tour manager, or marketing manager, where they develop tour itineraries, negotiate with transportation carriers and hotels, train and supervise guides, market the tours, and so on. These opportunities seem to be more abundant with the larger tour companies. At this level of employment, the skills and knowledge gained from a university program in recreation or tourism become very important, and about 75% of NTA companies require their mid- and upper-level managers to have a college degree or at least some college (National Tour Association, 2004a). The National Tour Association's "Certified Tour Professional" program is the premier certification in the industry, requiring a combination of experience, education, service, and a research paper.

There are also numerous instances where tour staff and managers have learned the business well and started their own companies. By starting small and contracting for transportation, a tour operator can get off the ground without a huge capital investment.

OTHER TRAVEL INDUSTRIES

Auto rental companies, railroads, and the RV industry do not have a proven record of opportunity for students of commercial recreation and tourism. However, they have important supporting roles in the overall travel industry. Therefore, this section will provide a brief inspection of these three industries.

Auto Rental Companies

The auto rental industry is tied closely to the airline industry. Of the $19 billion revenue from auto rentals (U.S. Census Bureau, 2004), about half the business comes from airport locations. This is because airline travelers are the most frequent rental car users. Traditionally, most of the rental car users were business travelers who rented the cars Tuesdays through Thursdays. This changed with airline deregulation and lower airfares, as more people became "discretionary flyers." Now 71% of the auto renters are pleasure travelers. This market is more weekend oriented, which helps pick up the slack in rentals and helps make the industry more cost efficient. With the increase in discretionary travelers, there has been intense price competition among auto rental companies. The average rental period for the leisure market is 3.8 days (Travel Industry Association of America, 2004). Cars average about 15,000 miles before they are removed from the fleet and sold.

This is an extremely competitive industry with thin profit margins. Rental companies are squeezed from two directions: the auto makers who have increased fleet costs, and a cost-conscious leisure market that is reluctant to pay higher prices, particularly since fuel costs have increased. Further cost increases have occurred in some tourism destinations as state taxes and airport access fees have been levied on car renters. However, car rental companies have learned that radical discounting and price wars have hurt their industry, and they have succeeded in bringing prices up a little. They have accomplished this by stressing their partnerships with hotels and airlines.

Innovations in the car rental industry include the use of more cars with the Global Positioning Satellite (GPS) technology, use of multilingual information kiosks, baggage lockers, changing areas for adults, and small shopping areas for travel convenience items.

Some rental car companies, particularly Enterprise Rent-A-Car, hire college graduates for most of their positions. Enterprise expects the young talent to learn the technical aspects of the business as they move up into management positions.

Railroads

Through the first half of this century, railroads were a prime carrier of American travelers. Then, improvements in air transportation and the development of the interstate highway system eroded the railroad's clientele base. Railroads and bus lines were left as the low-cost transportation alternative.

In 1970, most of the nation's rail system merged into one organization, the National Railroad Corporation, also called Amtrak, which is subsidized by the federal government. The rail lines connect about 500 communities in 46 states, and Amtrak has tried to eliminate or adjust less profitable routes, reduce management overhead, and retire outdated equipment. However, operating losses were $1.1 billion for 2003, on revenues of just $2.1 billion. This occurred even though riders increased to 24 million people (Miller & Associates, 2005). Congress has mandated that Amtrak achieve operational self-sufficiency, but many critics doubt this is feasible. A new plan for Amtrak was to develop several high speed (150–200 mph) cross-country routes. A problem is that the rail corridors for the "bullet trains" can cost as much as $20 million per mile, which is a huge investment for an industry that is already losing big money. Advocates for this system include environmental groups, urban planners, and tourism groups, who all agree that it would reduce road congestion and pollution and stimulate tourism. Detractors doubt that the federal government can make it work efficiently and suggest that the nation's railways be privatized (Luzadder, 2004). The future is not very clear.

Railroad travel is now being marketed as a distinctive experience. Railroads are touted as the scenic way to see America while enjoying comfortable accommodations, good food, lounge car entertainment, and planned activities such as bingo, movies, karaoke, and happy hour. Many senior citizens and fraternal groups find this is a good travel mode for a tour. One segment of rail travel that seems to be gathering steam is the historical railroad concept. Several short-line trains are linking tourists to historical destinations in Alaska, California, Colorado, West Virginia, and other locations.

In Europe, railroads remain a popular travel option, particularly among young tourists. The Eurail Pass, valid for unlimited travel for 21–90 days, is a good value. Rail travel is also important as a major connecting link between international airports and remote tourist towns and ski resorts in Europe.

Recreation Vehicles

An RV is considered to be a wheeled vehicle with temporary living quarters. This includes both motor homes (including truck campers) and towable units. Of the nation's 7.2 million RV owners, 47% are age 50 to 65, and 33% are younger than 50. This represents a change in demographics for an industry that once targeted retired persons as the number-one market (Recreation Vehicle Industry Association, 2005; Miller & Associates, 2005).

RV vacation costs are less than comparable trips by auto or air, and savings occur mostly in the area of accommodations and food. RV owners enjoy the family experience and the freedom as well as the cost savings. An overwhelming majority of RV owners think that RVs are the best way to travel with family and children. The RV industry has grown in recent years even though fuel costs have more than doubled.

An important trend is the growth of RV destination resorts (including time-sharing) having recreational amenities and programs. Another important trend is the increasing popularity of rental RVs, particularly by foreign tourists. The most popular RV destinations are Florida, Texas, and Arizona, but RV use for cold-weather activities such as hunting, skiing, and snowmobiling is gaining popularity. The leading trade association, the Recreation Vehicle Industry Association, promotes RV use with national advertising-centered themes such as, "Wherever You Go, You're Always Home." Further content about the RV industry is included in Chapter 10 in the section "Industry Profile: Campgrounds."

State and Regional Travel Councils

State and regional travel councils are often governmental or quasi-governmental organizations. They typically do not actually provide transportation, accommodations, or other consumable products or services. Instead, they serve as facilitators to the industry and, in this capacity, serve a very important role.

Lack of unity and coordination among the many sectors of the tourism industry is a serious threat to the efficiency and ultimate success of the industry. Tourism is particularly vulnerable to cannibalistic business practices, which do not contribute to the overall attractiveness of the destination. In response to this problem, many regions, states, and provinces have established travel councils. The mission statement of the Pennsylvania Travel Council, for example, identifies its role as

> *the membership-based organization, committed to the unification of the hospitality and tourism industry within the Commonwealth. Its primary purpose is to enhance the Commonwealth's political and economic environment, and to ensure the continued profitability of the industry and the Council's members. It also serves as the state's member association of the American Hotel and Motel Association (Pennsylvania Travel Council, 1999).*

In North Carolina, the state's travel council exists "to provide leadership, service and information in order to unite the various segments of the industry and assist in promoting and developing travel and tourism in North Carolina" (Travel Council of North Carolina, 1998). Beyond its unifying role, the state or regional travel council facilitates tourism through education and training initiatives, legislative advocacy, public information and destination marketing. Collectively, the state travel councils in the United States spend $603 billion to coordinate and promote tourism within their states.

Tourism council members usually include entrepreneurs in hotels and motels, resorts, bed and breakfast inns, ski operations and amusement parks, tour operations, tourist promotion agencies, retail establishments, colleges and universities, and government officials and industry suppliers. Membership usually numbers in the hundreds or thousands, but the leadership of the council is provided by a board of directors. Each board employs a small cadre of professionals who are usually college educated to coordinate their programs, marketing campaigns, and informational centers.

SUMMARY

The travel industry is a huge and complex network of transportation carriers, travel agencies, tour companies, hotels, attractions, and many other services. Historically, people traveled mostly for war, religion, or business, but pleasure travel has finally become a major component. There are significant differences between business and pleasure travel, as well as differences between domestic and international travel. Many of the trends in these areas can be attributed to changes in economic conditions, fuel availability, and political stability.

People travel for many reasons. Successful travel services must understand the motives of their particular markets, and strive to overcome any barriers to travel. Destinations and services for conservative psychocentric travelers would be quite different than those for the outgoing allocentric travelers. A major travel trend is the increasing popularity of weekend travel, particularly for families with two working adults who have too much difficulty coordinating careers to allow for extended vacations.

Opportunities exist in numerous travel industries: airlines, travel agencies, cruise lines, and several types of tour companies. In each, however, entry positions are low paying, but the benefits of free or discounted travel make the careers appealing. Advancement can occur if the employee has good interpersonal and communication skills, sound business sense, a knowledge of geography and the travel industry, and a desire to help others enjoy their travel and recreation.

Most of the individual travel industries are enjoying a period of relative prosperity and are recovering from the recession of 2000 and the terrorist attacks of 9/11/01.

SPOTLIGHT ON:

TAUCK WORLD DISCOVERY—THREE GENERATIONS OF EXCELLENCE

In the early 1920s, a young bank clerk named Arthur Taucknitz dropped a cigar box that was used to carry coins to the vault. He was fired! He went home and invented an aluminum coin tray that would not break, and, with partitions, it also eliminated the need for counting the coins. When Arthur took the tray to the bank he was offered his job back, but with this taste of entrepreneurism, he decided instead to travel New England selling his new invention to banks. The Taucknitz coin trays caught on and are still used in banks today, but it is not the tray that would become his legacy.

As Taucknitz traveled the Berkshires, he noticed that it was mostly other traveling salesmen who were enjoying the beauty of the area. He also noticed that most tourists wandered the area aimlessly in search of things to do, and they stayed in inferior hotels because they didn't know which ones were better. Thinking that his knowledge of the area would be of value to travelers, Taucknitz ran an advertisement in the Newark Evening News inviting people to join him on a New England Tour. Six people signed up and paid $49 each for their 7-day itinerary through the countryside in a Studebaker. From the beginning, he planned it as an all-inclusive price that would cover all the necessities. Guests stayed in the best hotels and saw the best sights. Although he planned the tour as a one-time event, word spread, and Taucknitz offered more tours. In 1925, he painted "Taucknitz Tours" on the side of a bus, decided he didn't like the looks of it, and changed the family name to Tauck.

As Tauck Tours grew through the years, three basic principles became the model for business:

1. Set a single price that includes everything necessary.
2. Create experiences beyond what individual travelers can get by themselves.
3. Always exceed customers' expectations.

The second and third principles can be a challenge, but Tauck Tours became famous for delivering on those promises. One approach is to include some "special touch," such as an extra attraction that is not included in the company brochure. Another is to encourage each tour director to maximize human interaction and set up highly memorable experiences. For example, in recent years, a tour director gave each passenger a rose as they entered Auschwitz, Poland, for a tour of the death camp, saying "sometime in the next hour you are going to feel compelled to put it down." At first, the tourists clutch the rose tightly, but at different times they are touched by emotion, and "for the rest of their lives they are going to remember where they put it down."

In 1958, Arthur Tauck Sr. retired and turned the company over to his son, Arthur Jr., who joined the company in 1954 as a tour director. Arthur Jr. took the company to new levels with a wide array of new services, including the use of air travel combined with bus tours to cross new destinations across the nation and

(continued)

overseas. When the Interstate Commerce Commission declared tour operators to be illegal if they crossed state lines, Arthur Jr. took the case to the U.S. Supreme Court and won the case. He joined with other tour operators to form the National Tour Brokers Association, which became today's National Tour Association.

In 1987, Arthur Jr.'s son, Peter, and daughter, Robin, took over as copresidents, and in June 2000 Tauck Tours changed its name to Tauck World Discovery. The change was made to reflect the company's style of experiential travel and their varied modes of transportation, which now include helicopters and ships, as well as planes and motor coaches. The biggest growth area is its cruise program, which grew 60% in 2005. They offer a selection of small "Elegant Yachts," "Expedition Vessels" serving 40 to 200 passengers, and high-class "Luxury Liners." Another new program is the family tours brand "Tauck Bridges." The company now serves over 100,000 clients a year with over 100 different tour itineraries. They remain true to their goal of providing each client with a "self-actualizing experience" where they "learn something about themselves that will impact them for the rest of their lives." In the process of growth through three generations of the Tauck family, the company has been recognized as the number-one tour company in the country in separate polls of tour industry professionals and experienced travelers.

Sources: Cogswell (2001); Cogswell (2000); Scutt (1996); Tobin (2005b); Tauck World Discovery (2005).

REFERENCES

American Hotel and Lodging Association. (2005). Governmental affairs-issue briefs. *Travel and tourism promotions.* http://www.ahla.com.

Bartlet, T. (1991, July 15). Cooperative trends among South Pacific nations. *Travel Weekly,* pp. 40–42.

Beekhuis, J. (1984). *The cruise industry: World tourism overview.* New York: American Express Publishing Corporation.

Chipkin, H. (2000, August 24). The pleasure lure: Trolling for profits in leisure waters. *Travel Weekly U.S. Travel Agency Survey 2000,* pp. 43–45.

Cogswell, D. (2000, July 31). Tauck redefines itself after 75 years. *Travel Weekly,* p.1.

Cogswell, D. (2001a, February 5). Fine-tuning the fine art of succession. *Travel Weekly,* p.1.

Cogswell, D. (2001b, December 31). Operators grasp for elusive cash flow. *Travel Weekly,* pp. 10–11.

Compart, A. (2005, January 24). Industry news. *Travel Weekly,* p. 14.

Corridore, J. (2004, May 20). Industry surveys: Airlines. *Standard and Poor's Industry Survey,* p.1–31.

Crossley, J., & Lee, B. (1994, June). Ecotourists and mass tourists: A difference in benefits sought. *Proceedings of the 1994 TTRA International Conference.* Miami Beach, FL: Travel and Tourism Research Association.

De Lollis, B. (2005, October 3). U.S. touts familiar images to woo foreign tourists. *USA Today,* p. B1.

Gee, C. M. (1984). *The travel industry.* Westport, CT: AVI Publishing Company.

Goeldner, C. R., Ritchie, J. R. B., & McIntosh, R. W. (2000). *Tourism: Principles, practices, philosophies.* New York: John Wiley & Sons, Inc.

Gunn, C. (1979). *Tourism planning.* New York: Crane Russak.

International Council of Cruise Lines. (2005, April 4). Cruise industry FAQs. http://www.iccl.org/faq/index.cfm. April 4, 2005.

International Ecotourism Society. (2005, August 20). Definition and ecotourism principles. http://www.ecotourism.org.

Jacobs, S. (2005, April 27). U.S. passport rule imperils tourism, Caribbean leaders say. *Orlando Sentinel*, p. A9.

Kiesnoski, K. (2005, April 25). More Americans head for Europe. *Travel Weekly*, p. 26.

Luzadder, D. (2004, October 18). High speed rail travel is going nowhere fast. *Travel Weekly*, pp. 1, 68–70.

Lenhart, L. (2005, October 25). Business travel recovery mode: Slow and steady. *Travel Weekly*, pp. 107–109.

Lewis, J. (1998, September). The development of rural tourism. *Parks and Recreation*, pp. 99–107.

Manor, R. (2004, March 18). Jet fuel costs take off, deal industry another blow. *Fresno Bee*, p. C3.

McDonald, M. (2004, October 25). Sales channels. *Travel Weekly*, pp. 25–31.

Miller, R., & Associates. (2005). *The 2005 travel & leisure market research handbook*. Loganville, GA.: Richard K. Miller & Associates, Inc.

Milligan, M. (2004, June 7). For airlines, cost of fuel adds to load. *Travel Weekly*, pp. 1, 58.

Milligan, M. (2005, May 16). Family ties: Hotels discover it's a kid's world. *Travel Weekly*, pp. 1, 20–21.

National Geographic Traveler. (2002). *The geotourism study: Phase I executive summary*. Washington, DC: Travel Industry Association of America.

National Tour Association. (2005b, October 21). NTA fact sheet. http://www.ntaonline.com/index.php?s = &url_channel_id = 24&url_subchannel_id = &url_article_id = 2078&change_well_id = 2 Oct. 21, 2005.

National Tour Association. (2005a, May). 2005-April NTA member needs survey summary. http://www.ntaonline.com.

National Tour Association. (2004a, September). 2004-July NTA member needs survey results. http://www.ntaonline.com.

National Tour Association. (2004b, February). NTA technology survey results. http://www.ntaonline.com.

Nickerson, N., & Ellis, G. (1991, Winter). Traveler types and activation theory: A comparison of two models. *Journal of Travel Research*, pp. 26–31.

Office of Travel & Tourism Industries. (2005). 2004 profile of U.S. resident traveler visiting overseas. http://www.tinet.ita.doc.gov.

Pennsylvania Travel Council. (1999). http://www.patourism.org.

Pfenning, A. (2003a, January 13). Sluggish economy must turn before travel industry regains its footing. *Travel Weekly*, p. 10.

Pfenning, A. (2003b, March 10). Travel agent compensation. *Travel Weekly*, p. 10.

Pfenning, A. (2005, January 10). Domestic travel lowdown: Short trips and hotel stays. *Travel Weekly*, p. 12.

Plog, S. C. (1974, February). Why destination areas rise and fall in popularity. *Cornell Hotel and Restaurant Administration Quarterly*, pp. 55–58.

Plog, S. (2002, February). The power of psychographics and the concept of venturesomeness. *Journal of Travel Research*, pp. 244–251.

Recreation Vehicle Industry Association. (2005). RV quick facts. http://www.rvia.org = / Media/fastfacts.htm.

Rodriguez, R. (2004, April 25). Cultivating tourism. *Fresno Bee*, p. B1.

Scutt, C. (1996, October 7). At Tauck, success is a family affair. *Travel Weekly*, pp. 80–85.

Shields, H. (1991). 1992 outlook for international tourism. *1992 Outlook for Travel and Tourism*, Washington, DC: U.S. Travel Data Center. pp. 25–36.

Sidron, J. (2004, October 24). Service fees. *Travel Weekly*, p. 55–57.

Sidron, J. (2005, January 10). Thai tourism pins hopes on rebuilding. *Travel Weekly*, p. 1,39.

Tauck World Discovery. (2005). http://www.tauck.com.

Tobin, R. (2005a, January 24). CLIA: Passenger numbers to surpass 11M. *Travel Weekly*, p. 14.

Tobin, R. (2005b, October 10). Tauck at sea expands, gives cruise products a boost. *Travel Weekly*, p. 59.

TNS-Plog. (2004, October 25). The travel consumer: the TNS-Plog American traveler survey. *Travel Weekly*, pp. 58–118.

Travel Council of North Carolina. (1998). http://www.visitnc.com

Travel & Tourism Executive Report. (1999a). Some travel trends through 2003. XX(3 & 4), p. 3.

Travel Industry Association of America. (2000). Fast facts. http://www.tia.org.

Travel Industry Association of America. (2004). *Tourism works for america*. Washington, DC: Travel Industry Association of America.

Travel Industry Association of America. (2005). Travel statistics and trends. http://www.tia.org.

Travel Weekly. (2004, October 26). 2004 survey highlights. *Travel Weekly*, p.13–18.

Travel Weekly. (2005a, August 8). Worldwide arrivals increase 10.3% in 2004, says WTO. *Travel Weekly*, p. 12.

Travel Weekly. (2005b, June 27). Hawaii tourism budget ranks no. 1 in U.S. TIA survey says. *Travel Weekly*, p.12.

Travel Weekly. (2005c, September 26). Adventure travelers say there's value in supplier integrity. *Travel Weekly*, p.12.

U.S. Census Bureau. (2004). 2002 economic census. Washington, DC: U.S. Census Bureau. http://www.census.gov/econ/census02/.

Yesawich, Pepperdine, Brown, & Russell. (2005, May 16). Motivation for leisure travel. *Travel Weekly*, p. 10.

Yiannakis, A. & Gibson, H. (1992). Roles tourists play. *Annals of Tourism Research*, pp. 287–303.

Weber, H. & Freed, J. (2005, September 15). Airlines file for bankruptcy. *Fresno Bee*, p. C1.

World Tourism Organization. (2004). Tourism Highlights 2004. http://www.world-tourism.org.

Chapter •••• 10

The Hospitality Industry

For this text, the hospitality industry will be considered to be those businesses that provide overnight accommodations, food and beverage service, and supporting amenities (such as hotel pools, shops, concierge, etc.) that contribute to the customer's leisure experience. In its pure form, the industry has only a few categories such as hotels, motels, resort condominiums, restaurants, bars and taverns, and so forth. However, there are also many ways in which the hospitality industry combines with the travel industry and/or the local commercial recreation industry. For example, campgrounds, meeting and convention services, summer camps, theme parks, casinos, and residential recreational communities are often considered to be part of the tourism industry as well as the hospitality industry.

Resorts are part of the hospitality industry, but they have a unique role because they link all the major categories of commercial recreation together. Resorts provide accommodations, food and beverage, recreational programs, retail services, and entertainment.

This chapter will examine several aspects of resort development and then consider the role of federal, state, and local government in the provision of tourism destinations and resorts and related economic development. The chapter will conclude with profiles of several specific industries within the hospitality field.

RESORT DEVELOPMENT

Resorts can be classified as theme resorts or variety resorts. A second approach is to consider them as comprehensive resorts or complementary resorts (Kelly, 1985). A theme resort, therefore, could be either comprehensive or complementary.

Theme Resorts are based on a particular type of natural resource or artificial attraction. Examples include resorts located at the ocean, ski areas, hot springs, historical attractions, or gambling towns. A problem for the theme resort is that it may be highly seasonal in nature and/or dependent upon a single interest that could change over time. Therefore, many theme resorts strive to diversify in order to stabilize their revenue base.

Variety Resorts offer a range of resources, attractions, and activities. Due to this diversity, they may be more capital intensive and/or labor intensive. Some variety resorts have a ratio of more than one staff per guest. Kiawah Island, South Carolina, is an example of a variety resort that offers numerous beach and aquatic activities plus golf, tennis, live entertainment, social activities, children's programs, shopping, and gourmet dining.

Comprehensive Resorts have control of their recreational resources and basic natural resources. Therefore, it is in their best interest to protect the overall ecology of the area. This can be costly and may involve development of an extensive infrastructure of roads, utilities, waste disposal system, and so on. Disney World is an example of a comprehensive resort, because it controls virtually all the land and infrastructure within its govern-mentally approved "improvement district."

Complementary Resorts have hospitality services, but the major natural resource or attraction of the area is located off-site. The resort has access to the resource or attraction, but not control of it. Obviously, this can be an uneasy situation, even though there is a complementary relationship between the resort and the resource. The town of West Yellowstone is a complementary resort for the major attraction, Yellowstone Park.

Why Develop Resorts?

Profit from the operation of a resort (sale of rooms, food, services, merchandise, etc.) is not the only reason to develop a resort. Other reasons for resort development include the following:

- **Profit from land development**—Resort property may be sold or leased for the development of condominiums, hotels, retail areas, and the like.
- **Land appreciation**—Property held by the resort or by local residents may appreciate with the development of a high-quality resort.
- **Boost adjacent business**—Tourism stimulates business for local merchants.
- *Economic development*—Government authorities often encourage resort development because it creates jobs and boosts tax revenues.
- **Political reasons and national/regional pride**—Resorts showcase an area and add to its image and prestige.
- **Tax reduction advantages**—Prior to tax changes in 1986, capital developments had numerous tax advantages such as investment credits, but these have been eliminated and tax rates have been reduced. Therefore, tax write-offs are no longer a significant reason to develop a resort. However, this could change again if Congress decides that certain tax incentives are needed to stimulate economic development.

Characteristics of Successful Resorts

Resorts must have several ingredients in order to be successful. They must be based on an attractive natural resource or have significant artificial physical attractions. In addition, the resort must be close to, or have good access to, a large population base. Lastly, it helps immensely to have a unique feature or gimmick that differentiates the resort from others.

Las Vegas is an example of a resort city that meets these criteria. Although there are natural resource attractions nearby (several national parks and Lake Mead), the city features numerous resort hotels with impressive amenities. Las Vegas is tied to major populations via excellent airline connections and an interstate highway to Southern California. Legal gambling is, of course, the unique gimmick, but several resort hotels have added other features. These include championship boxing and racing at Caesar's Palace; circus entertainment at Circus Circus; an erupting volcano, dolphin pool, and white tiger den at the Mirage; dancing water fountain light show at the Bellagio; an I-Max theater at the Luxor; King Arthur's Tournament at the Excalibur; and a shark reef aquarium at Mandalay Bay. There are several other characteristics that are common in many successful resorts:

- Development that is compatible with the environment.
- A political climate that advocates sustainable growth.
- Capacity of the electricity, water, and sewer systems to handle the development.
- Plenty of reserve capital to overcome unforeseen problems and delays in the development.

- Lack of manufacturing in the community.
- Comfortable and clean accommodations of a wide price range.
- A variety of shops and restaurants.
- A good internal transportation system.
- Plenty of long-term and short-term parking.
- Nearby medical services.
- An adequate commuter population for a labor source.
- Attractive, interesting, and themed architecture.
- Attractive aesthetic atmosphere, including scenic vistas, gardens, open spaces, parks, and so forth.
- A wide range of recreational amenities, including sports facilities, nightclubs, swimming pools, tennis courts, golf courses, fairs and festivals, fitness centers, youth recreation programs, trips and tours, social events, and recreational equipment rental.
- A variety of meeting and convention facilities.

Distinctive design, compatible with its beautiful natural setting, differentiates this resort in Moorea from other properties. (Photo: J. Crossley)

Resort Trends

There are several trends involving resorts that should be mentioned: mega-resorts and fantasy resorts, ecotourism resorts, all-inclusive resorts, spa resorts, and a new emphasis on experiential tourism.

Mega-Resorts and Fantasy Resorts are a popular attraction for the upscale tourist market. One of the grandest is the 3,700-room Mandalay Bay hotel in Las Vegas. The Mandalay Bay has a South Seas theme and features an 11-acre lake and a wave-pool beach where surfing can be offered. Another Las Vegas resort, the $1.9 billion Bellagio, is designed to resemble a small elegant city and is marketed as an "alternative to Paris."

The Bellagio features over $300 million in original artwork, a five-story conservatory, a dozen restaurants, and five swimming pools. In the Bahamas, the Atlantis resort has a 14-acre "waterscape" that includes a 3.2 million gallon open-air saltwater aquarium. There are over 100 species of fish, including sharks, rays, and barracudas in six exhibit lagoons. Guests can frolic in five pools with 40 waterfalls, slides, river rides, and fountains. Other fantasy resorts are operated in Arizona, Florida, California, Puerto Rico, and Australia.

Ecotourism Resorts are at the opposite end of the spectrum from the mega-resorts. Here, the emphasis is on limiting the number of tourists but maintaining revenues by getting them to stay longer and spend more. This is accomplished through the sustainable development of authentic natural, historical, and cultural attractions. Accommodations are typically rustic, and by some standards "unimproved," but a premium is placed on high-quality adventure and educational experiences at the destination. Ecotourism resorts are being developed on many small Caribbean islands and in Belize, Costa Rica, Fiji, Indonesia, Malaysia, and other locations.

All-Inclusive Resorts take the financial uncertainty out of vacations because the recreational activities, food, and sometimes beverages are paid up-front in one all-inclusive package price. Guests know what the vacation will cost before they leave home, except for gifts and souvenirs. Club Med was one of the leaders in this increasingly popular concept, and there are now at least 50 all-inclusive resorts in the Caribbean. Many are themed for singles, couples, families, beach activities, scuba divers, or other interests. Some Caribbean islands, such as Jamaica and the Dominican Republic, have areas where the majority of the hotels are all-inclusive family-oriented resorts. These resorts feature extensive recreational amenities and programs for all ages. Interestingly, though, Club Med resorts, once known for their "sea, sun, and sex" image, now count families as 65% of their customers (Flowers, 2000). It should be noted that a problem with these all-inclusive resorts is that the small local businesses fail to make much money from the tourists who stay on the resort property most of the time. Therefore, tourism planners need to be sure that their destination is not overcommitted to the all-inclusive resort format. Balance of several resort types is usually best.

Spa Resorts have existed for centuries, having their roots in Europe's many thermal hot springs where people went to relax and "take the cure" from alcohol or other ailments. Today's spa resorts feature fitness activities, healthy nutrition, yoga and other relaxation therapies, and many types of massage. Some have "new age" orientations with philosophic or spiritual programs. Other spa themes include quitting smoking, grief recovery, sexual health improvement, and detoxing. Another interesting trend is development of a "spa community" for year-round residence (Fitness Business, 2005).

Experiential Tourism Resorts are for vacationers who want more than just a change of scenery and nice amenities; they seek a richer and deeper experience. Therefore, some progressive resorts have decided to put their emphasis on the experiential and emotional aspects of their guests' vacations. For example, the 10,000-acre Alisal Guest Ranch and Resort in Solvang, California, opened a ropes challenge course to add to its "team-building" programs. The resort also teaches orienteering and has kayaking challenge activities (Carroll, 1999).

Government Lands as Tourism Destinations and Resorts

In 1916, the U.S. Congress created the National Park Service (NPS) to "conserve the scenery, natural and historic objects, and wildlife" and to keep them "unimpaired for the enjoyment of future generations." Little did they know just how much enjoyment would be generated by the system that now features about 388 areas, including national parks, national monuments, national recreational areas, national seashores, wild and scenic rivers, memorials, historical sites, and other areas. These areas have become major tourism destinations for millions of people each year. There are over 400 million visits to NPS sites each year, plus another 300 million to the 155 National Forests administered by the U.S. Forest Service. Millions of other visits occur in areas administered by the Bureau of Land Management, U.S. Army Corps of Engineers, and other federal agencies (Miller, 2005).

It is clear that the U.S. federal government has become a major player in the tourism industry, and part of that role is to provide a full range of hospitality services to the millions of visitors who come to recreate. In some cases, the federal agencies operate lodges, campgrounds, visitor centers, and other hospitality services. However, private enterprise concessionaires provide the majority of lodging facilities, food and beverage services, outfitter and guide services, ski facilities, marinas, and other hospitality and recreational services. In past years, many of the concession contracts were "sweetheart deals" that generated minuscule revenue for the government and gave the government little quality control over the concessionaire. These concession contracts have come under great scrutiny by public interest groups in recent years.

Unfortunately, problems still exist, including overcrowding, pollution, user conflict, crime, deteriorating facilities, invasion of exotic plant species, and the decline of the underlying natural resource. Strategies to cope with these problems include the dedication of higher user fees to renovation projects within the parks, limiting and zoning the public use, better design, more use of reservations and other demand controls, and more partnerships with various interest groups.

In addition to federal government lands, there are 5,842 state park areas that serve as recreational, environmental, and historical destinations. Many of these parks have campgrounds, interpretation centers, food service areas, and other hospitality services. Twenty-four states provide lodges that could be considered resorts, with an average of 55 rooms. Resort amenities include pools, golf courses, horseback riding, conference centers, interpretive programs, and other specialized activities. Some of the resorts are self-operated by the state and some are contracted out to concessionaires. There is expected to be some limited growth of state park resorts in the future (National Association of State Park Directors, 2005).

The Role of Government in State, Regional, and Local Tourism Development

States, provinces, and regional or local governments often have offices that are dedicated to the facilitation of new business and economic development in their geographic areas. Often, their efforts help to stimulate the development of tourism destination facilities such as resorts, hotels, stadiums, arenas, convention centers, restaurants, nightclubs, and shopping areas, as well as local transportation services. The Saskatchewan Economic and Co-operative Development, for example, has a mandate "to expand and strengthen the Saskatchewan economy by promoting, co-coordinating and implementing policies, strategies and services that encourage economic growth" (Government of Saskatchewan, 1999). Tourism, hospitality, and recreation are very often a major part of such efforts.

An economic development office does not usually provide much in the way of direct financial support, but it does help match entrepreneurs with investors and facilitate partnerships, which leverage human, financial, and other important resources. In other words, the job of an economic development office is to encourage, support, and facilitate business development. Such offices promote job creation and long-term economic growth by attracting new businesses to the area; help existing businesses to expand; assist emerging firms to obtain the human, financial, and technological resources necessary to prosper and grow; and provide assistance and training.

Convention and Visitor Bureaus (CVBs) also have an important role in the economic development of regions and cities. These organizations are typically financed by a combination of government tax revenues (often hotel occupancy taxes) and private sector funds. A CVB's primary role is to help bring in tourists who will fill up the hotels, restaurants, and shops. This can be accomplished by a variety of actions:

- Develop promotional materials and programs that present the entire area in a positive light and highlight reasons to visit.
- Help coordinate the promotional efforts of local hotels, restaurants, shops, and recreational attractions.
- Provide visitor centers and visitor services.
- Proactively solicit professional associations and companies to hold national and regional conferences and meetings in the community's convention center and/or hotels.
- Provide and manage convention and meeting facilities.
- Coordinate hospitality and visitor services for convention groups and other visitors who come to the area, working cooperatively with hotels and receptive tour operators.
- Host travel agents and travel writers and help them gain positive impressions of the area.
- Develop and/or help to coordinate and promote special events that will bring visitors.
- Provide, coordinate, or assist with training programs for individuals who work in the local hospitality industry.
- Help to represent the tourism and hospitality industry in the local, regional, and state political arenas.

INDUSTRY PROFILE: HOTELS AND MOTELS

Throughout ancient times and the Middle Ages, hotels or "inns" were just rooms within private dwellings. By the time of the Industrial Revolution in England, more people had begun to travel, and competition for the lodging business led to improvements. English inns soon gained a reputation for being the finest in the world, because they were clean and had friendly service. Eventually, English standards began to be emulated in other countries. In 1794, the City Hotel in New York became the first building in the United States to be erected specifically as a hotel.

A revolution occurred in 1908 in Buffalo, where Ellsworth Statler started the first of the modern commercial hotels. It had electric lights, private baths, fire doors, circulating water, full-length dressing mirrors, free morning newspapers, and courteous service. This led to a boom in hotel construction and to books on hotel management.

The Great Depression brought on the worst period in U.S. lodging history, and 85% of the nation's hotels went through some form of bankruptcy or other failure. World War II, however, revived the demand for hotel space, as millions of Americans traveled to defense plants or military camps. After the war, Americans took to the highways in autos, and there was a tremendous boom in the construction of motels along the roads.

In the 1960s, major hotel companies started to go after specific market segments. Hotels and motels were built for airport locations, or along the new interstate highways, and at resort areas. Several budget chains were started as well. By the 1970s, there was further specialization, with condominium and time-share developments at resorts, all-suite hotels, and more budget chains.

Overall Status of the Industry

There are about 55,000 hotels and motels in the United States, with a total of 4.4 million rooms. This is a $114 billion industry with about 1.7 million employees. About 75% of revenue comes from room rents. Food and beverage sales account for 18%, followed by telephone charges, facility rental, and other revenue, including recreation amenities. In a limited service property, room rents are 94% of revenue.

These revenues come from an average daily room rate of $86.41. Rates are highest in the Northeastern and Middle Atlantic states, at resorts, and at urban hotels. However, the largest segment of all properties are suburban and highway locations. Small properties are also the most numerous, as the great majority of hotels and motels have fewer than 150 rooms (American Hotel and Lodging Association, 2005; Graves, 2004).

Hotel occupancies dropped from a high of 71% in 1971 to a low of 59% in 2002. This was because the growth of demand did not keep pace with the construction of new hotels, and tourism dropped after the 9/11 terrorist attacks. The hotel industry rebounded to 62% occupancy rate by 2004. Occupancy rates tend to be higher in resort hotels, airport area hotels, and urban hotels, compared to suburban and highway hotels. Certain areas, such as Honolulu, New York City, Phoenix, and Orlando often have yearly occupancy rates in the 80% range. Occupancy is also higher in urban areas on weekdays when business travelers are in town, and on weekends at resort areas that are close to major population centers. An important part of the current profitability is the industry's ability to save money though improved marketing efforts and greater labor efficiencies (Graves, 2004; Miller, 2005; American Hotel and Lodging Association, 2005).

Hotel and Motel Marketing

Leisure travelers account for about 46% of total room nights at hotels and motels, and 54% of the customers are there for business, a conference, or a group meeting. However, 75% of all revenues come from business travelers (Miller, 2005). The businesspeople select hotels primarily due to location and previous experience with the hotel or chain. This is followed by hotel reputation, value for the dollar, and then price. For leisure travelers, however, value for the dollar is most important, followed by location, price, previous experience with the hotel or chain, and hotel/chain reputation (Pfenning, 2003). It is interesting to note, however, that most people choose to return to hotels primarily because of the courteous service. Cleanliness and the hotel's amenities are the next highest ranked reasons for returns.

Each year the Mobil Travel Guide announces its Five Star Award winners. Only about 30 hotels, resorts, and restaurants earn this prestigious award, which is proudly highlighted in the winner's marketing literature. To earn the award, a resort hotel must have a gracious lobby with tasteful furnishings and decor, elegant guest rooms, fine art, superior restaurants, meticulous landscaping, twice daily maid service, extensive recreational facilities, and the services of a social/recreation director.

To market its properties, most resort hotels utilize direct mailings to travel agencies, previous clientele, and targeted organizations and individuals. Web pages and links to destination Web pages have become very popular in recent years. Other marketing methods include corporate group discounts, newsletters, facility tours, radio ads, yellow-page ads, family discounts, and an outside sales force. "Frequent Stay" programs are used to build brand loyalty and influence prior customers to return.

Discounting is another common marketing tool. Many urban hotels give weekend discounts of 20 to 60% in order to spur weekend occupancy. Another approach is to give discounts or free nights to "Frequent Stay" guests after they have earned "points" based on previous stays. Senior citizen discounts are also common. Some hotels, instead of discounting their room prices, give "value added" upgrades, amenities, or discounts on meals.

Types of Hotel Operations

There are two major types of hotel/motel operations. Roughly 70% of lodging industry properties in the United States are affiliated with a national or regional brand, also called a *chain*. The remainder are primarily single-location operations termed *independents* (Graves, 2004).

Independents used to be the bulk of the industry, but they have lost ground to the chains. Independent operators/owners often have greater pride in their properties and have total management flexibility, but they typically lack the marketing clout and financial reserves of the large chains. If a small independent hotel or motel can fill a specialty niche within an area market, it can be very successful.

Chain Hotels and Motels offer consistency of product and name recognition. They are efficient due to volume purchasing, personnel training programs, standardized operating methods and procedures, national marketing programs, greater financial resources, and nationwide computer reservation systems.

Many hotel chain properties are built, owned, and operated by the parent company. This gives the company the most control. A hotel chain has three other choices: it may manage a property owned by someone else, it may lease out a property for another party to manage, or it may franchise out to another party to operate.

Figure 10-1 illustrates the organizational chart of a large hotel. Small hotels and motels perform most of the same functions, but people may have to fill several roles.

Hotel/Motel Classifications

In addition to being an independent or a chain property, hotels can be classified according to their primary function. Types include commercial hotels, airport hotels, economy properties, bed and breakfast inns, all-suite hotels, extended stay hotels, casino hotels, and resorts.

Commercial Hotels or Urban Hotels cater to business clients and small conventions. Center city locations are best for commercial hotels. Typically, they have excellent food and beverage facilities plus a variety of convenient services, such as valet laundry, concierge, and health clubs.

Airport Hotels are primarily a convenience to travelers, but some airport hotels are reaching out to other markets. For example, a large hotel at the Dallas-Fort Worth Airport markets heavily to convention groups. It can serve 5,000 at a banquet and create 50 different special events.

Economy or Budget Properties provide for the basic needs of vacationing families and budget-minded business travelers. Most guests stay only 1 or 2 nights and seek only clean accommodations with a TV. Economy hotels and motels have been one of the fastest-growing segments of the lodging industry, and some major chains have developed a "brand" of their own economy properties. Marriott's Fairfield Inn is an example. Rates at economy properties are typically 20–50% less than full-service hotels in their area.

Bed and Breakfast Inns are usually Victorian homes or renovated small hotels, lodges, or farmhouses. They offer sleeping accommodations and a breakfast in a charming and unique atmosphere. Rates are typically $100 to $180 a night. Target markets include business travelers who desire a change of pace, plus honeymoon and anniversary couples.

Highway/Roadside Motels usually provide overnight accommodations to travelers on their way to a final destination. In small towns, such properties provide the primary lodging facilities for business or recreational travelers staying several days or more. Few roadside motels have recreational amenities other than a small pool or play area. Since many roadside motels do not have the instant image that a chain-operated property enjoys, a favorable rating by the AAA (American Automobile Association) or Mobile and a Web site link to the destination can help attract customers.

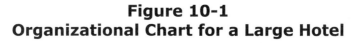

Figure 10-1
Organizational Chart for a Large Hotel

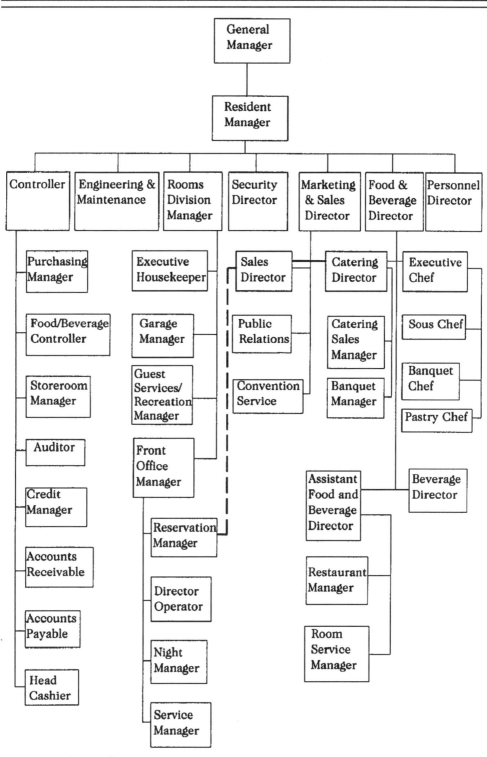

Source: Adapted from Lattin, 1985.

All-Suite Hotels offer accommodations with separate bedroom and living room/ kitchens. They are typically located in city centers and cater to business travelers, vacationers, and persons who are relocating.

Extended Stay or Residential Hotels are also usually in city centers and function as primary homes or as secondary homes for frequent travelers. The best residential hotels have suite accommodations plus housekeeping service and dining facilities.

Casino Hotels are often quite luxurious, although many are moderately priced. The idea, of course, is to make the profits through gambling revenues. Casinos are highlighted in a later industry profile.

Resort Hotels differ from other types of hotels in several ways. Most importantly, the target clientele is much different, as most resort hotel guests are on vacations. Groups and conventions are the second-largest segment, while only a small segment of guests are there on business. Length of stay is also longer at resort hotels, and guests are more interested in recreational amenities and programs. Most resort hotels have a bar/lounge, game room, meeting/conference rooms, restaurants, swimming pool, and sports/recreational facilities (combinations of tennis courts, night club, boating/fishing area, beach, golf course, playground, fitness center, shops, sauna/steam room/whirlpool, etc.).

Some resort hotels have relatively short seasons and have good occupancy only from late May through Labor Day. Winter-oriented resort hotels face the opposite seasonality. Another problem is that fewer tourists like to return to the same vacation resort year after year. A solution to both problems is diversification of off-season amenities and programs. Those resorts that solve this problem and serve an upscale market can be very profitable.

Hotel Operation Trends and Problems

Computer Technology, such as nationwide computerized reservation systems, has proven extremely beneficial to hotel chains. These systems allow reservations to be booked through travel agents, corporate travel departments, and airlines or directly by the customer over the Internet. Commissions to the travel agent can be tracked easily and paid centrally once a month. Guest check-in and check-out time is reduced, and customers are billed more efficiently. The computer systems also allow hotels to track and define their customer market segments, and the computer systems can provide a self-adjusting perpetual inventory of rooms by type and rate. Even small hotels can now afford a system because of the declining costs of computer technology. The Internet is also providing opportunities for more efficient purchasing of supplies. Overall, the advances in computer technology have proven to help hotels provide more services and at lower costs.

New Markets are being sought by hotels. Everyone is seeking the business of the 25,000 professional, trade, and fraternal organizations that hold conventions and conferences. Hotels give big discounts for convention business if it occurs in the off-season or shoulder season. About one third of conference attendees return someday to the same hotel, and the same number of convention travelers stay over an extra few days for vacation purposes. Many hotels have added fitness facilities or programs in order to draw the health-conscious, and other hotels have designated entire "no smoking" floors. Increased security is advertised in order to draw female executives, and compliance with ADA requirements should now be the norm. Many hotels are adding amenities aimed at enticing the business traveler: Internet access, built-in hair dryers, private-label toiletries, secretarial service, disposable swimsuits, personal computers, fax machines, morning newspapers, voice mail, and frequent-stay programs.

Brand Segmentation is a significant new strategy whereby major hotel chains offer three or more different choices of hotel types in order to capture a share of the market for each type. For example, Marriott Hotels offers Marriott Resorts, urban hotels (Marriott

Hotels), extended stay hotels (Residence Inns), all-suite properties (Town Place), mid-scale hotels (Courtyard), and economy hotels (Fairfield Inns), each under their own unique brand names. This approach is both a strategy for growth and a way to broaden a chain's customer base. At the same time, the chain is able to optimize corporate resources, management expertise, access to financial resources, and daily operations.

Opportunities in the Hotel/Motel Industry

Hotels and motels are one of the largest employers in the nation. Many of the positions, of course, are nonprofessional, such as room attendants, front desk clerks, bell staff, and porters. Even so, students who take these jobs while in school learn many of the practical, grassroots aspects of the business. Before they graduate, students can often move up to positions such as bell captain, concierge, front desk supervisor, reservations clerk, assistant housekeeper, sales representative, or night auditor. After graduation the student may be ready to move up to mid-level management positions such as front office manager, executive housekeeper, or guest service manager. With further experience the young professional may move up to be personnel director, sales manager, convention manager, marketing manager, assistant general manager, and eventually general manager.

It must be noted that many people currently in managerial positions came up through the ranks without academic training. The trend now, however, is to advance those employees who have combined academic training with practical experience. Most of the larger hotel/motel chains have training programs that prepare young professionals for managerial positions.

Some hotels and many major resorts employ recreational activity staff. In large programs there may be specialists for sports, fitness, golf, tennis, conference group programs, tours, aquatics, youth programs, or other activities. The recreation director for a major resort is usually a trained professional, and salaries tend to be in the $35,000 to $60,000 range, although some are higher.

Some resort recreation directors have succeeded in broadening the scope of their responsibilities to become directors of guest services, resort services, or resort operations. Such positions could have responsibility for not only the recreational programs and amenities but also concierge, bell staff, convention and meeting services, retail shops, golf, skiing, guest transportation, parking services, and grounds maintenance. These positions typically pay substantially higher salaries than the recreation directors earn.

Entrepreneurs with interest in owning their own hotel should first gain experience in the industry and start with buying or becoming a partner in a small property. Bed and breakfast inns are popular with entrepreneurs, but even these often take $400,000 or more to start.

INDUSTRY PROFILE: SKI RESORTS

Although skiing is usually considered a recreational activity (activity-oriented businesses are profiled in Chapter II), most of the revenues associated with ski vacations actually come through the hospitality industry. For example, the American Skiing Company, which owns seven of the largest ski resorts in the United States, reports that only 45% of its revenues come through lift tickets, including season passes. The rest comes from sales of lodging, food and beverage, real estate, retail goods, and other recreational activity (American Skiing Company, 2004). Since many skiers lodge, dine, and shop "off property" from the primary ski area, the percentage of revenue from actual skiing operations at the overall destination is further diluted.

The ski area industry was born in 1934 when a crude rope tow was installed on a hill outside Woodstock, Vermont. In 1936, Sun Valley, Idaho, became the first real ski resort when a mechanized chairlift was introduced. Sun Valley lured movie stars and helped give skiing a glamorous label. By 1955 there were 78 lift-served ski areas in North America (Ski Industries America, 1984). It soon became apparent that ski areas were excellent locations for hotels, lodges, condominiums, restaurants, and retail shops. Growth averaged 15–20% a year as skiing became the fastest-rising sport in the United States from 1973 to 1982. In 1975 there were about 1,000 ski areas, but many small areas failed, and the total is now around 492 (National Ski Areas Association, 2005) and many of them struggle to stay profitable.

The Ski and Snowboard Markets

Downhill skiing, cross-country skiing, and snowboarding in the United States involve about 15 million people, who account for about 57 million visits at ski areas. These figures have been fairly flat for about 20 years, and if not for the tremendous growth of snowboarding, the industry would be in serious decline (National Ski Areas Association, 2005; Miller, 2005).

Downhill skiers number about 6.8 million and represent about 45% of the overall market. The National Ski Areas Association classified skiers as beginners, core, or revivals. Beginners make up about 15% of the market and ski an average of 2.5 times a year. Unfortunately, about 85% of these participants drop out of the market in their first year. The core customers represent about 65% of the market, and they participate an average of about 7 days a year. Each year, about 20% of the core customers lapse into nonparticipation. The revivals are those who have returned to the sport. They represent about 25% of the market and participate about 5 days a year. It is clear that the future of the ski industry depends more on its ability to convert beginners into core participants than its ability to attract new skiers (National Ski Areas Association, 2005; Miller, 2005).

The prime market for the ski resorts are tourist families and adults with higher than average income. This tourist group is more likely to spend money for airfare, lodging, food, and retail products than are skiers from the local ski area. While they are likely to ski more often, the local skiers, including many students, are much more cost-conscious and don't need to spend much more than the cost of the lift ticket. Therefore, it is no accident that most of a major ski area's marketing budget is targeted at the tourist group.

Snowboarding is the fastest-growing segment of the winter sports industry. Participation rocketed from about 1.4 million participants in 1990 to 6.3 million in 2004 and accounts for about 42% of the industry (Miller, 2005). It is even more popular in the West, where snowboarders account for over 50% at many ski areas. Once looked upon as "outlaws" by skiers, snowboarders have saved some ski areas from losing money in an otherwise flat or declining downhill ski industry. While the sport is still 66% young male participation, young women and adults over the age of 35 are major growth segments. However, snowboarders are more likely to be local participants who drive to the ski areas and don't spend money on lodging and dining. Therefore, they are a less favored market. Overall, snowboarding will probably continue to make a big impact on the ski industry, bringing new, young participants to the resorts, while the number of aging baby boomer skiers declines.

Another market is cross-country skiers, who number about 1.9 million in the United States. Cross-country skiers tend to be older, more family oriented, and more educated. Almost half (48%) of all cross-country skiers are women (Miller, 2005). There are over 600 cross-country ski areas in the United States, but many people also ski across parks and golf courses, through forested areas, and in mountainous backcountry. This freedom to explore nature, plus the lower cost, help make cross-country skiing a popular sport.

Ski Area Development and Operation

The traditional wisdom for ski area location and design suggests the following:

- A minimum of 60–100 days of weather with 28 degrees or less and 70–100 inches annual snowfall.
- North-facing trails with beginner terrain at 10–15% slope, intermediate trails at 20–25% slope, and advanced trails at 30–50% slope.
- Minimum of 80-foot-wide trails with key runs 150–200 feet wide.
- Adequate natural drainage.
- Adequate water supply and electricity nearby to install snow-making equipment.
- Enough parking spaces for one car for every two skiers on peak days.
- A signage system to mark trails and provide skier safety information.
- Ski shops, food and beverage facilities, retail shops, and lodging that is contracted out or self-operated. All should have good access to the ski slopes and/or be linked by ground transportation.

Ski areas are expensive to develop and operate. Each ski lift typically costs several million dollars, grooming machines can cost over $200,000, and snowmaking equipment costs about $35,000 per acre covered. Skiers now expect well-groomed slopes and a system of high-speed detachable quad lifts to get them quickly up the mountain.

Figure 10-2 illustrates the organizational chart for a ski area that operates its own ski school and equipment rental but contracts out for the operation of food and beverage facilities, retail shops, and lodging.

Figure 10-2
Ski Area Organizational Chart

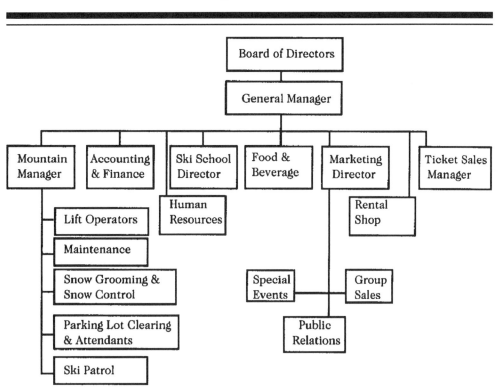

Cross-country ski areas require less capital development. A minimum of four to five kilometers of multiple-tracked trails should be available. Such an area could serve about 600 skiers a day. Base facilities for a small cross-country area should include a lodge with 3,000 square feet, snack bar, retail counter, and rental shop with 200 sets of equipment.

Trends and Problems in the Industry

Demographic changes in the United States have caused demand for downhill skiing to flatten out. This is because the active baby boomer generation has grown older, and the younger generations are more likely to take up snowboarding. Numerous strategies have been suggested to improve ski areas and serve skiers and snowboarders better:

- Improve services with variable-time lift tickets, more flexible hours for ski schools, and "ski guides" to assist intermediate and advanced skiers.
- Place more emphasis on women's interests and programs for children—the future lifeblood of the industry.
- Provide promotion and encouragement to skiers over age 45, a time when too many people quit the sport. Well-groomed runs, cleaner restrooms, and shorter lift lines are important to this group.
- Provide reinforcement for return clientele: welcome parties, social activities, etc.
- Provide incentives for first-timers: discount packages, free lessons, etc.
- Allow snowboarders to participate and provide special terrain for jumps, spins, and other maneuvers.
- Designate some terrain for "extreme" skiing in ungroomed backcountry, bowls, and wooded glades. Maintenance of such areas costs much less than for groomed runs.
- Provide credit card-size "access cards" with imbedded computer chips to be scanned for lift rides, meals, bus transportation and that also work as a hotel room key.
- Take advantage of the trend for aging boomers to spend less time on the slopes and seek other activities to fill their vacation time at the ski area.

A problem that must be dealt with is the off-season. Many ski areas are making major efforts to bring participants back during the summer. Common strategies include discount lodging, tram rides, hot air balloon rides, alpine slides, mountain climbing, tennis camps, water slides, music concerts, art shows, festivals, backpacking, horseback rides, mountain biking, golf tournaments, boating, windsurfing, fly-fishing, and white-water river trips.

Opportunities at Ski Resorts

Ski resorts have numerous employment positions in hotels, restaurants, and retail shops, but these opportunities are dealt with in other sections of this text. Most of the positions at the actual ski area are seasonal: ski instructors, lift attendants, ski patrollers, ticket sales persons, reservation clerks, snow grooming crew, ski area hosts/hostesses, and so on. A few students who gain experience in these areas may advance to the very few positions that are year-round at major resorts: mountain manager (and a corps of assistants), ski school director, and office manager. Commercial recreation and tourism graduates have also gained positions as communications director and assistant marketing manager, but both positions require additional background in communications and marketing. Virtually all of these positions, however, are hired from within the organization, or at least within a circle of contacts in the industry, which can appear to be a "good old boy" network. Some large ski areas have also employed a sports coordinator and an arts and entertainment coordinator to develop year-round programs.

INDUSTRY PROFILE: CASINO RESORTS

Another very different type of resort is the Casino Hotel Resort. What makes it different, of course, is the legalized gambling, or "gaming" as the industry prefers to call it. Casino gaming was only a $1 billion industry in 1975, but it has grown to become an industry with 833 legal casinos in 20 states and $44.5 billion in "wins" (wagers less payout) by 2003. Las Vegas and other Nevada casinos account for about 23% of the gaming wins, while Atlantic City brings in about 11%. About 24% of casino wins now come from the six states that allow water-based ("riverboat") casinos, and about 40% come from casinos on Native American lands (Graves, 2004). It is interesting to note that the riverboats and Native American casinos did not even exist before 1990. However, these gaming facilities come far short of the major casino resorts in Las Vegas and Atlantic City in generating revenue from lodging, food and beverage, and retail sales. In fact, gaming "wins" in Las Vegas yield only about 19% of the tourism revenue because the rest comes from non-gaming operations (Miller, 2005).

Slot machines are the most popular gaming attraction and account for about 60% of the typical casino's gaming revenue. Table games such as blackjack and craps account for most of the other casino gaming revenue (Graves, 2004). Casinos win without dishonesty because there is a house advantage built into every game.

The overall market of casino gamblers is a little older, slightly better educated and more likely to be white-collar workers compared to the general population of the United States. Among casino gamblers, slot machine players are generally considered to be older, less affluent, and less educated than blackjack and other table games players (Travel Industry Association of America, 2004; Miller, 2005).

Atlantic City and Las Vegas: Market Contrasts

There are tremendous differences in the markets of Atlantic City and Las Vegas casinos. The vast majority of Atlantic City's market are day visitors who arrive by auto and charter bus, whereas the average visit to Las Vegas is 4 days and almost half arrive by plane. The Las Vegas visitor spends much more on lodging, food, entertainment, and shopping and has a higher gambling budget. Whereas Atlantic City was once a classic seaside resort, it now markets itself as a gambling city. On the other hand, Las Vegas gained fame for its gambling, but it now markets itself as a complete tourism destination. Las Vegas has several golf courses, numerous parks, shopping malls, sports facilities, a water theme park, and several mega-hotel theme parks. Several hotels have children's activities and supervised programs. There are also boating, sailing, skiing, and water skiing opportunities within a short drive. Las Vegas is also very successful in attracting conventions, hosting 36 of the 200 largest trade shows in the United States (Miller, 2005).

Other Types of Casinos

Three other types of casinos deserve mention: water-borne casinos, Native American casinos, and historical Western town casinos. In 1991, Iowa was the first U.S. state to approve water-based (mostly riverboats) casinos. By 2000, there were 84 in Iowa, Illinois, Mississippi, Louisiana, Missouri, and Indiana. Their winnings total was about $10 billion in 2003 (Graves, 2004).

The Indian Gaming Regulatory Act of 1988 allowed Native Americans to operate whatever form of gambling that a state will authorize. By 2004, there were 354 casinos in 28 states, with casino winnings of about $17 billion (Travel Industry Association of America, 2004; Graves, 2004).

Historic Deadwood, South Dakota, began casino operations in 1989 and three Colorado towns, Central City, Black Hawk, and Cripple Creek followed in 1991. These four small towns earn about $758 million in winnings a year (Graves, 2004).

In theory, all these new casinos should stimulate tourism and bring prosperity to their communities due to higher employment, more business, and more tax revenue. However, an analysis of 55 counties that got new casinos indicated that the increase in overall business averaged just 4% a year; about the same as the rest of the nation. This suggests that much of this gambling is by locals rather than tourists, and that much of the gambling revenue is really just local money moving around in the economy. There are also statistics that show rises in crime rates in communities that have gambling (Shapiro, 1996).

Casino Resort Operations

There are several considerations in the planning and management of casino hotels/resorts that are somewhat different than for other types of hospitality businesses:

- Legislative controls, especially in New Jersey, are more complex. There are licensing and extensive investigation of personnel, conflict of interest regulations, and complex accounting requirements.
- Casino resort hotels are more labor intensive than other hotels because of the 24-hour activity. This drives operating costs up.
- Managers must be trained in handling a variety of problems that are unique to the industry: more transient labor, 24-hour operations, increased security, entertainment management, and gaming management.
- Lodging and/or food and beverage operations may be priced cheaply to be a marketing tool to draw customers, rather than being priced to make profits.

Due to the above problems, casino resorts have very high operating costs. In order to be successful, the casino must have a very high occupancy rate and entice its guests to gamble on the premises rather than at another casino. Successful casino operators see that their business is part of the overall leisure and travel industry. This is reflected in their pricing, marketing, and diversification to a wider range of recreational interests. One way that casinos build an identity is through a theme that may be reflected in facility design, decor, employee costumes, food, entertainment, and non-gaming recreational activities. Also, some casinos choose to focus on particular markets. For example the Boyd Gaming Company has sought to attract residents of Hawaii to its three casino hotels in Las Vegas. The unique strategy has proven to be successful, as Hawaiian visitors accounted for 63% of Boyd's room nights in 2003 (Graves, 2004).

Opportunities at Casino Resorts

Casino resorts have many of the same opportunities available in the hotel industry, but there are also some differences. One recreation student gained training at a blackjack dealers' school, then got an internship with a casino. After a few years, the student had advanced to a position supervising the gaming area of the casino. He was also given the opportunity to work with the marketing department to develop some new tour group business. Some casino resorts employ recreation staff to manage their youth programs, special promotional events, and recreational facilities. There is no defined career path for recreation/tourism graduates in the casino resort industry. Opportunities may be there, but they must be pursued on a case-by-case basis.

INDUSTRY PROFILE: TIME-SHARE RESORTS

Time-sharing, sometimes called vacation ownership, is the sale of luxury accommodations to numerous people, wherein the ownership and annual rights to use a unit are divided into increments of 1 or more weeks. Resort time-sharing was first developed and marketed in the French Alps in 1964 and has grown at a rate of about 16% a year

(American Resort Development Association, 2005a). By the mid-1970s, three things combined to bring this vacation concept to the United States:

1. Hotel and resort room rates escalated with inflation.
2. Condominiums and houses became so expensive that most Americans could not purchase vacation homes.
3. Americans began to realize that they did not have to own an entire vacation home in order to have dependable lodging available.

By 2005, there were over 5,425 time-share resorts in 100 countries worldwide, with about 1,668 resorts in the United States, mostly in Florida, South Carolina, California, Hawaii, and Colorado. Prices for fully furnished and equipped two-bedroom units average $15,789 for perpetual ownership of a week (American Resort Development Association, 2005b). However, smaller units in the off-season can be half that, and some luxury resorts command prices upwards of $30,000 for ownership of a prime week. Some people buy their time-shares through a resale service at prices that may be one third of the original price.

Time-shares can be a "fee simple" purchase, wherein owners gain full title to a specific unit for a specific week each year. Ownership of that week may be passed on to heirs or sold. Another approach is to purchase an individual interest or "right to use" license, lease, or membership. The buyer does not gain title, but does have the right to use a particular unit for a specific period of weeks for a fixed number of years. Variations of this method allow club members to use other units at other resorts in the same chain, or to have "floating time" right to use privileges within a particular season. About 70% of time-shares are now sold as floating time. A new approach that is gaining popularity is

Electronic slot machines enable gamblers to play faster and enable casinos to make more revenue. (Photo: J. Crossley)

the purchase of "points" that allow owners to trade their points for vacation weeks of different value, based on location, season, size, and so on. In almost every ownership system, the owners also pay annual maintenance fees that average $479 per week owned (American Resort Development Association, 2005a, 2005b).

Time-share Marketing

Time-share resort marketing has changed a lot in recent years. Once, the primary way to attract potential buyers to see the resort was through telemarketing or mailed invitations promising free gifts or free vacations at the resort. A one or two percent response rate to these methods, though expensive, would be cost-effective because the purchase price is often three times higher than the property and construction cost. Since time-shares are basically an "unsought good," they must be marketed aggressively.

Now there are over 50 million Americans on the "Do Not Call" list, and people are also very suspicious of bulk mail offerings and email spam. While mailings and telemarketing are still used extensively, more marketing programs now target referrals from current owners, sales of additional weeks to current owners, and promotions to in-house guests of hotel-resorts that include a time-share division. Another approach is the "off-premises contact" (OPC) such as sales staff placed in destination hotel lobbies or streetside kiosks. Here, a time-share tour—with incentive gift, of course—is pitched to a market that already has demonstrated an interest by coming to that destination for vacation.

The typical buyer of a time-share is 53 years old (median), married (84%), with a median household income of $85,0000, and likely (76%) to have attended college. Most time-share buyers (85%) are satisfied with their vacation style purchase because they like the certainty of knowing they have a high-quality and safe resort unit along with the flexibility to trade for vacations at other resorts. They also believe that time-share ownership makes economic sense over the long term (American Resort Development Association, 2005c).

Time-Share Exchange Services

There are several time-share exchange services, the largest being Resort Condominiums International, founded in 1974. By 2000, RCI had exchange service contracts with over 3,700 different resorts and over 3 million time-share owner/members. Each year about a third of the members trade their weeks and vacation at a different resort. In recent years, many hotels in resort areas have designated certain units or wings for time-share sales and exchange. This has helped improve the legitimacy of the time-share and exchange concept (Resort Condominiums International, 2005; American Resort Development Association, 2005c).

Time-share Resort Operations

The operation of a time-share resort is like other resorts and hotels in many ways. There are, however, some differences. Most of the guests arrive and depart on the same day of the week, the "turnaround day," usually Friday, Saturday, or Sunday. Between check-out time at 10:00 a.m. and check-in time at 4:00 p.m., all the units must be cleaned and prepared for the next wave of vacation weekers. This is a hectic time when all staff are very busy.

The regularity of the time-share week allows the resort recreation director to structure a very attractive program. The first evening, a get-acquainted buffet or social is very common. Recreational classes, trips, and special events can be promoted at this time to an essentially captive audience. From records of programs and attendance, interest patterns become clear over a period of several years. For example, owners of week number

20 may enjoy golf outings, while week number 5 owners enjoy bridge tournaments. The repeat nature of owners' visits also helps build social interactions that, in turn, help facilitate programs. Most large time-share resorts offer a wide range of recreational amenities and programs.

An important new trend is the commitment of several major hotel chains to the time-share concept. For example, Marriott Vacation Clubs, a division of Marriott International, has several dozen "vacation ownership" resorts, and Radisson, Hyatt, Hilton, Disney, and Embassy Suites have also opened time-share properties. The commitment of these companies has helped improve the overall reputation of the time-share concept.

Ultimately, the success of a time-share resort depends on several factors: the ability to keep high standards of quality, the satisfaction of time-share owners and guests, and the ability to sell the off-season and shoulder season weeks.

Opportunities in Time-Share Resorts

Time-share resorts often have many of the opportunities found in the hotel industry, plus a few more. All time-share resorts employ a team of sales people until the property is sold out. While many time-share sales staff are overly aggressive, it is possible to have sincere belief in the resort and communicate tastefully and ethically to prospective buyers. A successful time-share salesperson can earn excellent income through commissions, and some advance to management positions.

Large time-share resorts frequently employ recreation managers and activity directors. Salaries in the better properties have improved to very respectable levels, and advancement is possible to other positions in operations and even up to the property manager position.

INDUSTRY PROFILE: RECREATIONAL COMMUNITIES

There are about 6.6 million "vacation homes" in the United States that are used by their owners an average of just 8 weeks per year. These may include ski condos, beachfront villas, hunting cabins, golf resort condos, and lakeside retreats. Only 14% of these owners rent their vacation homes out to other people. The typical vacation home owner is 55 years old with a median income of $71,000, and the median price paid in 2004 for a vacation home was $190,000. About 20% of owners plan to use their vacation homes as a primary residence after retirement (National Association of Realtors, 2005). In addition, there are several million properties in retirement community complexes. All of these are types of residential/recreational communities.

People buy property in a recreational community because they want to take advantage of the recreational opportunities, to entertain business clients, to have a leisure environment for retirement, and/or because they are looking for an investment. Therefore, developers stress the following market considerations: (1) easy access to the area, (2) access to the primary recreational attraction, (3) rental potential, and (4) resale value.

Tax considerations can affect how long some people live in their recreation residence. Owners can rent out their vacation home for 14 days a year without losing their tax deduction for interest paid. If their property is used primarily for rental purposes, they cannot claim the interest expense, but can still claim all depreciation, maintenance, or other expenses for tax write-offs. Owners who split their occupancy more evenly can only charge off proportionate depreciation and maintenance for tax purposes.

Kelly (1985) classified recreational communities into three different types: retirement developments, mixed communities, and resource-focused communities. These, plus a fourth type, local recreational communities, are examined further below. One common feature is that most of these communities charge their residents a monthly fee to cover maintenance of the recreational facilities.

Retirement Developments are common in the Sun Belt area from Florida to California. Homes and condominiums are typically well integrated into a comprehensive land-use plan and adapted to the local climate, terrain, and aesthetics. Recreational amenities are prevalent, but mostly of a social nature: swimming pools, golf, social hall, and so on. Recreation programming may be provided by paid staff and/or through resident committees.

Mixed Communities have a combination of temporary and full-time residents and offer a range of recreational opportunities. Hilton Head, South Carolina, is a good example of a "mixed recreational community." Such an area has year-round residents, retirees, seasonal vacation homeowners, time-share properties, rental condominiums, and hotels for convention and tourist trade.

Resource-Focused Communities are developments based on a specific activity such as skiing or beach vacationing. There is less emphasis on full-time residents, and the development is designed for short-term visitors. This might mean proportionately more restaurants, nightclubs, retail shops, and recreational activities. Second homes and condominium projects in these settings are often affiliated with a property rental company. The property rental company markets the unit and handles reservations, check-ins, and maintenance. In return, they keep 40–50% of the rental revenue. Owners may stay in their properties a few weeks of the year but rent out the majority of the time. Owners may get only 50% of the income, but often have higher rental occupancy rates due to the marketing of the property rental company. A fast-growing concept in these areas is "fractional ownership," where ownership of a luxury resort home or condominium is held by just a few (4–12) individuals

Local Recreational Communities include apartment, condominium, and single-residence communities that are based on a recreational concept. Often, the concept is a golf course, marina, or sports facility. It is much more common now than 20 years ago to see residential areas sold because of their recreational opportunities. The Atlanta area has over 100 of these communities. One community, Bridgemill, has 2,700 homes, a golf course, a 2-acre aquatic center, 25 tennis courts, and a 6,000 square-foot clubhouse with complete gym (Kohl, 2003).

Opportunities in Recreational Communities

Many recreational communities employ full-time recreation coordinators and offer extensive programs. Some smaller properties may combine their resources with other such properties and jointly employ a recreation coordinator. This is also common with companies that manage several apartment complexes in one community.

Duties in managing the recreational programs and facilities for a residential community are somewhat similar to those in managing a municipal program. There are some differences, however, particularly in recreational communities that have major seasonal variations in residents. Special events rather than ongoing programs can be more popular in such settings.

INDUSTRY PROFILE: CAMPGROUNDS

Camping is one of the most popular recreational activities in North America. It is not surprising, therefore, that the provision of campgrounds is a large industry. There are about 8,500 commercial campgrounds in the United States (Travel Industry Association of America, 2004). Most of these campgrounds provide space, amenities, and services for the recreation vehicle (RV) camper or the family that is "car camping" (tents, etc., based out of their vehicle). Most campgrounds are very small and are privately owned single establishments with few recreational amenities. In many cases, these are sole proprietorships established to supplement primary sources of income already being generated from the land. Owners of gas stations, restaurants, small motels, and farms often provide small campgrounds to transient overnighters in an attempt to generate extra income. These mom-and-pop operations open and close down continuously. It is, however, the large chain-operated campgrounds that represent the greatest area of growth as a commercial recreation business.

Types of Campgrounds

Campgrounds can be classified as destination, overnight (or en route), and urban campgrounds. Each type is examined here.

Destination Campgrounds first emerged in the 1970s on the west coast. Several hundred acres are utilized with about half being used for campsites and half for recreational areas. Facilities are often very elaborate, including pool, clubhouse, tennis courts, sports fields, and even golf courses. Supervised recreation programs are recognized now as a great way to stimulate the social contact and satisfaction that leads to repeat business.

A popular variation of the destination campground is the membership campground. Space is sold just as with the time-share resort concept: fee simple title or right-to-use methods. Typically, there are no more than 15 owners per site. Members can also reserve or trade space at other camp resorts of the same chain.

The market for destination membership campgrounds is predominantly middle-aged and retired couples. Marketing schemes and sales pitches are similar to the time-share industry: mailed invitations and prizes to see the facilities. Sales costs can be 50% of the price. Persons who buy memberships but do not own RVs can rent a fully equipped RV at many of the destination campgrounds.

Overnight or En Route Campgrounds serve the needs of people traveling between destinations. Since most guests stay only one or two nights, recreational amenities are usually less extensive than at a destination campground. Nevertheless, there is usually a pool, a store, and a game room. Kampgrounds of America (KOA) is the largest private campground system in North America, and most would be considered as en route facilities. The initial fee to purchase a KOA franchise is not very high, but operators must also pay a small percentage of camping fees to the parent company. One trend in overnight campgrounds is to add more recreational amenities and programs in order to keep guests there for longer stays.

Urban Campgrounds serve RV travelers who need a place to hook up their vehicles (to electricity, water, and sewer service) while they are in a city. Spaces are very close together, and the majority of the facility may be asphalt. Nevertheless, some people stay at such locations for a week or more because of the attractions in the urban area. For example, the Circusland RV Park at the Circus Circus Hotel in Las Vegas offers 400 spaces, a variety of recreational attractions, Grand Slam Canyon (indoor theme park), and, of course, casino gambling.

Campground Operations

About 65% of revenues come primarily from space rental and related user fees while the rest is from auxiliary sources such as grocery store sales and recreational activity fees (Travel Industry Association of America, 2004). Most of the expenditures are for payroll. The peak season, as to be expected, is May through September. The average campground operates at just 43% of annual capacity.

To earn operating profits, a campground should be located on a major thoroughfare that is close to or en route to a popular natural resource or vacation attraction. An attractive environment with plenty of shade, vegetation, and a water source helps add to the ambiance. Recreational amenities and friendly service help gain repeat visitors. The facility should be marketed to out-of-state travelers and RV groups and with flyers at destination attractions. Yellow pages ads, Web sites, direct mail, and billboards are also used to attract visitors. In the off-season, it may be necessary to close down or offer alternative activities to draw business.

Opportunities in Campgrounds

The majority of campgrounds, being small, privately owned establishments, have little need for year-round employees other than the owner. Large campground chains, however, do present opportunities for the commercial recreation student. Many of the membership campgrounds such as Outdoor World employ recreation coordinators to develop extensive programs. Salaries have not proven to be very high; some are listed as low as $24,000 a year. However, there is reported to be opportunity to move up to positions managing the overall property or in coordinating recreation programs for several campgrounds in a region.

INDUSTRY PROFILE: RESTAURANTS

Public restaurants as we know them were in evidence in London as early as 1400A.D., and, within 200 years, the French had gained a reputation for serving fine food. In colonial America, restaurants were really just coffee houses and taverns. Most persons, however, still ate their three meals a day at home. The Volstead Act in 1919 changed this pattern, since it made the sale of liquor illegal. Taverns, therefore, were forced to increase their food service or close down. Improvements in refrigeration made it possible to transport beef and other foods that otherwise would spoil. As Americans left farmlands for the urban areas and became more mobile through automobile travel, they began to dine out more often. After World War II, the population increased dramatically, and more women sought jobs outside the home. All these factors led to a huge growth in the restaurant industry.

Today, about 47% of the American consumer's food dollar is spent dining out, up from 26% in 1960. The typical person consumes four to five meals prepared away from home per week. However, some populations, including singles, business people, and higher income families dine out more and spend more than half of their food dollars dining out. Overall, it is a $476 billion industry with 900,000 establishments and a growth rate of about 4% a year. Quality of food, convenience, price, and service are the traditional criteria for selecting a restaurant, but some people also seek atmosphere, amenities, and entertainment (Milton, 2004; National Restaurant Association, 2005).

Types of Restaurants

There are four types of restaurants that fulfill different roles in the leisure service industry: full-service, casual theme, limited service, and leisure theme restaurants.

Full-Service Restaurants have table service and typically middle-income to upscale customers. About half offer a varied menu, while the others are a variety of specialty restaurants for steak, seafood, Italian, Asian, and so on. The orientation may be that of a family restaurant, emphasizing variety of food and moderate price, or that of a fine dining restaurant emphasizing quality food and atmosphere. The average check is over $10 per person. The upscale restaurants make almost one fourth of their revenue from alcoholic beverage sales. This shows how dining out is often a form of social or business entertaining.

Casual Theme Restaurants include outlets such as Chili's, Bennigan's, and TGI Fridays who cater to young professionals and upscale students. Food selections are typically salads, sandwiches, Mexican dishes, and the like. Bar business is very important, and the marketing, therefore, emphasizes socialization. Many casual theme restaurants have "happy hours," special events, birthday parties, sports viewing, New Year's Eve parties, and other promotions to draw crowds.

Limited Service Restaurants, also called quick service or fast-food restaurants, are not all "burger joints." In fact, only about a third of fast-food restaurants have burger/beef orientations. The remainder are oriented toward pizza, chicken, ice cream, sandwiches, donuts, Mexican food, or other specialties. About 73 percent of food orders are take-out rather than dine in. McDonald's is the leading fast-food chain, with more than 13,600 U.S. outlets and 17,500 outlets in 120 foreign countries. Some chains have expanded too rapidly, and in recent years, several chains have suffered financial setbacks (Milton, 2004).

Increasingly, fast-food restaurants are using leisure amenities and activities to attract customers. Playground equipment, contests, discount toys, theme park coupons, birthday parties, and other promotions are common. McDonald's has an impressive record of community involvement through sponsorship of Special Olympics meets, Scout jamborees, youth sports leagues, fun runs, and countless other events. Many fast-food chains have become more health conscious, offering low-calorie salads and chicken dishes.

A fast-growing variation is the "quick casual" restaurant such as Boston Market or Panera Bread Co. These establishments offer more upscale food choices than other limited service restaurants and average $7 to $10 sales per person, which is several dollars higher than other fast-food establishments.

Leisure Theme Restaurants probably evolved in the early 1960s when Shakey's Pizza began to draw more people with its player piano, singing waiters, old movies, and cartoons than it did with its food. In the early 1980s, there was a tremendous boom in the construction of Chuck E. Cheese Pizza Time Theater and ShowBiz Pizza establishments. These are basically fast food establishments, featuring computer synchronized robotic characters that sing and dance. The two companies merged in the mid-'80s.

There are numerous video and arcade games and play attractions, plus dining rooms, TV viewing rooms, and party rooms. Some establishments serve 30 or more birthday party groups each Saturday. Special programs include sports team video parties, teen dances, and slumber parties. Several other chains, such as Jungle Jims, have recently joined the competition for this market.

Adult-oriented leisure theme restaurants are also common in many cities. Some feature bars, large screen TVs, video games, pool tables, dart game areas, and other attractions. Popular examples include the Dave and Busters chain and the ESPN Zone establishments.

In resort areas, themed dinner theaters have become common. In the Central Florida area near Disney World there are several dinner theaters, including Arabian Nights, Medieval Times, and King Henry's Feast. Each offers food and drink, music, races, jousts, and other entertainment based on a historical period theme.

Operations and Keys to Success

The operations of any type of restaurant involve a variety of tasks and jobs, which are illustrated in the organizational chart in Figure 10-3. In smaller restaurants, staff have to perform several of the tasks. There is no surefire formula for success, but the following factors contribute significantly:

- A good location near the population, accessible and visible.
- Good environment—a coordinated, clean, and tasteful theme.
- Qualified workers—this is currently the number-one industry problem.
- Good service—friendly, competent service that makes customers feel welcome.

Fine dining is one of the attractions and primary revenue sources at many hotels and resorts.
(Photo: Wintergreen Resort)

- Good food and beverage products that taste, smell, and look good.
- New product development to meet the changes in public taste.
- Value of the dollar—fair value for the total dining experience.
- Management controls—food costs held to about 31% of sales, liquor to 20% of sales, and labor to about 29% of sales, proper portion sizes, and inventory control.

There are several important trends in the restaurant industry. People are generally seeking more casual dining than in past years, and they desire greater menu choice, healthier foods, and choices in portion size. There is also continuing growth in the demand for take-out foods (including drive-through and delivered) and ethnic foods. "Dual branding" is also an important trend, whereby two or more food service providers operate out of the same building, sharing fixed costs and some promotional expenses. Examples include KFC and Taco Bell. Another important trend is the difficulty in finding dependable and qualified labor. Restaurants are using several strategies to counter this problem, including more employment of senior citizens and persons with disabilities, and more use of labor-saving technology. The majority of restaurants have also increased their training budgets in recent years in order to provide better service (Milton, 2004).

Opportunities in the Restaurant Industry

Restaurants employ more people than any other single retail business in the country. The vast majority of positions, however, are of part-time or nonprofessional nature. Nevertheless, positions such as cooks, waiters/waitresses, bus persons, and bartenders do provide essential background experience for persons interested in this field. Advancement to positions such as food and beverage controller, executive chef, dining room supervisor, purchasing director, and restaurant general manager require experience, and in some cases academic or specialized training. Few commercial recreation and tourism curricula offer sufficient coursework in this area, but restaurant management programs, hospitality programs, and cooking schools do. The average annual salary for managers in 2004 was $36,000 to $45,000, not including any bonus pay (National Restaurant Association, 2005).

Contrary to popular opinion, fast-food operations are usually more advanced in technology, methods, and operating procedures than are traditional full-service restaurants. Salaries for managers in quick service operations are also very competitive, but the hours are very long. Managers can also move up through the corporate structure to become training directors, district supervisors, and even franchise owners if they can get the capital.

Another area of opportunity is to work with a major hotel or resort as the banquet manager or catering manager. Both positions require the programming flair of a good recreation professional and the food service background of a restaurant management graduate.

Finally, some leisure theme restaurants have employed persons as special event coordinators. Recreation graduates have filled these positions successfully.

Figure 10-3
Sample Organizational Chart for a Large Restaurant

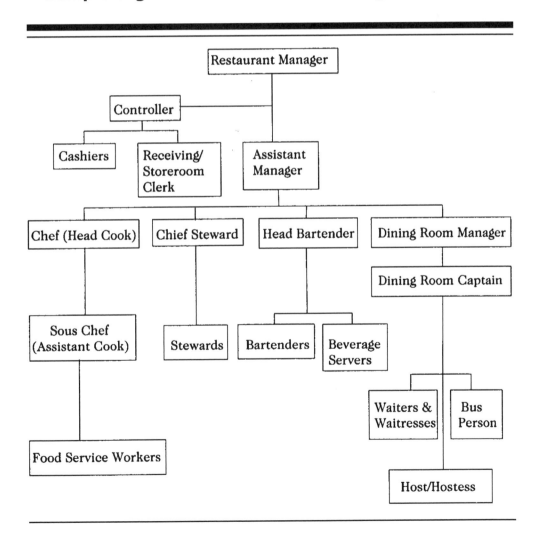

INDUSTRY PROFILE: CITY CLUBS, NIGHTCLUBS, AND TAVERNS

About 62% of American adults drink alcoholic beverages to some degree (Hanson, 2005). Although much of the consumption occurs at home and at restaurants, much of it also occurs at some type of club or tavern. Such facilities have been common in the United States since colonial days and, in fact, were the precursors of the restaurant industry.

Today, city clubs, nightclubs, and bars and taverns have similar functions: entertainment and social interaction at establishments serving alcoholic beverages and some food. There are about 70,000 drinking establishments in the United States, generating about $14 billion in revenue (Miller, 2005). Most are public nightclubs and taverns, but some are city clubs. Each type is briefly profiled in this section.

City Clubs provide an upscale environment for business people to socialize and conduct business. Most have an initiation fee over $500 and some are much higher. Food and beverage sales account for about half of the revenues, with another third from member dues. The remaining revenue comes from other sources such as overnight lodging or sports facility charges. Some city clubs have athletic facilities and swimming pools, but libraries, reading rooms, and meeting rooms are more common facilities.

Nightclubs feature entertainment in addition to alcoholic beverage service. The entertainment may be live music of many types, live comedy, or recorded music. Dance floors are a common amenity. Depending upon the state, clubs may be open to the public or may require memberships typically costing $25 or more.

Most nightclubs project some type of image, and more than anything else, the music defines the image: country and western, jazz, oldies, progressive rock, and so on. This image is enhanced by the furnishings, decorations, lighting, and the attire and attitude of the staff. Comedy clubs have also become popular. Nightclubs are a particularly challenging business because patrons are trendy in their tastes. A nightclub that is number one in a city may not even be in business five years later and, if they are in business, they are probably not the top club any more (Miller, 2005).

Bars and Taverns are typically smaller than nightclubs and have less emphasis on entertainment. As with nightclubs, profits at a successful tavern can be quite high, due in part to the excellent margin on alcohol sales. Beverage costs typically are only 15–25% of sales. Another reason for profitability, similar to nightclubs, is that labor costs are low. Cocktail waitresses, bartenders, and bar-backs are paid low hourly wages, but expect to earn more on tips. Two growth trends are in sports bars and microbreweries, the latter with 20% growth rates in recent years (Miller, 2005).

An important problem that has been recognized is the drunk driver. With the passage of Dram Shop Acts in most states, the responsibility for drunk drivers is shared by the server of the alcohol. Therefore, nightclubs and taverns now instruct bartenders and waitresses to stop serving patrons who are becoming intoxicated. They also serve more food and snacks to help neutralize the alcohol's effects.

Opportunities in the Club Industry

There is no clear career path for commercial recreation and tourism graduates to become managers or owners of clubs, nightclubs, and taverns. Numerous opportunities exist, however, for the student who learns the basics of bartending, food and beverage control, and customer service. Depending upon the setting, experience in managing entertainment and coordinating promotions is also essential. These are all skill areas that complement the social and business skills acquired in a commercial recreation curriculum. Experience and maturity are essential, however, and prospective club managers must regard the field as a business rather than as a personal playground. Otherwise, owners, managers, and staff have been known to give away and "drink away" the profits.

SUMMARY

The hospitality industry is composed of businesses that provide overnight lodging accommodations, food and beverage services, and supporting amenities. Federal and state government agencies have also become major providers of hospitality services at their parks and other recreational destinations. Specific types profiled in this chapter included hotels and motels, ski resorts, casinos, time-share resorts, recreational communities, campgrounds, restaurants, and clubs. There are many variations of businesses within each type of industry. Although each type of industry is different, there are several commonalities shared by successful businesses. The manager must know who the consumers are and what they expect. Services provided must meet those expectations. There must be a good location and a reliable labor source. Management must control costs and have a diversity of revenue sources. Finally, some types of resorts, hotels, time-shares, campgrounds, and recreational communities are very dependent upon having natural resource attractions that must be protected.

SPOTLIGHT ON:

THE WORK FAMILY RANCH

by Teresa Love, PhD, Radford University

Experience the renewing of your soul amidst the serenity and wildlife of our 12,000-acre oak woodland ranch. Whether you come in the golden summer or lush green spring, you will find a warm farm family welcome at our mountaintop home. The Work Family Ranch offers a fun-filled, down-home kind of getaway to experience and explore the unique adventures of ranch life.

George and Elaine Work, operators of the Work Family Ranch, use the invitation above to welcome guests to their Web site and their ranch. George and Elaine are a fourth-generation farm family who have made many contributions to California agriculture, including opening doors to farm stays within the state.

While bed and breakfast properties are prevalent and successful among travelers, farm stays are less well known. The typical New Zealand-style farm stay implies that the guests are integrated into the host family and take part in all the daily activities. The guests eat with the hosts, participate in chores, and learn the hardships and joys of working the land.

After several trips abroad, and having experienced New Zealand farm stays firsthand, George Work decided that the Work Family Ranch would be the perfect host for a farm stay program. After initial inquiries into starting the farm stay, George was informed by county administrators that he could not have paying guests eating and sleeping in his home. He asked what he could do and was told that he would need to change California legislation. George initiated a bill that would allow agriculturalists to operate farm stay operations. AB 1258 was signed in 1999 and put in effect in 2000. The Works were then able to open their doors to visitors.

Visitors to the Work Family Ranch can shadow the Works as they do whatever tasks need to be accomplished. This can range from chopping wood to helping a cow give birth.

(continued)

The Works primarily invite visitors onto the ranch to educate the public about agriculture and the realities of farm life. They want visitors to understand the value of environmental stewardship. Just as with any small business, the Works need to promote their product.

Conventional wisdom says that national publicity is a good thing for a small business, especially if the publicity is positive. In May 2004, NBC's *Today Show* featured the Work Family Ranch as one of several family-oriented vacation destinations. The story, which aired nationally and also appeared on the *Today Show* Web site, led to only one phone call from a prospective visitor.

A writer published a story in a hunting magazine about a new pocketknife he had field-tested. The writer only mentioned that he had taken the knife on a hunting trip on a ranch in Southern Monterey County. The article did not mention the Work Family Ranch by name. However, enough people tracked the ranch's name down that five calls from prospective visitors were generated from the article.

The Internet has been touted as the great leveling ground in terms of business promotion. Visitors have Web access to the Hilton chain as well as to small bed and breakfast inns. The Works' Web site, www.workranch.com, gets a lot of hits, but they are not seeing follow-up calls or business coming from the site.

The Work Family Ranch is listed with the California Association of Bed and Breakfast Inns (CABBI). Inclusion in CABBI has proved beneficial because the Works welcome children on their property while most B&Bs accept adults only.

George and Elaine are founding members of a marketing organization promoting agritourism operations on California's Central Coast. The Central Coast Agritourism Council is helping to promote agricultural awareness and agritourism operations. Through the Web site, www.agadventures., and area map, the Works are helping other operations invite visitors.

One form of promotion that has served the Works well is articles written by travel writers and included in major newspapers. In February of 2005, a story about the ranch appeared in the *Los Angeles Times* and led to a tremendous number of calls and interest in the farm stay program. Those contact calls led to several families coming to stay on the ranch.

As much as George and Elaine Work want to share their life and experiences with the public, marketing their property to visitors has proved difficult. They do not feel that any of the techniques they have used have been as successful as possible. Even though the Works are responsible for the allowance of farm stays in California, if they cannot find an effective way to market their program to the public, then they will need to forgo that part of their agritourism operation.

George and Elaine Work continue to explore better marketing techniques to promote their agricultural tourism operations so that the young fifth generation can continue to educate the public about the importance of environmental stewardship and the rewards of agriculture.

REFERENCES

American Hotel and Lodging Association. (2005). 2005 Lodging industry profile. http://www.ahla.com/pdf/Lodging-Ind-Profile-2005.pdf.

American Resort Development Association. (2005a). A consumer's guide to vacation ownership. http://www.arda.com.

American Resort Development Association. (2005b). Why vacation ownership. http://www.arda.org/AM/Template.cfm?Section = Why_vacation_ownership_1.

American Resort Development Association. (2005c). Industry fact sheet. http://www.arda.org/Content/NavigationMenu/IndustryInformation/IndustryFactSheet/Industry_Fact_Sheet.htm.

American Skiing Company. (2004). 2004 *Annual Report*. Bethel, Maryland: American Skiing Company.

Carroll, C. (1999, July 5). Alisal adds ropes course to team-building plan. *Travel Weekly*, p. 30.

Fitness Business. (2005, January). Top 10 spa trends to watch in 2005. *Fitness Business*, p. 28.

Flowers, G. (2000, February 21). Club Med's planned Colorado buy heralds start of North American push. *Travel Weekly*, p. 6.

Government of Saskatchewan. (1999). http://www.gov.sk.ca/govt/econdev/.

Graves, T. (2004, August 5). Industry surveys: Lodging & gaming. *Standard & Poor's Industry Surveys*, pp. 1–31.

Hanson, D. (2005). Alcoholic beverage consumption in the U.S.: Patterns and trends. http://www2.potsdam.edu/hansondj/Controversies/1116895242.html. November 24, 2005.

Kelly, J. (1985). *Recreation business*. New York: John Wiley & Sons.

Kohl, G. (2003). Life at the resort. http://www.atlantalifestyle.com/life_at_the_resort.htm. November 17, 2005.

Lattin, G. (1985). *The lodging and food service industry*. East Lansing, MI: The Educational Institute of the American Hotel and Motel Association.

Miller, R. (2005). *2005 travel & leisure market research handbook*. Loganville, GA: Richard K. Miller & Associates, Inc.

Milton, D. (2004, September 30). Restaurants. *Standard & Poor's Industry Surveys*, pp. 1–25.

National Association of State Park Directors. (2005). http://isu1.indstate.edu/naspd.

National Association of Realtors. (2005, March 1). Second home market surges, bigger than shown in earlier studies. http://www.realtor.org/PublicAffairsWeb.nsf/Pages/SecongHomeMktSurges05.

National Restaurant Association. (2005). Restaurant industry facts. www.restaurant.org/research/ind_glance.cfm.

National Ski Areas Association. (2005). http://www.nssa.org. November 11, 2005.

Pfenning, A. (2003, December 1). Biz, leisure travelers think alike when it comes to picking hotels. *Travel Weekly*, p. 10.

Resort Condominiums International. (2005). About RCI. http://www.rci.com/RCI/CDA/rciInfo/RCI_InfoDefault.jsp?request = RCI_AboutUsContent.

Shapiro, J. (1996, January 15). America's gambling fever. *U.S. News & World Report*, pp. 53–61.

Ski Industries America. (1984). *White paper on skiing*. McLean, VA: Ski Industries America.

Travel Industry Association of America. (2004). *Tourism works for America: 2004 annual report*. Washington, DC: Tourism Industry Association of America.

Chapter•••• 11

Local Commercial Recreation

This chapter deals with recreation products and services that are purchased by people in their home communities. For lack of a better title, "Local Commercial Recreation" is used. In some cases, tourists may account for much of the participation, but overall, it is the local residents who are the primary consumers. For example, Disney World, the largest theme park in the world, draws most of its revenue from tourists. Similarly, most of the other top 10 "mega-parks" such as Disneyland and Universal Studios, are major tourist attractions. However, most other theme and amusement parks are much smaller, and they draw their customers primarily from their local communities or metropolitan regions.

Local commercial recreation can be divided into three major groupings: recreational activity providers, recreational product retailers, and entertainment providers. Each category contains numerous recreation industries, some of which overlap into other categories.

Recreational activity providers include health clubs, racquet clubs, bowling centers, dance studios, golf courses, and summer camps. These businesses make their revenue primarily through the provision of recreation programs and facilities. Activity may occur as basic use of facilities (i.e., round of golf, individual fitness workout, etc.) or the activity may be a highly structured program, such as an instructional class, tournament, or league.

Recreation product retailers include sporting goods stores, arts and crafts shops, and stores selling scuba equipment, toys and games, bicycles, cameras, motorbikes, and music. Some provide a wide range of merchandise, and others are highly specialized. In many cases, recreation retailers also offer instructional classes and sponsor special events in order to draw and/or keep customers.

Entertainment providers include movie theaters, amusement parks, fairs and festivals, auditoriums and arenas, and pro sports. These businesses provide facilities where customers are essentially spectators for some type of entertainment (movies, concerts, sports events, etc.) or engage in non-active participation, such as riding a roller coaster.

The operation of a local commercial recreation business typically involves many of the task areas that have been discussed in previous sections of this text: marketing, recreation programming, retailing, facility management, and so on. Therefore, in order to avoid duplication, these task topics will not be covered again. As with previous industry profile chapters, the purpose of this chapter is to provide an overview of the operation of several important commercial recreation industries. Some of the smaller industries and the role of local government in commercial recreation will also be examined.

INDUSTRY PROFILE: SPORTS, FITNESS, AND HEALTH CLUBS

Sports, fitness, and health clubs have existed in various forms since ancient times. The Baths of Trajan in Rome included a swimming bath, running track, gymnasium, exercise area, courts for ball games, and refreshment rooms. Later, many European "health spa" resorts were based on the presence of a mineral hot springs. In Paris in 1847, Hippolyte Triat, a vaudevillian strongman, opened a gymnasium that may have been the first to charge a membership fee (Buck, 1999).

By the early 1900s, YMCAs began to exert an influence by offering sports facilities and programs. The Ys, though nonprofit, were pioneers in basketball, swimming, and weight training. Commercial health clubs also began to evolve, offering men's and women's exercise on alternating days.

As the sports and fitness movement grew, clubs tended to become oriented toward special interests. In the 1940s, Vic Tanny started a series of gyms in the Los Angeles area that were multipurpose facilities for weight lifting, swimming, bowling, and other activities. A friend of Tanny, Joe Gold, followed in the 1960s with a series of bodybuilder gyms. In the 1980s, numerous small clubs opened primarily as aerobics studios and figure salons. Now, clubs can be loosely classified as aerobics/figure salons, health clubs, bodybuilding gyms, tennis clubs, racquetball centers, or multipurpose clubs.

About half of adult Americans claim to exercise occasionally, but only 13% of the population, about 41 million people, are members of some type of sports, fitness, or health club. This participation drives a $15 billion industry of 26,830 membership clubs, of which about half are commercial and the other half are government or nonprofit operations (International Health, Racquet & Sportsclub Association [IHRSA], 2005).

Clientele at the various clubs differ somewhat, but most clubs attract young professionals, with 35- to 54-year-olds being the largest age group (37% of members). However, the 55-year and older age group is the fastest-growing segment, having more than tripled its membership since 1987. Secondary markets, particularly for off-peak daytime hours, are students, retirees, and night shift workers. Most members join the clubs to get in shape or to stay in shape, but clubs can also be a great setting for socialization and informal business contacts. On average, members attend 72 to 90 days a year (IHRSA, 2005).

Overall, the most common facilities are free weights, stationary bikes, climbers/ steppers, plate-loaded weight equipment, aerobic exercise area, and treadmills. Participation by women is slightly higher overall than participation by men, particularly in aerobic exercise and exercise walking (IHRSA, 2005).

Mini-Gyms, Aerobics Studios, Bodybuilder Gyms, and Other Health Clubs

Mini-Gyms and Aerobics Studios are the most elementary type of fitness facility. They typically are low overhead storefront facilities with a small exercise floor and limited equipment. However, they are also one of the fastest growing segments of the fitness industry. Curves, a no-frills fitness club for women, now has over 8,400 franchises. A typical Curves club has 8 to 12 hydraulic resistance machines, but no locker room, free weights, or aerobics classes. Club owners pay $29,900 for a franchise, equipment, and training, plus a monthly franchise fee of $395 (Canfield, 2004). Locations in strip-mall shopping centers offer good visibility and access, which is critical, since membership turnover is very high. Diversification into low-cost activities such as dance classes, yoga, martial arts, weight loss, and "spinning" can help these small businesses survive.

Bodybuilder Gyms, devoted to serious weight trainers, existed prior to the fitness boom. These gyms still exist in some areas but have little market share today. Most people seek a coed environment and a broader range of activities than is offered in the male-dominated gyms. Gold's Gyms are good examples of bodybuilder gyms that changed with the times to become more diverse in their offerings to women as well as men. Gold's is now considered a full service health and fitness club.

Health and Fitness Clubs offer a greater variety of facilities and services than do the salons and gyms. Facilities typically include an open exercise floor with sound system, variable resistance equipment, cardiovascular equipment, free weights, sauna, nursery, snack and juice bar, and whirlpool. Health and fitness clubs need 50,000 to 70,000 in population within a small radius in order to draw a sufficient membership of at least 1,000. Some clubs believe that it is impossible to sell too many memberships. For example, one club had 4,000 members yet had a capacity for only 100 people at a time. Fortunately, more managers now emphasize quality and are successful in keeping repeat customers.

Promotional efforts for health and fitness clubs begin two or three months prior to opening with direct mail and phone campaigns. A month prior to opening there are big newspaper ads, radio spots, and finally an open house. Some preopening campaigns raise most of the money needed to cover equipment purchase for the facility and much of the advertising costs.

Health and fitness club instructors are usually enthusiastic young men and women in good condition. They are employed at a ratio of one staff member for approximately 100 participants. There are more instructors on the floor when individuals use "personal trainers." This practice yields a very high profit margin, and some clubs promote the use of personal trainers aggressively. Unfortunately, some instructors learn what they know about fitness through crash training programs instead of through college programs in exercise physiology and fitness training. For management positions, sales background may be considered more important than knowledge of fitness and recreation. Recognizing the dangers of this practice, the American College of Sports Medicine offers a certification program for health and fitness club professionals. Other associations have begun to offer certification programs for aerobics instructors, weight training instructors, and managers.

Racquetball, Tennis, and Multipurpose Sports Clubs

Racquetball and tennis clubs feature indoor and outdoor court facilities, plus a pro shop and possibly some fitness facilities. Multipurpose sports clubs serve the widest range of fitness and sports interests, usually combining many of the features of the racquet clubs and health and fitness clubs.

Since they occupy considerable land, tennis and multipurpose clubs are usually located outside the center city area. Clubs should be within a 15-minute drive of the target market's workplace or residence. Many clubs are planned to have only 50 to 100 members per racquetball court and 25 to 50 members per tennis court in order to assure availability of playing time. However, by combining racquetball, tennis, fitness, and other facilities, higher ratios can be served by the multipurpose club.

The "average" multipurpose club has about 2,940 members and gross revenues of $2.1 million. Families constitute the largest membership category for racquet clubs, but single memberships are the largest group in multipurpose clubs. Most clubs charge an initiation or enrollment fee plus monthly membership dues, which combine to average $653 in revenue per member per year. These fees account for about 72% of the revenue at most clubs. Clubs' most profitable (by profit margin percentage) services are personal training, massage therapy, pro shop sales, aquatics programs, tennis programs, and food and beverage sales, in that order (IHRSA, 2005).

Personnel accounts for about half of the operating expenses of most clubs. It is interesting to note that fitness and multipurpose clubs pay out much more for marketing expenses than do the racquet clubs. This reflects the higher turnover of members at the fitness and multipurpose clubs, and, therefore, the need to advertise.

Recreation programs at racquet clubs and multipurpose clubs are much more extensive than at the health and fitness clubs. Leagues, tournaments, and classes are common for the racquet sports, and most clubs offer several types of fitness classes. Some clubs offer volleyball, basketball, gymnastics, swimming, fitness assessments, spinning classes, wellness programs, theme parties, trips, and children's day camps. A few clubs have become so innovative as to offer personal finance classes, nutrition classes, toy drives and Santa visits, "Fit for Two" aerobics class for pregnant women, "Stroll Aerobics" for infants, "Dad and Me" programs, "Ultra-Athlete" competitions, kayak lessons, scuba classes, golf simulator practice, in-line skating, and teen image workshops. Promotion of these activities is usually achieved through direct mail, mailed or e-mailed club newsletters, yellow pages ads, and special promotions. Figure 11-1 illustrates the typical organizational chart of a generic multipurpose club.

Figure 11-1
Organizational Chart for a Multipurpose Sports Club

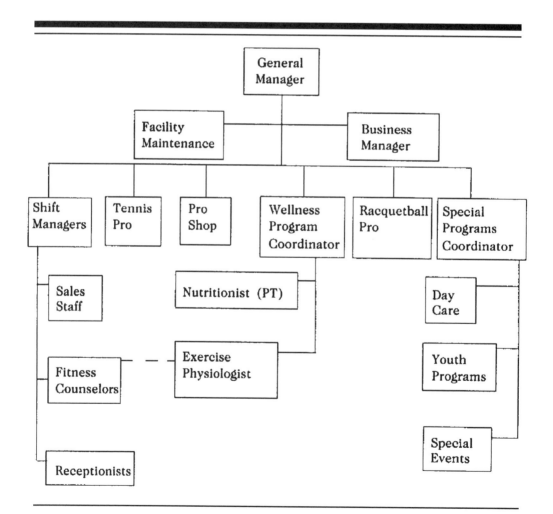

Operational Trends

While interest in fitness is high and still growing, demand for racquetball and tennis has leveled off (Roper Starch, 2004). A popular solution to this problem is to redefine and diversify the business. Aerobics and weight training are now the core of the industry, but a broader orientation to "wellness" is the emerging concept. This approach includes fitness and lifestyle assessment, health and nutrition programs, personal training, stress reduction, smoking cessation, and a wide range of sports and social activities.

In 1999, John McCarthy, Executive Director of the International Health, Racquet and Sportsclub Association, cited "10 Mega-Opportunities" for the new century (Cocchi, 1999). His predictions still seem to be on target at this time.

1. **Age wave opportunity**—Four million Americans turn 50 years old each year. Programs and marketing can help retain this segment as active members in clubs.
2. **Special populations**—Groups with special needs, especially arthritis sufferers, should get more notice.
3. **Benefits of exercise message**—Almost every day newspaper or television features a study about the benefits of exercise. Clubs need to tap into the delivery of that message.
4. **Sales and service training**—Customer service and hospitality skills need to become a bigger part of the sales presentation.
5. **Membership integration**—To counter high member attrition rates, clubs give more personal attention to new members throughout their first 120 days to encourage them to make exercise a permanent part of their lives.
6. **Health care industry integration**—Relationships with health care facilities have great potential, particularly to rehabilitate patients with injuries and chronic illness.
7. **Easy access**—Membership plans with shorter periods of 6 months to 1 year draw new business.
8. **"All of America" inclusion**—About a third of Americans are African, Asian, and Hispanic Americans, yet they are only 3% of club members. Promotions and programs for this market have great potential.
9. **Generation Xers**—Research shows that this group wants more excitement and variety. New programs need to address their interests and values more.
10. **Multi-generational clubs**—Family-oriented multipurpose clubs with a wider variety of activities are the most successful industry segment. Children's programs may cause parents to join too.

Opportunities in Sports and Fitness Clubs

To gain an entry-level position, career-oriented students should have a high level of proficiency in fitness, aquatics, racquet sports, and/or team sports. There are many part-time and some full-time positions as instructors in these areas. Beyond this level, programming and business skills are needed. Positions include youth programs director, tennis or racquetball director/pro, aquatics director, fitness program manager, night manager, and club program director. People in these positions develop new programs, supervise instructional staff, and manage facilities in their area. They may continue to teach group classes and private lessons and supervise other programs. They may also work as a shift manager, opening and closing the facilities, overseeing the front desk, and providing general supervision to all areas.

Many clubs also employ sales representatives on a full-time basis. Depending upon the club, this position may or may not require program background. Some clubs also employ food and beverage staff, retail shop staff, health and nutrition counselors, and exercise physiologists.

Prospective managers should have strong skills in at least one program area and a working knowledge of the other areas. Experience in sales, retailing, public relations, facility management, and personnel management are also critical. It appears that most manager positions are filled through promotions within the organization. Salaries for general managers average about $65,000 a year, while tennis directors average about $57,000, assistant general managers and fitness directors average about $42,000, and program directors average $30,000 to $40,000 depending on program area (IHRSA, 2005).

INDUSTRY PROFILE: GOLF COURSES AND COUNTRY CLUBS

Games similar to golf have existed since the Middle Ages, but the first golf course was started at St. Andrews, Scotland, in 1754. The first course in the United States was the St. Andrews Club in New York, which had six holes in 1888 (Cornish & Whitter, 1982). In just 100 years, the game has grown to involve about 33 million golfers in the United States. Although 78% of golfers are men, women are an important growth market, with about 1.4 million new female players since 2000 (National Golf Foundation, 2004a; Miller, 2005). Overall, golf has been one of the country's fastest-growing major sports because the baby boom generation now prefers golf over active sports such as tennis. However, the 495 million rounds of golf played in 2003 constituted the second of a two-year decrease since 2001. The bad economy has been blamed for this drop, which is expected to be temporary (National Golf Foundation, 2004b). The 18- to 39-year-old age group is the largest market (45% of rounds), followed by the age 50 and older market with 33% of rounds played (Miller, 2005).

Types of Golf Courses

There are two major approaches to the classification of golf courses: (1) type of course and (2) type of operation. The types of courses are regulation, executive, par three, and miniature. Types of operation include private membership/country clubs, commercial "public courses," and municipal courses operated by local government.

Regulation golf courses require about 130 to 150 acres and have a predominance of par four holes. Executive courses require less land and less capital. They have more par three holes than par fours, and the course can be played (by the busy executive) in less time. Par three courses have much shorter holes, but they can still be constructed so that they are challenging to play. As few as 10 acres may be needed, and the cost per hole for construction is much less than a regulation course. These courses can also be lighted for night play. Miniature golf courses are often developed as part of an outdoor entertainment complex at resorts, amusement parks, or along suburban highways.

Considering the other approach to classification, there are about 16,000 golf courses in the United States, of which about 50% are commercial public courses, 27% are private membership club courses, and the rest are municipal courses. Membership clubs and commercial public courses are contrasted in the next section.

Operations

Many of the membership golf courses function as private country clubs and have substantially more facilities than do public courses. The public courses often have bars and lounges, pro shops, and restaurants. Country clubs usually have these facilities, plus tennis courts, swimming pools, dance floors, better restaurants, meeting rooms, game rooms, and sauna/steam rooms.

Members of private country clubs pay initial membership fees that are often over $1,000, but may be $25,000 or higher. In addition, they pay monthly dues and/or greens fees. Public golf courses on the other hand make most of their revenue from the daily greens fees, which average $40. Either type of club may have significant food and beverage operations, but they generate more revenue in the membership clubs, because the clubs are used for many social functions.

Payroll is the majority expense and is slightly higher with membership clubs, reflecting their service orientation. Maintenance is a high priority and must be accomplished by knowledgeable professionals in horticulture or landscaping. Neither membership clubs nor public golf courses spend a high percentage of their revenues for promotion. The membership clubs typically have a stable number of long-term members, and the public courses typically draw repeating visits from a base of local residents.

Keys to Success

There are several keys to success in operating golf courses and country clubs. These include location, design and maintenance, retail operations, programming, real estate development, and finding ways to tap into the latent demand of 41 million potential golfers.

Location. The simple natural beauty associated with the location of a golf course is one of the game's most important drawing cards. Courses should capitalize on a beautiful landscape rather than alter the terrain artificially.

Efficient Design and Maintenance. Slow play reduces revenue by limiting the number of rounds played. A successful course presents challenge to the golfer without slowing play. This can be accomplished through proper design of the links, hole length, hazard placement, and greens design. In addition, good maintenance will help reduce the amount of time that golfers spend looking for errant balls. A competent starter also keeps play moving by getting foursomes started quickly.

Retail Sales. Food, beverage, and merchandise sales can contribute substantially to a golf course's success. High markups can be justified for many items purchased on impulse, such as balls, tees, caps, and drinks.

Effective Programming. A successful golf course finds ways to attract players on weekday mornings and early afternoons. One approach is to develop special programs and attractive prices for noncareer women and senior citizens. These programs can include lessons, mini-tournaments, and ladies' days. Another approach is to develop package deals for tourists and convention goers.

Real Estate Development. The majority of private and commercial golf courses constructed now are connected to real estate development. Without the sale of adjoining land for homes and condominiums, the money would not be available to build a tournament-quality course. By the same token, the presence of a quality golf course helps sell the real estate.

Tapping Latent Demand. The National Golf Foundation recommends several ways to reach the estimated 55 million individuals who are potential golfers. They suggest targeting women, mixed singles, junior golfers, and parents playing with children. They also suggest more dynamic pricing plans (time of day, day of week, group pricing, frequent player programs), and more emphasis on skills training beyond mere swing mechanics (strategy, course management, short game, etc.) that help golfers become more committed players.

Opportunities in Golf and Country Clubs

There are three different management career tracks in the golf course and country club industry: club pros, clubhouse managers, and greenskeeper/course managers.

Club pros have demonstrated a high level of playing proficiency and should have the ability to teach golf to groups and individuals. Many golf pros also manage the potentially lucrative retail pro shop and cart rentals. There is a Professional Golfers' Association (PGA) apprentice program that provides training in all areas of golf club operation. Numerous college level players with recreation degrees have done well in the PGA program.

Clubhouse Managers usually have backgrounds in the food and beverage industry and manage these services in the golf/country club. Sometimes they also manage the retail shops.

Golf Course Greenskeepers manage the staff who keep the course in great playing condition. Although some old pros have no academic background, many now have degrees in agronomy or landscaping. Top golf clubs pay good salaries to people who can make a course attractive and playable.

General Managers of golf courses and country clubs usually come from backgrounds as club pro or clubhouse manager. They must be masters at public relations to deal with the many diverse interests of members, and they must also have solid business skills.

INDUSTRY PROFILE: FAMILY ENTERTAINMENT CENTERS

The term *family entertainment center* is used to describe indoor and outdoor complexes that feature a variety of recreational attractions for a wide range of ages and interests.

Most outdoor centers are based around a combination of activities such as miniature golf, batting cages, bumper boats, mini-racers, video game rooms, and snack bars. Some outdoor centers are part of regional or national chain operations. For example, there are over 40 Malibu Fun Centers, and some of these facilities cost over $2.5 million to build.

Indoor entertainment/activity centers can include any of the same amenities that outdoor centers have. In addition, indoor centers may include bowling lanes, bumper cars, ice rinks, roller rinks, theaters, Laser Tag, indoor soccer, arcade games, climbing walls, and other attractions. There are two approaches to the indoor centers: the entertainment/activity center within a shopping mall, and the self-contained indoor entertainment center.

West Edmonton Mall in Alberta, Canada, is the largest entertainment and shopping mall in the world and home of the world's largest indoor amusement park with the world's largest indoor amusement park. It includes a water park with a 350-foot-long wave pool and 11 slides, a miniature golf course, a full-size ice hockey arena, a petting zoo, an aquarium, a life-size replica of Columbus's ship, the *Santa Maria*, 21 movie theaters, a casino, bowling lanes, rock climbing wall, bungee jump, and many other attractions. They sponsor parties, fund-raisers, company picnics, a marine life education program, and children's camps. Shopping in the mall is also world class, with 800 stores and services, 110 eating places, and a 235-room hotel (West Edmonton Mall, 2005).

The U.S. version of the mega-entertainment shopping mall is the Mall of America in Bloomington, Minnesota. This 520-store mall features the "Camp Snoopy" theme park with 26 rides and attractions, an aquarium, 50 restaurants, nine nightclubs, a LEGO play center, a flight simulator, a dinosaur museum, and a motor speedway (Mall of America, 2005).

Why have so much recreation in the malls? The answer is to help the malls survive the Internet shopping threat and the aging of the baby boomers. There are about 2,385 enclosed shopping centers in the United States, of which about 1,130 would be considered as "malls." About 130 of these are considered to be "lifestyle centers" which have a higher percentage of food services, movie theaters, and entertainment services (International Council of Shopping Centers, 2005). In all these venues, recreation and entertainment, including food and drink bring more people to the mall, they stay longer, and they visit on average two more stores. It's "shoppertainment."

Many cities now have self-contained indoor entertainment centers that are 100% recreation-oriented (as opposed to the shopping-oriented malls). Examples include the Discovery Zone, Jungle Jim's Playground, and Explorations, all facilities targeted to children ages 2–10, accompanied by their parents. These facilities typically charge an admission fee of $5 to $10 and are 8,000 to 25,000 square feet. To be successful, they need to have a variety of imaginative play options, be absolutely clean and sanitary, and offer parents clear visibility of their children.

Preteens, teens, and young adults are drawn to entertainment centers such as Sega's GameWorks facilities. There are 16 GameWorks centers, each having as many as 200 high-tech video and interactive games, music videos, and 12-player virtual reality games. Programs include corporate events, interactive team building, holiday parties, sports team parties, and graduation night events (Sega GameWorks, 2005).

The key concept with entertainment/activity centers is to provide a variety of recreational choices so that customers stay longer. When people stay longer, they try several activities and spend more money. Also, they tend to spend more for food, beverages, and souvenirs. Another advantage is that maintenance, operations, marketing, and administration are usually more cost effective with a centralized complex than with numerous separate and specialized facilities.

Some of the typical attractions of an entertainment/activity center are examined here in greater detail. It must be remembered, however, that each type often exists as a separate recreation enterprise.

Family entertainment centers draw customers with high-tech adventure simulation games.
(Photo: J. Crossley)

Bowling

Early bowling alleys were often smoke-filled hangouts of blue-collar working people, and the game's image was not associated with high status or wholesome family recreation. In the 1950s, however, the invention of automatic pin setters and ball returns sparked a growth in the game. Many clean, bright, multilane bowling centers were constructed and marketed as family recreational centers. Bowling participation grew dramatically, but dropped off again in the 1960s, as families were drawn to an increasing number of theme parks, shopping malls, and other attractions.

Bowling was rejuvenated again through good marketing and facelifts for the facilities, including automatic scoring, video playbacks, upholstered furniture, carpeting, color-coded balls, theme restaurants, video games, and day-care facilities. Bowling is now a $4.9 billion industry with about 3,100 commercial facilities (U.S. Census Bureau, 2004). However, participation has leveled off and changed. Once the league bowling "regulars" were the mainstay of the industry. Now, league bowlers are outnumbered by nonleague "casual bowlers" who do not want to commit to the regularity and structure of a league. They are less concerned with their scores and skills, but more interested in socialization.

There appear to be several keys to operating a successful bowling center (beyond the standard good location, sound management, good public relations, etc.). A solid core of league bowlers is still very desirable. Leagues usually fill at least half of the evening hours, but some lanes should be left available for nonleague open play. The best bowling centers also have successful daytime leagues for shift workers, women, and senior citizens, plus Saturday and summer leagues for youth. Secondly, there needs to be aggressive marketing for special events such as birthday parties, office parties, church group outings, youth events, and so on. The final key is that bowling centers need revenue-producing amenities such as restaurants, video games, day care, a billiards room, and possibly a nightclub (United States Bowling Congress, 2005; Mayhew, 2001).

Miniature Golf

Fully packaged miniature golf courses can cost $400,000 to develop because the costs may include land purchase (or lease), land preparation, a parking lot, utility installation, fencing, landscaping, night lighting, and a building for the office, restrooms, snack bar, and game room. A few multicourse sites in prime locations cost over $1 million to develop. On the other hand, a bare-bones outdoor course with no amenities can cost under $50,000. At the Putt-Putt Golf centers, surprisingly, only about 45% of the revenue comes from the course fee. The other 55% comes from the video game arcade and snack bar.

Overall, miniature golf has a good future, because it can be incorporated into larger recreational complexes or operated as a single enterprise. It has broad appeal, because everyone can play miniature golf, and it is cheaper than a ticket to the movies. It is also one of the few active things a family can do together. A final advantage is that course layout can easily be changed for variety, and, if unsuccessful, most of the course fixtures and structures can be sold or relocated.

Ice Skating Rinks

About 3% of the population of the United States participates in ice skating (Carini, 2000). There are, however, many different types of participants, and some ice rinks cater more to one type than another. The largest segment includes the many youth and young adults who desire open skating sessions and occasional instructional classes. There is also heavy demand in some locations for hockey games and team practices. Another segment consists of the figure skaters who need practice time on ice and individualized

instruction. Many of the rinks are provided by community park and recreation departments, while commercially operated rinks may be stand-alone facilities or rinks at major
shopping malls, family entertainment centers, or mountain resorts.

The major operating expenses for an ice rink are salaries, utilities, maintenance,
and insurance. Utilities are higher at ice rinks than at most other recreational facilities,
due to the cost of maintaining the ice. In order to cover the huge expenses, many ice rinks
stay open 20–24 hours a day. Hockey teams and figure skaters often use the less popular
hours for practice times. Revenue comes from public skate-time fees, concession stands,
pro shops, vending machines, hockey, private ice time, skate rentals, repair and sharpen-
ing, ice shows, and special events. Rinks that host major ice shows and skating competitions make more revenue from spectator fees and advertising/sponsorship charges (Ice
Skating Institute, 2005).

Skating demand falls off during the summer and some ice rinks close down or reduce their hours. Another quite profitable strategy is to conduct figure skating and ice
hockey camps.

A key aspect for efficient management is to design the facility so that it can be
supervised during slow periods by only one or two staff. Design that is centrally oriented
and connects the cashier's booth, control room, and rental facilities can accomplish this
objective.

Roller Skating and In-Line Skating

Roller skating became very popular in the United States in the 1950s, and in some
towns the local roller rink was the popular place for teens to meet on Saturday nights. As
with bowling, there was a major decline in the 1960s and early 1970s when theme parks
and shopping malls became popular. Many roller rinks closed down during this period.
Several events in the mid-1970s turned the sport around. Most importantly, the use of
polyurethane wheels gave skaters much more maneuverability and control. This technology was also combined with the disco dance craze to create roller disco. Skating rinks
installed high-tech sound systems and special-effect lighting to create an attractive atmosphere for teens and young adults. Participation may have peaked again in 1997 at 46
million skaters (both roller and in-line), as 2004 participation was down to 41 million.
Roller skaters account for only about 30% of the participation now, which is bad news for
skating rinks (Carini, 2000; Roller Skating Association International, 2005).

Skating is positioned both as part of the fitness movement and as "pop culture."
This is evident at many beach towns, where sidewalk skaters abound, entertaining people
with freestyling and slalom course acrobatics. Skating facilities typically cost about $1
million to build and have about 14,000 to 21,000 square feet including skating surface,
concession stands, video games, and a rental counter. In many ways, operation is much
like that of an ice rink, minus the ice. Revenues come from public skating periods (45%),
rentals (20%), snack bars (14%), pro shop (10%), video games (5%), and miscellaneous
events (5%) (Roller Skating Association International, 2005). It can be a profitable business if expenses can be kept down. A big problem is that there is little demand for skating
during morning and afternoon hours. Therefore, many rinks are closed much of the day
except for brief flurries of business in prime-time hours.

Opportunities in Family Entertainment Centers

With the diversity of businesses under this heading, there is no clear career path.
Managers for each type of facility need to have experience in that activity area as well as
general business skills, public relations ability, and personnel management skills. For
example, bowling lanes managers need to know about lane and pinsetter maintenance,
league scheduling, retail operations, facility maintenance, food and beverage manage-

ment, day-care center operations, and video game management. In other words, the manager must be a jack of all trades. While a commercial recreation degree provides important knowledge of programming, business, and management, practical experience is absolutely essential. Job announcements for managerial positions in these entertainment/activity centers seldom mention specific academic requirements, but do require practical experience. Such experience can be gained through part-time positions, for example: activity instructors, league coordinators, retail sales, front desk operations, maintenance staff, and so on.

INDUSTRY PROFILE: SPORTING GOODS RETAIL

One of the nation's first sporting goods stores, Abercrombie and Fitch, was founded in 1892. It gained a reputation for catering to affluent sports enthusiasts, and it outfitted personalities such as Teddy Roosevelt, Admiral Robert Perry, and Amelia Earhart. The store expanded to locations in numerous states, where it competed primarily with independent sports retailers. By the 1970s, however, Abercrombie and Fitch, plus other small chains and independents, were facing stiff competition from large chain stores. Often located at shopping malls, these new chains could purchase in large quantity, sell at a lower price, and afford more advertising. In 1977, Abercrombie and Fitch went bankrupt and was acquired by Oshmans Sporting Goods, the largest sports chain at the time (Hansard, 1983). Since then, Oshmans has been bought out by Gart Sports, which in 2003 was merged into the Sports Authority mega-chain. Meanwhile, many other independent sporting goods stores have suffered a similar fate as Abercrombie and Fitch.

While the mega-chain concepts are successful, they do not necessarily spell doom for all sports specialty stores. There is still a good market for well-managed specialty stores in product lines where service is most important. Actually there are numerous ways in which sporting goods reach the American public:

Department and discount stores usually carry at least a limited selection for the major sports in season. While product depth and service may be lacking, price is usually competitive.

Full-line sporting goods stores try to cover all the sports interests (with the exception of boats, snowmobiles, motorcycles, and other major capital items), while offering good product variety and service. Since there are many full-line chain stores, this approach dominates sales volumes in the sports industry. Some of these chains, such as The Sports Authority, are considered "category killers" because they can kill the competition with lower prices due to their bulk purchasing power (Wagle, 2004).

Specialty sports stores count on expertise, service, and depth of product lines to draw customers. Specialty stores often exist for boating, scuba diving, mountaineering/climbing, motorcycles, snowmobiles, snowboards, in-line skates, bicycles, hunting, fishing and skiing. Often an independent operator, it is usually necessary to diversify product lines for the off-seasons.

Pro shops and rental concessions are typically found at recreational facilities such as golf courses, tennis clubs, ski resorts, and the like. Rental equipment and convenience items are important products, as are specialty items with the facility logo.

Sports wholesalers sell primarily in quantity to small stores and to institutions such as schools, local recreation departments, camps, and YMCAs. Competitive, written bids are often part of the sales process.

Mail order and Internet venders often have specialty orientations. Some, such as L.L. Bean (outdoor equipment and clothing), offer high-quality products, while others offer cheap imitations.

Overall, the retail sporting goods industry is a very diverse industry with retail sales of about $28 billion a year. The largest sales categories are sports apparel and exercise and fitness equipment (Vanderwolf, 2005; Wagle, 2004).

In order to gain market share, the full-line stores and specialty shops must not only sell products, they must sell expertise, experience, and service. This helps create repeat business that is essential for success. Some stores also issue newsletters, teach clinics, lead trips, start activity clubs, and sponsor special events such as races, tournaments, or fun runs. Denver-based Gart Brothers, now part of the Sports Authority conglomerate, is a good example of such innovation. Their "Sports Castles" may have a ski machine hill, a golf driving cage with video camera, an adventure travel agency, basketball court, tennis court, boating pool, and meeting rooms for slide shows and classes.

Keys to Success

While there is no surefire formula for success, there are several characteristics that are often shared by successful sporting goods stores.

Product Line Buying can yield great savings for stores if the correct merchandise is purchased in quantity. Major chain stores have an advantage in this area and often employ professional buyers who study consumer trends. Trade shows are a good time to negotiate with the manufacturers, because factory managers usually attend and have considerable discretion on making deals. A good payment history helps the sporting goods store to get better prices and service from suppliers.

Store Location should match the needs of the particular market. For example, full-line sports stores need locations in regional or suburban shopping centers. These prime locations are justified by the high volume of drive-by or walk-by traffic. On the other hand, many specialty shops do not need such expensive locations, because their repeat customers know where to find them.

New Products and Innovations bring customers in who otherwise would not shop for replacements. For example, Calloway Golf's Big Bertha driver and various brands of "shaped" skis have generated sales from people who already owned perfectly good equipment.

Off-Season Strategy is important to carry the store through the year. Full-line sporting goods stores rotate their stock to carry whatever is "in" for the current season. Specialty shops may carry different but complementary product lines. For example, ski shops may carry tennis and water sports equipment in the summer.

Sales Staff and Service must be knowledgeable and experienced. It is also important to have the optimum level of staff: enough to give good service, but not overstaffed. Motivation of sales staff may be enhanced through commissions, bonuses, and recognition, in addition to an adequate base salary.

Opportunities in Sporting Goods Retail

Commercial recreation majors with advanced skills in several activity areas can be very valuable in the sporting goods industry, particularly if they also have retail experience. Employees who are accomplished participants can relate better to customers, can speak more knowledgeably about the equipment, and can discuss local opportunities for participation. In addition, such employees may be called upon to lead demonstrations and coordinate special programs and promotional events. Specialty shops in particular need staff who are both business-oriented and people-oriented, with expertise in the activity. There are, of course, those entrepreneurs who open specialty shops of their own. Some of the niches that may be the focus of a specialty retail store are scuba diving, skateboarding, in-line skating, surfing, windsurfing, trophies, climbing, skiing, hunting, fishing, soccer, hockey, golf, athletic shoes, outdoor adventure sports, or some combination of these.

Another approach is to work as a manufacturer's representative. This requires high knowledge of the activity and the product line and the personality to aggressively cover an assigned territory. Manufacturer's representatives conduct demonstrations, clinics, and training programs for retailers; coordinate special promotional events; and service their retail accounts by processing orders, handling product-related problems, and generally expediting business. Sometimes manufacturer's reps switch into retail management and vice versa.

INDUSTRY PROFILE: THEME, AMUSEMENT, AND WATER PARKS

In the early 1600s, several Russians operated a sled ride with a 70-foot vertical drop. It might be the first evidence of a business where people paid money to be terrified. Other amusements evolved over the years throughout Europe, but it was not until 1857 that a permanent amusement park, Jones Woods in New York City, appeared in the United States.

The industry really began to take off in 1884, when the first modern roller coaster was built at Coney Island, New York. For the next 40 years, amusement parks with roller coasters, rides, and carnival-type entertainment sprang up across the country. However, by the 1930s and 1940s, due to the Great Depression and World War II, the Industry declined into a lot of "kiddie ride"-type parks with carnival-type arcade games (Ruben, 1987).

Everything turned around in 1955 when Walt Disney opened Disneyland, the world's first theme park. Disneyland was different because it combined big, thrilling rides with a wide range of family entertainment. The facilities cost much more than any previous park, but more people attended, stayed longer, and paid more. Cleanliness and employee courtesy were cornerstones of the Disney concept, and the American public loved it.

A second Disney park, Disney World, opened in 1971. The 48-square-mile park near Orlando grew in stages and now includes the Magic Kingdom theme park, EPCOT (Experimental Prototype Community of Tomorrow), two water parks (Typhoon Lagoon and Blizzard Beach), an indoor interactive theme park (Disney Quest), a campground (Fort Wilderness), several entertainment and shopping areas (Disney's Boardwalk, Pleasure Island, and Downtown Disney), the MGM Studios theme park, an animal park (Animal Kingdom), a 200-acre sports complex (Wide World of Sports), a speedway, six golf courses, and 24 resort hotels. Many other parks have attempted to emulate the Disney characteristics of cleanliness, friendly service, and a family orientation.

Overall, about 328 million people visit the 600 theme and amusement parks and 476 water parks each year in the United States. There are 50 major theme parks that get over half this attendance. Total revenues are over $10.8 billion, and the industry employs over 500,000 people, many of them seasonally (International Association of Amusement Parks and Attractions [IAAPA], 2005; Miller, 2005).

Types of Theme, Amusement, Water Parks and Attractions

There are a variety of parks and attractions, each with a different approach to drawing crowds and showing them a good time. Each type is profiled below.

Cultural and Educational Parks are a remnant of the old-fashioned type of European park. Such parks feature formal greens, gardens, and fountains, with historical and educational exhibits. Musical entertainment may feature bands, string quartets, and choral groups. There are few of this type of park left in the United States.

Outdoor Amusement Parks are small and moderately sized parks that serve a metropolitan or regional market. These parks feature traditional thrill rides, carnival midways, and some entertainment. Most amusement parks lack a theme orientation for architecture, rides, and entertainment. Some of these parks draw as much as 50% of their business from group events such as company picnics.

Theme Parks differ from amusement parks in several ways. Primarily, a theme park is a family-oriented entertainment complex that has a particular subject as its theme. There is a major architectural concept throughout the park or in specified sections of the park. Theme parks tend to be larger and have a great variety of rides and attractions. Typically, more specialists are hired, especially in entertainment. Also, there usually are many specialty shops.

There are two areas of the country where a number of theme parks have clustered to form entire destination areas. The largest is Central Florida with the many Disney attractions, Sea World, Wet-'n'-Wild, Universal Studios, and many other specialty attractions. The other area is Southern California with Disneyland, Disney's California Adventure, Knott's Berry Farm, Universal Studios, Raging Waters, Six Flags Magic Mountain, Sea World, and numerous smaller specialty attractions. The Central Florida destination attracts a high percentage of tourists, whereas the Southern California attractions draw more of its attendance from the local area.

Water Theme Parks have become the hottest growth segment of the industry. The nation's 400 outdoor and 79 indoor water parks draw about 73 million visitors, but only 110 parks are considered "major." Many are small parks operated by small resorts and public recreation agencies. Large water parks feature wave action pools, "lazy river" rides, steep vertical drop slides, fountains, water spray cannons, and a variety of twisting flume slides. Water parks in some climates are a very "time intensive" business where money must be earned in a very short period of time. However, there has been tremendous growth in the number of indoor water parks that operate year-round. The Wisconsin Dells area has become a year-round tourism destination with a variety of outdoor and indoor water parks (Miller, 2005; Coy & Haralson, 2005; IAAPA, 2005).

Specialty Attractions exist in hundreds of cities and towns (and are not counted in the theme and amusement park totals above). They include wax museums, sports halls of fame, roadside attractions, specialty museums, and small animal/marine life attractions. A problem with many of these attractions is that they may hold visitors for only an hour. This is not long enough to justify a large admission fee, and it is not conducive to food and beverage sales. Therefore, marketing is extremely critical in order to draw pass-by traffic. Unfortunately, some of these attractions turn out to be disappointing tourist traps.

Operations

Over half of theme and amusement park revenue comes from admission fees (user fees and guest fees), while the rest comes primarily from food, beverage, and merchandise sales. Most of the operating expense for theme and amusement parks is for personnel.

Admissions. A centralized ticket system is preferred. An all-inclusive admission price entitles the customer to as many rides and shows as they desire. This approach has led to longer stays at parks, which in turn has boosted food and beverage sales. Another centralized admission method is to sell ride or show tickets in sets or coupon books. Usually, these are "value priced" (i.e., five coupons for $10, but ten coupons for $17). Either approach to centralized ticket sales minimizes the number of people handling money throughout the park, thus giving better efficiency and control.

Layout. Theme and amusement parks need to be designed with good inside and outside visibility. People inside the park should be able to see some of the other attractions in order to stay excited. People outside should be able to see some of the exciting action inside the park. Rides should be balanced: some wild, some mild, and some in between. In this way, different ages and temperaments will find something of interest.

Popular rides should be spread around the park so people will pass by the smaller attractions and concessions.

Facilities. In addition to rides of various types, theme and amusement parks are likely to have video game rooms, arcade games, concessions, gift shops, children's play apparatus, miniature golf, waterslides, restaurants, and show stages. Due to the need to draw repeat customers, many parks constantly add new attractions and renovate old ones. Since major rides such as state-of-the-art roller coasters can cost as much as $30 million dollars, changes tend to occur more with the smaller attractions and amenities.

Organization and Staffing. As much as 80 to 90% of the personnel at a theme or amusement park are seasonal employees, which can be a problem at the end of summer. Many parks have incentive programs that give bonuses for young employees who stay for the full season before returning to school. Figure 11-2 illustrates the organizational structure of a typical amusement or water park. It should be noted that the operations manager carries a major responsibility for the success of the park. It is a rare individual who has the technical and personal skills to perform this difficult job well.

Figure 11-2
Generic Organizational Chart for Theme, Amusement, and Water Parks

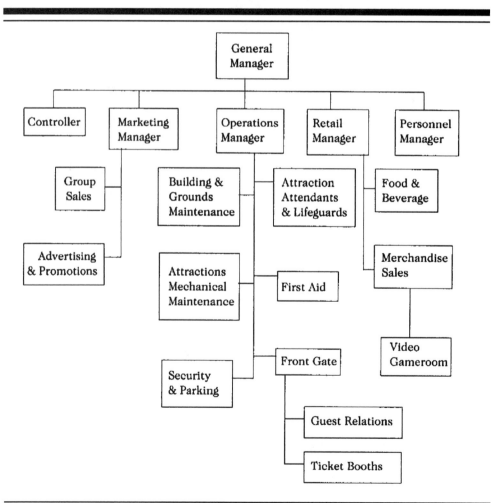

Marketing. The traditional appeal of theme and amusement parks is to preteens, teens, and young adults. Changing demographics are now causing most parks to think in terms of a broader market, particularly families, corporate groups, and even senior citizens. To reach these groups, parks are emphasizing increased beautification and diverse entertainment and food service. More parks are also working with tour operators to draw that trade. International tourists are also an important market at some parks, particularly those in the Orlando area.

The most common promotional methods for theme and amusement parks are radio, newspaper, yellow pages, Web sites, and direct mailings. Discount ticket kiosks and "hospitality desks" at hotels have also become popular in recent years, but some are tied to time-share sales promotions and thus make many people wary of buying at those outlets. Among large theme parks, television advertising is an excellent visual medium to capture the excitement. Therefore, a few parks use the majority of their advertising budget for television. There are five major market segments for theme and amusement parks:

- **Tourists**—the major market for large theme parks in destination areas such as Florida. Brochures in hotels and tourism informational centers and billboard advertising are good methods to reach tourists who have arrived in the area.
- **Local families**—people within a day's drive who visit mostly on weekends.
- **Children's groups**—schools, churches, recreation agencies, scouts, and other groups who come in buses on summer weekdays.
- **The evening market**—teens and young adults who come for entertainment, concerts, and dancing at night.
- **Corporate groups**—include consignment sales and group parties.

Keys to Success

Following the Disney example, a number of keys to success are suggested:

- The attraction must be clean, safe, secure, and comfortable.
- Having maintenance people visible and active in the park helps the cleanliness image and is a psychological deterrent to littering.
- Exciting rides will help gain repeat local attendance, particularly among teens.
- In order to attract an increasingly older market that includes many non-riders, parks must have more sit-down restaurants, more live entertainment, and better landscaping and aesthetics.
- It is critical to have a high "per-cap" (per person) revenue from food, beverage, and souvenir sales. These are increased when customers stay longer due to the park having more attractions.
- Employees must be personable and courteous, be trained well, and realize that they are "on stage" performers.
- If possible, the park should accumulate enough acreage to protect its adjoining buffer area from incompatible or unattractive developments.
- State of the art technology in rides and entertainment is more possible with computer technology to coordinate the timing of special effects.
- Discounts should only be used to bring in customers who otherwise would not come.
- Preventive maintenance for rides is absolutely essential for safe operation.
- Give people incentives to stay longer and spend more: morning coffee, afternoon snacks, magazines and sunscreen at the gift shop, lockers to keep things in, etc.
- Group sales are a key to success for pre- and post-prime season weeks.
- Good luck is essential, because a solid week of extremes in weather can ruin a season's profitability.

Industry Trends

There are a number of trends in the industry that should be noted (Miller, 2005; Krishnan, 2005; Coy & Haralson, 2005; Aquatics International, 2005; Travel Industry Association of America, 2005).

- Major theme park growth should continue in Asia as its middle income groups grow.
- There should be more growth of indoor water parks, which have increased from 18 in 2000 to 79 in 2004, particularly parks built in association with resort hotels.
- Parks continue to look for innovative yet less costly alternatives to expensive thrill rides.
- Due to concerns about both liability and terrorism, more emphasis is being given to safety.
- There is a positive correlation between attendance and gasoline prices, as some choose to vacation at closer theme parks rather than distant destinations.
- Small- and medium-size attractions are doing better in periods of weak economy than large parks are. This probably ties in to the correlation mentioned above.
- More natural habitats are being emphasized at animal theme parks such as the Australia Zoo, in Queensland, Australia.
- In order to attract the local market, many theme parks are selling discounted tickets and season passes to local residents.
- Some parks are trying two-tier price systems so VIP guests who are willing to pay significantly more do not have to stand in long lines.
- Parks are conducting more special events in order to compete with festivals and fairs.
- Parks are having more attractions that feature hands-on interaction with animals, a practice that is not favored by some environmental and animal rights groups.

Opportunities in Theme and Amusement Parks

Theme and amusement parks employ thousands of college-age students on a seasonal basis. In warm climates the opportunities are year-round. Most of the entry-level positions pay near minimum wage, yet require positive, outgoing personalities, good communication skills, and the ability to work with all types of people. Many of the managers of theme and amusement parks started in entry-level positions such as ride attendants, ticket salespersons, retail salespersons, maintenance staff, lifeguards, and guest relations staff. Each area of the park usually has several levels of positions, and good employees advance quickly through the levels.

Several large theme parks have college internship programs, but Disney's are the largest. The Disneyland and Disney World "College Programs" accept hundreds of college interns each year. In addition to the standard employee training program, interns attend business management seminars.

Experienced employees with good skills in personnel management, communications, and business can move up to mid-level management positions in personnel, marketing, group sales, promotional programs, merchandising, food service management, attractions operations, and guest relations. These department managers work extremely long hours for many days during the peak season, but may get extra-long vacations during the off-season. Many general managers and some department managers also receive bonus incentives if the park meets its goals for attendance, revenue, and/or operations. Overall, the theme and amusement park industry offers excellent opportunities for students who can work their way up to become creative problem solvers and humanistic managers.

OTHER LOCAL COMMERCIAL RECREATION INDUSTRIES

There are many other components of the local commercial recreation industry that present occasional opportunities for the recreation/tourism student. These industries include movie theaters, recreational and fantasy camps, craft and hobby shops, public assembly facilities, fairs and festivals, leisure publications, and recreational equipment wholesalers. This section will conclude with a brief review of several very creative entrepreneurial possibilities in local commercial recreation.

Movie Theaters

There are about 6,031 movie theaters in the United States with about 36,652 screens. This is an average of six screens per theater, but the large theater chains average 11 screens per site, indicating that the multiscreen concept is the industry norm. Movie attendance is about 1.5 billion people a year. However, this is only a third of the industry peak attendance of 4.5 billion in the late 1940s, before television became popular. Given these figures, it might be difficult to see how the industry survives financially. The answer is that ticket prices have increased significantly over the years, to an average of $6.21. This generates about $9.5 billion a year in box office revenues. Food and drink concession revenues add significantly more revenue, and in some theaters concession sales exceed revenue from ticket sales (Graves, 2004; National Association of Theatre Owners, 2005).

Drive-in theaters have not fared well at all, decreasing to about 402 locations from a peak of 5,000 in 1958. The rising value of land and cost of property taxes have squeezed profits and prompted owners to sell out in search of more profitable ventures. Many of those that are successful are using special events such as pony rides, miniature golf, and "tailgating" to attract more customers (National Association of Theatre Owners, 2005; Glusac, 2002).

Movie Theater Operations

Overall, the average theater gets to keep only about half of the box office revenue, because the other half goes to the movie distributor. For top hit movies, the distributor can get 70 to 90% of the first week's ticket sales (Wikipedia, 2005). It is, therefore, very important for a theater to have good concession sales. Typically, a theater earns an 85% margin on its concessions. Revenues can be increased through "value pricing" in which customers are encouraged to buy attractively priced larger sizes of drinks and popcorn. Most theaters are now also offering coffees, fruit juices, frozen yogurt, and ice cream, and some even offer beer, pizza, pastries, cocktails, and full dinners.

Theaters try to stimulate attendance by having discount nights, consignment tickets, Saturday children's matinees, family nights, midnight movies, and special promotional events. Drive-ins may use their asphalt areas during the daytime for giant open-air bazaars and "swap meets." Control of expense is very important, and the multiscreen theaters have a tremendous advantage due to economies of scale in their operations.

Even though revenues from the sale and rental of video movies have surpassed movie box office receipts, the motion picture theater business should continue to be a viable part of the entertainment industry. People enjoy the shared environment of seeing a first-run movie in a high-quality presentation environment.

Opportunities in Movie Theaters

There are few full-time positions in a movie theater. Most of the work can be performed by high school and college students in part-time jobs. Some theater chains prefer to hire college graduates for assistant manager positions. Much of this work involves supervision and training of the part-timers, but there are also financial responsibilities related to concession management and control of box office revenues. In addition, some assistant managers have responsibilities for arranging promotional events, screening films for future bookings, and working as a film projectionist. Assistant managers with experience may move up to fill managerial positions and positions in the regional offices of major chains.

Multiscreen movie theaters such as this 21-screen complex are the industry's major trend.
(Photo: J. Crossley)

Recreational and Fantasy Camps

There are about 12,000 recreation-oriented camps in the United States, but about 78% are operated by government and nonprofit agencies who try to break even on the operations. The others are private/commercially operated camps oriented to middle-income and upscale markets of youth and adults. Examples include ski, tennis, and golf camps at resorts; outdoor and nature camps; youth sports camps; and adult baseball camps that resemble major league spring training.

Recreational camps in the United States have revenues of about $11 billion. Most revenues from camps come from registration fees, which average about $2,500 for 4 weeks of a typical youth summer camp. However some upscale camps charge much more. Souvenirs and snack food and beverage sales can be important secondary revenue sources. Most expenses are for seasonal program staff and for facility upkeep. Promotion of camp programs is usually accomplished through direct mail, special interest magazines, and personal presentations to groups including camp "alumni" who are encouraged to bring along friends. Traditional summer camps are trying to diversify their offerings with new activities such as adventure sports.

Sports instruction camps are one of the fastest recreational growth trends. Many are operated as day camps with fees that exceed $100 a day. Camps that are cosponsored by professional teams or high-profile coaches and athletes seem to draw the best attendance. Adult "sports fantasy" camps also have become popular. For example, former baseball star Cal Ripkin offers a baseball camp, based at a Ritz-Carlton in Palm Beach Florida. Seventy-two adults pay $8,150 each for the three-day camp (American Camp Association, 2005; National Camp Association, 2005; Comarow, 2001).

There are many seasonal positions available in camps, but full-time positions are relatively scarce, because the typical camp employs just a few people year-round. Career-oriented individuals must have a broad range of experience, including maintenance and marketing, to justify their retention year round.

Crafts and Hobbies

The craft and hobby industry seems fairly resistant to economic downturns. This is because people enjoy crafts and hobbies (1) for personalized gifts, (2) for personal use, (3) for home and holiday decorating, and (4) as a revenue-producing hobby. These factors make it a fairly stable industry.

There are three primary ways to sell crafts. The most obvious is through a full-line crafts store or a specialty shop featuring products such as ceramics or leather works. Another outlet is Web sales and catalog sales, which are good ways to reach people with disabilities, shut-ins, and rural residents. Finally, there is a large wholesale market for sales to schools, camps, recreation agencies, and senior centers. Some craft stores utilize all three approaches. High quality and personalized service are extremely important because "word of mouth" is the primary way to reach new customers. Many shops offer special events and instructional classes to help stimulate customer loyalty.

Most craft stores are independently operated. It could therefore be an area for entrepreneurial pursuit, but the prospective operator should have a high level of crafts interest and experience before making such a commitment. Overall, it is a $30 billion industry with general crafts and needlecrafts as the largest segments (Hobby Industry Association, 2005).

Public Assembly Facilities

This category includes stadiums, auditoriums, arenas, convention centers, and performing arts centers. Forty-four U.S. cities are home to the 120 major league sports teams in football, baseball, basketball, and hockey. Minor-market sports (soccer, arena football, etc.) and minor league teams exist in hundreds of other cities, including 245 just in minor league baseball. Add in college teams, and it is now essential that almost every medium-size city (and virtually all major cities) have at least one arena, civic center, stadium, or auditorium. They are available not only for mainstream sports events, but also concerts, trade shows, motivational speakers, religious group gatherings, rodeos, wrestling, monster truck rallies, and so on. Some of the facilities are privately owned and operated, but many are public facilities that are operated in a commercial manner or contracted out to private corporations to manage.

Most revenue comes from the rental of facilities to sports teams and concert promoters, followed by food and beverage concession revenue. However, facilities are becoming very aggressive in generating advertising revenue. For example, one third of the revenues in minor league baseball comes from advertising on the scoreboard and on billboards around the stadium. Another third comes from ticket sales, and the final third from concession sales (Rowan, 2000). There are also major differences in concession revenue for different events. For example, people who attend convention and trade shows spend about $15 on food and beverages compared to just $2.35 spent by people who attend consumer shows, such as a boat show, Recreational Vehicle (RV) and camper show, and so forth. (Pricewaterhouse Coopers, 2004). At the major league level, advertising revenues can be astounding. For example, Federal Express paid $200 million for the rights to have the Washington Redskins' stadium named FedExField for 27 years.

Expenses are primarily for payroll. To meet these expenses, the key is to be highly scheduled. The Los Angeles Forum, for example, is in use two thirds of the time, which is a fairly full schedule. For convention and trade show facilities, 70% occupancy is considered as the practical maximum because time is needed between events for set-ups and move-outs (Pricewaterhouse Coopers, 2004).

Managers of many facilities have learned that special themes and events can greatly increase attendance. These include all types of spectator contests, fan-mascot interaction, autograph days, concerts, and fireworks displays. Minor league sports teams seem to be most progressive in using recreation programming in this way.

An important trend in stadiums and arenas is to build suites and areas for "premium seating." This can bring significant revenues to the venue. For example, at Purdue University's Ross-Ade Stadium, the installation cost for 34 suites and 567 "club seats" was $18 million, but the upgraded facilities bring in $4.3 million in new revenue a year. This means it will break even in less than five years and be a valuable revenue source for many years after that (Steinbach, 2005).

Commercial recreation and sports management majors have been successful in gaining many types of positions: event coordinators, concession supervisors, ticket office manager, sales and marketing staff, and even the marketing manager and general manager for facilities and sports teams. Entry-level salaries are moderate, but after an individual gains experience, there is potential for much better salaries in larger cities with larger facilities.

Fairs, Festivals, and Special Events

Fairs, festivals, and special events are a fixture of community life in almost every city, county, and state. About 40% of the U.S. population travels to some type of fair or festival each year (Travel Industry Association of America, 2005), and most Americans attend some type of event locally. There are about 3,250 major fairs and 10,000 major arts and crafts festivals held annually in the United States (Miller, 2005). There are even more music festivals, ethnic culture festivals, and other themed events every year.

Most fairs and festivals are operated as nonprofit but self-sustaining ventures through nonprofit community corporations, local parks and recreation departments, or organizations such as a convention and visitor bureau. There are also numerous commercially operated fairs, festivals, and special events and occasional regional fairs and world expos. Some events are big business, and there are over a dozen fairs that draw at least a million people. Overall, 33% of fair and festival participants attend arts and music festivals, followed by ethnic/folk/heritage festivals, county and state fairs, parades, food festivals, religious festivals, and a variety of other types of events (Travel Industry Association of America, 1999). It is important to note that these figures do not include major sports events, which draw millions of participants and spectators.

Overall, most participants in fairs, festivals, and special events are local residents, but some are planned primarily as tourism events. Such events have significant economic impact on a community and provide numerous seasonal jobs. An example is the New York City Marathon, which draws about 35,000 participants, of which at least 20,000 are from outside the region. In addition, there are about 2 million spectators, including many tourists. The direct spending of these participants totals several hundred million dollars.

Fairs, festivals, and special events revenue comes from gate receipts, parking revenue, sale of exhibition space, advertising rights and sponsorships, and a percentage of the revenue from contracted operators of rides, midway amusements, food and beverage stands, craft booths, and souvenir stands. For fairs, festivals, and major special events that have permanent capital facilities, another key to success is to earn significant revenue during the long off-season. This is accomplished through the profitable use of facilities for concerts, dances, wedding receptions, flea markets, private parties, trade shows, rodeos, and livestock exhibitions.

Large fairs, festivals, and events are managed by a combination of paid staff and volunteers. The full-time staff work in a variety of responsibilities: managing facilities; booking entertainment; developing promotional events; contracting with concessionaires, managing personnel; handling public relations, marketing; or group sales; and so on. Many of these positions can be filled by persons with commercial recreation training and experience.

Leisure Publications

Libraries and bookstores typically have a significant part of their inventory devoted to publications that are designed to inform the individual about leisure activities or tourism destinations. Further, most convenience stores, groceries, home repair stores, sports retailers, travel agencies, hobby stores, and other retailers also carry an inventory of publications related to leisure pursuits. Subscriptions to travel, hobby, and other leisure publications can be found in almost every home. Overall, leisure publication is a huge industry that has two main categories: books and periodicals

Leisure-related books are typically authored by people who have expertise in some form of leisure and wish to share it. Either a descriptive experience, instructional guidelines, or a combination of both can cause a reader to desire a similar experience. For example, John Muir wrote about experiences hiking through some of Northern California's pristine wilderness and inspired many wilderness hikers to similarly venture and explore. Ansel Adams photographed beautiful scenes in Yosemite National Park and other natural treasures and inspired millions of visits to the parks. Guidebooks are prepared by organizations such as the Automobile Association of America, state tourism offices, manufacturers, and many other types of organizations as well as individual authors.

Leisure-related periodicals include hundreds of monthly magazines with national and international distribution. A good example is Rodale Press, which publishes *Organic Gardening, Bicycling, Runner's World, Backpacker, Mountain Bike, Men's Health, Women's Health*, and others. The mission of Rodale Press "is to show people how they can use the power of their bodies and minds to make their lives better." In addition to these major publications, there are literally thousands of monthly and quarterly periodicals produced for specific local markets and/or special interest groups. Examples include the *Wasatch Sports Guide*, which covers outdoor recreational activities in the Salt Lake City, Utah, area, and the *Osceola*, which covers Florida State University sports for alumni and fans.

Career opportunities writing books, guidebooks, and articles for major national publications are very limited. Although some publishers will accept unsolicited manuscripts, most have a cadre of dependable writers already on staff or contract. Much better opportunities exist with the small local publications, which need versatile staff to write articles, solicit advertising, and find locations to place the publication for sale. Salaries are not high, but it is a good way to get started in the leisure publication business.

Recreational Equipment Manufacturers and Wholesalers

Recreational equipment manufacturers may sell directly to the customer, distribute to retailers and/or customers through a wholesaler, or sell through a retailer. The manufacturer may use any one or a combination of those strategies to maximize profits. Although some recreational equipment is purchased by tourists, most purchases are made by customers at retailers in their local communities or by mail-order or Internet purchase from their homes.

Manufacturers' representatives travel the country conducting sales training programs and equipment repair clinics for retailers. Manufacturers' reps also conduct numerous promotional events, such as equipment demonstrations, contests, and other special events that tie into their product line or market segment. These are positions that commercial recreation majors have excelled at, provided they have expertise in the product field. For example, a ski manufacturer representative may conduct free "demo days" at a ski resort, conduct an amateur race program, or sponsor a public relations appearance by an Olympic ski medalist, who races on that brand of skis, of course.

Along the distribution channels that provide equipment to the customer are wholesalers who exist to provide equipment at a reduced cost to retailers or directly to the customer. A wholesaler purchases equipment in volume, or represents the manufacturer to retailers, selling a quantity of equipment after a reasonable markup. This arrangement allows manufacturers to improve distribution of their products, and it allows retailers to gain quicker access to a wide variety of products though a few key wholesalers, who each may carry products from dozens of manufacturers. In this way, wholesalers convert the manufacturer's inventory into sales at a faster rate than the manufacturer could do it on its own. Both manufacturer and wholesaler share in the profits and the equipment gets wider distribution.

Recreational equipment wholesalers also market extensively to the "institutional market" of schools, camps, and community park and recreation departments in order to get large volume purchases. Wholesalers often have exhibit booths on the trade show floor of professional association conferences in an effort to meet as much of the institutional market as possible in a short time. Some commercial recreation majors have been very successful as representatives of equipment wholesalers.

Creative Entrepreneurial Recreation Examples

There are numerous opportunities in every community for enterprising people to start successful businesses that fill specialized niches in recreation. Some creative examples are illustrated below.

Hawaii Aloha Travel. At a time when many travel agencies are closing, Hawaiian residents Bruce and Yaling Fisher found a way to start a successful new agency. They knew that they could not compete with U.S. mainland travel agencies who sell outbound trips to Hawaii. Traditionally most travel agencies concentrate almost entirely on selling outbound trips. However, Bruce and Yaling decided to reverse this strategy and concentrate on selling inbound trips from the U.S. mainland to Hawaii, and they would do that by using the Internet. Yaling used the Internet to research all the competitors' fares and rates. Then she contacted the vendors (hotels, airlines, rental car companies, etc.) directly to secure their best rates. She conducts comparison cost analysis on a daily basis and develops travel packages that beat the major online booking services 90% of the time. Bruce studied Web search engines and how they rank Web sites. He discovered how to code Hawaii Aloha's Web site so it would appear in the top five of a search engine's listings for several keywords. Although clients' first contact with Hawaii Aloha is by Internet, Bruce or Yaling close each sale voice to voice by telephone. This allows more personalized service that many people still enjoy and it allows a travel package to be fine-tuned better. The concept has worked quite well, as Hawaii Aloha has about $2 million in sales each year (Covey, 2004).

Bob Watson's Bubble Maker Parties. Scuba diving instructor Bob Watson provides an introductory scuba experience in a birthday party format to children ages 8 to 12. The parties are carried out at a home swimming pool, and Bob provides all the equipment. Children wear inflatable vests that do not allow them to sink, but they get to use real equipment and they thoroughly enjoy splashing around and blowing bubbles (breathing through the scuba regulators). No more than four children are allowed in the pool at one time, and the cost is $99 for up to six children, with $15 for each additional participant. Bob suggests that families keep the guest list limited to the child's closest friends. The parties are booked though a local scuba diving shop, so Bob has virtually no overhead expenses other than a few sets of equipment (Keller, 2004).

Hydro Hounds. Deb Roberts, owner of Hydro Hounds in Laramie, Wyoming, says every dog has a water personality just waiting to be unleashed. She provides canine exercise and hydrotherapy to as many as 22 dogs each week. Some of the dogs come to her heated pool for specific reasons such as the need to rehabilitate an injury, recover from a surgery, or to build strength in a sensitive area before a planned surgery. Others are couch canines whose owners' want their pet to enjoy a fitness activity. One Rottweiler show dog comes for exercise to stay in top form and loves it so much he drags staff across the room to get to the pool. Roberts has developed her business with absolutely no paid advertising, just word of mouth from satisfied dog owners who want the best lives for their pets (Clotfelter, 2004).

LOCAL GOVERNMENT IN COMMERCIAL RECREATION

City, county, and special district park and recreation departments have become very active in providing high-quality facilities that traditionally have been offered by commercial enterprise. Examples include fitness centers, marinas, water theme parks, and indoor ice rinks. Other facilities, such as golf courses, campgrounds, and tennis centers have a long history of public agency management, but now many have been upgraded to levels where they compete directly with private enterprise. Why has this happened?

There are two primary reasons for the growth of "commercialized" public recreation. The first reason is that lack of a tax-based government budget has forced many public agencies to become more entrepreneurial. Facilities that are totally self-supporting through fees revenue take a lot of pressure off the budget. Further, if a facility can generate a true profit, those revenues can help offset the expense of other facilities and programs.

The second reason for the growth of commercialized public recreation relates to the escalating demands and expectations of the public. Many participants are no longer content with traditional basic public facilities such as a rectangular lap-swim pool or a poorly ventilated gym room with a multi-station weight machine. Instead, they want a wave pool with multiple slides, fountains, and a full-service snack bar. They want a bright, air-conditioned fitness center with state-of-the-art cardiovascular equipment and full range of variable resistance equipment, plus aerobics room, sauna and coed whirlpool bath.

In many communities, government has stepped up to provide the commercial-quality facilities. They may be funded through revenue bonds or general obligation bonds, but in almost every case, the facilities are expected to generate at least enough revenue to cover the operating expense, if not the capital development costs. Contracting the facility out for operation by private enterprise is another option.

Another area of commercialized public recreation is the provision of programs that generate revenue. This is very common with adult sports programs and instructional classes in the arts. However, in recent years, some agencies have tried to make all programs generate revenue. Further, public agencies have found that major special events can draw financial support from corporate sponsors, draw tourists to the area, and increase local sales tax and hotel tax revenue.

Some city park and recreation departments have started commercial-quality membership fitness centers. (Photo: J. Crossley)

Problems with Commercialized Public Recreation

Two potential problems can exist with commercialized public recreation. First, a true private enterprise can focus on whatever market segment it chooses, but a tax-supported public agency has to serve the interests of its entire base of residents. This includes low-income residents who may not be able to pay the higher fees of the improved public facilities. There are, of course, strategies for a public agency to use in these situations, including differential fee schedules, "scholarships," and so on. However, in large urban cities, with huge numbers of unemployed and low-income residents, the commercialized approach to public recreation may not be in the best interests of the people.

A second problem relates to the possibility that commercialized public recreation facilities may be "unfair competition" to local private enterprise. The public agency enjoys several advantages, including the ability to raise capital development funds at lower interest rates and freedom from paying property tax, sales tax, and income tax. It also has promotional advantages, and the probability of good relations with other governmental agencies involved with permits, police protection, and so forth. These advantages should enable the public agency to have a lower expense structure (unless wages and benefits are inflated due to union contracts) and thereby offer the facilities and programs at lower prices. Therefore, it is not surprising that some businesses have filed lawsuits charging the local parks and recreation agency with unfair competition.

Opportunities with Commercialized Public Recreation

Students in commercial recreation and tourism programs have proven to be very valuable employees in public parks and recreation programs. A student's extra coursework in marketing, accounting, economics, and business management fits perfectly with the demands of a commercialized approach to public recreation. Another opportunity area is with private enterprise that contracts for the management of public recreational facilities.

SUMMARY

Local commercial recreation businesses provide leisure products and services to people, primarily in their home communities. There are three major classifications of local commercial recreation, and each includes numerous distinct industries. Recreation activity providers include health clubs, racquet clubs, golf courses, bowling centers, and dance studios. Recreational product retailers include sporting goods stores, arts and crafts shops, toy and game stores, and sports specialty shops. Entertainment providers include theme parks, amusement parks, movie theaters, and fairs and festivals.

Many of the individual businesses within these industries function as national chains and/or franchises, but there are also opportunities for independent operators. Although the independents may be smaller, they can be successful by filling specialized niches within a given community.

Career opportunities exist in great numbers, but a recreation degree is not an automatic ticket to success. Students must have specific practical skills for entry level work in each industry. Some of the skills may be learned in an academic setting, but many are experience-based. Advancement to managerial levels is usually based on experience, even though the work tends to draw more heavily on the conceptual skills and knowledge gained in the academic program.

SPOTLIGHT ON:

TODD JOHNSON, DIRECTOR OF EVENT SERVICES

by Mary S. Wisnom, PhD

The city of Grand Rapids, Michigan, has seen tremendous growth over the last 20 years. In developing the downtown area it was decided that the city could benefit greatly from a large convention center. In February, 2005, after many years of planning and construction, DeVos Place opened its doors under the contracted management of SMG Corporation. SMG is a building management company owned by Hyatt Corporation that currently operates 74 arenas, 51 convention centers, seven stadiums, 34 performing arts centers, and 10 other recreational facilities around the world. Some of the most well known facilities that SMG manages are the Superdome in New Orleans, Soldier Field in Chicago, and Alltel Stadium in Jacksonville, Florida. DeVos Place is a state-of-the-art convention center located in the heart of downtown Grand Rapids. The multilevel DeVos Place provides 1 million square feet of space on a 13-acre riverfront site. It is equipped for meetings, conventions, and trade shows as well as performing arts and touring events, and it has the capability of hosting a variety of events simultaneously.

SMG also manages Van Andel Arena in Grand Rapids. Van Andel Arena is a 12,000-seat capacity sports and entertainment facility that hosts an average of 170 events a year. These include sporting events such as AHL and college hockey, basketball (from high school to NBA), arena football, motorcycle races, soccer, and wrestling. The arena also hosts a variety of special and family events, including concerts, ice-skating shows, and large theater productions.

The two facilities complement one another, each able to host a unique variety of events and programs. A noted difference in the operations is that Van Andel arena's primary purpose is to entertain those in West Michigan, whereas DeVos

(continued)

Place works to attract its clientele from all over the country. DeVos Place's sales staff works with other tourism agencies such as the local convention and visitor bureau, convention and arena authority, city, and local hotels to help generate business for the convention center.

In the two Grand Rapids operations, SMG employs 59 full-time and about 200 part-time personnel. To assist in the operation of DeVos Place, SMG employs a general manager, assistant general manager, five directors (event services, facilities, sales, marketing, and finance). Todd Johnson is the director of event services for SMG at DeVos Place. Prior to its opening, Todd was an operations supervisor, event coordinator, and ultimately the operations manager at Van Andel Arena. As director of event services, Todd's primary responsibility is to oversee the events and operations of DeVos Place, but he also assists with programs at Van Andel Arena. There are six event and operations managers who work with Todd to accomplish this task. With a bachelor's degree in recreation, parks, and leisure services administration (commercial recreation and facility management concentration) and having just completed an internship with Mile High Stadium, Todd decided that arena/convention management was the career he truly wanted. Upon returning to Michigan and learning of the plans to build an arena in Grand Rapids, Todd actively sought a position with SMG. When asked how he acquired the job, Todd replied, "My education was great, but my internship was the key." He stated, "The field is growing so quickly that individuals with experience in arena management are few and far between. When it came down to it, my internship experience got SMG to notice me and persistence got me the job." Todd's best advice for those seeking a career in arena/convention management is to "get experience in the profession."

Todd's attraction to arena/convention management came from the feeling that every day brings something different. Todd warns those interested in his career that arena/convention management is not all variety and adventure; it is hard work and long days. In order to be a successful director of event services, you need to be organized, be patient, be able to act appropriately under pressure, and have strong people skills. Todd also indicated that in this type of career, the good things definitely outweigh the bad.

For Todd Johnson, it is clear that arena/convention management is an exciting and challenging commercial recreation career. This type of career takes dedication, persistence, a desire for variety at the workplace, and a passion to please the customer. The growth of arena/convention management is inevitable. The opportunities for people with skills and experience are almost limitless.

REFERENCES

American Camp Association. (2005). ACA fact sheet. http://www.acacamps.org/media_center/about_aca/facts.php.

Aquatics International. (2005, September). 2005 waterpark survey. *Aquatics International*, pp. 34–37.

Buck, J. (1999, December). The evolution of health clubs. *Club Industry*, pp. 16–18.

Canfield, C. (2004, November 29). Fast-growing Curves shapes up as the McDonalds of fitness centers. *Fresno Bee*, p. B5–6.

Carini, M. (2000, April 27). Leisure products. *Standard & Poor's Industry Surveys*, 1–27.

Clotfelter, S. (2004, December 12). Swim gym. *Fresno Bee*, p. E4.

Cocchi, R. (1999, December). Growing in the next century. *Club Industry*, pp. 35–37.

Comarow, A. (2001, March 26). Fantasy camps offer a sweet swing at the real thing. *U.S. News & World Report*, p. 56–58.

Cornish, G. & Whitter, R. (1982). *The golf course*. New York: Rutledge Press.

Covey, M. (2004, March 22). A business plan that just clicked. *Travel Weekly*, p. 52.

Coy, J. & Haralson, B. (2005). What is a waterpark—really? http://www.jeffcoy.com/documents/articles/What%20Is%20a%20Waterpark---Really.pdf.

Glusac, E. (2002, November). Cultural icon: drive-ins USA. *Hemisphere*, p. 38.

Graves, T. (2004, September 9). Movies & home entertainment. *Standard & Poor's Industry Surveys*, p.1–25.

Hansard, D. (1983, October 16). Bagging wild game. *Dallas Morning News*.

Hobby Industry Association. (2005). 2002 nationwide craft & hobby consumer usage and purchases study. http://www.hobby.org/research.

Ice Skating Institute. (2005). ISI industry survey. http://www.skateisi.com/HTML/pubs/survey.cfm.

International Association of Amusement Parks and Attractions. (2005). U.S. amusement/theme parks & attractions industry—attendance & revenues. http://www.iaapa.org.

International Council of Shopping Centers. (2005). http://www.icsc.org. November 28, 2005.

International Health, Racquet & Sportsclub Association. (2005). http://cms.ihrsa.org. November 24, 2005.

Keller, G. (2004, April 20). Parties come true. *Fresno Bee*, p. E1–2.

Krishnan, A. (2005, May 10). Students analyze theme park trends. *Daily Bruin Online*. http://www.dailybruin.ucla.edu/news/articles.asp?ID = 33244.

Mayhew, D. (2001, August 19). Bowling for dollars. *Fresno Bee*, p. E1–2.

Mall of America. (2005). Mall of America fact. http://mallofamerica.com/about_moa_facts.aspx.

Miller, R. (2005). *The 2005 travel and leisure market research handbook*. Loganville, GA: Richard K. Miller & Associates, Inc.

National Association of Theatre Owners. (2005). Statistics. http://www.natoonline.org/statistics.htm.

National Camp Association. (2005). Camp facts. http://www.summercamp.org/media/article7.html.

National Golf Foundation. (2004a). Golf 20/20: Vision for the future. http://www.ngf.org

National Golf Foundation. (2004b). Rounds played in the United States: 2004 edition. http://www.ngf.org.

Pricewaterhouse Coopers. (2004). *2004 convention center report*. Tampa: Pricewatewaterhouse Coopers.

Roller Skating Association International. (2005). Industry stats. http://www.rollerskating.com.

Roper Starch. (2004, January). Outdoor recreation in America 2003. Washington, DC: The Recreation Roundtable. http://www.funoutdoors.com/files/ROPER%20REPORT%202004.pdf.

Rowan, R. (2000, September 4). Play ball! *Fortune*, pp. 310–326.

Ruben, P. (1987, May 4). The scream machines. *USA Today*, p. 5E.

Sega GameWorks. (2005). http://www.gameworks.com. November 28, 2005.

Steinbach, P. (2005, September). Honeymoon suites. *Athletic Business*, pp. 50–59.

Travel Industry Association of America. (1999, August 23). Types of festivals that draw travelers. *Travel Weekly*, p. 51.

Travel Industry Association of America. (2005). Travel statistics & trends. http://www.tia.org. March 28, 2005.

United States Bowling Congress. (2005). Bowling facts and figures. http://www.bowl.com. November 24, 2005.

U.S. Census Bureau. (2004). 2002 economic census. Washington, DC: U.S. Census Bureau. http://www.census.gov/econ/census02/.

Vanderwolf, J. (2005). *2005 sporting and athletic goods outlook*. Washington, DC: U.S. Department of Commerce, Office of Consumer Goods.

Wagle, Y. (2004, April 8). Retailing: Specialty. *Standard & Poor's Industry Surveys*, pp. 1–24.

West Edmonton Mall. (2005). http://www.westedmall.com/home/default.asp.

Wikipedia. (2005). Movie theater. http://en.wikipedia.org/wiki/Movie_theater. December 3, 2005.

Chapter ●●●● 12

The Career of the Future

Dramatic changes in demographics, the economy, the workplace, social structure, and lifestyles are occurring. It is imperative to recognize these changes and forecast coming events with some degree of accuracy in order to plan for a preferred future. One's view of the future is affected not only by past events, but also by attitude, intellectual orientation, and experience.

This chapter will review trends affecting the commercial recreation and tourism industry. This will help set the stage for a review of career strategies and opportunities. The chapter will conclude with a section that considers curriculum implications for commercial recreation and tourism academic programs.

A LOOK AHEAD FOR COMMERCIAL RECREATION AND TOURISM

Predictions about the future of commercial recreation and tourism are not a matter of agreement among industry authorities. Nevertheless, a review of the predictions and projections of Bandell, 2005; Bradsher, 2003; Campbell, 2004; Coy & Haralson, 2005; Fesenmaier, 2004; Foot, 2004; Glaeser, 2002; Godwin, 2004; Haard, 2005; Kelly, 2004; Mason, 2002; McArthur, 2004; Milligan, 2004; Pegg, 2005; Perdue, 2004; Romero, Hong, & Westrup, 2005; Schuster, 2002; Travel Weekly, 2005; World Future Society, 2005; and others does reveal some general consensus. Therefore, a variety of trend projections are presented here that should be of interest to both students and managers of commercial recreation and tourism enterprise.

Demographic Projections

- By 2020, people in the United States over the age of 50 will increase to 39% of the population. These people, in the peak of their earning years, will spend significantly for recreation and travel, including expensive travel packages, vacation homes, recreation vehicles (RVs) and other "big-ticket" items.
- By 2050, the number of people over 85 will increase five-fold. The seniors of the future will live longer, be healthier, and lead more active lives than today's seniors.
- Baby boomers are just now reaching retirement age, and this market segment will be a better market for recreation and travel than the current seniors market. This is because the baby boomers are more highly educated, wealthier, healthier, and more diverse in their leisure interests than the current seniors are.
- Generation Xers born between 1966 and 1980, embrace new technology more than the baby boomers and are more likely to use the Internet for travel purchases. They are cautious about longer distance travel due to safety concerns and shop for last-minute bargains.

Skateboarding and snowboarding shops serve two of the fastest-growing sports today.
(Photo: J. Crossley)

- Members of "Generation Y," born between 1980 and 1996, are going to be a tremendous market for travel because they are the first generation of kids to travel extensively with successful boomer parents. They will want flexibility and options and are wary of modern marketing tactics. They are more exposed to and accepting of cultural diversity, are computer and technology savvy, and are not as brand-loyal as their parents. They have lower attention spans, a low threshold of boredom, and favor less traditional sports such as "extreme sports."
- Asian-Americans and Hispanic-Americans will continue to increase in percentage of the U.S. population. Caucasians will represent only 53% of the population by 2050, down from 80% in 1980. The Hispanic market (actually two dozen different submarkets) is more likely than other markets to participate as a family group at amusement parks, on cruises, and on other trips.
- As populations increase there will be increased pressures on wilderness, the oceans, and other natural resources.

Economic-Oriented Projections

- Demands for development and consumption will have to be balanced with limits upon development of the earth and use of its resources.
- The needs of the community and society in general will have to be balanced by the willingness of people to pay for government services. Any decline in government responsibilities will, by default, open the door for commercial opportunity.
- Reliance on user fees for cost recovery will continue to increase in government-operated recreational facilities and programs.
- Significant tax incentives, infrastructure developments, and other inducements will be extended by government to private enterprises in order to lure recreation and tourism companies to revitalize urban and rural economies.
- A backlog of deferred maintenance projects in governmental recreation facilities will lead to difficult decisions to close some and/or contract their operations out to private enterprise.
- Home-based businesses and microbusinesses will be part of an entrepreneurial explosion, particularly among members of Generations X and Y.
- Due to mergers, a few very large companies will dominate certain industries: airlines, travel agencies, hotels, movie theaters, theme parks, sporting goods stores, and health and fitness clubs. Entrepreneurial opportunities will come in small markets and with specialty niches.
- People are spending more of their income on recreation and tourism, and this is expected to continue.
- American companies will seek more foreign business opportunities in an attempt to diversify their markets. Hotels, fast-food restaurants, and theme parks have already begun this move.
- The global wage gap is closing. This allows growth of middle income groups in developing nations, and these people will become consumers of recreational and tourism products.
- There will be increased interdependence among national economies partly because large multinational corporations will dominate many aspects of international trade.
- Increases in the minimum wage will cause businesses to become less labor-intensive wherever practical. Advances in technology will make this possible.
- A bimodal income distribution is emerging in the U.S., meaning the middle income group is shrinking while both the upper and lower income groups are growing.
- Over-consumption of oil based energy by industrialized countries will continue to deplete the fossil fuel resources thus driving prices higher. Public pressures for conservation and alternative energy sources will increase.

Social Structure Projections

- Immigrant entrepreneurship will forge new directions in commercial recreation through ethnic festivals.
- More mothers will work outside the home (from 18% in 1960 to 60% in 2005). This will generate need for more after-school programs.
- Multiple small meals and snacking ("grazing") will increase, while standard "three square meal" dining will decrease. Restaurants will accommodate this with a mix of big, little, and medium size meals during all hours.
- As more people strive to live healthier lives, restaurants will add more "healthy food" choices.
- More than 100 million people worldwide will telecommute to work by the year 2015. This will distribute wealth, save energy, reduce pollution, and change real estate values.

- Leisure markets will become more segmented in terms of values, subcultures, and styles. In response, marketing efforts will not just respond to desires, but will try to create them.

Activity Projections

- Participation will increase in the arts, walking, hiking, family picnicking, swimming, visiting beaches, adventure sports, extreme sports, cruises, outdoor sports events and concerts, visiting nature centers and historic areas, canoeing, gardening, stretching, bicycling, kayaking, rafting, rock climbing, caving, snowboarding, golf, backpacking, and amusement park attendance.
- Decline of bowling, roller skating, jogging/running, tennis, aerobics, horseback riding, hunting, fishing, power boating, water skiing, ice skating, bird watching, dance, needlework, sculpting, woodworking, racquetball, and skiing.
- Leisure consumption and participation will increasingly occur in off-season and off-peak hours, as the American work force continues to shift to less traditional scheduling of work hours.
- Activities that can be accomplished in short, discrete blocks of time will be preferred.
- A "search for meaning" will cause people to seek more substance and depth in their recreation. Ecotourism, cultural tourism, the arts, and other enriching experiences should flourish.
- New technologies, such as virtual reality simulations, interactive computer programs, and commercially viable underwater re-breathers, will create opportunities for many new leisure businesses.
- More people will seek to protect their precious recreational time from climatic inconvenience by participating at all-weather facilities such as malls and air-supported domes. These facilities will increasingly be used for golf, swimming, soccer, amusement parks, ice skating, wave pools, wall climbing, fairs and festivals, kayak river running, and other activities.
- Health and fitness clubs will continue to have success because adults and senior citizens will value health and fitness.
- Major shopping malls will increasingly function as social centers. Niche stores will thrive, but many department stores will fail and be converted to multipurpose centers offering multimedia entertainment, sports, fitness, and other recreational activities to a market of preteens, teens, and young adults.
- At-home recreational activities, such as gardening, home improvement, reading, and video viewing, should continue to increase.
- More businesses will strive to integrate a dining and entertainment experience. This means more dinner theaters, leisure theme restaurants, and microbreweries.
- Fitness programs will have a greater emphasis on stress reduction.
- Day-care programs will offer more creative activities for children to learn and play, including computer games, environmental activities, and interaction with senior citizens and people of other cultures.
- Space tourism will be fully operational by 2021 with an estimated 15,000 passengers taking off from Cape Canaveral and other locations.

Tourism Projections

- Short vacations and weekend travel will continue to increase among two-career couples who have difficulty in scheduling long vacations together.
- Worldwide tourism growth is expected to average 3% a year. This is higher than the overall world economy is expected to grow. It should be a $10 trillion business by 2015.

Basic accommodations characterize ecotourism resorts, one of the important trends in the tourism industry. (Photo: J. Crossley)

- Pent-up demand to visit the former Soviet Union, Eastern Europe, and Cuba (especially after Castro) will stimulate tourism to these areas, and there will be a corresponding boom of tourism infrastructure development.
- East Asia and the Pacific region are the fastest-growing destinations and will continue to receive record numbers of visitors.
- The most popular destination for Americans will continue to be the United States, and the number-one domestic magnet will continue to be Central Florida and Walt Disney World.
- Health tourism, ecotourism, cultural tourism, adventure tourism, and other forms of "life-enrichment tourism" will continue to be industry buzzwords and major marketing themes of the tourism industry.
- Safety may become the greatest concern for people when they plan vacations and other recreation. Destinations such as Vietnam, that are not tolerant of political dissenters, will benefit from having a perception as "safe harbors" for tourism.
- New aircraft will feature increases in capacity rather than speed. Double-level seating will enable planes to carry 800 to 1,000 people per flight.
- The airline industry will lose a share of total passenger miles traveled because more businesspeople will opt to communicate electronically rather than fly to meetings.
- Resorts will become more like theme parks providing more facilities, activities, and experiences for guests.
- Resorts will focus more on participation, interaction, and learning experiences as people seek to have a more complete and experiential experience.
- The cruise industry will expand significantly in Southeast Asia as Singapore strives to be the Miami of the Far East. Worldwide, the cruise industry will strive to broaden its appeal to include more young adults and families.
- More special events will be used to build awareness of a destination as a tourist attraction, even after the event is over.

- New niche markets will be the focal point of many travel agencies, tour operators, and destinations. There are already over 100 companies designing trips exclusively for female travelers.
- A smarter, less predictable consumer will drive new marketing trends.
- There will be more interest in "green" hotels and "green guest rooms" that create environmental savings through recycling and conservational measures.
- Many travel agencies will fail as airlines take more bookings online. Travel agencies will evolve to be travel consultants who serve their established client base with individualized services that airlines won't provide.
- State and local governments will become more active in promoting their areas as tourism destinations and will be more involved in providing facilities, services, and programs for tourists.
- The Internet will continue to increase in importance, not only for travel information and reservation purposes, but also for consumers to communicate helpful information to each other. Internet shopping for travel will be a popular recreational activity, much the way "window shopping" in a mall is enjoyed.

Operational Projections
- Companies will strive to better understand the cyclic nature of the business enterprise, the role that substitution plays in the choice of leisure pursuits, and the role of government and the advantages of collaboration.
- The entrepreneur will capitalize on technological innovation, including opportunities for e-commerce, the use of numerous software packages to automate and/or streamline operations, the role of virtual reality in the provision of leisure experience, and the educational potential for in-home preparation for leisure pursuits.
- Business will strive to understand its customers better, to the point of individualizing service delivery in order to meet customer needs. Strategies will include: expanding the service beyond a typical/traditional market, provision of deeper leisure experiences that are less consumptive, and allowing customers more choices and a greater role in the decision-making processes related to program design.
- The successful entrepreneur will be more adept at planning sound fiscal strategies that affect a rapidly changing business climate. These include more emphasis on the long-term profitability and sustainability of business rather than just short-term profitability, implementation of technological tracking devices for income and expenses, and more use of yield management technology for pricing decisions.
- Multiple-unit housing will continue to increase, and there will be more recreation provided through condominium associations, apartment management firms, etc.
- More resorts will become part of mixed-use developments, combining convention and conference centers, retail areas, medical facilities, recreational facilities, and communities for second homes, vacation homes, and retirement.
- Seasonal resorts will become year-round operations and build more indoor climate-controlled facilities.
- More government services will be contracted out to private enterprise. This should include opportunities in golf courses, auditoriums and arenas, campgrounds, lodges, food and beverage service, marinas, and so forth.
- Market fragmentation or "demassification" will force business to develop strategies to serve numerous niche markets that are very different from each other. Commercial recreation and tourism managers must select a market to focus on or provide real choices and options for several market segments.
- Bifurcation (going to either end of a continuum) seems to be where most of the growth is occurring. Under this concept, growth will occur in "mega-resorts" and small specialty resorts rather than midsize resorts. Similarly, we will have more Wal-Marts and specialty shops than midsize department stores.

- All-inclusive pricing will be used more frequently for theme parks, tours, hotels, and resorts, as people want to know the total price when planning their recreation.
- With a declining number of young employees for service industry jobs, employers may increasingly turn to retirees and immigrants, or they may export jobs, such as reservation centers and data processing, to overseas locations.
- Voice-activated computers the size of hand calculators will enable employees to translate several foreign languages and communicate directly with international visitors.
- Recreation programming, particularly special events, will be used more frequently by resorts, restaurants, bars/social clubs, recreational equipment retailers, and other businesses to draw new customers and to keep repeat customers interested.
- People will want to bring various forms of technology (i-Pods, cell phones, media players, etc.) with them while participating in recreation.
- More emphasis will be placed on security from crime and terrorism and on disaster management planning.
- Many resorts will take advantage of hiring a new type of seasonal employee, the individual on early retirement from corporate life or military careers. They can afford to live comfortably in resort communities because of retirement income, they are more mature and experienced, and they tend to be excellent employees.

Conclusion

By understanding these future directions, prospective commercial recreation and tourism professionals may improve their search for entrepreneurial opportunities and career advancement. The next section will present an overview of these career opportunities and suggest strategies for career development.

CAREERS IN COMMERCIAL RECREATION AND TOURISM

There are abundant opportunities for job placement in commercial recreation and tourism settings, many of which draw upon a recreation professional's strong programming, leadership, and communication skills. Most settings additionally demand abundant business acumen, whether it is learned as a part of formal education or acquired through experience. In fact, business educators are giving closer attention to the leisure industry as a place where business opportunities prevail. A well-prepared commercial recreation and tourism major can be just as competitive as a business major for many positions and actually have an advantage in some positions.

There are many settings in which to find employment—so many, in fact, that a job search may appear to be confusing. It is this apparent fragmentation that not only causes difficulty when searching for a suitable site for employment, but also causes fragmentation in professional preparation programs. For example, Figure 12-1 is a list of potential settings that, based upon projections of the future, may be among the best opportunities in commercial recreation and tourism.

The grouping of industries (travel, hospitality, and local commercial recreation) helps to focus the career search, because there are some similarities within each major field. In the following sections, it must be realized that the categories overlap. For example, the skills needed for success in a resort may actually be a combination of the skills needed in travel, hospitality, and local programming. Similarly, opportunities suggested are composite summaries for the major industry categories. Specific aspects were covered in the industry profiles in Chapters 9 to 11.

With more emphasis on technology in our educational systems, there will be a need for other employees who are strong in the "hyper-human skills" that include caring, judgment, intuition, ethics, inspiration, friendliness, and imagination (World Future Society, 2005). These are skills typically held by many of the people who are drawn to leisure service jobs.

Figure 12-1
Jamieson's Top 20:
An Unranked List of Potential
Employment Opportunities

1. **Visitor and conference management**—includes convention and visitor bureaus, meeting and conference planning.
2. **Cruise ship programming and management**—includes youth programs, fitness, shore tour excursions, social director, cruise director, marketing representative.
3. **Recreation consulting**—for companies, agencies, tourism planners.
4. **Youth programs**—commercial child care and recreation programs, programs for "at risk" youth.
5. **Ecotourism and agrotourism**—tour operators, wholesalers, destination development.
6. **Leisure entertainment**—includes entertainment malls, arcades, movies, and video.
7. **Outdoor and sports retailing**—includes many types of specialty shops and rental services.
8. **Special event management**—community events, road races, sports events, and tournaments.
9. **Leisure-oriented fund-raising**—for environmental causes, art organizations, schools.
10. **Corporate recreation services**—contracted to companies on individual program basis or contracted as total on—site operation.
11. **Campgrounds**—programming and management at membership campgrounds and other campgrounds.
12. **Adventure outfitters**—guides, marketing and management for river running, jeep tours, bicycle tours, jungle treks, scuba diving.
13. **Resorts, hotels, and residential communities**—recreation programming, guest services, marketing, and management.
14. **Tour management**—tour guides, operations directors, sales and management for tour operators, wholesalers, and destination receptive operators.
15. **Theme amusements and virtual reality centers**—includes theme parks, water parks, centers for virtual reality recreation.
16. **Cultural arts**—includes marketing and management of performing arts events, arts centers, galleries, museums.
17. **Tourism policy management**—includes local and state tourism bureaus, tourism promotion organizations.
18. **Wineries and leisure theme restaurants**—programming, promotion, and management.
19. **Party organizers**—contracted party services and suppliers for family events, reunions, company parties.
20. **Fair and festival management**—operations, marketing and management of local and regional fairs, centennials, and events.

Careers in the Travel Industry

The common thread in the travel industry is the transportation of people. Beyond that, the methods, amenities, and services differ according to the type of travel business. The primary employment areas are airlines, travel agencies, cruise ships, tour operations, convention and visitor bureaus, and travel promotion organizations.

As with all careers in the commercial recreation and hospitality industries, positions in the travel industry require a variety of personal qualities and skills: interpersonal communications, marketing, accounting, personnel management, public speaking, initiative and motivation, knowledge of leisure behavior, organizational aptitude, attention to detail, and so on. These and other personal skills are discussed further in the career development section of this chapter. Some of the particular skills needed for most travel industry careers include knowledge and ability in

- geography of the United States and the world, history, and social customs;
- computer reservation and ticketing systems;
- transportation carriers and systems;
- United States and international regulations regarding travel;
- foreign language; and
- global awareness.

Positions in the travel industry tend to be perceived as glamorous. Many employees get the opportunity to travel to world-famous resorts as part of the job and/or get great savings on personal travel. Long hours, low pay, repetitive work, and inconsiderate customers, however, often temper the glamour. Salaries are better after significant experience has qualified a person to advance into management positions. Experience is essential, because a degree alone seldom qualifies a person for a management position. For persons interested in starting their own travel agency, tour company, or other travel service, there is typically more chance of success in appealing to a specialized market.

Hospitality Industry Careers

The common thread in the hospitality industry is the provision of overnight accommodations, food, beverage, and related amenities. Within this industry, career paths are interesting and diverse in hotels, motels, resorts, restaurants, campgrounds, nightclubs, time-share condominiums, recreational communities, and meeting/convention services. Particular skills and knowledge needed for success in the hospitality industry include the following:

- Marketing and sales skills.
- Food and beverage preparation, service, and management.
- Housekeeping management.
- Facility maintenance and safety.
- Front desk and reservation systems.
- Foreign languages—particularly with hotels having an international market.
- Meeting and conference planning.

Students interested in hospitality careers will probably be employed in a variety of positions before reaching their position of choice. Entry positions generally require less than a college education, and some people have advanced to top management without a formal education. People who move up from entry level or who enter from specialized training/educational programs may fill mid-management positions. Top-level management positions tend to favor college-educated individuals who have gained varied experience while moving up through the ranks. Management-level salaries can be quite good in the hospitality industry, and there are many benefits, particularly with large chains. For example, management-level employees may be able to vacation at greatly reduced rates at the resort properties of other hotels in the chain.

Careers in Local Commercial Recreation

Local commercial recreation businesses provide activity programs, retail products, and entertainment to people primarily in their home communities. Since each of these types of businesses differ greatly from the others, each type will be reviewed separately.

Activity/Program Providers include health and fitness clubs, racquet clubs, multipurpose sports clubs, golf courses, skating rinks, bowling lanes, dance studios, and party services. In each case, the business provides facilities and staff for its customers to engage in a particular type of recreational activity, often as a designed program. Some of the particular areas of expertise needed in this career area include the following:

- A high level of knowledge and proficiency in the program areas.
- Background knowledge for a particular skill area—this may include advanced skills and teaching ability, exercise physiology, coaching theory, etc. in golf, tennis, fitness, aquatics, or other activity.
- Maintenance and management skills for specialized facilities: pools, golf courses, ice rinks, tennis centers, and so on.
- Membership sales technique.
- Recreation programming ability for a variety of program formats: classes, clinics, leagues, tournaments, trips and tours, demonstrations, clubs, special events, and so forth.

Entry-level positions typically require the employee to work directly in the program area, teaching classes, supervising leagues, directing tournaments, and maintaining the facility. There may also be some retail sales work required, as well as membership sales work. Managers are usually involved more in personnel management and training, facility scheduling and program development, marketing, and financial management.

Local Recreation Retailers include stores and specialty shops that sell sporting goods, boats, arts and crafts supplies, toys and games, and so on primarily to local customers. Some of the particular skills necessary in this area are as follows:

- In-depth knowledge of the product line.
- Direct sales and customer service ability.
- Inventory management, including purchasing, stock control, and merchandise display.
- Product service and repair.
- Sales force management and motivation.
- General programming skill for product-oriented promotions and special events.

There are numerous entry-level positions in recreation retailing that do not need to be filled by degreed staff. These positions typically receive a low hourly wage, but they may also receive sales commissions and bonuses. Managers usually have sales experience and perform more work in the areas of marketing, purchasing, personnel, and financial management. At the managerial level, the skills and knowledge gained in a college degree program become more applicable. In addition to a base salary, many managers participate in profit sharing or bonus programs. It is not unusual, particularly in small specialty shops, for the manager to be an owner or part owner in the business.

Entertainment Providers include movie theaters, amusement parks, water theme parks, arenas and auditoriums, and fairs and festivals. Although some of the customers are tourists, most are local residents. Some of the specialized areas of skill and knowledge needed for success in this industry include:

- Technical aspects of entertainment productions, including staging, lighting, sound systems, graphic projection, and so forth.
- Artistic aspects of entertainment production plus booking, contracting, and management of entertainment acts.
- Maintenance and management of specialized facilities: arenas, performing arts centers, theaters, auditoriums, amusement attractions, and so on.
- Ticket office and ticketing systems management.
- Event marketing and securing of sponsorships.
- Management of food and beverage concessions and souvenir stands.
- Event security, crowd control, and facility safety.

As with other types of local commercial recreation, there are numerous positions that do not require a degree. Entry-level hourly wages are low, and there are few opportunities for tips or commission. Therefore, high school and college students perform much of the work. Experienced employees can move up to mid-level management positions. Some of these positions, however, may also be seasonal or part-time, particularly with water parks, amusement parks, and fairs and festivals that have seasonal periods of operation. Skills and knowledge gained through college programs are most applicable at upper-management positions. Again, experience is a prerequisite for advancement.

CAREER DEVELOPMENT

Students who are interested in a career in commercial recreation and tourism will encounter several barriers. Each must be overcome to gain a good entry-level position on a career track. The barriers are fragmentation of the field, uncertainty of the business, and position variety.

Fragmentation. It should be very clear from reading the past several chapters that the commercial recreation and tourism industry is extremely diverse and fragmented. There is no professional association that bridges the spectrum of industries and provides career guidance, contacts, and job placement service. Rather, there are separate professional associations for hotels, restaurants, travel agencies, tour companies, theme parks, campgrounds, sporting goods stores, golf courses and country clubs, fitness centers, racquet clubs, resorts, and many others. Some offer career guidance and job placement service, but all offer the opportunity for professional contacts. The student would be well advised to investigate membership in two or three associations and strive to attend state, regional, or national conventions whenever possible. The conventions provide an excellent opportunity to interact with the professionals, attend workshops, and apply for internships and full-time positions at scheduled job marts.

Uncertainty. The second barrier is the uncertainty of the business. Since commercial recreation and tourism are dependent upon economic and market conditions, a major decline can result in reduced profits, personnel layoffs, and business closings. Even when business is booming and an employee has an excellent evaluation, there is no guarantee for sustained employment. A thriving company may be purchased by another company who decides to bring in a new management team. There are three major strategies to cope with the uncertainty barrier. First, have a variety of skills and experience areas in order to pursue jobs in several different industries. This increases your chances to enter an industry that happens to be in a growth stage at the time. Second, make solid contacts with professionals in the industry, because inside information from peers is the best way to find out about good opportunities. Third, live a notch below your income level in order to save enough money to withstand a temporary setback. Rather than take the first new job that comes along, it may be more prudent to hold out a little longer for the job that is right for you.

Position Variety. The third barrier involves the variety of positions within many of the industries. Some positions may offer the best entry-level opportunity, but others may offer the best career track. For example, a recent graduate might have the opportunity to work as a front desk clerk or as the assistant recreation director at a resort hotel. The recreation position might initially pay better and offer the better professional challenge. However, the front desk position might lead to a management-training program and eventually to a higher position such as assistant manager or general manager.

Part of career development is to position oneself for future employment. Five strategies help accomplish this goal:

- Utilize the time in school to develop career skills such as foreign language, communications, computer literacy, and sales technique, whether or not they are required in your program.
- Gain a variety of practical experiences through part-time employment while in school. Emphasize the quality of the work experience over the money received.
- In both of the above, concentrate on improving personal skills such as attention to detail, patience, writing, interpersonal relations, dependability, public speaking, etc.
- Consider fieldwork and internship opportunities that are well structured to provide you with exposure to all aspects of the business.
- Concentrate on academic courses that provide a balance of quantitative skills and qualitative skills. The program should not be overloaded on the end of activity skills or on the other end—accounting and finance.

The remainder of this section will examine the topics of career skills and personal skills mentioned in the first three strategies above. The final section of this chapter will address curriculum implications of the last two items above.

Career Skills in Commercial Recreation and Tourism

The commercial recreation or tourism specialist needs a variety of skills that may differ from public sector training. This distinction may be made between commercial recreation and tourism business and public programs, because there are different ultimate goals and often different clientele. Understanding those differences is important in developing career skills through post-secondary education and experience. It is important to have business competence with a grounding in leisure/recreation/tourism studies in order to deal with the bottom-line profitability of a business and with characteristics of leisure/recreation/tourism participation.

Generally, an aspiring commercial recreation and tourism professional should have an understanding of the motivations and attitudes of participants as well as the social, political, and physical factors that affect his or her recreation/tourism environment. In addition, functional business skills should be attained to determine what the business must accomplish and how to accomplish it.

The career skills needed by commercial recreation and tourism professionals can best be summarized as:

- Adaptability to the rapidly changing needs of customers and their choices that drive business.

- The technical or nuts-and-bolts skills and knowledge of their particular industry.
- Ability to connect to the wide range of technological support systems that drive marketing, finance, operations, and leisure experience enhancement.

Personal Skills and Attributes Needed in Commercial Recreation and Tourism

An important feature of career development in commercial recreation and tourism is the need for certain personal skills and attributes. Such characteristics must be an integral part of an individual's personality or must be developed through awareness and experience. They are not directly teachable through an academic curriculum, although they should be reinforced in this setting. Commercial recreation and tourism managers have mentioned the following personal skills and attributes often as essential for entry-level employment and success on the job:

- **Self-confidence**—Part of the development of self-confidence comes in mastering a course of study successfully. Similarly, as one progresses in a job, people advance when they are ready for the increased responsibility. One of the best avenues for self-confidence is mastering the tasks that are required for a position.
- **Flexibility**—Most commercial recreation and tourism positions demand long hours, working a variety of responsibilities. In catering to a passenger, hotel guest, or activity center member, many demands are on the employee's time. The ability to work with different people, work a variety of hours, work long hours, use a variety of skills, and respond to change is important for success.
- **People skills**—People contact requires an extroverted individual or at least someone with assertive and friendly skills in dealing with people. Most commercial recreation and tourism businesses are customer-service intensive, and the ability to work with people is imperative.
- **Self-motivation**—Persons entering the field of commercial recreation and tourism often enter at the first rung of the career ladder and must demonstrate their motivation in order to advance. For example, a student with a BS degree took a job in the room service division of a luxury hotel. He was able to computerize the service operation and was soon promoted.
- **Empowerment**—Professionals in commercial recreation and tourism must have the ability to empower and excite their employees to perform at high standards. The traditional role of the manager as an authoritarian boss has given way to a style of coaching and facilitating.
- **"Big Picture" vision**—Managers and upwardly mobile employees must be able to see how their company fits into the overall industry and society in general. They must have a vision of where they and the company can go to fulfill their potential.
- **Creativity**—Uncommon problems require uncommon and creative solutions. One way to expand vision and creativity is to read widely in many diverse areas of business, arts, sciences, social sciences, and humanities.
- **Attention to detail**—This quality is related to organizational skill development, but is one step beyond simple task organization. The requirements of managing a successful people-oriented business necessitate an ability to see that all aspects of the operation are running smoothly. A missed detail can result in a very dissatisfied customer.
- **Entrepreneurship and initiative**—Professionals in commercial recreation and tourism are expected to take leadership in developing new ideas, making decisions, and being innovative. While following job responsibilities is important, taking the initiative to solve problems, improve procedures, and find new opportunities are definite pluses in employment.

- **Patience**—Most commercial recreation and tourism managers started at entry level and moved up in the field. Students pursuing this field would benefit from being patient in career development. Too many students think they can start off as managers, but in reality they lack maturity and understanding of the industry. Patience and hard work will help overcome this shortcoming.
- **Stability**—Due to high turnover rates in the field, those with greater stability are able to progress more rapidly as openings occur. Most hotels promote from within, as do fitness centers, sports clubs, theme parks, retail chains, and other local commercial recreation and tourism ventures.
- **Placement skills**—Campus placement centers can help with the development of an application letter and a resume, plus improve a student's interviewing technique and job search skills. These skills require the student to understand their goals in order to best represent their education and experience to an employer.

Obviously, an outgoing, confident, poised, organized, and positive individual will be more successful than one who does not readily display those traits, so these attitudinal variables are at the base of others mentioned here. The above personal skills are attainable by anyone who has the desire to achieve them. By practicing certain select qualities, a person's weaknesses may be overcome before actual employment.

CURRICULUM IMPLICATIONS

The field of commercial recreation and tourism requires certain essential skills as previously discussed. Some of these skills are developed best through practical experience, while others are developed, or at least introduced, through academic programs. Therefore, many universities have developed commercial recreation and/or tourism programs to respond to the academic needs of the industry. This section will examine the components of a well-balanced academic curriculum in commercial recreation and tourism. These components include core courses, business courses, specialization courses, other supporting courses, and fieldwork or internship programs. Depending upon credit hours and semester length, some curricula may offer more than one course to address each topic area.

Core Courses

The student should gain a firm understanding of the overall recreation/leisure service field. This includes coursework in the following areas:

- **Leisure industry foundations**—basic history, philosophy, social and economic impact, service providers, and interrelationships of the entire leisure industry.
- **Leadership and supervision**—leadership theory, principles, and practices as applied to participants, staff, and volunteers. Also customer service training.
- **Recreation programming**—needs/interests assessment, program areas and formats, program structure, operations, and evaluation.
- **Leisure behavior**—background in the psychology, sociology, and economics of individual, family, and group leisure, including tourism-related behavior.
- **Physical resources planning and management**—principles of master planning, site planning, facility design, maintenance, and operations management for outdoor and indoor areas and facilities.
- **Introduction to commercial recreation and tourism**—an overview of the nature of commercial recreation and tourism, including behaviors, impacts, industry regulation, and the major components of the industry. Also business concepts applied specifically to commercial recreation and tourism settings.

- **Operations and feasibility study in commercial recreation and tourism**—advanced applications of business principles and economics to the operation of commercial recreation and tourism enterprise. Also the feasibility study process and steps to start a new business.
- **Computer applications**—to develop skills in the use of spreadsheets, databases, graphic presentations, Web use and Web page development, and special applications such as program registration, memberships, facility scheduling, and so forth.

Business Courses

Each student should have coursework in five or more of the following areas:

- Accounting
- Human resources management
- Economics
- Business writing and communication
- Budgeting and financial management
- Management principles
- Principles of marketing
- Business law
- Small business management and entrepreneurship
- Optional subjects: retail sales and management, real estate development, international business, and so on.

Specialization Courses

Each student should take a cluster of courses in one or more of the following specialization areas:

- Travel and tourism
- Hotel/motel management
- Restaurant/food services management
- Fitness and sports management
- Retail Sales and management
- Arts/entertainment management
- Outdoor recreation and resources management
- Convention and meeting planning
- Adventure-based recreation
- Public assembly facility/event center management

Other Supporting Courses

To provide a well-rounded background, the student should take as many of the following courses as possible:

- Public speaking
- First aid and CPR
- Foreign languages
- Activity courses (depending on career interest): sports and fitness, outdoor recreation, art, theater, music, and so forth.

Fieldwork and Internships

The most effective way to secure a quality initial experience in commercial recreation and tourism is through fieldwork or internship with an established business. This is because fieldwork or internship is (or should be) more than just a part-time or seasonal job. It is an opportunity to have an intensive, work-based exposure to a broad range of operations within a company. Certainly the student should expect to perform some regular and productive duties in at least one division of the company. The bonus, however, is that the intern usually has a unique opportunity to observe and/or work with many other divisions of the company, thereby enriching the experience. The student should seize this opportunity, even if it requires 20 hours of volunteer work beyond the standard workweek.

Fieldwork and internships vary in length, intensity, and requirements set by the business and the university. Perhaps the best system is to have a three-credit fieldwork early in the academic program (sophomore year), followed by a 10–15 credit internship late in the program (junior or senior year). The fieldwork serves as an exploratory experience in which the students can test their interest in a practical setting, 10–20 hours a week. The internship should be more of a culminating experience, in which students receive a professional-level work challenge. To get the most from the opportunity, it requires a full-time, 40- to 70-hour-per-week commitment.

Some students strive to gain an internship placement that will lead directly into a full-time professional-level position or lead to industry contacts that will accomplish the same objective. It is also important to select an internship with a company that gives the student a high-quality and varied experience. Unfortunately, some students accept higher paying internships with companies that return little educational benefit to the student. Therefore, the student must be cautioned to consider the quality of the internship experience first and the pay second.

Another area of concern is the length of the fieldwork or internship commitment. Universities are often tied into 10-week quarters or 15-week semesters that may not coincide with the needs of the company, either for starting and ending dates or for duration of the program. It may be necessary for the student to sacrifice some personal vacation time or even forego a quarter/semester of school in order to be available when the company requires. For example, some hotels and resorts want interns for 6-month commitments.

A final area of concern regards out-of-state internships. There are many out-of-state resorts, theme parks, tour operators, and other companies with excellent internship programs. Sometimes these out-of-state positions pay less and/or have higher housing costs than convenient local placements. Again, the student must decide if his or her priorities are on having a high-quality experience or on cost and expediency. The student who plans ahead and saves money while in school is in a better position to choose the high-quality experience, which in the long run usually pays higher dividends.

It should be mentioned that the Resort and Commercial Recreation Association (RCRA) publishes a monthly job bulletin that lists numerous internships as well as full-time positions. RCRA and other professional associations also have job marts at their annual conventions.

COMMERCIAL RECREATION AND TOURISM INTERNET RESOURCES

This concluding section will provide a variety of Internet resources that should be useful to students in conducting a search for job opportunities. Since Web sites change frequently, don't be surprised if an address is not correct when you check it. If this hap-

College students find opportunities for internships and career-track positions at the job fairs of professional conferences such as the Resort and Commercial Recreation Association.
(Photo: J. Crossley)

pens, try a Web search for the primary organization using yahoo.com, google.com, or one of the other search engines. Some of these sites are industry specific, while others are general in nature, with categories for certain industries.

ActionJobs.com: http://www.actionjobs.com
Adventures in Hospitality Careers: http://www.hospitalityadventures.com
American Hospitality Academy: http://www.americanhospitalityacademy.com
AOL Careers: http://www.AOLCareers.com
Association of Collegiate Conference and Events Directors International—Jobs:
       http://acced-i.colostate.edu/imis_web/StaticContent/3/Jobs/job.htm
Athletic Business—Classifieds: http://www.athleticbusiness.com/classfieds
AthleticLink.com—Job Seekers: http://www.athleticlink.com/JobSeekers.asp
Career Builder: http://www.careerbuilder.com
Club Managers Association of America—Executive Career Services: http://www.cmaa.org/
       ecs/index.htm
Cool Jobs: http://www.cooljobs.com
Cool Works: http://www.coolworks.com
Connected International Meeting Planners Association—Career Center: http://
       www.jobtarget.com/home/index.cfm
Disney Careers: http://corporate.disney.go.com/careers/index.html
Ehotelier.com: http://www.ehotelier.com
Entertainment, Hospitality, Travel & Resort Jobs Page:
       http://www.nationjob.com/hotelhcareers.com
Entertainment Services and Technology Association—Job Board: http://www.esta.org/jobs/
       index.php

Eventplanner.com—Employment Board: http://eventplanner.com/boards/employment.html

Fitness Management Classified Ads: http://www.fitnessmanagement.com/FM/marketplace/classifieds

Fun Jobs: http://www.funjobs.com

Hospitality 1st: http://www.hospitality-1st.com

Hospitality Online—Job Search: http://www.hospitalityonline.com/jobs

Hospitality Careers: http://www.hospitalitycareernetworks.com

Hotel Career Solutions: http://www.hotelcareersolutions.com

Hotel Jobs Network: http://www.hospitalityjobs.com

Intern Jobs: http://www.internjobs.com

Internship Programs: http://www.internshipprograms.com

International Association for Exhibition Management—Career Center: http://iaemorg.expoexchange.com/CareerCenter/ccintro.htm

International Association for the Leisure & Entertainment Industry—Classifieds: http://www.ialei.org/helpwanted.aspx

International Association of Amusement Parks and Attractions—Career Opportunities: http://www.iaapa.org/modules/Careers/index.cfm?fuseaction = Menu

International Association of Assembly Managers—Career Opportunities: http://iaam.org/IAAM_News/Pages/NLcareerlist.htm.

International Association of Convention & Visitor Bureaus (Online Career Opportunities): http://www.iacvb.org/iacvb/career_center/cbvjobops.asp

International Association of Conference Centers—Job Board: http://www.iaccnorthamerica.org/resources/index.cfm?fuseaction = JobBoard

International Facilities Management Association—JOBnet: http://www.ifma.org/career/index.cfm

International Festivals and Events Association—Job Bank: http://ifea.com/resources/jobbank.asp

International Health, Racquet & Sportsclub Association—Job Connection: http://www.ihrsa.org/jobs

International Special Events Society—ISES USA Chapters: http://www.ises.com/chapters/usa.cfm

Jobs in Paradise: http://www.jobsinparadise.com

Jobs in Hospitality, Convention, and Tourism: http://www.unlv.edu/Tourism/jobs.html

Job Monkey: http://www.jobmonkey.com

Luxury Hotel Jobs: http://www.luxuryhoteljobs.com

Meeting Professionals International—Job Bank: http://www.mpiweb.org/CMS/MPIweb/MPILandingPages/CareerResourcesLanding.aspx

Meeting Connection: http://www.themeetingconnection.com

Meeting Exchange: http://www.mmaweb.com/meetings/meetingboard

Meetings Industry Mall—Directory: http://www.mimegasite.com/mimegasite/index.jsp

Monster: http://www.monster.com

Mountain Resort Community Employment Connection: http://www.jacksonholenet.com/area_info/employment.php

Mpoint.com—Job Board (jobs for planners): http://jobs.mpoint.com

National Intramural-Recreation Sports Association—bluefishjobs: http://www.bluefishjobs.com

National Park Service—Employment Information: http://www.nps.gov/personnel

National Recreation and Park Association—Career Center: http://nrpa.jobcontrolcetner.com

Navy's Morale, Welfare, and Recreation Employment Opportunities—Personnel and Benefits: http://www.mwr.navy.mil/mwrprgms/personnel.html

NCAA News Online—Employment Opportunities: http://ncaa.thetask.com/market/jobs/browse.php

Online Sports Career Center: http://www.onlinesports.com/pages/CareerCenter.html

Overseas Jobs: http://www.overseasjobs.com

Preferred Jobs: http://www.preferredjobs.com

Professional Convention Management Association—Careers: http://careers.pcma.org/home/index.cfm?site_id = 518.

Recreation Resources Service—Job Service Bulletin: http://www2.ncsu.edu/ncsu/forest_resources/recresource/newjsb.html

Resort and Commercial Recreation Association—Job Bulletin: http://www.R-C-R-A.org/

ResortJobs.com: http://www.resortjobs.com

Ski Resort Jobs: http://www.coolworks.com

Society of Independent Show Organizers—Job Listings: http://www.siso.org/live/SISO/JobPostings

SpecialEventSite.com—Employment: http://specialeventsite.com/IndustryInfo/Employment

Sponsorship.com—Job Bank: http://www.sponsorship.com/jobbank

Sporting Goods Manufacturers Association—Employment Opportunities: http://www.sgma.com/

Summer Jobs: http://www.summerjobs.com

Themed Entertainment Association—Job Board: http://www.themeit.com/job.htm

Theme Park & Amusement Park Jobs: http://www.themeparkjobs.com

Theme Park Career Center: http://www.themedattraction.com/careers.htm

Trade Show Exhibitors Association—Career Center: http://careercenter.tsea.org/

Tradeshow Week Magazine Classified Bulletin Board: http://www.tradeshowweek.com/index.asp?layout = classifieds

Travel Jobs: http://www.traveljobs.com

Travel Jobz: http://www.traveljobz.net

United States Army—Morale, Welfare, and Recreation Employment Opportunities: http:www.mwrjobs.army.mil.

United States Office of Personnel Management: http://www.usajobs.opm.gov

United States Olympic Committee—Jobs: http://www.olympic-usa.org/12211.htm

Wine and Hospitality Jobs: http://www.winecountryjobs.com

Women Sports Jobs/Women Sport Services: http://www.womensportjobs.com

Work In Sports: http://www.workinsports.com/home.asp

World Leisure Jobs and News: http://www.worldleisurejobs.com

World Waterpark Association—Classifieds: http://www.waterparks.org/classifieds_new.asp

SUMMARY

While it is difficult to predict the future, numerous authors have made a number of well-thought-out projections based upon analysis of current trends. These trends include changes in leisure lifestyles and participation by different demographic groups, increased importance of computer technology, and the globalization of business and culture. Other authors have made a variety of projections about social and economic trends, recreation and tourism activity, and selected operational considerations for leisure-related business.

Career opportunities should continue to grow in the travel, hospitality, and local commercial recreation industries. A common theme is that career tracks typically start in relatively low-paying entry-level positions before movement into management-level positions is possible. Students need to gain practical industry skills to complement their education in order to have career opportunities. Further, a variety of personal skills such as self-confidence, flexibility, people skills, motivation, creativity, attention to detail, and entrepreneurship are essential.

Academic programs in commercial recreation and tourism can significantly help a student to gain the educational background necessary for a career. Programs should include a core of courses related to the overall leisure industry, some business courses, and a cluster of specialized courses in tourism, hospitality, sports management, arts/entertainment management, outdoor recreation, or other area depending on the student's interest. A short fieldwork experience and a substantial internship are also key elements in preparing a student for a career.

SPOTLIGHT ON:

AL BEARSE—RED JACKET RESORTS
by Cathy DeLeo, Lyndon State College

Everyone who lives on Cape Cod is in the tourism and hospitality business in one manner or another. As a summer destination for beachgoers and ocean lovers in southeastern Massachusetts, residents know and understand the importance of tourism to their economy. While 3 million visitors each year impact roads and grocery lines, the influx of visitors supports a booming trade for the many suppliers of the industry.

Al Bearse started working as a crew member with a charter boat company while in high school. He then worked for a newly established ferry service between Cape Cod and Nantucket Island, performing the many office duties needed to manage schedules and budgets and meet customer needs. Some of the lessons learned early on have helped Al in his current position as director of sales for Red Jacket Resorts, New England, a group of seven family-owned upscale resorts. By the time Al entered college, he already had a solid work ethic and an understanding of the value of quality customer service. Al states, "A student who is a 'wanna-be'—someone who is passionate about working in the lodging and hospitality business—is one who will succeed." Al notes that an outgoing personality and basic training in hospitality are requisites to enter this profession.

As an undergraduate at Lyndon State College in Vermont, Al majored in both ski resort management and business administration. He volunteered in the marketing department at Burke Mountain, a midsize destination resort in Vermont's Northeast Kingdom. This helped him secure an internship at the resort, which led to his promotion to manager of marketing and sales upon graduation. His next career move led him to a season with Ragged Mountain in New Hampshire as director of marketing. His diverse background was put to use in many areas, including loading chairlifts on New Year's Day! By the time Al moved into the hospitality and lodging business he had been earning in the high $40,000 range. At the time, he never could have predicted his present position with the family-run Red Jacket Resorts, but he has always preferred the more personal, noncorporate atmosphere and is happy that he still is not wearing a suit and tie on a daily basis (though he does have a few in his closet). Still under 30 years old, Al could not guess where his career path may lead, but he knows he has never enjoyed skiing so much now that he can experience it as a guest rather than a "person in charge."

(continued)

Personal traits that have helped Al succeed thus far include those important for any manager in the hospitality business: self-confidence, flexibility, people skills, motivation, initiative, attention to detail, and stability. Amiable and easygoing, but very organized and adept at planning, Al loves the challenges and opportunities in his job. He is a perfectionist with high standards of quality, is very self-motivated and always follows up on details. Al will admit that the recreation degree and the specialty of ski resort management require some interpretation for many employers who may not realize the strong hospitality and service background inherent in the discipline. His business degree was essential in his daily tasks involving economic forecasting, marketing strategy, and sales management. Another critical skill in this business is the ability to communicate. Al feels that his written and verbal communication skills were key in his success, along with his "people skills."

In the early years, Al recalls his day always included at least one "daily challenge," and he was never afraid to learn from his mistakes. His advice to entry-level workers and new graduates is to keep an open mind, and if you don't love what you do, you're in the wrong profession. Al loves what he does.

REFERENCES

Bandell, B. (2005). Space tourism. *The Business Journal.* http://www.msnbc.com.

Bradsher, K. (2003, January 6). Vietnam, poor but orderly is now tourists' safe haven. *Bangkok Post.* p. 11.

Campbell, A. (2004). Entrepreneurship, rural America, and elections. *Small Business Trends.* http://www.smallbiztrends.com/2004/11/entrepreneurship-rural-america-and.html

Coy, J. & Haralson, B. (2005). 17 predictions on future resort development. http://www.jeffcoy.com/documents/articles/17%20Predictions%20on%20Future%20Resort%20Development.pdf.

Fesenmaier, D. (2004). Searching for experience: Technology-related trends shaping the future of tourism. In K. Weiermair & C. Mathies (Eds.), *The tourism and leisure industry: Shaping the future* (pp. 285–299). New York: The Haworth Hospitality Press, Inc.

Foot, D. (2004). Leisure futures: A change in demography? In K. Weiermair & C. Mathies (Eds.), *The tourism and leisure industry: Shaping the future* (pp. 21–33). New York: The Haworth Hospitality Press, Inc.

Glaeser, J. (2002, Winter). Millennials, the new generation boom proves to be highly desirable market. *California Parks & Recreation,* pp. 30–34.

Godwin, N. (2004, March 16). Hispanic travel hot and getting hotter. *Travel Weekly,* pp.1, 47.

Haard, N. (2005). USA consumer trends. http://trc.ucdavis.edu/NormanHaard/sld058.htm

Kelly, J. (2004). Leisure investments: Global supply and demand. In K. Weiermair & C. Mathies (Eds.), *The tourism and leisure industry: Shaping the future* (pp.105–119). New York: The Haworth Hospitality Press, Inc.

Mason, K. (2002). Future trends in business travel decision making. *Journal of Air Transportation,* 7(1), 47–68.

McArthur, S. (2004, January/February). Selling to Gen Y. *RCI Ventures,* pp. 18–21.

Milligan, M. (2004, May 17). Gen X are new travel trendsetters. *Travel Weekly,* p.4.

Pegg, S. (2005). *Future trends in leisure.* Unpublished course materials. University of Queensland, Brisbane, Australia.

Perdue, R. (2004). Skiers, ski bums, trust fund babies, migrants, techies, and entrepreneurs: The changing face of the Colorado ski industry. In K. Weiermair & C. Mathies (Eds.), *The tourism and leisure industry: Shaping the future* (pp. 209–225). New York: The Haworth Hospitality Press, Inc.

Romero, P., Hong, S., & Westrup, L. (2005, March). *Trends worth talking about*. California and Pacific Southwest Recreation and Park Training Conference. Sacramento, California.

Schuster, P. (2002, Winter). Baby boomers present parks & recreation with new market opportunities. *California Parks & Recreation*, pp. 28–34.

Travel Weekly. (2005, December 5). WTTC: Tourism a $10 trillion business by 2015. *Travel Weekly*, p.12.

World Future Society. (2005). Top 10 forecasts from Outlook 2005. http://www.wfs.org/forecasts.htm. May/9/2006.

Appendix ••••

Account executive—The salesperson with an airline, hotel, or tour operator who manages a particular piece of business.

Add-on fare—Air fare to the city where a tour originates.

Advance purchase excursion fare (Apex)—A "supersaver" for international flights.

Affinity group—A target market group of people who belong to a membership organization.

All-inclusive tour—A tour that includes round-trip transportation plus a package tour of hotel, transfers, local tours, and possibly meals for one price.

Allotment—The number of airline seats, hotel rooms, and so forth that a tour company has allocated for group sales. May also be called "blocks."

American plan (AP)—Breakfast, lunch, and dinner included in the lodging package.

Bank—A group of flights of one airline that converge on a hub, trade connecting passengers, and depart from the hub within a short period of time. One late plane bringing numerous connecting passengers can delay the departure of the entire bank of flights.

Boilerplate language—The section of a tour contract or brochure that explains all the legal terms and conditions.

Budget hotel—Reasonably priced accommodations with bathroom but few other amenities.

Bulk fare—A net contract rate on a certain block of airline seat, contracted by a tour company.

Calendaring—Listing the entire schedule of a group tour so that no dates or tasks are overlooked. This includes all payment dates.

Circle trip—A journey with stopovers that returns to the point of departure.

Class F—First-class airfare; the wide seats and extra service in the front of the plane.

Class Y—Coach airfare in the middle and rear of the plane.

Commercial rate—A special rate agreed upon by a company with a hotel or car rental firm.

Connecting flight—One that requires passengers to get off one flight and change to another flight.

Consolidators—Companies that buy blocks of slow-moving tickets from airlines and resell them to the public at a discount.

Continental plan—A hotel rate that includes continental breakfast.

Customized tour—A tour package that has been designed from the ground up to meet a client's particular needs.

Deluxe hotel—A top-grade hotel. All rooms have private bath, standards are high.

Destination management company—A company at a destination that handles arrangements for tourists once they arrive. See *ground operator*.

Direct flight—Not necessarily a nonstop flight, but passengers stay on the same plane to their final destinations.

Dorm—A room shared by four or more persons who might be strangers. Accommodations may be beds, cots, or bunk beds.

Double occupancy rate—Price per person if two people share a room.

Double room—Room with one double bed for two persons.

Double room rate—Total price of a room that is shared by two persons.

Drop-off charge—A fee charged by a car rental company to defray the cost of returning the auto to its original location.

Escorted tour—Tour in which an escort or tour manager accompanies the participants.

Escrow account—Funds, typically customer deposits, placed in a financial institution for safekeeping.

European plan—A hotel rate that includes bed only; meals are extra.

Excursion fares—Individual fares requiring round-trip travel to be completed within specific time limits.

Executive coach—A luxury motor coach seating 25 or less and including TV, galley, wet bar, and so forth.

Extension—A pre- or post-tour optional excursion that is booked for clients in addition to their basic tour package.

Familiarization tour (fam trip)—A trip offered to travel agents and travel writers to acquaint them with a destination and its services. All or part of the cost may be covered by the sponsoring airline, hotel, convention bureau, and so on.

Final documents—The tickets, vouchers, tour documents, badges, baggage tags, and information in a pack that is sent to clients at least 3 weeks prior to departure.

First class hotel—An average comfortable hotel.

FIT—Foreign independent tour. A tour booked for an individual, couple, or family that is not a group tour.

Fly/drive tour—An independent tour featuring use of a rental car.

Full pension—A European term for a hotel rate including three meals a day.

Gateway—City, airport, or area from which a tour departs.

Ground operator—A company that provides on-site services (tour guides, ground transfers, hotel arrangements, and so on. for a tour. Also known as a receptive tour operator, inbound operator, and destination management company. They operate the land program at the destination, but are not usually the wholesaler that created the tour package.

Group inclusive tour (GIT)—A discounted fare, usually for international flights, available for a group of people (minimum may be 5, 10, or more), who travel on the same flight.

Guaranteed share—Tour company pairs single travelers of the same sex, or company will not charge a single supplement.

Guaranteed tour—A tour guaranteed to operate unless canceled by an established cut-off date (usually 60 days from departure).

Half board—Breakfast and either lunch or dinner included in a lodging package.

High season supplement—Additional charge imposed during the busiest time of the year.

Hub and spoke—A concept wherein an airline uses a central point for connecting flights to numerous destinations. This reduces the overall number of direct flights that would have been necessary to connect all the perimeter destinations.

Incentive travel—A trip offered as a prize, often used to reward employees in sales positions.

Independent tour—Package tour for individuals who wish to travel on their own, without an escort.

Joint fare—A discount fare wherein a traveler flies one airline to a gateway city and takes another airline to the final destination.

Land operator—A company that provides local travel services, sightseeing, guides, etc.

Land price—The cost for the land arrangements only: hotel, local tours, activities, and possibly meals.

Manifest—The final list of passengers.

Modified American plan (MAP)—Breakfast and dinner included in the lodging package.

Net-net—The basic, non-commissionable cost of an airline ticket, hotel room, or tour, plus applicable taxes and services charges.

Net rate—A wholesale rate to be marked up for resale to the consumer.

Ocean front room—Hotel room directly facing the ocean.

Ocean view room—A room from which you can see the ocean; usually on the side of the hotel.

Open jaw—A round-trip flight, but the person returns from a different place than the original destination.

Open ticket—A ticket, valid for transportation between certain points, indicating no specific reservation.

Option date—A deadline at which time the air, hotel, or tour space will be released if a deposit is not received.

Outside sales agent—A salesperson, usually on commission basis, who does not work in the regular sales office, but instead brings in business from outside.

Override—An extra commission paid by a travel carrier or hotel as a bonus for volume business.

Passport—Official government document certifying identity and citizenship, permitting a person to travel abroad.

Pension—A European term for guesthouse or small inn.

Private bath—A bath inside your room.

Q, V, or M fares—Computer names for various promotional air fares that may carry marketing names such as "Paradise Holiday."

Rack rate—The list price for a lodging unit, the highest rate listed. This is usually charged to drop-ins or persons contacting the establishment directly. Package deals are usually cheaper.

Run-of-the-house—A flat group rate offered by a hotel.

Semiprivate bath—A bath outside your room shared with occupants of one other room.

Service charges, gratuities, and taxes—A fixed percentage automatically added to room and meal charges. Taxes may be set by city, state, and federal governments.

Shared bath—A bath between two rooms and available to occupants of each.

Single room—Room with one bed for one person.

Single supplement—Additional fee for single persons not sharing a room.

Standby fares—Discounted and conditional fare for persons willing to risk replacement on a full flight.

Stipend—A sum of money provided to a tour manager to cover personal expenses otherwise not included in the tour. Also called a *Per Diem*.

Supersaver—A discounted fare, usually for domestic round-trip flights that must be booked and paid for a specific number of days before flight time. There may be requirements for staying a specific number of days and/or a Saturday night (so business travelers do not take advantage of a bargain designed to lure discretionary travelers).

Table d'hote—A fixed-price meal as opposed to an a la carte selection.

Tariff—A published list of supplier rates or fares.

Tour-basing fare—Fares only on certain routes that require advance purchase of a land package.

Tour desk—A service desk in a hotel lobby that sells optional tours.

Tourist class hotel—A budget hotel with few private baths and limited services.

Tour shells—Brochures (of resorts and carriers) containing artwork and graphics but without written copy, which are then overprinted by tour operators or wholesalers.

Transfer—The ground transportation, usually by van or bus, that takes passengers from the airport to their resort or hotel.

Travel package or tour package—A combination of whatever a tour operator decides to offer. It may include airfare, lodging, ground transfers, meals, entertainment, and/or activities.

Twin—A hotel room with two single beds for two guests.

Twin room—Room with two beds for two people.

Visa—Official authorization added to a passport permitting travel to and within a particular country.

Vouchers—Documents issued by tour operations to be exchanged for lodging, meals, sightseeing, and the like.

Index